The Psychological Consequences of Being a Black American

The Psychological Consequences of Being a Black American:

A Sourcebook of Research by Black Psychologists

ROGER WILCOX
Ohio University

JOHN WILEY & SONS, INC. NEW YORK • LONDON • SYDNEY • TORONTO

This anthology is respectfully dedicated to Joy Ann Wilcox for being always helpful and reassuring and Dr. Herman G. Canady for being so forceful and productive throughout his life in ways that lend great dignity not only to his own Black people but to the rest of humanity as well.

Preface

This book is the result of a course I offered at Wilberforce University entitled "The Research and Writing of Black Psychologists," which attempted to make psychology relevant at a university where the student body is almost exclusively Black. The most straightforward approach seemed to be to assemble the published works of black psychologists and present them as the substance of a general readings course.

Careful examination of the collected speeches, articles, and symposia showed that considerable attention had been focused on the implications or consequences of being a Black American in the hope of developing understanding and awareness in this most complex area of human interaction and concern. This book brings together the articles and speeches that were most directly concerned with the psychological issues of the Black American, and essentially furnishes a tentative beginning for a viable and meaningful Black psychology. As one might assume, the major focus of the research and writing has been in the area of education with particular emphasis on learning, intelligence testing, and achievement testing. There is a vast amount of research available concerning Black Americans and the articles included here are only representative of the work that has been published. Since the content of this book has been restricted to the contributions of Black psychologists (excluding collaborative efforts) I felt that additional bibliographical material would be of value to the student interested in understanding some of the topics in greater detail. Therefore, one of the features of the book is a related bibliography of material involving the psychological study of Black Americans.

I hope the book will make a contribution toward the development of racial awareness and pride in the sense that the student can gain some appreciation of the nature and scope of the contribution that Black psychologists have made to the development of psychology in America. However, the book does represent somewhat of an artificial dichotomy in that the overall research of Black psychologists does not essentially differ from the research of other American psychologists. Although it may be understandably true that many Black psychologists are concerned with the consequences of being Black, a great many (perhaps a majority) are equally concerned with and are productive in the areas of theoretical and applied psychology. In this respect it might be well to single out the research of Dr. Leslie H. Hicks in *primate behavior and physiology,* Dr. Gloria T. Chisum in *radiation flash-blindness,* Dr. Bernard W. Harleston in *verbal processes,* and Dr. Reginald L. Jones in the *exceptional child.* Even though many more authors could have been mentioned, the work of these four is representative of the considerable breadth of interest and involvement of Black psychologists.

Whenever possible, articles of historical interest have been included to demonstrate the continuity of concern within the psychological research literature for the problems of being Black. Of particular interest are the three papers of Professor Emeritus Herman Canady whose work represents some of the very early material published by a Black psychologist related to social action. In this same vein is the early paper on the development of the self-concept in Negro children by Drs. Kenneth and Mamie Clark, surely two of the most prestigious of the Black psychologists.

The article by Dr. Martin Luther King, Jr. has been included in the hope that it will inspire a number of Black college students to consider a career as a research worker in the social sciences. Obviously there is still much to learn of the consequences of being Black, and a truly significant contribution toward this understanding can and must be made by Black scholars who have lived the experience but who bring to their research the training and insight of professional study in the behavioral sciences.

I express a deep sense of gratitude to the many Black psychologists who originally made their work available for use in my course, and also for providing certain papers that have not appeared elsewhere. Specific recognition has been accorded on the initial page of each contribution to indicate permission of the authors and publishers to include copyrighted material in this volume. A personal mention of gratitude that implies no responsibility is offered Dr. Brendan Maher who read an earlier version of this book and who provided valuable and perceptive criticism concerning its content. Finally, I express my appreciation to the Wilberforce University community for making me aware of the relevance and importance of Black psychology; with my own myopic involvement in research, it would never have occurred to me if they had not pointed it out.

ROGER WILCOX

Contents

The Psychological Consequences
of Being a Black American

PART I

Cultural Disadvantage, Minority Groups, and Exceptional Children

Before discussing the actual contents of this section, a brief comment is in order regarding certain aspects of this collection. This book has a number of features that may be helpful to the student or researcher, and among these is its emphasis on the critical examination of scientific data concerned with the psychology of being a Black American. Each paper represents the work of a trained behavioral scientist who focused his education and experience on a specific problem and, as such, should be read not only for its content but also for the way in which the particular problem was approached. In psychology we call this latter facet of research experimental design and it indicates the way in which the experimenter decided to examine the problem in which he was interested. This is a crucial point because the reader should carefully consider the ways in which the authors in this collection attempted to prove their point or belief (Clark and Clark, 1939), demonstrate their concept (Gore and Rotter, 1963), or demonstrate statistical differences (Jenkins and Randall, 1948).

The set of references at the end of each article are all related to the subject of the various articles, and provide useful surveys of relevant research and writing. In addition, each section of the book includes a bibliography of references that should be useful to the reader since they provide up-to-date sources where additional explanatory research can be found. It is important to bear in mind that a considerable amount of research and writing has been devoted to Black Americans, and the many sources cited here are only a small part of the available research. The *Journal of Negro Education* remains the best current source for material in Black psychology and should be carefully read by anyone interested in developing an increased understanding of the psychology of Black Americans.

The papers in this section deal with the more general effects of being culturally and racially disadvantaged. This is a complex topic and the selections indicate the extent to which researchers have considered these effects. Generally we have assumed that severe disadvantage will have some effect on the people involved, but the problem has been to isolate the various factors in order to more clearly understand the effects of being disadvantaged. All too often, such global conceptualizations as *disadvantaged* are not helpful because they fail to specify the nature of the harmful interaction between the person and his environment.

The paper by Atchison (1955) explores the basic area of the measurement of growth and development in a group of mentally retarded Negro children while Jones, Terrell, and De Shields (1967) report more specifically on the intellectual and performance abilities of preschool children from lower income families. Drs. Green, Hofmann, and Morgan (1967) examine the specific effects of cultural deprivation on intelligence, achievement, and cognition, while Brazziel and Terrell (1962) report their attempt to develop scholastic readiness in culturally disadvantaged first graders. At a more complex level of psychological analysis, Dr. Regina Goff (1954) examines the consequences of cultural rejection on the educational aspirations of minority group children.

1 Some Effects of Deprivation on Intelligence, Achievement, and Cognitive Growth

ROBERT L. GREEN, LOUIS J. HOFMANN, & ROBERT F. MORGAN[1]

It is perhaps fitting that the initial selection of this book is a literature review of some of the cognitive effects of being deprived. Each section of the paper presents the results of research studies in terms of (1) personal characteristics (age, race, etc.), (2) context characteristics (grade level, parental education, etc.), and (3) measurement characteristics (type of psychological test, race of examiner, etc.). Dr. Green and his associates survey a great deal of information, and with careful reading this selection offers a general overview of many of the papers to be presented later.

Many assumptions have been made concering the probable effects of extended periods of non-schooling. A typical assumption is that basic learning such as the attainment of verbal concepts, reading comprehension, and arithmetic reasoning can be acquired more readily in a formal school setting with a teacher trained in educational methodology. However, a review of the literature indicates that the above assumption, so often taken for granted, rarely has been empirically assessed. This lack of psychological research on the effects of non-schooling stems from the national trend of universal school attendance.

There is, however, a body of research focusing on such factors as the impact of the environment on school achievement with varying individual and measurement characteristics. There are a few studies touching on selected aspects of the cognitively deprived child. What studies there are can be organized into the areas of (1) intelligence, (2) achievement, and (3) cognitive growth.

SOURCE. Reprinted from *Journal of Negro Education*, 1967 36, 1, 5–14, with permission of the author and the publisher.

[1] This article is based on research supported by cooperative research project #2321, U.S. Office of Education. The authors' current affiliations are: Michigan State University, Yeshiva University, and Hawaii State Hospital, respectively.

INTELLIGENCE DISADVANTAGE

Examination of the research to date shows that an individual's intelligence in the school context in not independent of many aspects of that context, nor of several personal characteristcs brought to the schooling situation, nor of certain aspects of the tests used to measure intelligence while in the educational context. Specifically, the variables can be schematized as follows: (1) *Personal Characteristics*—(age, sex, race, motivation); (2) *Context Characteristics*—Immediate (socio-economic class, parental education and marital status, number of siblings, radio in the home, grade level, and amount of prior education), General—(national stress [war versus peace], population density [urban versus rural], caste limits [degree of segregation], and cognitive deprivation); (3) *Measurement Characteristics* (time emphasis [speeded versus non-speeded items], examiner [color and attitude], and language emphasis [verbal versus non-verbal items]).

Personal Characteristics

The individual represents a composite of the fixed factors of his heredity, and these factors provide a basis for the molding influence of the environment. The limits of a general intelligence or an adaptational aptitude may well be spelled out by individual heredity. However, the two fixed characteristics which past research has indicated as highly relevant to intelligence and schooling are sex and race.

Arlitt (2) found that Negro girls aged 5 and 6 intellectually excelled the Negro boys of the same ages in Philadelphia and New Orleans. Anastasi and D'Angelo (1) found that, in Northern mixed and unmixed neighborhoods, five-year-old white girls surpassed white boys in intelligence while Negro boys surpassed Negro girls of the same age levels. The difference was more pronounced in racially unmixed neighborhoods. Thus, at an age where white and Negro intelligence is equatable, the general trend is that girls outperform the boys, but as the degree of caste limitation is increased, the relationship may reverse itself. Unfortunately, Arlitt's pooling of Negro children from segregated New Orleans and unsegregated Philadelphia precludes confirmation of Anastasi's findings.

Just as the influence of sex on intelligence typically tends to favor one sex over the other but may reverse with certain caste limitations, race as an influence on intelligence typically tends to favor one race over another (whites over Negroes in the United States). This influence may also fluctuate according to the severity of caste limitations.

Of the literature cited here, four studies used white and Negro comparison groups of school children. (Only groups actually tested by the author in question are being considered as "comparison groups".) In three of the four studies (1, 18, 8), children drawn from Nothern integrated schools and areas were tested. In all three, no significant I.Q. differences were found between races. One did find Negroes to be significantly lower on the Colored Raven Progressive Matrices (CRPM) I.Q., but they attributed this to deficiency in a special skill since no significant difference was found on the Stanford-Binet I.Q. On the other hand, in the fourth study (24) in which the sample was drawn from a segregated community, Negroes were found to have significantly lower Binet or Otis I.Q.'s than whites. These data suggest race, in itself, has no effect on general aptitude except in the context of severe caste limitation.

Five studies (Arlitt, 2; Higgins and Sivers, 18; Kennedy et al., 23; Tomlinson, 38; Young and Bright, 40) testing intelligence at different ages all found the I.Q. of Negro children to decrease with age. Higgins and Sivers also found the I.Q.'s of white children (from the lower socio-economic class) to decrease with age. Tomlinson found the biggest jump to be between ages 4 and 5 suggesting either a critical period, a traumatic effect from introduction into a school situation, or both. In all cases, white and Negro intelligence were comparable when tested from ages 4 to 6. The apparent negative effect of schooling context over time on the intelligence of lower-class white and Negro children is certainly contrary to what is normally expected of the education process.

The motivation to perform well on an intelligence test can influence the resultant I.Q. This variable fits better under the rubric of individual characteristics rather than with the measurement variables since three studies show motivation may often, regarding Negroes, be a permanently depressed personal characteristic independent of the testing context. Miner (30) suggests that this depressed motivation definitely lowers the measured I.Q.'s of many Negroes. Roen (35) agrees and links the depressed motivation to a lack of self confidence, and Davidson (11) attributes it to a lack of social goals in the face of limited opportunity. Thus, the attitudes reinforced in a Negro by his educational context will shape the motivational level which, in turn, determines how open the child's intelligence will be to growth in that same educationl context.

Context Characteristics

Among the factors in a child's immediate context studied as germane to its intellectual growth are socio-economic class, parental education and marital status, number of siblings, the presence of a radio in the home, the amount of prior education, and grade level. Five studies (2, 19, 22, 4, 23) show intelligence to increase with increasing socio-economic status of the individual or his family. A sixth study (21) points out that, of sixteen Negro children with an I.Q. over 160, none had parents in lower than middle-class socio-economic status. The lowest educational level among the parents was high school graduation. Horton and Crump (19) also found, in the comparison of three-year-old Negro children of high and low intelligence, that the mothers' education, the number of siblings, and the number of married parents differentiated the groups. Intelligence increased with decreasing number of siblings and decreasing frequency of unmarried parents. Robinson and Meenes (3), in testing Negro third graders on I.Q., did not find that any of the above factors correlated significantly with intelligence, but they did find that having a radio in the home did. Lorge (27) tested intelligence before and after a twenty-year interval and found change to depend greatly on the education received in between. Thus, intelligence is not only related to schooling, but also may be contingent to an extent on its continuation.

Recently, a group of investigators reported a study in depth of children in a Southern county whose schools had been closed for several years to prevent integration (14). The predominantly low educational level of the parents offered little alternate instruction at home. Intelligence, achievement, social, and demographic data were collected for approximately 1700 children aged 5 to 22. The sample was divided into those having had no schooling whatsoever (No Education group) and those receiving at least some out-of-county education (Education group). The mean I.Q. score of the Education group (still victims of some non-schooling) was approximately 80. Up to the age of 8, this was also the mean I.Q. for the No Education group; after age 8, the overall mean I.Q. of children without any formal schooling averaged 65. I.Q. for both groups appeared to be lower, the older the age group tested. Thus, in an actual sample of children undergoing the non-schooling treatment, measured intelligence level appeared to be dependent upon formal instruction at all ages.

One final factor occasionally linked to the intelligence of a child is the grade in which he happens to be. Lacy (24), for example, found the I.Q.'s of Negro children to decrease with increasing grade, finally leveling off between sixth and twelfth grade. Lorge (27), however, emphasized that years of school attendance and the highest grade completed are not always the same thing; i.e., grade level is not synonymous with the time exposed to education nor is it synonymous with age. In the South especially, children of quite advanced age are found in the early grades since promotion is contingent on a fixed level of achievement. Another study suggests that grade level in itself influences intelligence only as it correlates with age;

e.g., Kennedy *et al.* (23), studying Southern Negro children (where age and grade are not as highly correlated as elsewhere in the United States), found no significant difference in I.Q. by grade level but found a very significant difference by age.

In terms of the general context, national stress was reported to have depressed I.Q. in Holland's schools during World War II (12). Based on that study, increasing population density appears to lead to increased intelligence. Coppinger and Ammons (9) found the I.Q.'s of Louisiana Negroes to be higher in urban than rural areas. Kennedy *et al.* (23), in their survey of five Southern states, found no significant difference between rural and urban Negro I.Q.'s but did find a significantly higher urban I.Q. than either one of the latter two. All of Jenkins' (21) Negro children who earned I.Q.'s of 160 or higher came from major cities. He suggests that only the cities have the recognition methods and necessary facilities to nourish exceptionally intelligent Negro children.

The effects of caste limits on intelligence have been discussed throughout this section, especially under the topic of race and sex. Low socio-economic status, as applied to all races, and segregation and discrimination against minorities (predominantly the Negroes) provide a general context against which the intelligence (and achievement) of the minorities involved is far from independent.

Measurement Characteristics

As previously mentioned, a low caste group may have typically depressed achievement motivation to carry into an intelligence testing situation. Items depending heavily upon high motivation will therefore present more difficulty for a group of this nature than would items not as heavily motivation-weighted. Davidson *et al.* (11), in comparing the intelligence test results of white and Negro psychoneurotics, definitely found the Negroes performing better at passive (unspeeded) attention problems than at active (speeded) attention problems. Bean's (3) administration of a verbal and non-verbal I.Q. test to Lousiana Negro eighth graders and his conclusion (that since both elicited low scores, cultural opportunity—verbal test—alone is an insufficient explanation for low Negro I.Q.) is suspect because both tests were speeded.

Pasamanick and Knobloch (32) found Negro children at age 2 (in their third I.Q. test session) showing sudden decline in verbal responsiveness to a white examiner. This illustrates that attitude, empathy, color, all the things an examiner's manner and appearance convey to the subject, may be relevant variables even at the tender age of two years.

An attempt has often been made to differentiate the intelligence of different groups on the basis of verbal versus non-verbal (or performance) intelligence tests. Occasionally, non-verbal measures are labeled "culture-free." However, the high correlation usually seen between verbal and non-verbal I.Q. tests suggests that they have a lot in common. Predictably then, "verbal" and "non-verbal" differences will be contradictory in different studies depending mostly on sampling error. For example, in testing the I.Q. of Southern Negro children both Bean (3) and Kennedy *et al.* (23) found verbal items to elicit lower I.Q.'s while Homer (16) and Newland and Lawrence (31) found non-verbal items to elicit lower I.Q.'s Clarke (8), in a Northern comparison between white and Negro children, found the Negroes superior on verbal items. In general, past opinion has been that Negroes are at a disadvantage with the verbal items and at an advantage with non-verbal since the latter are supposedly more free from the effects of cultural deprivation. However, the research does not consistently support this notion.

As previously mentioned, Higgins and Sivers (18) found Negroes to fall below whites on the Colored Raven Progressive Matrices (CRPM), a "culture-free" I.Q., although the Stanford-Binet showed no significant differences for the same groups. Levinson (26) demonstrated that Jewish children, initially scoring equally well on verbal and non-verbal items, showed higher verbal than non-verbal I.Q.'s after two years in a Yeshiva Day School that emphasized verbal facility. Thus, intelligence tests, influenced to an extent by the presence or absence of verbal training, are also influenced by training and acculturation in general. Neither the intelligence tests nor the children who take them are ever "culture-free."

ACHIEVEMENT DISADVANTAGE

Although, as the preceding section has demonstrated, intelligence is no longer considered to be a single general factor invariable for the individual, it still can be treated as a relatively stable set of aptitude limits. Between these limits fall the achievement levels elicited by specific tasks. Logically then, achievement should be sensitive to the same variables as intelligence and, in addition, fluctuate with factors of its own. Past research shows this to be the case. Of the research to be cited in this section, some refer to the same factors as the preceding section while others focus in unexpected directions. The variables to be presented can be schematized as follows: (1) *Personal Characteristics* (motivation, health, attention span, verbal ability, and imagination); (2) *Context Characteristics*—Immediate (socio-economic class, home conditions [number of parents, number of siblings, parents' education, parents' emphasis on self responsibility, degree of physical punishment, verbal environment], school conditions [verbal facilities, remedial programs]), General (caste limits [degree of segregation] and cognitive deprivation); and (3) *Measurement Characteristics* (time emphasis, examiner, language emphasis).

Personal Characteristics

Schultz (36), when testing the achievement of Florida ninth graders, found high achievement to be inversely correlated with the number of days absent from school. This might be due to ill health causing reduced exposure to educational content. Ransom (33) found good health to correlate with good achievement. He also found attention span as well as health to be relevant to achievement for Atlanta first graders. Scott (37), after testing Oregon fifth and sixth graders, decided reading ability is the key to ability in other areas such as arithmetic and social studies. It was noted in the preceding section that all intelligence tests correlate somewhat with verbal ability (even the "non-verbal"). It would seem, then, that the development of verbal ability is a crucial factor in both intelligence and achievement. Finally, Milner (29) suggests that imagination may be a relevant variable as low scorers on a mental maturity test had relatively less of it than the high scorers.

Context Characteristics

Among the immediate contextual variables, once again socio-economic class and certain home conditions apply. Curry (10) found that scores of Southwestern white sixth graders on a standardized achievement test increased with socio-economic class rise with the exception of the highest scoring group which seemed to be independent of class level. Another finding was that parents' occupation levels correlated with a child's achievement.

Schultz also found achievement relating to number of parents, number of siblings, and parental education level—all in the expected direction. Milner confirmed the importance of parental education in her study and added the observed significant effects of a warm emotional and highly verbal family environment (correlated with high achievement) and high incidence of physical punishment (correlated with low achievement). Ransom also stressed the relevance of home conditions in general.

Willis (39), in his study, found differential progress in a remedial reading program varying with the amount of verbal facilities (number of books in the library) the school had to offer. A group of white ninth graders in Nashville showed greater improvement than an equally intelligent group of Negro ninth graders. The enrichment program itself facilitated reading ability in both groups. Brazziel and Gordon (5) also reported facilitating effects when a special program (Higher Horizons) was transplanted from New York to a Southern segregated Negro seventh grade. By stressing self-concepts, self-expression, imagination, and better parent-teacher relations, reading and arithmetic performance showed improvement.

Green *et al.* (14), in their study of educationally deprived children found the *Education* group to attain higher mean grade equivalent scores than the *No Education* group on all subtests of the Stanford Achievement Tests at all age levels. Both groups achieved at lower levels than a comparison group from a neighboring (similarly rural) county. Schooling made the greatest difference for spelling and language at early ages and for arithmetic at older ages; paragraph meaning and paragraph comprehension showed relatively uniform differences at all age levels investigated. Educationally deprived children as old as 17 demonstrated imperfect time-telling ability on a time-telling test. The 14- through 18-year-olds did not tell time significantly better than the neighboring county's schooled third and fourth graders. Thus, the overall effect of the absence of local schools was a depression of readiness skills at all age levels, even for children who had been exposed to a little formal education.

Among the general contextual characteristics, caste limitations again appear to be important. Hansen (17) presents statistics to show that the integration of Washington, D. C., led to higher Negro achievement without depressing the achievement level of the white children. This was attributed to the more efficient pooling of resources although it is probable that the cessation of separate education involves cognitive effects as well as resource-using efficiency. Recently integrated areas offer excellent research situations for relating the cognitive variables to achievement. An additional finding in this area by McQueen and Churn (28) is that, on the whole, elementary school students in a long integrated western community do not significantly differ in achievement according to race.

Cognitive deprivation, whether of educational, social, or cultural nature relates to both intelligence and achievement in the school situation. It, therefore, has been included in the preceding variables schema without discussion since the next section will present the handful of pertinent articles in some detail.

COGNITIVE DISADVANTAGE

The published papers touching on cognitive deprivation, while few in number, compensate for their low frequency with a richness in ideational quality. These contributions may be schematized as follows: *Personal*

Characteristics (emotional atmosphere, lack of teacher interest, social deprivation and restrictions); (2) *Critical Age Period* (I.Q. spread, educational facilities for deprived children); and (3) *Perceptual Deprivation Experiments in the Laboratory* (lack of cognitive deprivation, importance of cognitive deprivation).

Personal Characteristics

The enrichment programs mentioned in the preceding section showed relative success in raising the achievement level of the school children exposed to such programs. Deprivation forms the other side of the coin and is, the literature suggests, the more important side. Brazziel and Terrell (6), for example, reported a first grade class receiving abundant interest and encouragement to reach the fiftieth percentile of an intelligence test after seven months while three control classes receiving apparently lukewarm attention and interest fell between the thirteenth and sixteenth percentiles. Thus, an enriched emotional atmosphere secured average performance while slight deprivation of teacher interest tremendously depressed the measured intelligence.

This emotional deprivation on the teacher's part, with its apparently devastating effects, has been observed to be more frequent with selected groups of children. Deutsch (13) noted that the teachers of Negro children often reinforce negative self-images in their students by their verbal behavior.

The social deprivation and restriction inherent in most institutions may also hamper a child's intellectual development. Green and Zigler (15) reported retarded performance on monotonous tasks to occur with institutionalized retarded children but not with non-institutionalized retarded children and normals.

Green *et al.* (14) found several pronounced cognitive effects of non-schooling in their sample. For both deprived groups, the predominant admired model was one or the other parent. Peers, teachers and professional figures were rarely chosen. Occupational aspirations, positively related in the sample to educational aspiration, were found to be higher in the *Education group*. However, the realism of the vocational choices was not significantly related to the amount of non-schooling. The average self-concept of ability for both groups of educationally deprived children did *not* differ significantly from the neighboring county's children or from a large sample of Northern children. This was attributed to either an unintentionally biased sample, an unexpected independence of self-concept from schooling, or to the nation-wide interest and attention (and testing) the deprived children were receiving.

Critical Age Period

There also seems to be evidence for a critical age period during which the effects of deprivation may be maximized. Jackson (20) puts this time period between nine months and kindergarten age as judged by the jump in I.Q. spread. Levine (25) suggests that the crucial time for developing the capacity of environmental interpretation, symbolism, and language is between the ages of 2 and 4. He recommends educational facilities for lower socio-economic class children who might otherwise be deprived of adequate stimulation from their surroundings during these critical years. Milner (29) (discussed in the preceding section) also advocated preschool training programs for emotionally deprived children.

Perceptual Deprivation Experiments in the Laboratory

Bruner (7) takes the deprivation problem out of the necessary past monopoly of field experiments by connecting perceptual deprivation experiments performed under the close control of the laboratory with cognitive deprivation occurring daily in the lives of thousands of children. Lack of cognitive deprivation, Bruner maintains, is prerequisite to a child's capacity for adaptive inference in dealing with his environment. Deutsch (13), Brazziel and Terrell (6), and Green and Zigler (15) have pointed to the importance of cognitive deprivation via a child's teacher or his institutional surroundings.

The effects of social and cultural deprivatioin have then been sifted for years. Educational deprivation's effects have been touched upon only recently. Research must move quickly to catch up with the flood of the *suggested* disadvantage of inferior or aborted education on intelligence, achievement, and the many facets of cognitive growth. To what extent and in what ways are the formalized means of cultural transmission central to adaptation to the environment? It has taken psychology a long time to formulate the question in testable terms. The answers are only just beginning to emerge.

Bibliography

1. Anastasi, Anne and D'Angelo, Rita Y. "A Comparison of Negro and White Preschool Children in Language Development and Goodenough Draw-A-Man I.Q.," *J. Genetic Psychol.*, 81: 147–165, 1952.
2. Arlitt, Ada Hart. "The Relation of Intelligence to Age in Negro Children," *J. Applied Psychol.*, 6:378–384, 1922.

3. Bean, L. "Negro Responses to Verbal and Non-Verbal Test Materials," *J. Psychol.*, 13:343–350, 1942.

4. Blanks, A. C. "A Comparative Study of Mentally Bright and Mentally Dull Negro High School Seniors (with reference to personality, background, school achievement, interest, ambition, and school marks), *Dissertation Abstracts*, 15:1200–1201, 1955.

5. Brazziel, W. F. and Gordon, Margaret. "Replications of Some Aspects of the Higher Horizons Program in a Southern Junior High School," *Journal of Negro Education*, 33:107–113, 1963.

6. Brazziel, W. F. and Terrell, Mary. An Experiment in the Development of Readiness in a Culturally Disadvantaged Group of First Grade Children," *Journal of Negro Education*, 31:4–7, 1962.

7. Bruner, J. S. *The Cognitive Consequences of Early Sensory Deprivation.* Cambridge, Massachusetts: Harvard University Press, 1961.

8. Clarke, D. P. "Stanford-Binet Scale "L" Response Patterns in Matched Racial Groups," *Journal of Negro Education*, 10:230–238, 1941.

9. Coppinger, N. W. and Ammons, R. B. "The Full-Range Picture Vocabulary Test: VIII. A Normative Study of Negro Children," *J. Clinical Psychol.*, 8:136–140, 1952.

10. Curry, R. L. "The Effects of Socio-Economic Status on the Scholastic Achievement of Sixth Grade Children," *Brit. J. Educ. Psychol.*, February, 1962.

11. Davidson, K. S., *et al.* "A Preliminary Study of Negro and White Differences on Form I of the Wechsler-Bellevue Scale," *J. Consult. Psychol.*, 14:489–492, 1950.

12. de Groot, A. D. "War and the Intelligence of Youth," *J. Abnormal and Social Psychol.*, 43:596–597, 1948.

13. Deutsch, M. *Minority Group and Class Status as Related to Social and Personality Factors in Scholastic Achievement.* Society for Applied Anthropology, Monograph No. 2:1–32, 1960.

14. Green, R. L., *et al.* *The Educatonal Status of Children in a District Without Public Schools.* Cooperative Research Project No. 2321, United States Office of Education, Department of Health, Education, and Welfare, 1964.

15. Green, C. and Zigler, E. "Social Deprivation and the Performance of Retarded and Normal Children on a Satiation Type Test," *Child Development*, 33:499–508, 1962.

16. Hammer, E. F. "Comparison of the Performance of Negro Children and Adolescents on Two Tests of Intelligence, One as an Emergency Scale," *J. Genetic Psychol.*, 84:85–93, 1954.

17. Hansen, C. F. "The Scholastic Performances of Negro and White Pupils

in the Integrated Public Schools of the District of Columbia," *J. Educ. Sociology*, 36:287–291, 1963.

18. Higgins, C. and Sivers, Cathryne H. "A Comparison of Stanford-Binet and Colored Raven Progressive Matrices I.Q.'s for Children with Low Socio-Economic Status," *J. Consult. Psychol.*, 20:265–268, 1958.

19. Horton, C. P. and Crump, E. P. "Growth and Development XI: Descriptive Analysis of the Backgrounds of 76 Negro Children whose Scores Are Above or Below Average on the Merrill-Palmer Scale of Mental Tests at Three Years of Age," *J. Genetic Psychol.*, 100:255–265, 1962.

20. Jackson, E. Grant. "The Impact of Environment on Racial Achievement," *J. Human Relations*, 6:47–53, 1958.

21. Jenkins, M. D. "Case Studies of Negro Children of Binet I.Q. 160 and Above," *Journal of Negro Education*, 12:159–166, 1943.

22. John, Vera P. "The Intellectual Development of Slum Children: Some Preliminary Findings," *Panel: Programs for the Socially Deprived, Urban Child*, 1962.

23. Kennedy, W. A., Van De Riet, V., White, J. C. Jr. *The Standardization of the 1960 Revision of the Stanford-Binet Intelligence Scale on Negro Elementary School Children in the Southeastern United States.* Cooperative Research Project No. 954, United States Office of Education, Department of Health, Education and Welfare, 1961.

24. Lacy, L. D. "Relative Intelligence of White and Colored Children," *Elementary School J.*, March, 1926, pp. 542–546.

25. Levine, D. U. "City Schools Today: Too Late with Too Little?" *Phi Delta Kappan*, 44:80–83, 1962.

26. Levinson, B. "Subcultural Values and I. Q. Stability," *J. Genetic Psychol.*, 98:69–82, 1961.

27. Lorge, I. "Schooling Makes a Difference," *Teachers College Record*, 46:483–492, 1945.

28. McQueen, R. and Churn, B. "The Intelligence and Educational Achievement of a Matched Sample of White and Negro Students," *School and Society*, 88:327–329, September 24, 1960.

29. Milner, Esther. "A Study of the Relationship Between Reading Readiness in Grade One School Children and Patterns of Parent-Child Interaction," *Child Develop.*, 22:95–112, June, 1951.

30. Miner, J. B. *Intelligence in the United States.* New York: Springer Publishing Co., Inc., 1957.

31. Newland, T. E. and Lawrence, W. C. "Chicago Non-Verbal Examination Results of an East Tennessee Negro Population," *J. Clinical Psychol.*, 9:44–46, 1953.

32. Pasamanick, B. and Knobloch, Hilda. "Early Language Behavior in Negro

Children and the Testing of Intelligence," *J. Abnormal and Social Psychol.*, 50:401–402, 1955.

33. Ransom, Katharine A. "A Study of Reading Readiness," *Peabody J. Educ.*, 16:276–284, January, 1939.

34. Robinson, Mary Louise and Meenes, M. "The Relationship Between Test I Intelligence of Third Grade Negro Children and the Occupations of Their Parents," *Journal of Negro Education*, 16:136–141, 1947.

35. Roen, S. "Personality and Negro-White Intelligence," *J. Abnormal and Social Psychol.*, 61:148–150, 1960.

36. Schultz, R. E. "A Comparison of Negro Pupils Ranking High with Those Ranking Low in Educational Achievement," *J. Educ. Sociology*, 31:265–270, 1958.

37. Scott, Carrie M. "The Relationship Between Intelligence Quotients and Gain in Reading Achievement with Arithmetic Reasoning, Social Studies, and Science," *J. Educ. Research*, 56:322–326, 1963.

38. Tomlinson, Helen. "Differences Between Pre-School Negro Children and Their Older Siblings on the Stanford-Binet Scales," *Journal of Negro Education*, 12:474–479, 1944.

39. Willis, L. J. "A Comparative Study of the Reading Achievements of White and Negro Children," *Peabody J. Educ.*, 17:166–171, November, 1939.

40. Young, Florence M. and Bright, H. A. "Results of Testing 81 Negro Rural Juveniles with the Wechsler Intelligence Scale for Children," *J. Social Psychol.*, 39:219–226, 1954.

2 Use of the Wechsler Intelligence Scale for Children with Eighty Mentally Defective Negro Children

CALVIN O. ATCHISON[1]
Tennessee Agricultural & Industrial State University, Nashville, Tennessee

Professor Atchison's rather technical paper examines the nature of the difference between *Verbal* and *Performance* IQ observed in mentally retarded Negro children. Dr. Atchison shows that these children seem to differ from either normal Negro children or comparably retarded Caucasian children in that their measured *Verbal* IQ is greater than their *Performance* IQ. Part III of this book takes a closer look at the concept and the measurement of intelligence of normal Black children, but the interested reader should consult some of the sources cited in either of the research bibliographies in order to gain the background necessary to thoughtfully deal with the problem of intelligence testing with minority group members, since this is among the most complex and assuredly the most provocative issues in Black psychology (Professor Brazziel's *A Letter from the South,* 1969, this collection).

Since the publication of the Wechsler Intelligence Scale for Children in 1949, many studies have been released regarding its usefulness in the diagnosis of children. A review of the literature seems to indicate that most of those studies have been concerned with the reliability and validity of the test. Since the scale is a downward extension of the Wechsler-Bellevue Scale for Adolescents and Adults (4), many examiners apply almost the same diagnostic values to the various subtests and the two scales (Verbal and Performance).

SOURCE. © 1955, American Association of Mental Deficiency by permission of *American Journal of Mental Deficiency.*

[1] The data for this paper were collected while the writer was employed as school psychologist with the Division of Special Education, Charlotte City Schools, Charlotte, North Carolina.

A search of the literature failed to reveal any research project which dealt with the relationship between verbal ability and performance ability of mentally defective Negro children. The purpose of this paper is to give a summary of findings resulting from a three-year period of screening of retarded children for special class placement in the Charlotte, North Carolina public schools. It is the hope of the writer that this critical examination will point up some worthwhile areas for further investigation.

Test patterns gathered on defective Negro children, unlike those obtained on normal Negro children, have shown frequent recurrences of Performance IQ scores which are low relative to Verbal IQ scores on the WISC. It is, of course, necessary to know the etiology involved in any group of defective Ss before generalizations concerning test patterns can be made. The higher Verbal IQ relative to Performance IQ is to be expected when a number of organic cases is included in the sample. Sloan and Schneider (3) found that, in general, the Performance IQ's of mental defectives were consistently higher than the Verbal IQ's. On the other hand, Gurthie and Pastovic (1) found a higher mean Verbal IQ than Performance IQ. It was intended in the construction of the scale that no difference between the two averages on the WISC would occur when representative samples are used.

Because of the discrepancies which have been noted between Verbal IQ's and Performance IQ's, it appeared worthwhile to analyze the IQ scores of a group of Negro mental defectives, in order to determine if such a discrepancy occurs in a sample of this nature.

PROCEDURE

The IQ scores of 80 mentally defective Negro children (54 males and 26 females) were tabulated from the case record files. The Ss ranged in age from 6 years, 8 months, to 13 years, with a mean age of 9 years, 6 months. All full-scale scores were tabulated from the sum of 10 sub-tests (digits span and mazes omitted), and none of the Ss had a full scale IQ on the WISC above 69.

TABLE 1

WISC Verbal and Performance Results for 80 Negro Mental Defectives

Scale	Mean	SD
Verbal	66.3	6.5
Performance	56.8	8.7

All Ss were without handicap or disability in the upper extremities which would make manipulation impossible. Diagnostic evaluations made by public health authorities working in conjunction with the schools showed no evidence of organic pathology or sensory incapacity.

RESULTS

Table 1 presents a summary of the test results.

Those subjects who scored relatively low on verbal tended to score low on performance also. On the other hand, those who scored higher on verbal did not tend to score higher on performance. Thus it appears that the relationship between verbal scores and performance scores for mentally defective Negro children may be different from that found for normals.

A CR of 9.79 was obtained which indicated that the hypothesis of no difference between the verbal and performance means could be rejected beyond the .01 level. A Pearson r of .39 ± .07 was obtained when the Ss' standings on Verbal and Performance scales were correlated. This correlation is significant beyond the .01 level of confidence.

Although it is believed that none of the Ss was of the brain damaged variety, the possibility of incorrect diagnoses cannot be ruled out.

It became obvious during the testing that the Ss had difficulty in understanding instructions. Possibly the incidence of low scores was due at least in part to this difficulty. It is also worth noting that some of the Ss, had they been evaluated in terms of Verbal IQ alone, would not have been classified as mentally defectives.

SUMMARY

Data were obtained on 80 feebleminded Negro boys and girls in order to determine if there was a difference between Verbal and Performance IQ scores obtained on the WISC. An analysis of the scores yielded significant results, the verbal mean exceeding the performance mean. These results indicate that equal Verbal and Performance IQ's on the WISC may not be characteristic for Negro children classified as familial defectives. Further work is needed to see if similar results would be obtained for larger samples of Ss falling in this category.

References

1.   Gurthie, G. M. and Pastovic, J. J. "Some Evidence of the Validity of WISC," *J. Consulting Psychology*, 1951, 15, 385–386.

2. Seashore, H. G. "Differences between Verbal and Performance IQ's on the Wechsler Intelligence Scale for Children." *J. Consulting Psychology,* 1951, 15, 62–67.

3. Sloan, W. and Schneider, B. "A Study of the Wechsler Intelligence Scale for Children with Mental Defectives," *Am. J. Mental Deficiency,* 1951, 55, 573–575.

4. Wechsler, D. *Manual for the Wechsler Intelligence Scale for Children.* Psych. Corp., New York, 1949.

3 *Intellectual and Psychomotor Performance of Preschool Children from Low-Income Families*[1]

ROY J. JONES, DAVID L. TERRELL, & JAMES I. DE SHIELDS
Institute for Youth Studies, Howard University

The question raised by this article arises in nearly every selection of the book; namely, what effect does the disadvantaged environment have on the psychological development of those who mature within it? The final answer to this question remains to be developed, but the available research invariably shows the effects to be negative. It may be that some children are affected more than others, but the effects themselves are generally negative. It is interesting to note that fully one-third of the preschool children originally tested dropped out of the study before it was concluded because of moving, absence, or unwillingness to cooperate. This highly unstable aspect of the disadvantaged environment is simply another of the primary characteristics of such environments and, quite predictably, will have certain undesirable effects on the children living there.

The purposes of this study were: (a) to appraise the level of intellectual and psychomotor functioning of a sample of preschool children from low-income families in the Cardozo School District of Washington, D. C. at the beginning of the preschool experience; (b) to determine whether changes in intellectual and psychomotor functioning occur in these preschool children after exposure to the preschool program and; (c) to de-

SOURCE. Reprinted from PSYCHOLOGY IN THE SCHOOLS, 1967, IV, 3, 257-259, with permission of the author and Psychology Press, Inc.

[1] This study was supported by a contract with the United Planning Organization of the Greater Washington, D.C. Metropolitan Area. Funds utilized were part of a grant to that organization by the Office of Juvenile Delinquency and Youth Development, U.S. Department of Health, Education and Welfare.

20

termine whether the changes, if they occur, are significantly different from a comparable group of children not exposed to the preschool experience.

METHOD

Sample

Sixty of the children enrolled in the five preschool centers of the Washington, D.C. anti-poverty program were randomly selected for study. Nineteen children who met the eligibility criteria who were not enrolled in this or other preschool programs served as the control group.

Data analyses conducted on four demographic variables—broken homes, overcrowding, number of siblings and combined family income—indicated that these two groups were drawn from a common population.

The measure of psychomotor functioning used in this study consisted of the number of months credit earned on the psychomotor or nonverbal subtests at the year V level of the Stanford-Binet Intelligence Test Form L-M. These subtests are: Picture Completion, Folding a Triangle, Copying a Square, Pictorial Similarities and Difference II, Patience, Rectangles, and if appropriate, Tying a Knot. It should be pointed out that scores obtained on these subtests were not interpreted as the psychomotor mental age of the child. Similarly the derived scores were not considered as representative of the maximum psychomotor abilities of each child.

The testing was conducted in the mornings in private rooms which were removed from the area of other preschool activity.

The tests were administered during two different time periods, December–January, 1964–65 and July–August, 1965. The mean interval between pretesting and posttesting was seven months.

RESULTS AND DISCUSSION

Although 60 subjects, one-third of the preschool population, were originally randomly selected, results for only 40 subjects are reported here because of the attrition which had occurred by posttest time. The attrition was due to the fact that some of the children had moved from the area, were absent at the time of posttesting or were uncooperative. The high attrition rate for this preschool sample, in all probability affected the obtained results.

The range for the IQ scores obtained was 66–137 for pretesting, and 71–133 for the posttesting. The mean pretest IQ was 96.3 while the mean posttest IQ was 99.6.

The three points increase in the mean IQ score upon posttesting was not statistically significant. There were however, 13 individuals whose IQ scores increased by ten or more points upon posttesting. One of the subjects had an increase of 20 points and a change in IQ classification from high average to superior. Another subject had a 25 point increase in IQ classification from borderline defective to average. There were also four cases with losses of at least ten points in IQ score, and in one case there was a loss of 20 points.

Some of the factors which could be responsible for these extreme variations are attitude, interest, or emotional state of the subject or of the examiner. As pointed out by Anastasi (1961), preschool testing is a highly interpersonal process and qualified examiners may obtain appreciably different results from the same subjects.

A comparison was made between the performance of males and females. The results of this comparison indicated that while the mean IQ of the males of 100.0 was six points higher than the mean of 94.1 for the females, this difference was not statistically significant.

The analysis yielded a t of 1.30 for the pretest and a t of 1.57 for the posttest. This finding is inconsistent with those reported by other investigators. Freeman (1963) in his review of studies in this area, points out that girls, as a group, score higher than boys on the standardized tests of intelligence until about age six or seven. A closer examination of factors influencing the obtained results for this population seems warranted.

There was a marked increase in the psychomotor scores from pre- to posttest. The pretest mean was 1.48 and the posttest mean was 2.35. The obtained difference is significant at less than the .001 level of confidence.

A factor which must be considered in any interpretation made of this finding is the normal physiological maturation of the preschool child which may produce increased muscular coordination and/or general improvement in psychomotor ability. Another factor which must be considered is the nature and the effect of the play activity which is an integral part of the preschool curriculum.

The type of play activity included in this program is designed to enhance psychomotor performance. Consideration must, however, be given to the nature of the tests used to measure psychomotor performance. It is necessary to undertake a rigorous examination of the sub-tests in an effort to determine their reliability in measuring psychomotor functioning and their predictive value with respect to subsequent school achievement.

The average family income for the children who had taken both tests was $4,448.90. Analysis of the data indicated a positive relationship between family income and mean IQ. The correlation between income and IQ is .39. Although the positive correlation of .39 is relatively low, it is significant at the .05 level of confidence.

When an analysis was conducted using the median income, statistically significant differences in IQ were found for those above the median income and those below the median income for the group. The mean IQ for the above the median group was 100.2, while the mean IQ for the below the median group was 94.9.

The literature is replete with studies attesting to the association between income and intelligence (Jones, Terrell, DeShields, Taylor, & Fishman, 1966). Parents with higher socioeconomic status are able to provide more cognitive stimulation for their children than parents of lower socioeconomic status.

The fact that this difference would be expressed with families whose median incomes is less than $900 above the often used $3,000 poverty cutoff point has obvious implications for the planner and the researcher.

A comparison was made between the Stanford-Binet test performance of the preschool enrollee and the children not enrolled during the different testing periods (time and staff limitations precluded a posttest of the not enrolled group). There were no statistically significant differences for the following comparisons: (a) results obtained on the first testing of the experimental group, whose mean IQ was 96.3 with the results obtained on the control group whose mean IQ was 98.8; (b) the average mean IQ of 98.0 of the first and second testing of the experimental group with the mean IQ or 98.8 of the first testing of the control group.

The absence of a statistically significant gain in IQ of the children enrolled in school over those not enrolled should not be interpreted as being indicative of a lack of effectiveness of the preschool experience in stimulating cognitive development.

It may be argued that the time between pre- and posttesting was not long enough to expect significant increases in cognitive development.

McHugh (1943) has reported, however, a significant mean rise in IQ scores of a group of public school children who were tested upon entering kindergarten and retested in as short a time period as two months.

It may also be argued that the effects of this experience may not be discernible until much later. Deutsch (1964) contends that the effect of the preschool experience is more likely to differentiate between the two groups significantly at the fifth grade level than it is at the first grade level. Some differentiation, however, does occur at the first grade level.

When the possible differential effect that a particular preschool center might have on intellectual performance of the preschool enrollee was examined, no statistically significant differences were found between centers. This preschool sample was drawn from a common population with respect to broken homes, overcrowding, number of siblings and combined family income. The experience gained at the five different preschool centers did not differentially affect the intellectual performance over the first seven months of exposure to these centers for these children whose backgrounds are essentially the same.

It should be emphasized that to measure the ultimate effect of the pre-school experience, it will be necessary to obtain evaluative criteria six years after exposure to the program. It is also important to ascertain the progress of these children at periodic intervals and to continue to contrast their progress with the progress of the children not exposed to the pre-school experience.

From measures taken in such studies, it may be possible to generate some predictive indices of school performance at later ages for this segment of the population.

References

Anastasi, A. *Psychological testing*. (2nd ed.) New York: MacMillan, 1961.

Deutsch, M. The disadvantaged child and the learning process. In F. Reissman, J. Cohen, & A. Pearl (Eds.), *Mental health of the poor*. New York: Free Press of Glencoe, 1963. Pp. 173–187.

Freeman, F. S. Intelligence. In A. Deutsch & H. Fishman (Eds.), *The encyclopedia of mental health*. New York: Franklin Watts, 1963. Pp. 872–881.

Jones, R. J., Terrell, D. L., DeShields, J. I., Taylor, J. O., & Fishman, J. R. The net impact of the Cardozo demonstration project: First Annual Report. Washington, D. C.: Institute for Youth Studies, Howard University, July 1966.

McHugh, G. Changes in IQ at the public school kindergarten level. *Psychological Monographs*, 1943, 55(2).

Terman, L. M., & Merrill, M. A. *Stanford-Binet Intelligence Scale-Manual for the Third Revision Form L-M*. Boston: Houghton Mifflin, 1960.

4 An Experiment in the Development of Readiness in a Culturally Disadvantaged Group of First Grade Children

WILLIAM F. BRAZZIEL & MARY TERRELL
Coordinator of General Studies, Norfolk Division of the Virginia State College
First Grade Teacher, E. A. Harrold School, Millington, Tennessee

Brazziel and Terrell report the results of a project in which they attempted to develop readiness for school in disadvantaged first grade children. The work is significant for two reasons: (1) it shows that severely disadvantaged children can be tutored and assisted to the point where they closely resemble their more fortunate counterparts in intellectual ability and interest, and (2) it is an excellent example of the *Control Group* versus *Experimental Group* research design. This is one of the basic designs utilized in the behavioral sciences, and derives from the fact that we begin with two comparable groups and expose one, the *Experimental Group*, to the conditions whose effects we are interested in investigating. Since the *Control Group* does not receive the experimental treatment, the results of the research are assessed by considering the final differences between the two groups (see Tables 1, 2, and 3 in particular).

The great challenge to the schools in America which teach the poor, and thus the culturally disadvantaged groups, is that of overcoming the operation of age-grade decrements in intelligence and achievement in their pupil populations and thereby of developing children and youth who can realize the American dream of equality of economic opportunity regardless of the circumstances of birth. As a rule, the child from the disadvantaged home will come to the school slightly less prepared in both literacy

SOURCE. Reprinted from *Journal of Negro Education*, 1962, 31, 4-7, with permission of the senior author and the publisher.

and social learnings than will his more fortunate middle or upper income counterpart. As a result he carries from the school a disproportionately smaller gain in learning. This decrement is reflected in a gradual decrease in intelligence and achievement test scores as the child moves through the school. Generally, such children can be expected to "lose" 15–20 points in intelligence by the end of junior high school and to be from two to three years "behind" in school work. The solution to this inexcusable devastation of human potential is, perhaps, a corps of teachers who will search very diligently for ways and means to narrow the cultural gaps very quickly upon induction into school of the disadvantaged child and to keep it narrowed as he moves through it.

PURPOSE

The purpose of this study was to test the hypothesis that a guidance approach to registration and school induction and an intensified teacher-parent approach to the creation of reading and number readiness would overcome the ravages of the cultural heritage of a disadvantaged group of first grade children.

METHOD

Twenty-six Negro first grade children in the E. A. Harrold School of Millington, Tennessee were used as an experimental group and three first grade sections of 25, 21 and 20 children respectively were used as control groups. The majority of the children were from farm or part-time farm families. The majority could be classified as culturally disadvantaged. The experimental group was registered and inducted into the school under a system which included the following innovations:

1. Participation of the teacher in the pre-school physical examinations of the children and the use of knowledge gained therefrom to plan with parents and to do classroom planning.

2. Two separate registration days, one each for parents and pupils. The parents spent the day going over the rhyme and reason of the readiness period, the first grade work and the school generally. The pupils spent the day in orientation and socialization. Each group had a special luncheon prepared and a spirit of ease and fellowship was achieved.

The parents were met weekly for the six weeks of the readiness period in an hour or so of group work on the progress of the program plus personal conferences on problems. A 30-minute educational television program commercially sponsored was watched daily by the children in the homes. The program was of an enrichment nature consisting mainly of travelogues. The children were given the experiences of the Scott Foresman Readiness Series consisting of six weeks of intensified activity to develop perception, vocabulary, word reasoning, ability and will to follow directions. The children began "reading" exercises on the first day even though the majority of the group was memorizing or improvising from pictures.

A test on some phase of readiness was given each week. The tests were taken from the 1960 series of the *Weekly Reader*. The Readiness Checklist of the *Reader* was also used. The Metropolitan Readiness Test was administered at the end of the six weeks readiness period. At the end of seven months of study, the Detroit Intelligence Test was administered to the group.

RESULTS

A tabular analysis of the study contains data for the following findings.

1. The experimental group scored at the 50th percentile, the national average, on the readiness test which was given at the end of the readiness period. The control groups scored at the 16, 14, and 13th percentile respectively. The difference in readiness scores of experimental and control groups was significant at the .01 level of confidence. (See Table 1.)

2. The scores of the experimental group approached the symmetry of the normal curve of development while the control group scores were skewed sharply left.

3. The experimental group when compared to the four groups of the previous year which had been taught by the same corps of teachers,

TABLE 1

A Comparison of Experimental and Control Groups on the Metropolitan Readiness Test at the End of the Readiness Period (6 weeks)

Group	Number	Mean Reading Readiness	Mean Number Readiness	Mean Total Readiness	Percentile Rank
Experimental	26	48.2*	18.3*	66.0*	50*
Control A	25	38.1	6.7	48.7	16
Control B	21	35.9	7.0	48.5	14
Control C	20	36.5	5.0	45.0	13

* Differences significant at .01 level of confidence. (Test of t).

TABLE 2

A Comparison of Experimental and Control Groups on Previous Year
Tests of Readiness

Group	Number		Mean Reading Readiness		Mean Number Readiness		Mean Total Readiness		Percentile Rank	
	'59	'60	1959	1960	1959	1960	1959	1960	1959	1960
Experimental	26	26	42	48*	12	18*	59	66*	35	50
Control A	28	25	39	38	9	6	48	48	16	16
Control B	28	21	35	36	8	7	45	46	13	14
Control C	23	20	34	36	8	6	42	45	10	13

* Differences Significant at .01 level of confidence.

showed a significant gain of 15 percentile points over the class taught by
the experimental teacher and 34, 37 and 40 percentile points over the control groups. (See Table 2.)

4. The experimental group scored slightly above the national average
on the intelligence test which was administered in the spring. Their score
(106.5) was 16 points above the general expectations for culturally-de-
prived children as revealed by the literature. Their score was 15 points
above the score compiled by second grade county Negro children in the
1959 statewide testing program in Virginia Schools. (Tables 3 and 4.)

CONCLUSIONS AND IMPLICATIONS

An efficacious combination consisting of a direct parent-teacher partner-
ship, permissive regimentation, test wisdom development, excellent materials and energetic uninhibited teaching seems to have been the main
discovery of this study.

TABLE 3

A Comparison of Intelligence Quotients of Experimental Group with Cronbach
Indices for Culturally Disadvantaged Children

Group	Mean Intelligence Quotient	Standard Deviation
Experimental	106.5	13.2
Cronbach Indices*	90	—

* From Lee Cronbach *Esssentials of Psychological Testing*, New York: Harper
and Co., 1960.

TABLE 4

A Comparison of Intelligence Quotients of Experimental Group with Virginia School Children* in Grades Two and Seven

Group	Mean Intelligence Quotient	Standard Deviation
Experimental (First Grade)	106.5	13.2
Virginia City White, Grade 2†	100.4	—
Virginia County White, Grade 2	99.8	—
Virginia City Negro, Grade 2	94.1	—
Virginia County Negro, Grade 2	91.4	—
Virginia City White, Grade 8‡	102.0	—
Virginia County White, Grade 8	100.0	—
Virginia City Negro, Grade 8	90.0	—
Virginia County Negro, Grade 8	85.0	—

* *Report of the Virginia Testing Program* 1959–60, Richmond: Virginia State Board of Education.
† Kuhlman—Anderson Test M = 101.6.
‡ California Mental Maturity Test M = 100.0.

As Allison Davis so well said some ten or twelve years ago, when the battle against the then-widely-prevailing concept of inherent intellectual inferiority was first joined, to be poor is not necessarily to be ill-educated but such a circumstance increases the likelihood of one's being so. The findings of this little study might well be duplicated by alert and committed teachers and parents of disadvantaged children everywhere. It would seem particularly imperative that such a form of uninhibited thinking and planning and teaching should come to the Negro child who in addition to the yoke of poverty, must also bear the cross of economic bigotry.

As one warms in the reflected goodness of a group of sharecropper's children who are performing as Americans in a public school, it is almost impossible to escape the chill of the dismaying realization that a continuation of this glorious circumstance, and others like it, will depend directly upon the expertise of an additional corps of six or seven elementary-school and five or ten high-school teachers, and that this will and bent for the needed personal invention might not be harbored in every classroom and supervisory office. This does not have to be. And it should not be if the goals of universal education are to be realized fully.

5 Some Educational Implications of the Influence of Rejection on Aspiration Levels of Minority Group Children

REGINA M. GOFF
Morgan State College, Baltimore, Maryland

Dr. Regina Goff has examined the effects that cultural rejection may have on the level of aspiration of minority group children. Essentially this paper deals with the extent to which cultural rejection will cause a person to reconsider what he may be able to achieve or produce, and because of the rejection and lack of support from his social environment, settle for a much less significant level of achievement than might otherwise be the case. She utilized the survey method in her report, another very powerful and useful research technique (see Shelton, 1965; and Shelton, 1968 for other examples of the survey technique), and also looks at two separate age groups, 6 to 8 and 12 to 14, in order to examine the relationship of age to the perception and effects of such cultural rejection. Her discussion is an exceptionally thoughtful and candid statement regarding certain long-term effects of maturing in a culture that offers active rejection of one's person and beliefs.

This study is concerned with the social pressure of rejection as it acts as a barrier to effective intellectual and social functioning of minority group children. The purpose is to consider approaches in guidance which may offset attitudinal and action patterns which follow rejection and which subsequently interfere with goals or aspiration levels of the individual who is rejected.

The term is used in the sense of a feeling state which represents a response to specific overt action patterns such as being barred from activities and institutions freely attended by others. The act of rejecting is essen-

SOURCE. Reprinted from *Journal of Experimental Education,* 1954, **23**, 179–183, with permission of the author and Dembar Educational Research Services, Inc.

tially a dispatching of annoyers to which the designated individual responds with discomfort. An assumption made is that attitudes have a pervasive effect on behavior; that goals personally anticipated have an "inner structure"[1] which reflects attitudes of confidence; that experiences subsequent to the original goal-setting may depress attitudes and thus deflect the individual from anticipated paths leading to the attainment of the goal. Further, ways of thinking concerning the self become habituated through time in terms of social reinforcements. The individual thus learns to place values on himself in terms of positive or negative experiencing. It is the desire here to indicate how educational experience may contribute to positive conditioning with reference to the self.

In analysis of the problem, there is presented, first, an exploration of the probable strength of intervening annoyers and interferences through an appraisal of the picture which a designated group of children have of themselves, including, among other things, their own evaluation of their abilities and the concomitant goals which they have set. This is followed by a consideration of actual achievement as it is found in adult members of the same group. The probable strength of annoyances in forestalling the realization of goals may be indicated by the consistency or discrepancy existing between goals of young group members and actual achievement as it is found in mature members of the same group. The approach thus followed includes, a presentation of original, empirical data on the children studied and a summary of the findings. Next, a comparative statement of the status of adult members of the same group, and finally interpretations and implications with reference to offsetting the effects of rejection.

DESCRIPTION OF THE STUDY

One hundred twenty children, including 60 boys and 60 girls were interviewed in Durham, North Carolina, in the summer of 1951. Represented in the group were 6 to 8 year old children and those aged 12 to 14. Equal members were in each group. Two age groups were used in order to note any changes in attitudes or outlook during the years of growing awareness, deepening perception, the acquisition of new knowledges, and new realizations concerning individual abilities. Upper and lower income groups are also represented in recognition of the fact that individuals in different social and economic groups "act in response to their cultural

---

[1] Kurt Lewin, et al. "Levels of Aspiration," in *Personality and Behavior Disorders*, Vol. II (New York: Ronald Press, 1944), p. 335.

training, to their particular system of socio-economic rewards."[2] Contrast in social experiencing and training result in subjective intellectual and emotional reactions which result in contrast in thought, feeling, and action.

Questions asked centered around successes or failures in competitive out-of-school activities (games and sports) in which they freely engaged; ranking of the self in relation to in-school academic performance; ambitions, goals or aspiration levels, and major wishes held. Where one places himself, reflects personal feelings of potentialities, confidence, and worth of self. Ambitions or goals are natural consequents of self-evaluation. That there may be wishful thinking rather than objective, realistic evaluations, is a possibility. Nevertheless, such thinking furnishes a basis for action. In-school and out-of-school performances were considered to note any possible differences in ranking of the self in freely chosen activities and those which are adult imposed tasks. Wishes, revealing unfulfilled desires or "formulated aspirations" indicate sensitivity to lacks. This ego involved sensitivity provides vulnerable areas in personality structure on which negative pressures may make immediate and noticeable inroads.

The qualitative data from the interviews are categorized and later quantified in terms of percentage in various categories. In order to obtain significant differences in responses according to age level and economic bracket, where appropriate, the chi-square technique was employed.

In giving results obtained, it is recognized that 6 to 8 year old children, because of limited experience, may present fanciful conjectures. Nevertheless, if such should be the case, it is not amiss to place credence in responses inasmuch as phantasy has its origin in experience, real or vicarious, and thought patterns emerge from such content. It may be added that 12 to 14 year old children may voice social expectations or approved-of-goals rather than true individual expectancies. However, in 46% of the cases, the ambitions of children differed from parental expectations of them which might indicate some genuine personal concern on the part of the subjects.

STATEMENT OF FINDINGS

  I. Competency in in-school and out-of-school activities

  A. In freely chosen out-of-school activities, lower income children indicated a decrease in confidence with increase in age. (Significant at the .01 level of probability.)

---

[2] Allison Davis. "Light from Anthropology," in *Cultural Groups and Human Relations*, Conference on Educational Problems of Special Cultural Groups (New York: Bureau of Publications, Teachers College, Columbia University, 1951), p. 84.

B. Feelings of inadequacy in relation to school subjects were notable in the low income group. But 33% of the girls at each age
level felt competent, while 63% of the younger boys and 37%
of the older had feelings of academic success.

C. Upper income girls indicated rising assurance with age increase
in relation to both in-school and out-of-school activities. (Significant at the .02 level of probability.)

D. There was no significant difference in levels of confidence expressed by 6–8 year old, lower and upper income boys. Older
upper income boys expressed more assurance in relation to
school subjects than the comparable lower income group. (Significant at the .02 level of probability.) However, there was
greater reluctance on the part of upper income boys to make
decisive statements concerning out-of-school activities. Statements such as "Maybe I do as well," "Sometimes," were typical.

E. Results obtained indicate that feelings of worth exist to some
extent in all groups and are found most often in younger children. In the upper income group, children rank themselves as
equally competent or better than their peers more often than
they rank themselves as decisively less capable.

F. Lower income girls hold least feelings of assurance and self-
esteem.

II. Ambitions held, presented according to age, sex, and income level
and in order of first three preferences

A. Lower income group:
Boys: 6–8—Firemen and policemen (26%); brickmasons,
builders, mechanics (24%); lawyers (20%) 12–14—Big
league ball players (40%); doctors (27%); contractors
builders (14%)

Girls: 6–8—Teachers (34%); movie stars, dancers, models
(15%), cooks (14%)
12–14—Teachers (30%); movie stars, dancers, models
(15%); secretarial activities (10%)

B. Upper income group:
Boys: 6–8—Policemen and firemen (34%); builders and mechanics (32%); agents in real-estate offices (14%)
12–14—Doctors and lawyers (46%); scientists, "biologists", "chemists" (20%); architects (10%)

Girls: 6–8—Teachers (34%); nurses (26%); home makers:
mothers (24%)

12–14—Teachers (37%); movie stars (27%); secretaries (14%)

C.   Seventy-nine percent of the lower income boys and 33% of the girls felt that they would reach their goals, while 53% of the upper income boys and 67% of the girls made decisive statements of assurance.

D.   Lower income children held money and lack of opportunity as major interferences while the upper income children named ill-health, physical disabilities, bad luck, and death as possible interventions.

E.   Lower income girls expressed least security with reference to probable success.

III.   Expression of wishes presented in order of first three choices

A.   Lower income group:
Boys: 6–8—Toys (Only wish expressed.)
12–14—Money, clothes
Girls: 6–8—Clothing, food, homes
12–14—Improved physical appearance, homes, families, and money

B.   Upper income group:
Boys: 6–8—Toys, pets
12–14—A wide spread of desires was reported from the acquisition of Eagle Scout badges, success in occupation, money for philanthropic purposes, to more sober wishes for good health to eternal life
Girls: 6–8—Toys, pets
12–14—As above, wishes were divergent with no heavy localization in any particular category. These included distribution from personal luxuries and travel to fulfillment of social needs; "places for colored children to swim," skating rinks, admittance to the "big library."

C.   Particularly in the lower income group were findings similar to those of Gray[3] in which wishes were more in terms of the material and concrete than in terms of the abstract; happiness, health.

[3] S. Gray. "Wishes of Negro Children," *Journal of Genetic Psychology*, LXIV (1944), pp. 225–237.

SUMMARY OF FINDINGS

A glance at trends throughout the findings reveals, with reference to lower income girls, a straight line relationship between low confidence levels, little anticipation of success, and feelings of deprivation as revealed by wishes in areas which contribute to inner securities. Similarly, a thread of continuity appears to run through the findings with reference to the remainder of the group reporting. In general, feelings of confidence are expressed more often than not, positive attitudes of competence exist more frequently than negative ones, ambitions are directed toward occupations which yield substantial economic returns, success in areas of performance are most often expected, and wishes generally are in terms of further self-enhancement.

While these children have no doubt experienced ego-deflation in their movement in the larger world, they evidently see them as isolated from the context of life of the future. There probably exists at these ages no generalized notions of the impact which a totality of rejecting episodes of the larger world may have on the fruition of ambitions. When asked to state conditions which might interfere with the realization of goals, but two mentioned rejecting experiences and conflict in inter-group relations although a much larger number had no doubt experienced unfavorable situations.

THE ADULT POPULATION

If we now turn to the adult population of Negroes in American life, we find but 2.6% of the total group in the professions with more than half that number in the teaching occupations and the remainder spread thinly as doctors, trained ministers, and lawyers. Discriminatory and rejecting practices in industry have leveled the ranks of Negro workers to unskilled and semiskilled employment. Hardly 5% of the total Negro population can be considered in the upper income bracket. How much of the discrepancy which we note between children's confidence levels, their ambitions and wishes toward improvement and adult reflection of lack of fruition of these can be attributed to outright techniques of economic and social discrimination and rejection, or to misjudgment of ability, and how much to apathy or a giving up in the process of development is hardly discernible. Yet, the question appears worthy of consideration. It is highly probable that aspiration levels are lowered, confidences shaken, and wishes abandoned because of psychological omissions in training and guidance. It is also likely that much by way of prevention of wastage of ability and warping of personality could be achieved if, before their inception, effort were made to offset negative attitudinal patterns which are barriers to achievement. While the Negro group was used for the illustrative purposes, it would appear appropriate to assume that the same principles apply to any individuals in comparable unfavorable situations for common causes are present despite other variables.

INTERPRETATIONS AND EDUCATIONAL IMPLICATIONS

As indicated, lower income children showed a marked feeling of inadequacy in relation to school subjects. It is possible that attitudinal patterns stem most directly from early home and cultural influences. In other words, these children have learned a particular response pattern. They have no social heritage akin to scholarly production, nor perhaps do they even have family exposures which reflect a tradition of schooling. Such omissions generate an unfamiliarity with abstract symbols and attendant feelings of shyness concerning them. The discernible trend to feel more at ease in physical games and sports may be worthy of attention. The school might recognize the role of feelings of competence in physical activities from the point of view using these initial security reactions for the development of generalized feelings of adequacy. Praise and commendation following successful endeavor in deliberately chosen games which require thought as well as skill, with this requirement pointed out to the child, releases latent streams of inspiration which invoke motivation to tackle problems with similar requirements in other areas. A greater measure of successful anticipation will accompany effort, and early tendencies to feel incompetent in relation to diverse tasks will be eased.

Incidentally, a factor influencing attitudes toward success in out-of-school activity is absence of adult domination and censure. The child, relieved of the tension of straining for goals set by adults unreservedly directs attention and enthusiasm to the experience at hand. Also, he probably chooses those activities in which he has demonstrated his competence. Teachers might well assume a "background" or "hands off" attitude, thus avoiding unnecessary intrusions which set up emotional restraints.

The discernible trend of decrease in confidence level with increase in age in lower income children has implications for the basic problem—the probable force of the impact of rejection. Greater receptivity, less resistance to social depressors characterize the individual who already has initial feelings of inadequacy and whose confidence level is continuously lowering. In such instances, there are hardly notions of success freely entertained nor high goals set with reference to the larger competitive world.

Lower income girls merit special attention for their reactions indicate a greater sensitivity with reference to the self. A cue is given here for the building of thought patterns, outgrowths of experience, which negate feelings of self-limitations. Otherwise, circumstances of rejection will be accepted as a natural consequence of imagined inadequacy. A capable person may thus never discover latent abilities and as a consequent waste inherent talent.

The contrast furnished by the upper income girls, in which there is increase in self-confidence with age increase, may reflect among other things more considerate classroom treatment. Not infrequently, children from "better" families" are academically favored or given a place of importance which serves to nourish the ego and to influence effort and output. If the difference in feelings of competence can be attributed in part, to interpersonal parent-child, teacher-pupil relations, it is incumbent upon parents and teachers to begin in the early stages of the child's life, particularly low-income children, to contrive planned activities which provide opportunity for independent performances which give status in the respective groups. This in turn provides satisfactions which bolster the ego.

Older upper income boys revealing less confidence than girls in the same group, no doubt have a greater attunement with reality. There is more movement and mingling outside the home and classroom with greater opportunity for sharp person to person comparisions and increased awareness of group standards. Outlooks, as a result, are less hopeful.

As indicated, feelings of worth exist to some extent in all groups. Where found, these positive attitudes may be thought of as "security anchors" which, if strengthened, may, figuratively speaking, provide a basis for the building of a reserve of "ego energy" which in turn holds the individual fast when he is faced with annoyers designed to deflate.

It is interesting to note in relation to occupational choices, that irrespective of socio-economic level and roles of parents, ambitions of children were directed away from more menial types of employment. The increasingly large number of picture magazines and comic strips high-lighting activities of the world outside the home may have some bearing on choices made. An influence, too, may be the recent advent of a few Negroes in occupational avenues previously closed to them. An indication of social direction of a given time is revealed by the beliefs and values held by the children of the culture.

A question sometimes arises with reference to the advisability of giving the growing child a full view of the social world of which he is a part, and of his possible position and treatment within it. As stated earlier, the Negro child voiced little evidence of seeing a relationship between future success in chosen fields and his particular group membership. Is it wise to tell a child of underprivileged parents and deprived homes, or a child of a minority group that he might not be invited to play with some children whose parents consider them better; that he will not be allowed to enter some theaters and restaurants; that adult members of his group are not welcome to live in some neighborhoods and may be bombed out; that there are industries and firms which will not hire them? Is there a risk of unduly planting seeds of inferiority and antagonism? Is it better to let the individual smack up against the culture without forewarning? Perhaps either approach as stated is inadequate. However, if revealing the culture carries with it a "readiness for," a full view of the larger world appears feasible. An approach tinged with self-pity or hatred, rather than understanding, is detrimental. However, if the growing individual were made aware of annoyances and interferences there would more likely be wholehearted cooperation in training designed to weaken the impact. Further, there would follow increased determination to succeed in desired ends.

Though recurring patterns of rejection, mobilized by the culture have persisted through time, few behavioral responses conceived of as psychological defenses have been suggested for withstanding them. However, such insightful training seems a possibility. Teacher training institutions might consider even further than at present the social and psychological role of future teachers and emphasize the meaning of social morality, the study of social-psychological problems, principles of mental hygiene and guidance, and dynamics in human relations. The examination of causal sequences in behavior, attempts to offset the effects of known but uncontrollable causes, the utilization of experimental data in the area of human relations, and use of findings from socio-psychological studies in child guidance would all appear to be aids in filling the notable gaps in the training of minority group children.

Bibliography for Part I

Bayley, N. Comparisons of mental and motor test scores for ages 1–15 months by sex, birth, order, race, geographical location, and education of parents. *Child Development,* 1965, **36**, 379–411 (a).

Bender, Eugene I. Reflections on Negro-Jewish relationships: the historical dimension. *Phylon, Atlanta University Review of Race and Culture,* 1969, **30**(1), 56–65.

Bullough, Bonnie. Alienation in the ghetto. *American Journal of Sociology* (March, 1967), **72**, 469–478.

Canty, Donald. *A Single Society: Alternative to Urban Apartheid.* New York: Frederick A. Praeger, 1969.

Clark, Kenneth B. *Dark Ghetto: Dilemmas of Social Power.* New York: Harper & Row, 1965.

Cravioto, J. Malnutrition and behavioral development in the preschool child. *Pre-School Child Malnutrition.* National Health Science, Public, 1966, No. 1282.

Cravioto, J., De Lincardie, E. R., and Birch, H. G. Nutrition, growth, and neurointegrative development; an experimental and ecologic study. *Pediatrics,* 1966, **38**, 319–372.

Dreger, R. M., and Miller, K. S. Comparative psychological studies of Negroes and whites in the United States: 1959–1965. *Psychological Bulletin,* 1968 (Monogr. Suppl. 70, No. 3, Part 2).

Duncan, O. D., Featherman, D. L., and Duncan, B. Socioeconomic background and occupational achievement extensions of a basic model. Final Report, Project No. 5-0074 (EO-191) U. S. Dept. of Health, Education, and Welfare, Office of Education, Bureau of Research, May, 1968.

Frazier, E. F. Problems of Negro children and youth resulting from family disorganization. *Journal of Negro Education,* 1950, **19**, 269–277.

French, J. R. P., Jr., and Raven, B. The bases of social power. In D. Cartwright and A. Zander (Eds.), *Group Dynamics* (2nd ed.) Evanston, Ill.: Row Peterson, 1960. Pp. 607–623.

Geber, M., and Dean, R. F. A. The state of development of newborn African children. *Lancet,* 1957, 1216–1219.

Green, Robert L., and Hofmann, Louis J. A case study of the effects of educational deprivation on Southern rural Negro children. *Journal of Negro Education* (Summer, 1965), 34, 327–341.

Hardy, J. B. Perinatal factors and intelligence. In S. F. Osler and R. E. Cooke (Eds.), *The Biosocial Basis of Mental Retardation*. Baltimore, Md.: The Johns Hopkins Press, 1965. Pp. 35–60.

Harrell, R. F., Woodyard, E., and Gates, A. I. *The Effects of Mothers' Diets on the Intelligence of Offspring*. New York: Bureau of Publications, Teachers College, 1955.

Hill, A. C., and Jaffee, F. S. Negro fertility and family size preferences. In T. Parsons and K. B. Clark (Eds.), *The Negro American*. Cambridge, Mass.: Houghton-Mifflin, 1966. Pp. 134–159.

Hodges, W. L., and Spicker, H. H. The effects of preschool experiences on culturally deprived children. In W. W. Hartup and N. L. Smothergill (Eds.), *The Young Child: Reviews of Research*. Washington, D. C.: National Association for the Education of Young Children, 1967. Pp. 262–289.

Jensen, A. R. The culturally disadvantaged and the heredity-environment uncertainty. In J. Helmuth (Ed.), *The Culturally Disadvantaged Child*, Vol. 2. Seattle, Wash.: Special Child Publications, 1968.

Jones, H. F. The environment and mental development. In L. Carmichael (Ed.), *Manual of Child Psychology* (2nd ed.) New York: Wiley, 1954. Pp. 631–696.

Krippner, Stanley. Race, intelligence, and segregation: The misuse of scientific data. In Barry N. Schwartz and Robert Disch (Eds.), *White Racism*. New York: Dell, 1970.

Loehlin, J. C. Psychological genetics, from the study of human behavior. In R. B. Cattell (Ed.), *Handbook of Modern Personality Theory*. New York: Aldine, in press.

Miller, Carroll L. Educational opportunities and the Negro child in the South. *Harvard Educational Review* (Summer, 1960), 30, 195–208.

Moynihan, D. P. Employment, income, and the ordeal of the Negro family. In T. Parsons and K. B. Clark (Eds.), *The Negro American*. Cambridge, Mass.: Houghton-Mifflin, 1966. Pp. 134–159.

Nelson, G. K., and Dean, R. F. *Bulletin of the World Health Organization*, 1959, 21, 779. Cited by G. Cravioto, Malnutrition and behavioral development in the preschool child. *Pre-School Child Malnutrition*. National Health Science, Public, 1966, No. 1282.

Ovington, Mary White. *Half a Man: the Status of the Negro in New York*. New York: Schocken Books, 1969.

Pettigrew, Thomas F. *A Profile of the Negro American*. Princeton: D. Van Nostrand, Inc., 1964.

Raymond, Richard. Mobility and economic progress of Negro Americans during the 1940's. *American Journal of Economics and Sociology,* 1969, **28**(4), 337–350.

Schmuck, Richard A., and Luszki, Margaret Barron. Black and white students in several small communities. *Journal of Applied Behavioral Science,* 1969, **5**(2), 203–220.

Skeels, H. M., and Dye, H. B. A study of the effects of differential stimulation on mentally retarded children. *Procedural Address of the American Association for Mental Deficiency,* 1939, **44**, 114–136.

Social Education. Minority Groups in American society. 1969, **33**(4), 429–446.

Spuhler, J. N., and Lindzey, G. Racial differences in behavior. In J. Hirsch (Ed.), *Behavior-Genetic Analysis.* New York: McGraw-Hill, 1967. Pp. 366–414.

Tyler, L. E. *The Psychology of Human Differences* (3rd ed.) New York: Appleton-Century-Crofts, 1965.

Vernon, P. E. Environmental handicaps and intellectual development: Part II and Part III. *British Journal of Educational Psychology,* 1965, **35**, 1–22.

Walters, C. E. Comparative development of Negro and white infants. *Journal of Genetic Psychology,* 1967, **110**, 243–251.

Wilcox, Roger. Music ability among Negro grade school pupils: Or, I got rhythm? *Perceptual and Motor Skills,* 1969, **29**, 167–168.

Wilcox, Roger. Further ado about Negro music ability. *Journal of Negro Education,* 1970, in process.

Zigler, E. Familial mental retardation: a continuing dilemma. *Science,* 1967, **155**, 292–298.

PART II

Racial Integration: Academic and Social Implications

The articles in this section examine the implications of racial integration for Black Americans. It is obviously not enough to integrate the races; a very significant issue revolves around the educational and social implications of the integration itself. Dr. Jenkins' (1954) early paper focuses on the problems likely to be generated by widespread racial integration and is frankly prophetic. As President of Morgan State College, Dr. Jenkins was called on to summarize a three-day conference on racial integration in education and in so doing addressed most of the significant issues involved. Dr. Green (1966) examines the various problems in social learning that will arise as a result of scholastic integration, while Dr. Williams (1968) surveys certain components of Southern Negro students' attitudes toward integration. Finally, Drs. Green and Morgan (1969) examine the effects of Prince Edward County's Black children resuming their schooling following its disruption by civil rights litigation.

6 Problems Incident to Racial Integration and Some Suggested Approaches to These Problems — a Critical Summary

MARTIN D. JENKINS
President, Morgan State College

Dr. Jenkins has reviewed and summarized the papers that were presented to the Conference on the Courts and Racial Integration in Education (Howard University, April, 1952), and presents what is essentially a blueprint for the requisite overall problem of racial integration *in education*. His paper is a scholarly, detailed, and straightforward statement of the many educational problems related to racial integration. Dr. Jenkins considers the ramifications of educational integration for the students, their Black and white teachers, and also the institutions. In addition, he makes some candid, significant comments about Negro colleges and universities that merit careful consideration. The interested reader should review the papers of the entire conference (*Journal of Negro Education*, 1954) in order to gain the perspective necessary to meaningfully appreciate Dr. Jenkins' insight of nearly 20 years ago.

Our responsibility at this final session is to summarize in critical fashion the assumptions, findings, and conclusions of a three-day conference. This is not an easy task. All of the participants in this conference are distinguished persons whose views demand respect and consideration. Simply to summarize these views would not be too difficult. To be critical, however, in a personal sense, would be presumptuous. I must, perforce, assume the role of a Quaker moderator and attempt to express "the sense of the meeting" in a not too uncritical fashion. The larger value of this conference lies in the critical summary and evaluation each delegate will make for himself.

The present paper is concerned primarily with the educational and

SOURCE. Reprinted from *Journal of Negro Education*, 1954, **21**, 411-421, with permission of the author and the publisher.

social problems incident to racial integration in education. The appraisal of court action and the development of cooperative acceptance are to be covered by other papers and will consequently be given only peripheral attention here.

It is desirable at the outset that the scope and limitations of this conference be explicitly defined. The conference is concerned primarily with racial integration in *education* and only incidentally with integration in other areas of American life. This is due in part to the fact that the proceedings are to be published in the Yearbook issue of a publication devoted to educational problems. It is due in larger part, though, to recognition of the facts that the public school is the symbol of democracy and equal opportunity and that the segregated school is more than simply an educational institution—it is an instrument of policy and a symbol of subordinate status. Education, consequently, becomes the center of attraction in the struggle against segregation.

The discussions have been confined largely to Negro-white relationships in this country. The integration problems of the Mexicans, the orientals, and the foreign-born have been only incidentally considered. Despite this neglect, these too are problems which America must face and solve.

Implicit in the thinking of the membership of this conference are several basic assumptions, the most important of which are the following:

Racial segregation and discrimination are incompatible with the ideals of a democratic society and a violation of the Christian ethic. Disabilities and distinctions based on race, therefore, have no place in American life; their entire removal is a desirable and necessary goal.

This would appear to be a self-evident proposition in our society in accordance both with constitutional guarantees of individual liberty and the concept of brotherhood inherent in the Christian faith. This assumption probably is held, implicitly at least, by a majority of the American people. Except for a small minority of racists, even those who oppose racial integration present their objections to the removal of racial disabilities in terms of time and timing.

Attitudes in the area of race relations are rapidly changing to the extent that there is a readiness on the part of the dominant racial group to accept racial integration in education now to some extent and in some situations, and ultimately throughout the country and in all areas of American life.

The dynamic character of race relations is, of course, a matter of fact. In the area of education the admission of Negroes to Southern graduate and professional schools, the increasing integration of Negro students and teachers in schools and colleges of the North, the deterioration of racial segregation practices in the educational programs sponsored by the armed services have all been accomplished without friction and indeed with the general acceptance of the white groups concerned. Integration works anywhere it has been tried.

Racial integration, although in accordance with the principles of our social organization, is contrary to historic and current practice. Its functional incorporation into the social fabric, therefore, has created and will create opposition and tension.

We are all creatures of our culture. Deep-rooted behavior patterns, such as those involved in racial relationships, are not easily and readily changed. The protection of vested interests, whether concerned with the material fact of economic competition or the psychic fact of maintenance of the ego, inevitably constitutes a barrier to change. It is recognized that in the implementation of racial integration there will be individual casualties, in an economic and social sense, among both Negroes and white persons.

Finally, in its deliberations the conference implicitly accepted Thompson's definition of the term *racial integration*: " 'Full racial integration in education' means that schools will be established and maintained where the admission of students; the employment of teachers, non-teaching personnel, administrative officers, and members of boards of control; and participation in the official life of the school by all concerned are based upon aptitude, ability, and character rather than race."

It was not clearly understood by all participants that the mere admission of Negro students to schools and colleges from which they formerly were excluded, or the token employment of a Negro teacher are, by definition, only steps toward integration as conceived by this conference, that *desegregation*—i.e., the mere admission of Negro students to existing institutions for white people—does not constitute *integration* proved a serious source of confusion to some.

It was held by others, correctly, I think, that true integration goes far beyond the mere physical fact of non-segregation; that it involves as well a feeling of acceptance and a sense of belonging on the part of the participating individuals.

THE PRESENT STATUS OF RACIAL INTEGRATION IN EDUCATION

Provisions for the education of Negroes have been greatly improved throughout the South, particularly during the last decade, largely, but not entirely, as a result of legal pressures exerted by and under the direction of the National Association for the Advancement of Colored People. The principle of "separate but equal" facilities has been generally adopted by the dominant racial group and in many, many localities a real effort is being made to bring Negro schools up to the level of their white counterparts. Nevertheless, by all objective criteria, facilities and opportunities for Negroes are still greatly inferior to those for whites.

Negro students are currently enrolled in graduate and professional schools, and in some instances undergraduate curricula in institutions formerly restricted to white students, in 12 Southern states and the District of Columbia. These steps toward desegregation have taken place without incident and with the general and sometimes enthusiastic acceptance of students and faculty. Except in a few parochial schools, racial segregation at the level of elementary and secondary education is universal practice throughout the South.

With a few important exceptions, full racial integration in education does not now exist in any state or any section of the country. Significant steps toward integration are being made in the Northern tier of states and in a number of communities, particularly in Connecticut, New Jersey, Minnesota, and the far Northwest where teachers, as well as students, are being assigned to classes freely without regard to race, and Negroes are appearing with increasing frequency as members of governing boards of the public schools.

Despite these instances of real progress, however, only a very small minority of the Negro population of the North is experiencing full integration and the trend toward desegregation in the South is substantially limited to a few Negro students at the graduate and professional level.

Not a single conference participant expressed satisfaction with the *status quo* or with the progress that has been made in improving the educational opportunities of Negroes—as substantial as this progress has been. Despite this, there has been exhibited a considerable degree of optimism concerning prospects for future progress.

A complex of factors has operated to make possible now a basic change in social pattern which would have been almost inconceivable a quarter of a century ago. The Rooseveltian "New Deal" with its emphasis on the underprivileged; the impact of court decisions; the ideological conflict with communism; the rise of nationalism among the darker peoples of the world; the increasing educational level and political power of the Negro people; the industrialization of the South; the increased sensitivity of religious leaders to social problems; the scientific and practical demonstrations of the abilities of Negro individuals; the cumulative effect of many local incidents of violation of racial mores; and full employment with a resultant decrease of economic conflict have all combined to create a social atmosphere which makes positive progress in race relations possible —indeed inevitable, so long as these factors continue to operate.

That last clause—so long as these factors continue to operate—is tremendously important. Perhaps the conference participants are too optimistic in their (almost) unanimous assumption that the curve of progress in racial integration will continue its upward course in geometric progression. One important aspect of the struggle for full citizenship rights lies in the maintenance of a social atmosphere conducive to further progress.

BASIC PRINCIPLES AND PROBLEMS

From the proceedings of this conference there have been developed areas of agreement on basic issues involved in the problem of racial integration in education.[1] These areas of agreement which may be regarded as *basic principles,* are as follows:

1. Present patterns of racial segregation and discrimination tend to deprive our society of the best resources of the Negro race and to weaken our nation in its ideological conflict with non-democratic powers.

2. The fight for the admission of students to schools and colleges, the employment of teachers and administrators and the selection of governing boards without respect to race must be carried on relentlessly and with increased vigor by all those who are devoted to the democratic way of life.

3. The struggle for racial integration must be conducted within the constitutional framework of our government and with the utilization of tactics appropriate to a democratic society.

4. Racial integration in education is part of a larger complex involving integration in other areas such as employment, housing and government. It is necessary and desirable that the problem of racial integration be attacked on many fronts—legal, political, educational, governmental—rather than on a single front.

5. Participation in the areas of public interpersonal relations such as employment, schooling, housing, politics, civic activities and other public services, without discrimination on account of race, is a basic right which must be guaranteed every citizen by law.

6. It is not possible to establish "separate and equal" facilities. The best education of all students, from the elementary through the graduate level, can be achieved only under conditions of racial integration in our society.

7. Educational institutions organized on the basis of race must redefine their purposes and seek to serve a clientele on a non-racial basis where this is legally permissible.

8. Integration practices are not to be selective and applicable only to a

---

[1] No votes were taken during the conference. Although there was no articulate disagreement, it is probable that some delegates do not fully subscribe to the principles stated.

few. The token admission of a few Negro students to schools and colleges formerly restricted to white persons and the token employment of a few Negro teachers in schools and colleges cannot be regarded as satisfactory even as a step toward integration.

There were a number of areas in which there was a considerable amount of disagreement and in which the conference could not arrive at a consensus. The more important of these areas of disagreement, which are termed her *problems,* will now be briefly considered.

THE ROLE OF THE NEGRO COLLEGE UNDER INTEGRATION

The conference gave considerable attention to the question of what will happen to the Negro institutions of higher education, both public and private, under conditions of desegregation and integration. These colleges were established and are now supported to afford opportunities which were and are not available to Negroes at the institutions attended by white persons. There is no question but as racial bars are lowered the role of the segregated college will change. The extent and direction of this change cannot now be predicted nor can any general statement be made which will apply equally to the future of every existing institution.

It was the consensus of this conference that under conditions of full racial integration some of the present Negro colleges will be discontinued but that many will and should continue to exist, but as institutions serving all the people. It is felt that the first casualties will be the weaker colleges and those geographically adjacent to the stronger existing white institutions. In view of the anticipated increase in college enrollments in the years ahead, most of the publicly-supported institutions will be retained as a part of the states' system of higher education. A majority of the existing privately-supported colleges for Negroes will continue to exist to serve a clientele on an integrated basis and thus join the scores of private colleges now serving their respective communities in the South. The racial composition of the staffs of both existing white and Negro institutions will undergo a process of gradual change and integration.

The land-grant colleges for Negroes pose a special problem because of their highly specialized curricula and because their programs are not comparable in scope and quality with white land-grant colleges in the same region. With Negro students freely admitted to the state universities and land-grant colleges, existing institutions for Negroes need no longer strive to become prototypes of the presently-organized white institutions. If these institutions are to survive at all in their land-grant function, their program must be reorganized to offer specialized curricula for the benefit of all of the people of the state. The danger here, of course, is that, under such arrangement an attempt may be made to perpetuate present patterns of inferiority and segregation and thus force continued appeal to the courts. There is need for serious and critical thinking with respect to the purposes and program of the existing land-grant colleges. The only alternative to the ultimate abandonment of the land-grant phase of their work is a redefinition of function in terms of service to all citizens of the state.

I sense the majority opinion of this conference to be that the Negro colleges have the responsibility of "working themselves out of a job," not necessarily as colleges but as segregated institutions. It is recognized that in the process there will be casualties among both administrators and teachers, and immediate losses to communities through being deprived of cultural centers. In the final analysis, though, Negroes will benefit through improved educational facilities and increased opportunities for employment and adjustment in the general society. I may add that little attention was given, other than in the area of employment, to losses which will come with integration.

Adjustment of Negro Teachers and Administrators

The severity of the adjustment problem to be faced by Negro staff members depends in large measure upon the abruptness of change and whether, as anticipated, a large portion of existing institutions will be retained. Eventually, Negro teachers will take their places beside their white colleagues in schools and colleges throughout the nation. The short-term problem is one of individual competence and the willingness of institutions and communities to accept Negro teachers in non-segregated classrooms.

Just as in other areas of American life where racial segregation practices have been altered, institutions and communities throughout the nation will come to accept Negro teachers and administrators on the basis of their professional ability, as is being done now in a number of Northern cities and states. Negro teachers must be prepared to compete not as a unit but as individuals and with all others engaged in similar lines of work. As pointed out in this conference by Miller, "Only as the individual is willing to work harder, study longer, express himself more precisely, delve more deeply into research can he expect to achieve the goals he and his people have set for themselves. The Negro is, at this point, in the same position as representatives of other minorities. He cannot escape such rivalry nor can he hope to gain his place on other terms."

Adjustment of Negro Children and Youth to the Integrated Situation

Almost entirely neglected in this conference was the problem of the adjustment of the Negro child or youth who participates or shares directly in a racially-integrated situation in high school or college. Since this problem was not considered, I can only call attention to the fact that children and youth do, and will, in the beginning at least, have difficulties in academic and social adjustment. The effect of these problems both on the individual and on the process of integration demands careful consideration and study.

ELEMENTS OF A PROGRAM FOR THE FUTURE

The very topic of this conference has served to place emphasis upon the legal approach and to divert attention from other important techniques for achieving integration.

It is recognized that there is no alternative to court action in the elimination of segregation in the schools and colleges of the nation. It is clearly the sense of this conference, however, that racial integration in education cannot be achieved by court decisions alone. Other tactics, techniques, or approaches must be utilized concurrently to achieve racial integration. These things will seem "old hat" to members of this audience; as familiar as they are, though, they are essential.

Before considering each of the several approaches, I wish to make two observations which are relevant to the grand strategy of achieving racial integration.

First, it is a matter of considerable significance that there was little indication in this conference of any willingness to compromise at any point. Nevertheless, it is universal social and political experience that deep-rooted issues on which the protagonists hold tenacious views are resolved through compromise. At the risk of being termed an appeaser, I believe that we must be prepared to compromise, not on basic principle, but on intermediate adaptations at many points.

Second, it is imperative that in our struggle for democracy we preserve the democratic tradition of respect for minority viewpoints. There is observable a tendency to be impatient with persons whose views with regard to a particular tactic to be employed differ from the majority view. We must, of course, maintain and insist upon a solid front on the basic issue of the elimination of racial segregation from American life. Let us, though, recognize that there are choices in strategy and that persons of the highest integrity may often select different alternatives to arrive at common objectives.

Education

Certainly no thoughtful person would deny that racial integration in education can be achieved in a fundamental sense only if it is acceptable to

—or at least not rejected by—a majority of the dominant racial group. It follows, then, that education—and we may include in the term "good" propaganda—is a desirable and necessary tactic.

The 13th Yearbook of the Journal, *Education for Racial Understanding* (1944) explored in much greater detail than was possible in the present conference the question of how the educational process might be effectively utilized. It was pointed out that the immediate function of education is to change the attitudes of the majority racial group through the utilization of schools and colleges, the church and religious organizations, organized labor, advancement organizations, government agencies, mass communication media and personal contacts.

An action program on the basis of the findings of the 13th Yearbook is necessary and desirable. To be guarded against, however, is the tendency to restrict education to verbalization and to allow talk to become a substitute for action. The effectivenes of education must be judged not simply by increased knowledge but in terms of changed behavior.

There is need, too, for redirecting the attitudes of Negroes themselves with respect to the problem of racial integration in education. The Negro people generally must be brought to understand the limitations placed upon them by segregation practices. In our segregated schools and colleges advantage must be taken of the opportunity to teach our youth democratic viewpoints and techniques for achieving racial integration.

Political Pressure

Negroes are becoming an increasingly significant factor on the American political scene. They are voting in the South to a greater extent than ever before and in many Northern states and communities they constitute the balance of political power. The emergence of this group has exerted tremendous influence on the alignment of diverse groups within the two major political parties and in isolated instances has resulted in tangible and observable gains for the masses of the Negro people.

The use of the ballot for social reform in a democracy is a basic and legitimate procedure. Effective utilization of this instrumentality to attain racial integration in education entails the delineation of definite goals, political education in schools and on the adult level, intensified campaigns on the local level to increase the number of registrants and voters, and the education of candidates on the issues of race.

It must be clearly recognized, however, that for a minority group to structure an election on the basis of race alone would be fatal to the attainment of its objectives. What is indicated is the support of genuinely liberal candidates, regardless of party affiliation, who exhibit a readiness to incorporate Negroes into the fabric of American life.

Statutory Enactment

The 14th Amendment to the Federal Constitution, which guarantees the individual the full privileges and immunities of citizenship, due process and the equal protection of the laws, provides the constitutional basis for the legal attack on racial segregation. The Constitution, however, "means what the Supreme Court says it means" and in a more fundamental sense means what the people clearly demand that it mean. Interpretations in the area of civil rights, as in others, vary, therefore, with changes on the personnel of the Court and with changes in the climate of public sentiment.

The enactment of legislation should be sought at both the Federal and state levels which specifically prohibit racial segregation in education. A number of states have already enacted such legislation with varying degrees of effectiveness. The experience at New Jersey, whose constitution provides that "no person shall be denied the enjoyment of any civil or military right, nor be discriminated against in the exercise of any civil or military right, nor be segregated in the militia or the public schools, because of religious scruples, race, color, ancestry, or national origin," (Art. 1, Sec. 5) suggests that with the appropriate techniques and social climate, racial integration in education can be achieved.

Legislation which assures the tenure and seniority rights of teachers should also be sought. It is to be emphasized, however, that the experience of states such as Illinois shows that mere adoption of such legislation will not assure integration. Desirable if not essential concomitants are, determination of state officials to administer the law with firmness and the imposition of financial sanctions on school districts for non-compliance.

While it is unrealistic to anticipate the enactment of such legislation in the Southern and border states in the foreseeable future, this is a basic and effective approach to promote integration involving both students and employed personnel.

Enlisting the Support of Liberal Southerners

In my experience, there are many, many Southerners, call them "cultural sports" if you will, who are ready not only to accept but to work for racial integration. They are to be found at all class levels and at all ages but particularly among the younger generation. As Granger pointed out at an earlier session, "The intensity of the spirit of liberal reform in the South has probably been exaggerated by professional optimists as seriously as it has been underestimated by determined pessimists. Nevertheless, it is a fact that such a spirit does exist and is growing steadily. There has been too little recognition and examination of that growth by the very people who have most to profit from it."

Utilization and Cooperation of Advancement Associations

Our advancement organizations, the National Association for the Advancement of Colored People, the National Urban League, the American Council on Human Rights, the religious and fraternal councils and committees have done a magnificent job in promoting the cause for human rights in this country. Without these organizations, especially, in this connection, the NAACP, the upsurge in educational opportunities for Negro youth would certainly not yet have occurred.

The very holding of this conference has vital meaning for these organizations. The process of sitting down and discussing problems with officers of other organizations having similar goals, and legal, educational, and governmental leaders from all sections of the country cannot fail to yield fruitful values. This procedure will serve to keep the leadership of these advancement organizations in close touch with the field and to avert the minor, and sometimes major, conflicts of policy. I would urge these organizations to provide for the calling of periodic conferences such as this one as a technique for testing the validity and feasibility of projected lines of action.

Utilization of Non-Racial Organizations

We have had the common experience in this conference of considering the racial question involved as if it exists in a vacuum; as if it is unrelated to all the other social, economic and political forces operating in our society. This is not altogether fair criticism, for among the participants have been representatives of labor, the church, and government. But it is a substantially valid comment in that the discussions have been couched almost exclusively within the framework of Negro-white relations.

Recognition must be given to the fact that the problem of racial adjustment touches many facets of American life. The indirect approach to racial integration, through identifying our interests with the basic objectives of labor, the church, political organizations, and the like, may in a fundamental sense be just as effective as direct attack. Let us, then, cooperate with and become a part of all those movements and organizations in American life which have as their objective improvement of the welfare of the people.

CONCLUSION

This has been a fruitful conference and it has made a significant contribution to race relations in this country. I believe it will come to be regarded as one of the important milestones in the exciting, if sometimes halting, journey this country is making toward a truly democratic society. There were a number of areas of disagreement as to tactics, as to immediate outcomes to be sought. But the main lines, the important lines, are clear and unmistakable.

Perhaps the most important single outcome of this conference is the demonstration of the absolute unanimity of Negro leadership that racial segregation must be abolished from American life. There was not a single dissenting voice. So far as Negro leadership is concerned, the doctrine of "separate and equal" facilities is dead as an objective or as a satisfactory solution.

There is full agreement, further, that there is no alternative to legal action "to secure these rights" and that seeking favorable judicial decisions is a continuing urgent necessity.

There is a consensus that judicial decisions will not in and of themselves result in integration. An essential concomitant is the development of favorable racial attitudes among the dominant racial group. The implementation of a supplementary program along the lines suggested in this paper is an urgent responsibility of our leadership.

We say to America and to the world that racial segregation is incompatible with the ideals and goals of our nation; that it prevents our country from exploiting in full the resources inherent in the Negro people and thus weakens our domestic economy; that it provides for our opponents in the world-wide ideological struggle a potent weapon for enlisting the support of darker peoples throughout the world and thus weakens our international position. We believe that the attainment of our goals, therefore, will serve the vital interests of our nation.

7 After School Integration — What? Problems in Social Learning

ROBERT L. GREEN[1]

It is a sad commentary on America's actual ability to implement educational integration that Dr. Green should be concerned with many of the same issues so ably discussed by Dr. Jenkins nearly 15 years earlier. However, the intervening period had shown that integration often meant "remedial placement" for Black youngsters because of their lack of facility with the many standardized ability and achievement testing programs. This was often equivalent to *de facto* segregation. The problem of school integration turned out to be even more complex than many had imagined, and Dr. Green further details certain related problems and implications. The interested reader would do well to consider the work of Dr. Robert Rosenthal and his associates (1969) on educational problems with disadvantaged children. Dr. Green's paper is an exceptionally thoughtful and comprehensive examination of the total educational environment following racial integration.

A totally integrated school must include more than biracial enrollment. Open and positive communication at all social and educational levels is paramount in overcoming the complex problems related to the transition from segregated to integrated education. Remedial classes based on standardized achievement tests results can lead to intraschool de facto segregation and may retard positive interaction. Teachers assigned to integrated schools should be of demonstrated competence and should not be the recipients of a "last chance" teaching assignment. While teachers and counselors sharing race in common with students may lead to more easily established positive interactions and identification, the opportunity for wholesome interactions with competent staff of another race must not be ignored. School integration should occur at the early elementary levels to allow minority group students to profit from quality education throughout their academic careers.

SOURCE. Green, R. L., "After School Integration—What? Problems in Social Learning.", THE PERSONNEL AND GUIDANCE JOURNAL, 44, 1966, 7. Copyright 1966 by the American personnel and Guidance Association and reproduced by permission.
[1] Robert Lee Green *is Assistant Professor, Department of Counseling, Personnel*

The premise of this paper is that incorporating Negro or other minority students into an all-white school for the first time may bring about an interracial school but not necessarily an integrated school. An interracial school is one in which students of varying racial backgrounds are found; an integrated school is one in which students of varying racial backgrounds are found *and* a mutual interaction between them occurs. Mutual interaction between all segments of the student population is necessary if meaningful social and academic learning is to occur.

An observer of an elementary school, a secondary school, or a college that has a large white student population and a substantial number of Negro students can readily find clusters of Negro students in the school cafeteria, the school library, or the student union, although there is no official policy restricting them to certain areas. One explanation may be that Negro students for some reason segregate themselves from the white population although it is equally likely that white students sit together and segregate themselves from their Negro peers. The same pattern of group voluntary segregation can be observed in the union buildings or cafeterias of many eastern, western, or midwestern colleges and universities that, in some instances, have had substantial Negro student populations for years, a fact which suggests that voluntary group segregation does not necessarily decrease even though minority group students are consistent members of the school population.

Given these observations, how can school integration result in meaningful social learning for all children? What are the most effective roles for educators in promoting positive mutual interaction between all segments of the student population?

TRANSITIONAL OPPORTUNITIES

A crucial stage in bringing about meaningful social learning between white and Negro students is the transitional period when Negro students are first introduced into a formerly all-white school. As a result of living in an all-Negro community and attending predominantly Negro schools, which in most instances are admittedly educationally inferior to exclusively white schools, many Negro children experience difficulty in meeting the educational standards of the "new school" when integration first occurs. Numerous research studies indicate that Negro students score lower on standardized achievement and aptitude tests than their white counter-

Services, and Educational Psychology, College of Education, Michigan State University, East Lansing. This paper was delivered in part at the Third Annual Symposium on Urban Education at Yeshiva University, May 24, 1964.

parts (Bullick, 1950) and initially achieve at a lower level in their course work (Green & Farquhar, 1965). Many educators, in attempting to cope with this problem, group youngsters on the basis of their measured achievement level on nationally standardized tests. When this is done, one finds within such schools a "special class" for "slow learners" which, in many cases, is simply an all-Negro class. These youngsters are often labeled as "slow learners," "retardates," or youngsters unable to benefit from regular classroom instruction. Rather than regarding these youngsters as being *educationally* retarded, teachers frequently perceive them as being *intellectually* retarded and therefore incapable of benefiting from new and meaningful school experiences. As a consequence, what is in effect initially planned as school integration results in intraschool *de facto* segregation (Riessman, 1964). The latter approach inhibits and may actually reverse meaningful integration and social learning.

One suburban school district in the Detroit area is currently facing this problem. When grouping on the basis of the students' performance on standardized achievement tests, it was found that a high percentage of Negro students in the eleventh and twelfth grades were in special classes for "slow learners." School counselors in this situation were not aware of the fact that correlations between standardized achievement test scores and actual achievement (grade-point average) of Negro students are often low. In a recent study (Green and Farquhar, 1965), no correlation was found between the verbal score of the School and College Ability Tests (SCAT) and grade-point achievement for a sample of eleventh-grade Negro high school students. With the same sample, academic motivation was a more crucial factor and a much better predictor of school achievement than standardized aptitude test scores.

A similar phenomenon is being observed in Prince Edward County, Virginia (Green, Hofmann, Morse, Hayes, & Morgan, 1964) with a group of Negro students who were deprived of formal schooling for a four-year period. Many of these students performed from three and one-half to five years below grade level on standardized achievement tests, yet their present actual achievement level is inconsistent with their standardized achievement test scores. When grouping solely on the basis of standardized achievement test scores brings about intraschool *de facto* segregation, white students tend to regard Negro students as being "different," and Negro students perceive themselves as being "different," since they are in special classes. The notion of "difference" frequently centers around feelings of inferiority on the part of the Negro student and feelings of superiority on the part of the white student. In other words, the Negro group is not only considered to be different, but is also considered to be intellectually inferior to the white student population. Intraschool *de facto* segregation on the academic level which comes about during this transitional period leads to other forms of segregation, i.e., students who attend classes together are more likely to become friends with youngsters in their own classrooms, and these friendships are apt to be carried over to cafeteria, library situations, athletic events, and school assemblies.

Another adverse effect of intraschool *de facto* segregation is the reinforcement of the negative self-perception of many Negro students. A considerable body of research associated with the self-concept indicates that good concepts of self are associated with such desirable characteristics as low anxiety (Lipsitt, 1958), and generally good adjustment, popularity, and effectiveness (Mussen and Porter, 1959) in group relations. Furthermore, poor self-concepts are associated with academic underachievement. Recent research (Grambs, 1964) also indicates that many Negro students have developed very negative self-images as a result of the experiences that they have had with the dominant society. They perceive themselves as being worthless, ineffectual, and in general, not wanted by society. When placed in a school system in which their educational limitations are emphasized, this tends to reinforce their low self-esteem. Teachers in the latter school situation are aware of the fact that Negro students are in special classes and the notion that the deprived students are intellectually inferior may be reinforced. This also may become a rationale or an excuse for classroom teachers to provide inadequate instruction for such youngsters, i.e., "they cannot profit from quality instruction." Furthermore, teachers who regard certain students as being unable to benefit from quality instruction may not encourage them to become involved in aspects of the school situation which would more likely result in positive social learning (i.e., French club, band, etc.).

THE ROLE OF THE SCHOOL ADMINISTRATOR

One problem that has come about over a period of time is related to the perception that teachers have concerning an integrated school. There are teachers who perceive an assignment to an integrated school as an academic affliction. An assignment to such a school is frequently perceived as a loss in status; i.e., the greater the number of Negroes or non-whites in such schools, the lower the school is ranked on the academic status pole.

In a large urban school community in which a prospective teacher was being interviewed for a position, there was some question as to whether or not she should be hired since her undergraduate school record was rather inadequate, as was her student teaching evaluation. After a lengthy discussion by the school hiring committee, it was decided to offer her a probationary position in a school which had the highest Negro population, the highest dropout rate, and whose members ranked high in family disorganization, physical illness, and residential mobility. The prospective teacher was told that if she did an excellent job of teaching during her probationary period at this school, she would be promoted to a higher prestige school within the system. In effect, the school administrators in this case had perceived this integrated school as being one of low status and communicated this attitude to prospective teachers by consequently assigning teachers to it who were low in academic qualifications. Communicating negative attitudes to teachers who will work in depressed areas reinforces the perceptions that they may already hold concerning students who attend such schools. Grambs indicates that recent studies show many teachers to entertain a Negro stereotype:

"Studies of their attitudes toward children show that the Negro child is rated lowest in all rankings of groups on a Bogardus-type social-distance scale (Grambs, 1950). The original study was completed 13 years ago; teachers in training in 1963 gave the same responses. Attempts to change teachers' attitudes through human-relations workshops and special courses have reached very few" (Grambs, 1964).

Gottlieb (1963), in assessing the views of Negro and white teachers toward students in a northern urban school community, found differential perceptions of those students by their teachers. White teachers typically selected test items indicating that Negro students are "talkative, lazy, high-strung, rebellious, and fun-loving," while Negro teachers perceived the same students as being "happy, cooperative, energetic, ambitious, and fun-loving." However, most teachers agreed that the children did not possess qualities usually associated with middle-class children. They were not perceived as being "cultured, poised, or sophisticated." The above findings support the notion that Negro and white teachers in depressed schools may have differential impressions of the students, but, in general, they both perceive that the children do not possess the "desirable qualities of middle class school children."

Furthermore, Negro and white teachers who teach in depressed areas are aware of the fact that their schools are perceived as being "low status" and "low prestige" schools which may cause them to have lower self-esteems when assigned to disadvantaged areas. School administrators should reassess their perceptions of schools that become integrated or that are located in depressed areas of the city and attempt to change the negative attitude and perceptions that teachers might have pertaining to such schools. The professional challenge of teaching in such schools should be stressed, higher salaries offered, and special consultative assistance by school personnel experienced in dealing with school-learning problems should be a part of the regular school program. It is crucial that educators foster the idea that an assignment to a school in a depressed area can be a worthwhile experience rather than a form of punishment.

COMMUNICATION AND INTEGRATION

During and immediately after the transitional period, an attempt to open communications between Negro and white students might alter intraschool *de facto* segregation. During this period it is crucial that school administrators encourage Negro students to become involved in the total school life. There seems to be no problem in getting Negroes involved in the athletic aspect of social learning. However, athletics is only a minute segment of the total school activities. A general ethic of American society is that we should be athletically excellent. Athletics, as a route to social mobility, have long been extolled. However, it should now be clear that while it is a desirable outcome that students achieve athletically, it is undesirable to focus the Negro students' attention on athletics to the detriment of other methods of achievement.

Indicative of the major society's regard for athletics was a United States Senator's recent comments of the effect that professional boxing had on social mobility for certain disadvantaged youth. Boxing, however, has possibly been least effective in this regard, and the ratio of successes to failures is probably far lower than in any other sport where Negroes actively compete. It would be an exceedingly interesting project to find out whether Cassius Clay and Sonny Liston are more popular models for Negro youth than Elgin Baylor, Arthur Ashe, Bill Russell, and Henry Carr (since education was related to the athletic push of the latter four athletes).

Boxing models, if found more popular, may be as much related to the lack of necessary educational qualifications, as they are related to the intrinsic popularity of the most successful participants. Educators should be wary of limiting the alternatives of successful Negro athletes. There may often be a press on the part of teachers in disadvantaged schools toward excellence in the field house rather than in the classroom.

Negro students should be encouraged to join various language and literary clubs, art clubs, band, future teachers club, etc., rather than assuming that "deprived students" are uninterested in such activities.

Another significant factor is the involvement of Negro parents in the activities of the school. It can be met by actively encouraging them to attend and become active in the PTA and other school related activities. Encouraging parents to become more personally involved in the activities of the school might promote more academic and social interest on the part of the students.

CURRICULUM

Another significant factor related to a lack of communication, awareness, and positive perception on the part of the Negro and white students is related to curriculum development and the absence of the role of minority groups in our history. Many Negro and white students are totally ignorant of the historical role that the American Negro has played in the development of America. As a matter of fact, it may be safe to say that the history of the Negro has been systematically excluded from our school textbooks. A more realistic appraisal of the Negro involvement in the development of our society would in itself allow the Negro student to develop a more favorable self-perception, and at the same time, allow white students to develop a more accurate perception and understanding of the Negro's participation. Rather than devote a special paragraph to only the contributions of George Washington Carver, Booker T. Washington, and Ralph Bunche, the technological and scientific contributions of the Negro throughout his entire history should be presented in an objective manner. Pressures from civil rights organizations such as the Detroit NAACP have recently caused school administrators to become concerned about the problem. In the latter case, supplementary materials were provided regarding the historical achievements of the American Negro.

However, historians make a basic error when they assume that Negroes should receive a special place or annex in our history and literature books. Historians have the obligation to present the Negro as a part of the whole rubric and not as a special group with its own aims, goals, and accomplishments. This might be accomplished more adequately by showing pictures of past Negro leaders without any attempt to render this a special issue. Only when racial characteristics are a necessary part of the history (the Civil War, the Underground Railway, etc.) should the race of the individual be emphasized.

TEACHER PREPARATION FOR DEPRESSED AREAS

An important factor related to teacher effectiveness in integrated schools is the ability and desire on the part of the teacher to work with children of varying social, religious, ethnic, and racial backgrounds. Needless to say, teachers who have the ability but not the desire to work in integrated areas will experience difficulty.

Teacher training programs should not overlook the special social and academic problems that often result when minority group students first integrate a school or school district. Language difficulties, lack of academic motivation, and poor home situations are well known. Haubrich (1963) recognizes this problem when he says: "One discovers very quickly just how interrelated is the social and educational context when the unique relationship between money, occupation, home and school comes to the teacher's classroom."

One meaningful approach in teacher training programs would be to expose education majors to integrated school settings early in their academic training career. Too often young people complete their college careers with minimal or no exposure to the "inner-city" school with its multitude of problems. Early exposure would allow students to assess their ability and desire to teach in other than a middle-class, racially homogeneous school. Programs such as the Student Education Corps at Michigan State University and the Hunter College Project in New York allow early teaching experience with more than the usual amount of professional assistance. In addition to the regular student teaching program, the Hunter College Project allows for weekly school conferences in which all subject-matter areas meet—a close relationship between college and school personnel in order to continually assist the student teacher in becoming a more adequate teacher and a regular program of community visits discussed with supervisors and other students participants. In the final analysis, the most crucial factors related to teacher success in integrated school areas are the ability to learn and benefit from one's experience and the desire and motivation to work in such areas.

COUNSELING

Counselors should recognize that when counseling the Negro student in Detroit, the Puerto Rican youngster in Harlem, or any non-white student, he will be confronted with an individual presenting a unique and complex set of needs and problems. So unique are the needs of the non-white student that some writers have proposed that white counselors are unable to see society as Negroes do, which prevents a positive counseling relationship from developing (Phillips, 1960). Negro students, due to their experiences in a predominantly white and often hostile world may view a sympathetic white counselor with suspicion. In other special circumstances, a white counselor confronted with a Negro may find it difficult to develop rapport. However, this is not to say that only Negro counselors can counsel Negro students. This notion would be almost commensurate with the thesis that only Negro teachers can teach Negro students. (Such an argument could be reversed.) With a special knowledge of the needs of the Negro gained by studying his psychological and sociological background, a sensitive and sympathetic white counselor can structure an atmosphere that will allow the non-white student to express himself freely.

A meaningful relationship with a representative of the group that he perceives as being hostile and rejecting could well bring about a positive attitudinal change.

Among the many psychological needs of the Negro student, basic acceptance is paramount. A recent study (Blodgett and Green, 1966) found that the Negro high school students felt basically rejected by both their school and home environment. Their feelings of rejection were complicated by a high rate of broken homes and material deprivation. The latter problems of non-white students often lead them to expect the "worst" in their relationships with adults. A well-trained, sensitive counselor, irrespective of race, may be able to offset the non-white students' past negative experiences with society.

EARLY SCHOOL INTEGRATION

School integration should come about at the early elementary levels so that Negro students can profit from quality education and social interaction throughout their elementary school careers, rather than being introduced into an all-white school situation at the junior or senior high school level. Present data indicates that there is a systematic decline in aptitude and achievement test scores with time when students remain in a school environment that is not stimulating, and there is enough evidence to support the contention that predominantly Negro schools are not academically stimulating (Green, et al., 1964).

When school integration does come about relatively late in the youngster's school career, these children may need special educational assistance in achieving the educational objective of the school. The research of Deutsch (1960) indicates that the lower-class Negro child at times receives about one-half to one-third less instructional time in the elementary grades than does the white child even when socio-economic status is controlled. In the same schools that Deutsch sampled, as much as 80 per cent of the school day focused on discipline problems and organizational detail. If similar students are integrated into a white junior or senior high school level, a significant portion of the assumed academic training that most youngsters receive at this period is completely lacking and must be accounted for. Frank Riessman (1964) points out that certain activities that could be put into effect can help the youngster through the crucial transitional period:

"Most of the catching up should be done in intensive after-school programs—afternoons, weekends, summers, vacations—can all be utilized. Homework helpers, tutors, teachings machines, educational TV, specially trained teachers, and the best existing teachers and supervisors (master teachers) should be utilized. These programs should key on reading, basic knowledge and school know-how, test-taking skills, how to do homework, make outlines, participate in class, take notes, etc. The assumption should be made that these students are ignorant and uninformed rather than unintelligent, non-verbal, lacking in motivation and the like. The parents must be intensively involved in supporting these after-school programs. Dr. Samuel Sheppard's approach to involving parents in the Banneker District of St. Louis might provide an excellent model."

However, integration at the early school levels will prevent many of the educational deficiencies that are so apparent at the later elementary and upper school levels without diluting the academic program and might allow adequate social learning for both Negro and white students.

The general question of this paper was "After School Integration—What?" Certainly, educators must seek to minimize rather than maximize differences between the minority and majority student when integration occurs. Remedial programs during the transitional period should be carefully scrutinized in order to decrease the negative psychological effects of "special classes" which might make "catching up" more difficult. Students who need extra or remedial help should spend a good portion of the school day in regular classrooms. Furthermore, constant evaluation and careful counseling should be a part of the program to allow disadvantaged students to move rapidly to a regular academic schedule. Finally, teacher and inservice training programs are crucial and should focus on the educational challenge of teaching in integrated schools rather than on the pitfalls of such an experience.

References

Blodgett, E., & Green, R. A junior high school group counseling program. *J. Negro Educ.*, Winter, 1966 (in press).

Bullock, H. A. A comparison of the academic achievements of white and Negro high school graduates. *J. educ. Res.*, 1950, 44, 179–192.

Deutsch, M. Minority group and class status as related to social and personality factors in scholastic achievement. *Soc. Appl. Anthropology Monograph*, 1960, 2, 1–32.

Gottlieb, D. Teaching and students: the views of Negro and white teachers. Unpublished paper, Michigan State Univ., 1963.

Grambs, Jean D. Are we training prejudiced teachers? *Sch. Soc.*, 1950, 71, 196–198.

Grambs, Jean D. The self-concept: basis for re-education of Negro youth. In Kvaraceus (Ed.), *Negro self-concept: implications for school and citizenship.* Cooperative Research Project G-020, United States Office of Education, Department of Health, Education, and Welfare, 1964.

Green, R., & Farquhar, W. W. Negro academic motivation and scholastic achievement. *J. educ. Psychol.,* 1965, *56,* 241–243.

Green, R., Hofmann, L., Morse, R., Hayes, Marilyn, & Morgan, R. *The educational status of children in a district without public schools.* Cooperative Research Project No. 2321, United States Office of Education, Department of Health, Education, and Welfare, 1964.

Haubrich, V. F. Teachers for big-city schools. In Passow (Ed.), *Education in depressed areas.* New York: Columbia Univ., 1963.

Lipsitt, L. P. A self-concept scale for children and its relationship to the children's form of manifest anxiety scale. *Child Develpm.,* 1958, *29,* 463–472.

Mussen, P. H., & Porter, L. W. Personal motivations and self-conceptions associated with effectiveness and ineffectiveness in emergent groups. *J. abnor. soc. Psychol.,* 1959, *59,* 23–27.

Phillips, W. B. Counseling Negro pupils: an educational dilemma. *J. Negro Educ.,* 1960, *29,* 504–507.

Riessman, F. Integration: the key to quality education for all. Unpublished paper presented at Michigan State Univ. Symposium on School Integration, May, 1964.

8 Cognitive and Affective Components of Southern Negro Students' Attitude Toward Academic Integration[1]

ROBERT L. WILLIAMS
Department of Psychology, University of Tennessee

The question of whether or not there is a discrepancy between the emotional and intellectual aspects of Black students' feelings toward academic integration is a significant one because of the obvious effect that very negative feelings would have on their ability to perform in the integrated classroom. Dr. Williams examines both the intellectual and emotional attitudes of Blacks toward the integrated classroom and reports that the high school students in his study showed far more philosophical than emotional proclivity for integrated schools with the bulk of their apprehension centered around white peer acceptance, fairness of white teachers, and ability to achieve in such settings.

A. PROBLEM

Numerous studies (5, 8, 13, 14) have appraised the attitudes of white students toward academic integration, but comparatively few have dealt with the attitude of Negroes. Available research ostensibly implies that the Negro is totally committed to integration in the schools (2, 3, 4). However, the Negro's cognitive support of integration may not be duplicated in affective components of his attitude. For example, Rubin (12) found that most Boston Negroes favored open housing, but that few were willing to make the initial move into white neighborhoods opposed to integrated housing. Similarly, interaction with white students for the first time may be construed as a threatening experience by the Negro.

SOURCE. Reprinted from *Journal of Social Psychology*, 1968, **76**, 107–111, with permission of the author and The Journal Press.
[1] Received in the Editorial Office, Provincetown, Massachusetts, on July 28, 1967. Copyright, 1968, by The Journal Press.

For years Negroes in the South have been forced to judge themselves in the context of the second-class citizenship assigned them by whites. In addition, white racists have persistently insisted that Negroes are innately inferior to whites. Consciously or unconsciously, many Negroes are driven to question their basic adequacy as persons. When the Negro is initially thrust into an interactive and competitive situation with whites, his feelings of inferiority may erupt with great intensity. Research has demonstrated that even when Negroes receive objective confirmation of mental ability comparable to that of whites, in interracial experiences they are still inclined to feel inadequate and respond subserviently (6). This affective dimension is also evident in Pugh's finding (11) that Negroes in segregated institutions are better adjusted to the social life of their schools than Negroes in integrated settings. Likewise, Negro teachers in recently desegregated public schools manifested more resistance toward biracial interaction and more often requested to be excused from interracial participation than did white teachers (9).

The present study is concerned with the cognitive and affective reservations of Negro students toward academic integration. It also attempts to evaluate the relationship of sex to intensity of antiintegration sentiment. Although the Negro female typically has enjoyed a more stable position than the Negro male in a segregated society, the opposite may be true in the integrated setting (1).

B. METHOD

1. Subjects

The 212 Ss, 72 males and 140 females, were randomly selected from a segregated Negro high school in the deep South. Most of the Ss were scheduled to attend integrated schools the following year and were aware of the ensuing integration.

2. Procedure

An expanded form of Komorita's School Segregation Scale (7)[2] was administered to all Ss. This scale, originally developed for use with Caucasians, primarily deals with philosophical or cognitive endorsement of ra-

---

[2] The Expanded Form of Komorita's School Segregation Scale has been deposited as Document number 10064 with the ADI Auxiliary Publications Project, Photoduplication Service, Library of Congress, Washington, D. C. 20540. A copy may be secured by citing the Document number and by remitting $1.25 for photoprints, or $1.25 for 35-mm. microfilm. Advance payment is required. Make checks or money orders payable to: Chief, Photoduplication Service, Library of Congress.

cial integration. However, items relating specifically to the Ss' association with local whites and their expectations relative to academic and social experiences the following year in integrated settings were included. The latter items focus on feelings, such as positive anticipation, confidence, insecurity, apprehension, and ambivalence, which the Negro may attach to these real experiences and thus provide some index of affective acceptance of integration.

The 55-item expanded Komorita scale is a Likert-type instrument which requires the S to mark his response to each item along a six-point scale from "I agree very much" to "I disagree very much." Participants were not required to sign their names and were assured that their responses would not be revealed to teachers or administrators.

C. RESULTS

The dependent variable in the investigation was affinity for academic integration. The independent variables were attitudinal component (cognitive *vs.* affective) and the sex of the Ss. To assess cognitive acceptance of integrated experiences, the E identified 22 items related to the general issue of academic integration; a concomitant set of 22 items concerned with feelings toward local integration provided a measure of affective affinity for academic integration. The Ss were given 1–6 points credit for each item, with the smaller scores indicative of greater endorsement of integration. A total cognitive score based on the responses to the 22 cognitive items and a total affective score based on the 22 affective items were computed for each S. Examples of cognitive and affective items are included in Table 1.

TABLE 1

Sample Cognitive and Affective Items from Expanded Komorita Scale

Items	Mean score
Cognitive	
1. The Negro should be accorded equal rights through integration.	1.539
2. Since segregation has been declared illegal, we should integrate schools.	2.427
3. Integration of the schools will be beneficial to both white and Negro children.	2.106
Affective	
1. I would prefer to attend Carver (the Ss' school) rather than a white school, such as City High or Central.	4.804
2. I look forward to having white classmates.	3.376
3. I could learn just as much by remaining in an all-Negro school.	5.122

A 2 × 2 mixed design analysis, with attitudinal component (cognitive vs. affective) as the within factor and sex as the between, yielded an F ratio of 200.189 ($df = 1/210$, $p < .005$) for the cognitive-affective dimension. No significant interaction or sex difference was obtained. A comparison of the attitudinal means demonstrated that the Ss' cognitive endorsement was greater than their affective endorsement of integration. A mean cognitive score of 68.62 indicates that the mean individual item score was 3.119 or "slightly agree" with prointegration items and "slightly disagree" with antiintegration statements. In contrast, a mean of 88.25 for the affective segment denotes an individual item mean of 4.0113 or "slightly disagree" with prointegration items and "slightly agree" with antiintegration declarations.

D. DISCUSSION

The results of the present study demonstrate that Negro students in the deep South may experience considerable personal conflict in the transition from segregated to integrated settings. Most students indicated philosophical commitment to the integration movement, but expressed affective disquietude concerning local integration. This reaction might be explicated in the context of Miller's (10) approach-avoidance paradigm. As long as actual integration is some time and distance away, the Negro may express commitment without major apprehension; but once integration is imminent, the prospect of face to face confrontation with whites may prove more threatening than positive commitment to integration will counteract.

The findings of this study indicate that the Negro's affective reservations center around such concerns as white peer acceptance, fairness of Caucasian teachers, and his achievement in the integrated milieu. Students on the whole expressed some degree of agreement with such items as "I believe that Carver (present Negro school) is one of the best schools in the county," "I would prefer to attend Carver rather than a white school, such as City High or Central," "I could learn just as much by remaining in an all-Negro school," "I would feel more comfortable in a Negro than an integrated school," "I fear that white students would make fun of me," and "I would enjoy social activities more in a Negro than an integrated school." In contrast, they generally disagreed with such statements as "I look forward to having white classmates," "I feel that my grades will improve in an integrated school," "I would prefer white rather than Negro teachers," and "I believe that I would get a better education in an integrated than all-Negro school." These responses signify a willingnesss to maintain the *status quo* and to avert emotionally or to delay actual academic integration.

E. SUMMARY

An expanded form of Komorita's School Segregation Scale was administered to 212 Negro adolescents in a segregated southern high school. The scale included items pertaining to the general philosophical issue of integration and statements related to emotional affinity for local academic integration scheduled to begin the following year. The students expressed significantly greater ($p < .005$) philosophical endorsement of integration than emotional proclivity for actual integration in the local setting. An analysis of specific responses indicated that most of the Negro's affective insecurities centered around white peer acceptance, fairness of Caucasian teachers, and his achievement in integrated settings.

References

1. Ausubel, D., and Ausubel, P. Ego development among segregated Negro children. In A. H. Passow (Ed.), *Education in Depressed Areas*. New York: Bur. Pub., Teach. Coll., 1963. Pp. 109–141.
2. Brink, W., and Harris, L. The Negro Revolution in America. New York: Simon & Shuster, 1964.
3. Greenberg, H., Chase, A. L., and Cannon, T. M., Jr. Attitudes of white and Negro high school students in a West Texas town toward school integration. *J. Appl. Psychol.*, 1957, **41**, 27–31.
4. Grossack, M. M. Attitudes toward desegregation of southern white and Negro children. *J. Soc. Psychol.*, 1957, **46**, 299–306.
5. Hyman, H. H., and Sheatsley, P. B. Attitudes toward desegregation. *Sci. Amer.*, 1956, **195**, 35–39.
6. Katz, I., and Benjamin, L. Effects of white authoritarianism in biracial work groups. *J. Abn. & Soc. Psychol.*, 1960, **61**, 448–456.
7. Komorita, S. S. Attitude content, intensity, and the neutral point on a Likert scale. *J. Soc. Psychol.*, 1963, **61**, 327–334.
8. Lombardi, D. N. Factors affecting changes in attitudes toward Negroes among high school students. *Diss. Abst.*, 1962, **23**, 1413–1414.
9. Mays, N. Behavioral expectations of Negro and white teachers on recently desegregated public school faculties. *J. Negro Educ.*, 1963, **32** (3), 218–226.
10. Miller, N. E. Liberalization of basic S-R concepts: Extensions to conflict behavior, motivation, and social learning. In Sigmund Koch (Ed.), *Psychology: A Study of a Science*. New York: McGraw-Hill, 1959. Pp. 196–292.
11. Pugh, R. W. Comparative study of adjustment of Negro students in mixed and separate schools. *J. Negro Educ.*, 1943, **12**, 607–616.

12. Rubin, M. The Negro wish to move: The Boston case. *J. Soc. Iss.*, 1959, **15**(4), 4–13.

13. Stephenson, C. M. The relation between the attitudes toward Negroes of seniors in a school of education and their major subject. *J. Educ. Res.*, 1955, **49**, 113–121.

14. Young, R. K., Benson, W. M., & Holtzman, W. H. Change in attitudes toward the Negro in a southern university. *J. Abn. & Soc. Psychol.*, 1960, **60**, 131–133.

9 The Effects of Resumed Schooling on the Measured Intelligence of Prince Edward County's Black Children[1]

ROBERT L. GREEN
&
ROBERT F. MORGAN
Michigan State University
St. Bonaventure University

When the Prince Edward County (Virginia) schools were closed in 1959 to avoid desegregation, nearly 1700 Black children were left without schools to attend. This deplorable condition continued for nearly four years, and in their very thoughtful paper Drs. Green and Morgan examine the effects on the children's intelligence of both having been out of school and then resuming school. The paper requires careful study since it is one of the most detailed analyses of intelligence test data in the literature. The authors show that children with at least some education surpassed those with no schooling at all on any measurement used, and that the predeprivation schooling experience determined much of the effect of not being able to attend school.

In the spring of 1959 one of the most unusual and debilitating events in the history of American public education occurred. To prevent desegregation of the public schools, officials of Prince Edward County, Virginia, closed these schools for a total of four years to their County's children. While most of the white children's families could afford the tuition to a segregated private school during this period of time, nearly 1700 Negro children lacked even this alternative. For the school year of 1963–1964,

SOURCE. Reprinted from the *Journal of Negro Education*, 1969, 38, 2, 147–155, with permission of the senior author and the publisher.

[1] This paper was delivered in part at the annual meeting of the American Psychological Association in September, 1965. Support for the Research derived from Cooperative Research Project #2498 U. S. Office of Education, 1966.

through the efforts of the United States Department of Justice and six Virginia educators, a private school system was at last made available to all the County's children. Enrollment in this school system, the Prince Edward County Free School Association, included those black children still residing in the county as well as six of their white peers. The next fall (1964) regular public schools were reopened by court order.

In an earlier study, based on tests of the county black children directly after their four years school deprivation, Green and colleagues (1964) found the measured intelligence to be significantly depressed at all age levels. Children who had never attended school were the most seriously affected, with mean differences as great as 30 I.Q. points between the no education groups and partial education controls.

For purposes of this study, follow up testing was made following the reintroduction of education, private then public, into the lives of these children. The social upheaval in Prince Edward County in its consequent multiple tragedy of non-schooling for hundreds of children, if the literature of published papers were any guide, would have serious negative effects on each child's achievement, attitudes, and intelligence (Green, Hofmann, and Morgan, 1967). It seemed essential, however, to validate and categorize these effects, both those of immediate nature (Green et al., 1964) and those following strenuous efforts of re-education (Green et al., 1966). While quality of educational environment has long since been related to measured intelligence (e.g. Miner, 1957), a field study such as the present one offers a chance at better defining the direct intellectual impact of this environment, or its absence.

GENERAL PROCEDURE

Experimental Design

Standardized intelligence measures were made of the black children of Prince Edward County before (1963), during (1964), and after (1965) the resumption of public schooling which followed their extensive four year period of educational deprivation.

The two basic groups of interest were those children having no education whatsoever during the years (1959–1963) in which the schools were closed, the NO EDUCATION group, as opposed to those children who received *some* formal education during this period, the SOME EDUCATION group. It should be noted that the latter group averaged only 1.5 years of such formal education during the four years of deprivation.

Population and Sample

Approximately 1700 black school children were initially left without public schooling in 1959. This was the basic population of interest, and it should be noted that this report refers only to the educational status of the black children. Although informal estimates of how many Caucasian children not receiving formal education during this period range as high as 300, these children were not available for testing purposes.

Naturally, many of the 1700 children left Prince Edward County permanently. It has been postulated that this may have been a selective migration with the brightest students most likely to have left or received some education. Unfortunately, pre-1963 I.Q. data are not available. Therefore, to the extent this may be true we must be cautious about placing too great an emphasis on observed differences between the SOME EDUCATION and NO EDUCATION groups pending further data. However, I.Q. changes in both groups from 1963 to 1964 or 1965 as a result of renewed schooling remain a major focus of this paper. Nevertheless, there were several hundred children in both the SOME EDUCATION and NO EDUCATION group samples drawn for testing in 1963 (Green *et al.*, 1964) for whom an equivalent number was available for the 1964 and 1965 testings (Green *et al.*, 1966). Samples were drawn randomly from this school-age population.

Instrumentation and Data Collection Methods

Intelligence was tested by the Stanford-Binet Intelligence Scale (Form L-M) and the Chicago Non-Verbal Examination (CNV). Both group (CNV) and individual (Binet) testings were conducted at either the senior high school or one of three elementary schools in the County. Graduate students in education and psychology from Michigan State University assisted in collecting the bulk of the data. Trained school psychologists from the Detroit public schools and from Michigan State University administered the individual intelligence tests.

The data were collected within the confines of the school classroom with teachers serving as proctors and test aides. Due to the cooperation and assistance of these teachers and the administrative staff, the test atmosphere facilitated good test-taking behavior on the part of the students.

It was noted during the collection of the 1963 data that many of the subjects exhibited behavior indicating that they were completely unfamiliar with the rudiments of test-taking procedures, including the comprehension of verbal directions. Such difficulties as the inability to use a pencil appropriately (or coloring a picture when asked to "draw a frame" around it) were no longer apparent after the one year of formal schooling.

STUDY A—INDIVIDUAL TESTING

Subjects

The full sample consisted of 288 children (SOME EDUCATION and NO EDUCATION groups) whose intelligence was individually assisted in July, 1963. A sub-sample was randomly drawn from those still available for testing in April, 1965—after a year and a half of formal schooling. The re-tested sub-sample consisted of 35 males and females drawn from the original SOME EDUCATION group and 31 males and females drawn from the original NO EDUCATION group. All Ss were from 9 to 17 years of age at the original 1963 testing.

Results

Table 1 shows the median I.Q. for both the SOME EDUCATION and NO EDUCATION groups before and after the resumption of formal education. As indicated, there was a slight median increase in I.Q. at all three age levels for the EDUCATION group. However, the Sign Test (Siegel, 1956) showed that none of the increases were statistically significant.

TABLE 1

I.Q. of SOME EDUCATAION vs. NO EDUCATION Groups in 1963 and 1965

Age in 1963	N	Median I.Q. 1963	Median I.Q. 1965	% Ss Increasing IQ from '63–'65	Sign Test Probability
		Some education group			
9–11	12	92.0	97.0	67	.15
12–14	16	77.5	83.5	62	.21
15–17	7	87.0	91.0	57	.45
		No education group			
9–11	16	62.5	67.5	86	.002
12–14	11	57.0	75.0	82	.01
15–17	4	68.5	68.0	50	.75

Within the NO EDUCATION group, statistically significant gains in measured intelligence were made by the 9–11 and 12–14 age groups. The 15–17 NO EDUCATION group was the only age category that indicated no appreciable change. (Note, however, the N at that age level was relatively small.) From this table, it appears as though the NO EDUCATION group alone showed significant gains in I.Q. after formal education.

In both 1963 and 1965, at all age levels, the SOME EDUCATION group performed at a significantly higher I.Q. level than the NO EDUCATION group. In both 1963 *and* 1965, the most dramatic difference due to partial education occurred at the earlier age level (9–11) in which a 30-point difference in measured intelligence was obtained. It should be noted that the 9–11 year old group, for the most part, had had no formal education before the closing of the schools in 1959. (See Table 2.)

TABLE 2

I.Q. of SOME EDUCATION vs. NO EDUCATION Groups in 1963 and 1965

Age in 1963	Some Education Group		No Education Group		Difference	U*	P
	N	Median IQ	N	Median IQ			
For the year 1963							
9–11	12	92.0	16	62.5	29.5	3	.001
12–14	16	77.5	11	57.0	20.5	3	.002
15–17	7	87.0	4	68.5	18.5	4	.07
For the year 1965—After universal schooling							
9–11	12	97.0	16	67.5	29.5	17.5	.002
12–14	16	83.5	11	75.0	8.5	34	.02
15–17	7	91.0	4	68.0	23.0	4	.07

* Mann-Whitney U.

It is interesting to note that the low point in median I.Q. is at the 12–14 year old age level in 1963 for both groups. Although the SOME EDUCATION group in 1965 demonstrated the same low point at ages 12–14, the NO EDUCATION group showed an increase in 18 I.Q. points at this age level to put the 12–14 age level at a higher median I.Q. than either of the other age levels of the NO EDUCATION group.

DISCUSSION

That the NO EDUCATION group, rather than the SOME EDUCATION group, made the only significant gain in measured I.Q. was an interesting finding. Apparently the introduction of formal schooling had the most dramatic effect upon those who were most deprived. This finding suggests that even the most severely deprived children can make significant gains when educational deprivation is altered.

The most dramatic gains were made by the 12–14 year old NO EDUCATION subgroup. (See Table 1.) This may have been a critical age for improving abilities assessed by the Stanford-Binet or, more likely, for overcoming the debilitating effects of interrupted education.

For the SOME EDUCATION group of 1963 and 1965 and the 1963 NO EDUCATION group there was a drop of I.Q. from the first (9–11) to the second (12–14) age level. This might be a result of two opposing factors. One factor would be the cognitive disadvantage of a segregated low budget school system. This decline in I.Q. with successive years of age for segregated black school children has been frequently observed (Kennedy, Van De Riet, and White, 1961; Green et al., 1967). While it might be expected that the cognitive disadvantage of an inadequate school system would have an increasingly depressive effect across all age groups, the data here suggest that for some reason the elder group of 15 to 17 year olds show *less* disadvantage than the younger 12 to 14 year olds. A possible explanation for this might be the fact that school deprivation for the elder group occurred after the first several crucial years of schooling. Since the 15 to 17 year old group had more schooling than the 12–14 year old group before the schools were closed, the additional time spent in school possibly had a positive impact on the measured I.Q. of this age group. Thus, even when education is inadequate it is sometimes better than none at all. However, sampling error could also account for the increase in I.Q. from the 12–14 to the 15–17 year old age group since the positive increase measured in I.Q. is in contrast to the earlier findings of Kennedy et al., 1961, and Green et al., 1967.

STUDY B—GROUP TESTING ON A NON-VERRBAL MEASURE OF INTELLIGENCE SUBJECTS

From the full population of SOME EDUCATION and NO EDUCATION school-age children of Prince Edward County, a sample of 528 Ss was drawn and tested on a group-administered test of intelligence in May, 1964. Pre-measures from this same instrument had not been collected during the 1963 testing period. Hence, a pre- and post-education analysis was not possible. Ss ranged in age at the time of testing from 8 to 17 years of age.

INSTRUMENTATION

The Chicago Non-Verbal Examination was administered so that minimal emphasis would be on S's comprehension of complex verbal instructions.

Results and Discussion

In spring, 1964, after nine months of "Free Schools" and before the reopening of the public schools, the mean I.Q. of the SOME EDUCATION group excelled the mean I.Q. of the NO EDUCATION group at all age levels; this was statistically significant at nearly all age levels. Thus, the non-verbal measure with substantially more Ss at each age level paralleled the findings of the Stanford-Binet. (See Table 3.)

TABLE 3

Mean Non-Verbal I.Q. of SOME EDUCATION vs. NO EDUCATION Groups in 1964 as a Function of Age in 1964

Age in 1964	Some Education Group			No Education Group			Mean Difference	t
	N	Mean IQ	SD	N	Mean IQ	SD		
8	18	95.7	15.1	46	87.4	13.5	+ 8.3	2.05**
9	21	90.3	15.9	62	80.8	11.4	+ 9.5	2.53**
10	12	90.7	17.6	45	77.3	11.7	+13.4	2.48**
11	18	85.7	20.6	36	76.0	15.5	+ 9.7	1.77*
12	24	81.5	16.2	36	68.4	14.9	+13.1	3.17***
13	25	82.4	16.2	27	72.8	14.8	+ 9.6	2.23**
14	27	86.4	13.7	30	77.9	12.0	+ 8.5	2.50**
15	14	92.7	15.8	36	78.9	14.4	+13.8	3.43***
16	14	91.2	12.6	17	82.5	17.9	+ 8.7	1.69*
17	4	89.8	11.4	16	81.4	12.6	+ 8.4	1.28
Sum:	177			351				
Mean:		87.6			78.3		+ 9.3	

*p < .10.
**p < .05.
***p < .01.

Note that the age groups of interest are much closer in mean I.Q. differences as a function of SOME EDUCATION versus NO EDUCATION when the non-verbal measure was used in 1964 than either the 1963 or the 1965 measures as gauged by the Stanford-Binet. Although degree of educational deprivation was significant in effect on both measures, the verbal I.Q. measure appeared to be more sensitive to it. This is even more striking considering that the Chicago Non-Verbal manual (Brown, 1940) cautions "in comparison with the Stanford-Binet, it (Chicago Non-Verbal Examination) seems to rate the dull children somewhat lower and the bright ones somewhat higher" (page 34). On the contrary, the non-verbal test seems to have assessed the deprivation of verbal skills as so powerful as to have shrunk the expected measurement differences. Verbal and non-verbal test results are comparatively listed by year of testing in Table 4.

As is often observed in younger educationally deprived or disadvantaged children, the mean I.Q. decreased with increasing age (See Table 3) for

TABLE 4

Median I.Q.'s for Ages 9–11, 12–14, and 15–17 in 1963 for the Years 1963, 1964, and 1965

Year Tested	Instruments	Antecedent Conditions	SOME EDUCATION GROUP						NO EDUCATION GROUP					
			N 1963	MIQ 1963	N 1964	MIQ 1964	N 1965	MIQ 1965	N 1963	MIQ 1963	N 1964	MIQ 1964	N 1965	MIQ 1965
1963	S-B	4 yrs. of no PEC Schooling	12	92.0	16	77.5	7	87.0	16	62.5	11	57.0	4	68.5
1964	CN-V	1 yr. PEC Free Schools	54	85.7	66	86.4	18	89.8	117	76.0	73	77.9	33	81.4
1965	S-B	1 yr. Free Schools and nearly 1 yr. Public School	12	97.0	16	83.5	7	91.0	16	67.5	11	75.0	4	68.0

Key: N—Number.
MIQ—Median I.Q.
S-B—Stanford-Binet
CN-V—Chicago Non-Verbal.

both the SOME EDUCATION and NO EDUCATION groups. (This does not mean the more schooling, the less intelligence but rather the more years of inferior schooling, the further behind the growth of intelligence falls in comparison to the better educated children upon whom the I.Q. norms were established.) The negative product-moment correlation between age and I.Q. for the 8–11 age range was significant, however, only for the NO EDUCATION group ($r = -.191$, $n = 189$, $p < .05$). On the other hand, the measured I.Q. of the sample seems to have increased with age for the older children of age 12 to 17. This was true for both the SOME EDUCATION and NO EDUCATION groups; their significant positive correlations of age with I.Q. for 12–17 year olds were $+.256$ ($n = 108$, $p < .01$) and $+.303$ ($n = 162$, $p < .01$). What might have brought about this increase? Once again, it is necessary to look at the differential education history of those below and above age 12 in 1964. Five years earlier, in 1959, the public schools were closed. Since public schooling in Prince Edward County begins at age 6 (there is no kindergarten), no child under 12 in 1964 probably ever had the experience of public schooling before the schools were closed in 1959. Thus, the 8 to 11 year olds (as of 1964) of the NO EDUCATION group had a common total lack of educational experience prior to the deprivation period. Thus, the longer they were out of school, the more depressed the I.Q. and the resulting significant negative correlation of I.Q. with age. On the other hand, children 12 and over in 1964 did have predeprivation school experience; the older they were, the more years of education they had before the public schools closed. This could be the basis for the significant positive correlation of I.Q. with age for the children of age 12 to 17. This was, of course, the same explanation found relevant in the discussion of the Stanford-Binet data.

In summary, it was again demonstrated that both age and degree of educational deprivation appeared critical to measured magnitude of intelligence. The non-verbal measure found smaller mean differences in I.Q. as a function of degree of deprivation than the verbal measure used before and after its administration. Nevertheless, the I.Q.'s of those children with even sporadic education (SOME EDUCATION group) excelled those having no education at all (NO EDUCATION group). This difference held at all ages regardless of the measurement used to assess it. It would seem that the amount of predeprivation school experience may also have implications for post-deprivation measured intelligence and the responsiveness of this measured intelligence to retraining.

References

Brown, Andrew W. *Manual of Directions for the Chicago Non-Verbal Examination.* New York: Psychological Corporation, 1940.

Green, Robert L., Hofmann, L., and Morgan, Robert F. Some Effects of Deprivation on Intelligence, Achievement, and Cognitive Growth. *Journal of Negro Education,* 1967, **36**, 5–14.

Green, Robert L., Hofmann, L., Morse, R. J., and Morgan R. F. *The Educational Status of Children During the First School Year Following Four Years of Little or No Schooling.* Cooperative Research Project No. 2498, United States Office of Education, Department of Health, Education and Welfare, 1966.

Green, Robert L., Hofmann, Louis J., Morse, Richard J., Hayes, Marilyn E., and Morgan, Robert F. *The Educational Status of Children in a District Without Public Schools,* Cooperative Research Project No. 2321, United States Office of Education, Department of Health, Education and Welfare, 1964.

Kennedy, Wallace A., Van De Riet, Vern, and White, James C., Jr. *The Standardization of the 1960 Revision of the Stanford-Binet Intelligence Scale on Negro Elementary-School Children in the Southeastern United States.* Cooperative Research Project No. 954, United States Office of Education, Department of Health, Education and Welfare, 1961.

Miner, John B. *Intelligence in the United States.* New York: Springer Publishing Company, Inc., 1957.

Siegel, Sidney. *Non-Parametric Statistics.* New York: McGraw-Hill Book Company, Inc., 1956.

Bibliography for Part II

Amerman, Helen. Perspective for evaluating inter-group relations in a public school system. *Journal of Negro Education* (Spring, 1957), **26**, 108–120.

Ausubel, David P., and Ausubel, Pearl. Ego development among segregated Negro children. In A. Harry Passow (Ed.), *Education in Depressed Areas.* New York: Bureau of Publications, Teachers College, Columbia University, 1963, 109–141.

Bell, Reginald. A study of the educational effects of segregation upon Japanese children in American schools. Ph.D. dissertation, Stanford University, November, 1932.

Blevins, Audie L. Migration rates in twelve Southern metropolitan areas: a "push-pull" analysis. *Social Science Quarterly*, 1969, **50**(2), 337–353.

Coles, R. *The Desegregation of Southern Schools: a Psychiatric Study.* New York: Anti-Defamation League, 1963.

Forbes, Jack D. Segregation and integration: the multi-ethnic of uni-ethnic school. *Phylon, Atlanta University Review of Race and Culture*, 1969, **30**(1), 34–41.

Glazer, Nathan, and McEntire, Davis. *Housing and Minority Groups.* Berkeley: University of California Press, 1960.

Goldberg, Louis C. Ghetto riots and others; the faces of civil disorder in 1967. *Journal of Peace Research*, 1968, **2**, 116–132.

Haddad, William F., and Pugh, G. Douglas (Eds.) *Black Economic Development.* Englewood Cliffs, N. J.: Prentice-Hall, 1969.

Kain, John F. *Race and Poverty: the Economics of Discrimination.* Englewood Cliffs, N. J.: Prentice-Hall, 1969.

Katz, Irwin. Review of evidence relating to effects of desegregation on the intellectual performance of Negroes. *American Psychologist* (June, 1964), **19**, 381–399.

Katz, I., Goldston, Judith, and Benjamin L. Behavior and productivity in biracial work groups. *Human Relations*, 1958, **11**, 123–141.

Lesser, Gerald S., Fifer, Gordon, and Clark, Donald H. Mental abilities of children from different social class and cultural groups. *Monographs of the Society for Research in Child Development*, 1965, **30**, No. 4.

Lott, A. E., and Lott, B. E. *Negro and White Youth.* New York: Holt, Rinehart & Winston, 1963.

Lupsha, Peter A. On theories of urban violence. *Urban Affairs Quarterly,* 1969, 4(3), 273–296.

Mearns, E. A., Jr. Part 4, Virginia. In United States Commission on Civil Rights, Civil Rights, U. S. A.—public schools, Southern states. Washington, D. C.: United States Government Printing Office, 1962. Pp. 155–217.

Pettigrew, T. F. Regional differences in anti-Negro prejudice. *Journal of Abnormal and Social Psychology,* 1959, **59**, 28–36.

Reissman, Leonard. Readiness to succeed: mobility aspirations and modernism among the poor. *Urban Affairs Quarterly,* 1969, 4(3), 379–396.

Rogers, Tommy W. Migration attractiveness of Southern metropoliltan areas. *Social Science Quarterly,* 1969, **50**(2), 325–336.

Rosenthal, Robert, and Jacabson, Lenore. *Pygmalion in the Classroom: Teacher Expectation and Pupils' Intellectual Development.* New York: Holt, Rinehart & Winston, Inc., 1968.

Stallings, F. H. A study of the immediate effects of integration on scholastic achievement in the Louisville public schools. *Journal of Negro Education,* 1959, **28**, 439–444.

U. S. Commission on Civil Rights. Racial isolation in the public schools. Vol. 1. Washington, D. C.: U. S. Government Printing Office, 1967.

Weinstein, Eugene A., and Geisel, Paul N. Family decision making over desegregation. *Sociometry* (March, 1962), **25**, 21–29.

Wilson, A. B. Educational consequences of segregation in a California community. *Racial Isolation in the Public Schools,* Appendices, Vol. 2 of a report by the U. S. Commission on Civil Rights, Washington, D. C.: U. S. Government Printing Office, 1967.

Wolff, Max. Segregation in the schools of Gary, Indiana. *Journal of Educational Sociology* (February, 1963), **36**, 251–258.

Wolman, T. G. Learning effects of integration in New Rochelle. *Integrated Education* (Dec., 1964–Jan., 1965), **2**, 30–31.

Zurcher, Louis A., Jr. Stages of development in poverty program neighborhood action committees. *Journal of Applied Behavioral Science,* 1969, **5**(2), 223–267.

PART **III**

Intelligence and Achievement

The papers in this section deal with the testing of intelligence and achievement levels in Black children, and not only present results but also carefully examine the very nature and utilization of psychological testing.

Dr. Canady (1943), Katz and his associates (1964), and Brazziel (1969) all examine the theoretical and practical problems associated with minority group testing and present a number of cautions that warrant very serious consideration. Dr. Jenkins' (1948) very important paper develops the idea that there is literally no upper limit to Negro intelligence, and that the more appropriate concern is the distribution of intelligence within a race rather than between races. Drs. Peters (1960), Horton and Crump (1962), and Professor Roberts and his associates (1965, 1966) present the results of intelligence tests given to various groups of Negro children and discuss both the implications of the results and also the problems related to such testing.

10 The Problem of Equating the Environment of Negro-White Groups for Intelligence Testing in Comparative Studies[1][2]

HERMAN G. CANADY

Department of Psychology, West Virginia State College

In the late 1930's Dr. Canady had developed the thoughtful notion that it would be more meaningful to consider the range of intelligence test scores *within* a race than any observed differences *between* races, and in so doing made available a most helpful and productive viewpoint for research in racial intelligence. Having established this perspective, he then saw the need for a very careful analysis of the factors that might be related to intelligence test scores. In this paper he reviews the many problems involved in attempting to equate the environments of Negro and white groups for comparative studies of intelligence test data. The paper begins with a careful historical review of fact and conjecture concerning Negro-white cultural and experiential differences, and systematically develops the viewpoint that these differences are so great as to preclude the equating of the two environments. This is a significant point, because so many attempts had been made to experimentally equate environments in order to arrive at a literally valid measure of the intelligence of the races. Professor Canady shows that such equality cannot be arranged.

A. INTRODUCTION

In the psychological investigation of the American Negro, no problem has attracted so much attention as the question of the inherent intellectual superiority of whites over Negroes. The problem has been approached in

SOURCE. Reprinted from the *Journal of Social Psychology*, 1943, **17**, 3–15, with permission of the senior author and The Journal Press.

[1] Received in the Editorial Office on July 18, 1941.

[2] This article is part of a larger study, directed by Dr. A. R. Gilliland, made possible by a fellowship grant from the General Education Board.

89

many different ways (27), but with the coming of the intelligence test, it was felt by many that perhaps an instrument had finally been devised which would make it possible to study with complete objectivity the relative ability of these "races."[3] The studies may be divided into two groups, (a) tests of children and (b) tests of adults, particularly in the Army draft. Comparisons are then made in at least two ways (a) the percentage of overlapping and (b) intelligence quotient. In both cases, the test standings of Negroes have suffered in comparison with whites[4] because of their poorer social environment which consists of such factors as socio-economic level of the home, schooling, and community influences. Together, these conditions constitute a serious handicap in making scores on the intelligence tests.

It has been sometimes suggested that in order to obviate the difficulties introduced into Negro-White comparisons by social considerations, a better procedure would be to equate the two "racial" groups, and then see which is the superior. Some of the more recent studies have included an attempt to equate the groups for one or more background factors. For example, Phillips (39) visited the homes of Negro and white children whom he tested and equated the environmental elements by pairing each Negro boy with a white boy of approximately the same age and home conditions. Murdock (36) attempted to eliminate school training by selecting her Negro subjects from public schools of New York City and comparing them with white children from corresponding grades. Mayo (30), attempting to eliminate the same factor, compared white freshmen students from the University of South Carolina with Negro freshmen students from Benedict and Allen University (both schools located in South Carolina). Peterson

[3] "Race" here, and throughout this article, refers to a large group of persons possessing in common certain physical characteristics which are based upon heredity. Whenever the concept is used it will be enclosed in quotation marks to indicate that it cannot be applied except in the loosest sense. Some psychologists, e.g., Anastasi (1), take the view that racial classification is so difficult a matter as almost to preclude investigation of comparative racial intelligence. For readable accounts of many of the difficulties of "race" classification, see Huxley and Haddon (23); also Herskovits (22). Perhaps we should also stress the fact that as concerns the American Negro the word "race" is a sociological term. Herskovits (20) has shown that this group constitutes a population which is "probably less than one-fourth unmixed Negro descent" (pp. 10–18), and that the average American Negro is as far removed in respect to racial traits from the pure Negroid type as he is from the average Caucasoid type. Yet the old patterns of racial prejudice tend to persist, and those suspected of possessing the slightest strains of "Negro blood" are classified sociologically as Negroes.

[4] The reader who is interested will find a comprehensive discussion of the techniques and results in the 1934 *Yearbook of the Journal of Negro Education* (26), as well as in several briefer reviews by Pinter (40), Yoder (52), Viteles (47), Garth (16), Witty and Lehman (50), Klineberg (27), Freeman (15), and Anastasi (1).

(38), in some of his studies endeavored to avoid the common difficulty encountered in comparing Negroes with whites on the basis of school grades (in which Negroes are generally a year or more older than the whites) by choosing all his subjects at age twelve. He also tried to compensate *in part* for the condition of inferiority of opportunity on the part of the Negro by selecting them (in Nashville, Tennessee) from social areas which he believed to be superior to those areas represented by his white subjects. McGraw (31) recently made an interesting attempt to eliminate the effects of social status by comparing the test standing of Negro and white infants under one year of age.

These ingenious attempts to eliminate or measure certain factors other than "race" which influence test standing in order to make a *fair* comparison of Negroes and whites have yielded results which show still a definite superiority on the part of whites. Before any reasonable interpretation can be made of the data, it is necessary to point out certain difficulties inherent in the method. This paper, therefore, will be concerned with a critical discussion of the recent attempts to equate the background of Negro-white groups for intelligence testing in comparative studies.

B. DIFFICULTIES IN EQUATING NEGRO-WHITE GROUPS

It is difficult to equate fully Negro and white groups with any exactness but even if it were possible, it would by no means be conclusive. The results obtained in this manner could not be generalized, but would apply only to the particular samples studied. For example, if we matched a group of Negroes and whites for socio-economic status it might be argued that they were exceptions, and could not be taken as representative of white or Negro groups in general. The former might represent the lower end of the white socio-economic distribution and the latter a central or slightly superior segment of the Negro distribution. In spite of statistical and other checks on the validity of a sample, this remains a constant problem and possible soure of error in all Negro-white comparisons.

Another possible source of error inherent in all attempts to equate Negro and white groups is that of implying, if not assuming, that the school, home, or occupation represents the sum total of the cultural conditions which act to stimulate a growing child, or the sole measure of environmental equality. In thinking of "environment," we should, and many do, recognize that the present school, or the present home, or the present occupation does not mark the limit of the social setting of the Negro or any child.[5] We should include in the picture the record of education and lit-

[5] Perhaps we should stress the fact that every child lives in an involved world,

eracy of parents and members of the immediate family, the presence or absence of various cultural items (such as books, magazines and newspapers, moving pictures, radios, and the like), as well as community influences. In considering the Negro's environment, special significance should be given to the effects of several centuries of slavery, his minority status, segregation, illiteracy, intellectual stagnation, family disorganization, and low occupational and economic status.

1.   *Limitations of Measures of Environment*

It is true that an objective estimate or some of the major environmental constellations can be made by use of one of several available scales which purport to measure home environment, social status, and socio-economic level.[6] The limitations of these measures of environment, when applied to Negro groups, have been recognized by several writers (7, p. 66; 24, p. 182; 41, pp. 431–432). For example, inspection of the scales reveals that they are largely concerned with the material aspects of environment, and that their chief criterion is possession. Anyone familiar with Negro life and culture knows that:

"One cannot reason glibly from the presence of fine furniture, rugs, and other appointment, or luxuries in Negro homes, to certain 'standard' social status, for generally speaking, the cultural values of the two groups differ. One is reminded in this connection of the observation of Booker T. Washington in his *Up From Slavery.* He makes the point that often in the cabins of the newly emancipated slaves one would encounter sewing machines but nobody in the house could sew; ornate clocks, but no one who could 'tell time'; reed organs with nobody to play them" (41, p. 431).

Furthermore, the hierarchy of occupations is not the same for Negroes and whites in the United States. Consequently, a different occupation may represent a different socio-economic level in the two groups. The classification of postal workers is a case in point. Taussig places "mailman" in Group II on his scale, along with semi-skilled workers and the like. The Negro postal worker certainly enjoys a higher relative status than this within the Negro group. A large number of Negroes who have partially or

---

subjected to a number of environmental forces simultaneously. He is seldom solely under the influence of the home, apart from community influences. A description of all the possible environmental forces operating upon the child during any given time or period in his developmental process entails a task of Herculean propositions. Even more difficult is the description of all the environmental forces that have been operating upon him at various times in the past. See Wellman (48).

[6] A summary of the most comprehensive and widely used scales has been given recently by Leahy (28).

fully prepared themselves for professional occupations, having found difficulty in entering upon or succeeding in their chosen line of work, passed the Civil Service examination and entered the postal or railway mail service. This tends to raise the general educational level of this class of workers to a relatively higher status than would be expected. Moreover, there is a high degree of stability attached to the occupation which automatically reacts favorably on the general economic and social status of individuals thus employed. The education, therefore, and general social status of persons engaged in postal and railway mail service are approximately equal to that of Negro professional workers, the large majority of whom are teachers.

Again, it would show a lack of understanding to argue that, absolutely, "a Negro college president represented the same socio-economic level as does a white college president, the fact is that they are alike only in name. But measured either by training, experience in administration, or salary, the distance from common labor to college president for the Negro is less than for the white."

Differences in occupational opportunities might also be mentioned in this connection. It can hardly be denied that, to a very great extent the Negro's economic status is thrust upon him. The kind of competition he has to face in his search for a job has been described by Johnson (25), Nearing (37), Spero and Harris (45), and Feldman (12). These writers point out that Negroes do not enter all occupations in the same proportions as do native-born white wage earners. There is a piling up of workers in the unskilled and semi-skilled jobs, balanced by a scarcity of opportunity in the skilled and professional occupations.

Low incomes influence housing, recreation, cultural advantages, nutrition, and family life, all of which have been shown to be correlated with standing in intelligence tests in varying degrees. Furthermore, unstable and poorly paid occupations—low incomes, large families, and definitely restricted educational opportunities—all these and other influences work to hold Negro children within circumscribed social, economic, and educational boundaries within which their fathers have lived.[7]

Thus, all uses of objective measures of environment in an attempt to equate Negro-white groups is unwarranted for the following reasons: (a) there is a fundamental difference in attitudes toward the material aspects of environment; (b) the hierarchy of occupations is not the same for both groups; and (c) opportunities for employment in the higher positions are far from equal.

[7] For an interesting discussion of the profound effect the occupation of the Negro child's father usually has upon his general social, economic, and educational status, see Bell (2).

2. Educational Inequalities

The *sine qua non* of comparison must be first, a dependable measurement of each "race"; second, a representative sample of each "race"; and third, identical or not significantly different environmental conditions—especially educational opportunity (11, 17). Let us note very briefly certain features of Negro education in the United States. In the southern states the per capita expenditures for the education of whites were reported as being, on the average, more than four times as large as those for Negroes, while the inequality increased as the counties were more densely populated with Negroes. It was disclosed further, that the southern states appropriated for higher schools for whites nearly 20 times as much as for higher schools for Negroes. The salaries of Negro teachers in the South are so meager that the standards are of necessity low; and the quality of instruction also must be very poor, for it is extremely doubtful whether the better Negro intellects could be attracted to the work. Whatever school attendance laws existed in the southern states were not enforced with Negro children, contributing to serious retardation. In addition to these unfavorable conditions, the average length of the school term varied from 94 days in Mississippi to 183 days in Delaware. The Negro schools and classes are frequently overcrowded and inadequate, so that two or three short sessions a day are arranged to accommodate all the children.

Thus in the southern states, the Negro child is a product of extremely inadequate and poor schooling. The position of the Negro in the northern states is much more favorable with respect to educational facilities, although they are not always the equal of those provided for white children.[8]

It is very difficult, therefore, to equate experimentally for educational opportunity, especially in the South, because of the sheer inequality of opportunity in public schools for Negroes and whites throughout this area.

3. Differences in Cultural[9] Background

Of equal importance are the cultural differences between the two groups. Most students of the social sciences are agreed that the Negro slaves did not come to America as savages and culturally naked (21). It

[8] For details of Negro education, see Caliver and Greene (9), Bond (6), Johnson (25), and Caliver (8).

[9] The term culture is here used in its anthropological sense to refer to a relatively well-defined system of folkways and customs effective throughout a community, nation, or larger area, and can be regarded, roughly, as including those factors in the individual's background that psychological usage comprises in the term "environment."

has been shown that the majority of the slaves brought with them a cultural background that might be regarded as highly sophisticated[10] and "can be called 'primitive' only in the technical sense of the word—that is, of a folk who have never developed a written language" (18, p. 88).

There is, however, a lively controversy as to whether there are African survivals in the present-day behavior of the American Negro. The argument against the retention of aboriginal tradition is as follows: the conditions of slavery were such that a large part of the Negro's aboriginal culture was of necessity lost. He was separated from his fellow-tribesmen, taught a new language, and inducted both subtly and forcibly into the culture of the white master. In other words, it is argued that because Negroes and whites have been compatriots for over three hundred years their present culture and behavior are identical (14).

It is easier to assume that because Negroes and whites are compatriots their culture is necessarily identical in all important respects, than it is to prove the point. Such a community of culture is actually far from being a fact. A common culture implies, not only substantial conformity in tradition, religion, recreation, education, economic status, and the like, for all members, but also adequate participation in cultural opportunities. Since there are marked deviations in many of these cardinal aspects arising by reason of historical and social conditions (25, 53), the cultural setting of the American Negro is radically changed, however much it may seem superficially to be identical with that of whites.

Moreover, Herskovits (21) has shown that the African background has greatly influenced the patterns of New-World Negro life. The cultures can be placed on a scale of decreasing intensity of Africanism in behavior. He writes:

". . . the Africanisms of the Guiana and Haiti have persisted more strongly than elsewhere in the New World, the amount of Europeanization of New World Negroes increasing as Jamaica, Brazil, and Cuba are reached, being more intensive in the other West Indian Islands and southern portions of the United States, and becoming almost complete when the culture of the urban northern Negroes is considered" (21, p. 266).

Although the American Negro's accommodation to European custom has been far-reaching, nevertheless Herskovits finds that many forms of his present-day behavior are readily recognizable as of African origin, that is,

[10] Murdock (35) writes: ". . . contrary to popular prejudices, the Negro peoples display, on the average, a more complex development of government, art, industry, and material culture than the non-literate inhabitants of any other great continental area" (p. xiv).

manifestations of the carry-over of aboriginal customs. For example, Africanisms in religious beliefs and practices, music, dance, folklore, attitudes, and certain aspects of motor behavior are generally observable in the United States (19).

It is unnecessary to elaborate upon the fact that intelligence tests are constructed from materials which their authors take for granted but which are frequently quite foreign, and thus unfavorable, in this context to the Negro. Psychologists have tended to slight this circumstance because they readily make the assumption that the culture of Negroes and whites is identical. A moment's reflection, however, has shown this to be far from the case. Hence, the Negro is at a decided disadvantage in taking our current intelligence tests, and this handicap will be reflected in the Negro's group performance on these tests. It appears, therefore, that cultural differences make very difficult and complex the problem of equating Negro-white groups.

4. Socio-Psychological[11] Factors

Furthermore, even if one could equate for certain background conditions it would still be doubtful that the socio-psychological factors could ever be equated. The Negro is compelled to live in a relatively closed cultural environment (some have characterized it as "a psychical, often a physical ghetto," 6, p. 8) where the concept of inferiority goes mainly unchallenged. His forced society tends to establish inferiority patterns of adjustment and leaves little or no place for the play of a strong, aggressive will, the type, say of the "empire builders" of white society (29). This state of depression and retardation is well-illustrated in an observation by King who found in his study of West Virginia Negroes that

"boys and girls tended to drop out of school just about the age of puberty. When he asked them why they wished to leave school, he was frequently told that they saw no reason to stay on since they would never be permitted to do the kind of work for which a more advanced education would fit them. As they came to realize that they could never be any-

[11] The term socio-psychological refers to the dynamic, functional relation between culture and personality, or to the influence of the folkways on the individual. A number of ethnologists (3, 4, 5, 32, 33, 34) have presented data showing that the experiences of people living in different cultures and social environments vary in such a way as to lend different meaning to their actions, stimulate the development of totally different interests, and furnish diverse ideals and standards of behavior. The importance of motivation, interests and similar factors in intelligence-tests performance has been repeatedly emphasized by Klineberg (27), Freeman (15), Anastasi (1), Terman (46), and others.

thing but laborers or house servants or quarrymen, it seems to them a waste of time to continue with their education."[12]

Prolonged subjection will not only produce complete acquiescence, as evidenced in these children, but also a consciousness of belonging to an "inferior" or helpless group and a certain uniformity of behavior determined by common experiences.[13]

Since the Negro represents a minority more sharply set off than any of the country's other minorities, the utmost caution must be exercised in equating Negro and white groups. The gap between the groups is enormous, and tradition prevents it from being bridged by the Negro. He is under a handicap which no amount of intelligence can quite overcome. No amount of achievement will permit a Negro to share privileges denied on account of "race," even though shared as a matter of right by the most illiterate white person in the community (53). He may, however, be recognized as a superior by virtue of his achievement, nevertheless he is dubbed inferior by virtue of belonging to the Negro "race." The feeling that he is a member of a despised and abused "race," that he is discriminated against in his own country solely because of "race," tends to curb his age-expansion tendencies and profoundly disturbs his personal equilibrium.[14]

It is a question, then, whether psychologists can ever equate experimentally for these and other subjective and highly elusive problems of culture and their profound influence upon the mental reactions of Negro children.

C. CONCLUSION

It would seem that the materials in this paper leave no choice but to assume that there is no basis for equating Negroes and whites by reference to similarity of environment. It is a question, therefore, whether Negro-white differences in intelligence-test scores can ever be changed except by such a radical change in social and economic condition of Negroes in

[12] Cited by Klineberg (26, p. 94).

[13] Several of the Iowa studies of *IQ* changes have revealed important experimental findings in this connection: (*a*) continued residence in an inadequate environment has a leveling effect on intelligence. In other words, changes in brightness tend to be related to the general *IQ* level of the group (42, 43); (*b*) the mental level of a child is significantly related to the amount and character of environmental stimulation (10, 44).

[14] For a frank and human discussion of one intelligent Negro attempting to escape personality strains caused by class barriers, see Williams (49); an interesting and rather realistic account of personality disintegration in a Negro brought about by frustration will be found in Wright (51).

America as shall provide comparable opportunities.[15] It might be possible by a sufficiently extensive investigation to make a comparable sampling of the "races." Perhaps the Army test approaches such a sampling. It is hardly possible, however, to secure data which will be unaffected by differences in environmental influence without a more widespread and radical control of social and economic conditions than a mere scientific experiment can provide.

Finally, we should note that it is no longer considered a respectable procedure to measure and judge individual mentality against what Benedict (4) calls "arbitrarily selected normality." Instead, the relativity which has come to be so prominent in other fields of science grows apparent here, for it becomes evident that the mental reactions which make an individual atypical in one culture may fit him perfectly for another; and the low *average* scores made by Negroes on intelligence tests, standardized chiefly on northern whites, may represent a lack of adjustment to the latter's culture.

References

1. Anastasi, A. Differential Psychology; Individual and Group Differences in Behavior. New York: Macmillan, 1937.
2. Bell, H. M. Youth tell their story; a study of the conditions and attitudes of young people in Maryland between the ages of 16 and 24; conducted by the American Youth Commission. Washington, D. C., American Council on Education, 1938.
3. Benedict, R. F. Anthropology and the abnormal. *J. Gen. Psychol.*, 1934, **19**, 59–82.
4. ————. Paterns of Culture. Boston: Houghton Mifflin, 1934.
5. Boas, F. Race, Language, and Culture. New York: Macmillan, 1940.
6. Bond, H. The education of the Negro in the American social order. New York: Prentice-Hall, 1934.
7. Caliver, A. A background study of Negro college students. *U. S. Off. Educ. Bull.*, 1933, No. 8.
8. ————. Secondary education for Negroes. *U. S. Off. Educ. Bull.*, 1932, No. 17.

[15] It may be argued that since social, economic, and educational opportunities are unequal in America, the low *average* score made by Negroes on intelligence tests is to be regarded as a disease of society rather than evidence of group incompetence. This concept of "society as the patient," of the "sick society," has recently been analyzed by Frank (13).

9. Caliver, A., and Greene, E. G. Education of Negroes: a 5-year bibliography 1931–1935. *U. S. Off. Educ. Bull.*, 1937, No. 8.

10. Crissey, O. L. Mental development as related to institutional residence and educational achievement. *Univ. Iowa Stud. Child Wel.*, 1937, 11, No. 1.

11. Estabrooks, G. A. The question of racial inferiority. *Amer. Anthropol.*, 1928, 30, 470–475.

12. Feldman, H. Racial Factors in American Industry. New York: Harper, 1931.

13. Frank, L. K. Society as the patient. *Amer. J. Sociol.*, 1936, 42, 335–344.

14. Frazier, E. F. The Negro Family in the United States. Chicago: Univ. Chicago Press, 1939.

15. Freeman, S. Individual Differences: The nature and causes of variations in intelligence and special abilities. New York: Holt, 1934.

16. Garth, T. R. Race Psychology: A study of racial mental differences. New York: McGraw-Hill, 1931.

17. ————. White, Indian, and Negro work course. *J. Appl. Psychol.*, 1921, 5, 14–25.

18. Herskovits, M. J. The ancestry of the American Negro. *Amer. Schol.*, 1938–1939, 8, 84–94.

19. ————. Acculturation and the American Negro. *Southw. Pol. & Soc. Sci.*, 1927, 8, 211–224.

20. ————. Anthropometry of the American Negro. New York: Columbia Univ. Press, 1930.

21. ————. Social history of the American Negro. (In) Murchison, Carl (Ed.), *A Handbook of Social Psychology*. Worcester: Clark Univ. Press, 1935. (Pp. 207–267).

22. ————. The American Negro: A Study in Racial Crossing. New York: Knopf, 1928.

23. Huxley, J. S., and Haddon, A. C. We Europeans: A Survey of "Racial" Problems. New York: Harper, 1936.

24. Jenkins, M. D. A socio-psychological study of Negro children of superior intelligence. *J. Negro Educ.*, 1936, 5, 175–190.

25. Johnson, C. S. The Negro in American Civilization. New York: Holt, 1930.

26. Journal of Negro Education: Yearbook Number III. The Physical and Mental Abilities of the American Negro. Washington, D. C.: Department of Education, Howard University, July, 1934.

27. Klineberg, O. Race Differences. New York: Harper, 1935.

28. Leahy, A. M. The measurement of urban home environment. Minneapolis, Minn.: Univ. Minnesota Press, 1936.

29. Long, H. H. Some psychogenic hazards of segregated education of Negroes. *J. Negro Educ.*, 1935, 4, 336–350.

30. Mayo, M. J. The mental capacity of the Negro. *Arch. of Psychol.*, 1913, No. 24.

31. McGraw, M. B. A comparative study of a group of southern white and Negro infants. *Genet. Psychol. Monog.*, 1931, **10**, 1–105.

32. Mead, M. Coming of Age in Samoa; A Psychological Study of Primitive Youth for Western Civilization. New York: Morrow, 1928.

33. ————. Growing up in New Guinea. New York: Morrow, 1930.

34. ————. Sex and Temperament in Three Primitive Societies. New York: Morrow, 1935.

35. Murdock, G. P. Our Primitive Contemporaries. New York: Macmillan, 1934.

36. Murdock, K. A study of race differences in New York City. *Sch. & Soc.*, 1920, **11**, 147–150.

37. Nearing, S. Black America. New York: Vanguard Press, 1929.

38. Peterson, J., and Lanier, L. H. Studies of the comparative abilities of whites and Negroes. *Men. Meas. Monog.*, 1929, No. 5.

39. Phillips, B. A. The Binet tests applied to colored children. *Psychol. Clin.*, 1914, **6**, 190–196.

40. Pintner, R. Intelligence Testing: Methods and Results. New York: Holt, 1931.

41. Price, J. St. Clair. Negro-white differences in general intelligence. *J. Negro Educ.*, 1934, **3**, 424–452.

42. Skeels, H. M., and Fillmore, E. A. Mental development of children from underprivileged homes. *Genet. Psychol.*, 1937, **50**, 427–439.

43. Skodak, M. Children in foster homes: a study of mental development. *Univ. Ia. Stud. Child. Wel.*, 1938, **16**, No. 1.

44. Skeels, H. M., Updegraft, R., Wellman, B. L., and Williams, H. M. A study of environmental stimulation: An orphanage preschool project. *Univ. Ia. Stud. Child Wel.*, 1938, **15**, No. 4.

45. Spero, S. L., and Harris, A. L. The Black Worker. New York: Columbia Univ. Press, 1931.

46. Terman, L. M., and Merrill, M. A. Measuring Intelligence; a guide to the administration of the new revised Stanford-Binet tests of intelligence. Boston: Houghton Mifflin, 1937.

47. Viteles, M. The mental status of the Negro. *Ann. Amer. Acad. Pol. & Soc. Sci.*, 1928, **140**, 166–177.

48. Wellman, B. L. The meaning of environment. (In) *The Thirty-Ninth Yearbook of the National Society for the Study of Education Intelligence: Its Nature and Nurture, Part I.* Bloomington, Ill.: *Pub. Sch. Pub.*, 1940. (Pp. 21–40.)

49. Williams, P. I am a Negro. *Amer. Mag.*, 1937, **124**, 59–161.

50. Witty, P., and Lehman, H. C. Racial differences: The dogma of superiority. *J. Soc. Psychol.,* 1930, 1, 394–418.

51. Wright, R. Native Son. New York: Harper, 1940.

52. Yoder, D. Present status of the question of racial differences. *J. Educ. Psychol.,* 1928, 19, 463–470.

53. Young, D. American Minority Peoples. New York: Harper, 1932.

11 The Upper Limit of Ability Among American Negroes

MARTIN D. JENKINS[1]

This paper is an interesting classic since it advances the notion that there is literally no upper limit to the intellectual ability of Negroes. Thus, it makes permanent a particular approach to the conceptualization of racial intelligence that Professor Canady had argued for as early as 1937 (see Canady, 1937, this volume). Specifically, Dr. Canady had argued that the crucial question evolved around the nature and range of intelligence *within a race* and not, as had usually been the case, the nature and range of intelligence *between races*. Dr. Jenkins presents considerable data to show that the Negro race has a large supply of extremely gifted persons; indeed the highest score achieved on the Stanford-Binet Intelligence Test (IQ = 200) was that of a young Negro girl. The paper is significant for its having established a more sensible and comprehensive concept of *racial intelligence*. In Part IV of this book, Dr. Jenkins and Constance Randall further analyze some of the differences between very superior and unselected Negro college students in an attempt to enumerate some of the characteristics of superior college students.

More than three decades of psychometric investigation among American Negroes has yielded a rich fund of information concerning this population group. Perhaps the most generally known finding, and certainly the most emphasized, is that when "comparable" groups of whites and Negroes are tested, the Negro group is almost invariably inferior to the white in psychometric intelligence (intelligence as measured by psychological tests). Preoccupation with the significance of the low *average* performance

SOURCE. *Scientific Monthly*; LXVI, 399–401, 1948. Reprinted by permission of the author and *Science*.

[1] Professor Jenkins (Ph.D., Northwestern, 1935) has taught at Virginia State College, North Carolina Agricultural and Technological College, and Cheyney Training School for Teachers; since 1938 he has been teaching at Howard University. A specialist in educational psychology, Dr. Jenkins became interested in gifted children while studying for his doctorate.

of Negro groups has served to divert attention from an equally important phenomenon—the variability of the group, and especially the upper limit reached by its really superior members.

The question of the upper limit of ability among Negroes has both theoretical and practical significance. Psychologists generally attribute the low average performance of Negro groups on intelligence tests to cultural factors. It is well known that Negroes generally experience an inferior environment; and there is certainly no question but that an inferior environment tends to depress the psychometric intelligence. There are, however, many Negro children who are nurtured in an environment that is equal or superior to that of the average white child. Thus, we may hypothesize that *if race in itself is not a limiting factor in intelligence, then, among Negroes whose total environment compares favorably with that of the average American white, there should be found a "normal" proportion of very superior cases, and the upper limit of ability should coincide with that of the white population.* This hypothesis is especially attractive from a negative aspect; thus, if very superior individuals are not to be found in the Negro population, the environmental explanation would clearly be inadequate to account for the phenomenon. The existence of such individuals, on the other hand, would afford additional evidence, but not absolute proof, of course, of the validity of the environmental explanation of "racial differences" in psychometric intelligence.

The practical significance of the question is apparent. If Negroes are to be found at the highest levels of psychometric intelligence, then we may anticipate that members of this racial group have the ability to participate in the culture at the highest level. In these days of reconsideration of the role of the dark races throughout the world, this question has more than mere national significance.

Analysis of the literature relating to the intelligence-test performance of Negro children reveals that a considerable number of these children have been found within the range that reaches the best 1 percent of white children (I.Q. 130 and above) and at the level of "gifted" children (I.Q. 140 and above). There are at least sixteen published studies that give an account of Negro children possessing I.Q.s above 130; twelve of these report cases above I.Q. 140. These investigations were made by different psychologists in various localities and under varying conditions; moreover, the I.Q.s were derived by a number of different tests. Further, the populations studied were located almost exclusively in Northern urban communities. Consequently, one may not justifiably generalize, from a composite of these studies, concerning the incidence of Negro deviates. It is of significance, however, that of the 22,301 subjects included in the thirteen studies for which N's are reported, 0.3 percent scored at I.Q. 140

and above, and fully 1 percent scored at I.Q. 130 and above. These percentages are similar to those obtained from a "normal" I.Q. distribution of American school children.

Of especial significance are the cases of very bright children of Binet I.Q. 160 and above. It may be estimated that fewer than 0.1 percent of school children are to be found at or above this level. As the I.Q. rises above 160 the frequency of occurrence, of course, decreases. Statictically, cases at or above I.Q. 180 should occur about once in a million times, although they actually occur with somewhat greater frequency. In his classic California study of the gifted, Terman found only 15 children testing as high as I.Q. 180; and Hollingworth reports: "In twenty-three years seeking in New York City and the local metropolitan area I have found only twelve children who test at or above 180 I.Q. (S-B)." It is apparent then, that children who test upwards of Binet I.Q. 160 are extreme deviates in psychometric intelligence and representative of the very brightest children in America.

I have assembled from various scores the case records of 18 Negro children who test above I.Q. 160 on the Stanford-Binet examination. Seven of these cases test above I.Q. 170, 4 above I.Q. 180, and 1 at I.Q. 200. Two of these cases were tested initially by me; the other 16 were reported by psychologists in university centers and public school systems. Analysis of the case records indicates that these children during the early years of their development, at least, manifest the same characteristics as do other very high I.Q. children: originality of expression, creative ability, and surpassing performance in school subjects. Some of these children, but not all, are greatly accelerated in school progress. Two, for example, had completed their high-school course and were regularly enrolled university students at age thirteen; both of these subjects were elected to Phi Beta Kappa and earned the baccalaureate degree at age sixteen.

It is of some significance that all these children were found in Northern or border state cities (New York, Chicago, Washington, and Cincinnati). No Southern Negro child, so far as I have been able to ascertain, has been identified as testing at or above Binet I.Q. 160. It is certain that among the 80 percent of the total Negro population that lives in the Southern states, children with potentiality for such development exist. Whether the fact that no children with this development have been discovered is due to lack of environmental opportunity and stimulation, or merely to lack of identification, is not surely known.

I am not attempting here to show that approximately as many Negro children as white are to be found at the higher levels of psychometric intelligence. There appears little doubt that the number of very bright Negro children is relatively smaller that the number of bright white children in the total American population. Nevertheless, it is apparent that children of very superior psychometric intelligence may be found in many Negro populations, and that the upper limit of the range attained by the extreme deviates is higher than is generally believed.

The performance of extreme deviates at the college and adult levels has not yet been extensively studied. Such evidence as is available, however, indicates that at maturity, as in childhood, some Negroes are to be found at the highest level of psychometric intelligence. In a recent unpublished study conducted at Howard University, it was found that of approximately 3,500 Negro freshmen entering the College of Liberal Arts over a period of seven years, 101 scored in the upper decile, and 8 in the upper centile (national norms) on the American Council on Education Psychological Examination. In a more extensive study, the National Survey of Higher Education of Negroes, there were, among 3,684 students in twenty-seven Negro institutions of higher education located chiefly in the Southern states, 23 cases in the upper decile and 4 in the upper centile on the A.C.E. Psychological Examination. It is of some significance that in the same study 12 upper decile cases are reported among the 105 Negro students in two Northern universities (almost half as many as were found altogether among the 3,684 students in the twenty-seven Negro colleges). This contrast is in accord with the general but undocumented opinion that among Negro college students there are proportionately fewer extreme deviates in psychometric intelligence in the Southern segregated colleges than in the Northern nonsegregated institutions.

The Army General Classification Test data assembled during World War II have not yet become fully available. One may predict with a fair degree of confidence, however, that these data will reveal some Negro cases at the very highest levels of performance. In view of the fact, however, that the Negro selectees were predominantly from communities that provide inadequate provision for the educational and cultural development of Negroes, we may expect that a very small proportion of the total population will be found at the higher levels of performance. Subgroups which have had a normal cultural opportunity should, in accordance with our hypothesis, yield an appreciable proportion of superior deviates.

The findings of the studies cited in this article support the hypothesis formulated at the outset. In some population groups there is to be found a "normal" proportion of Negro subjects of very superior psychometric intelligence, and the extreme deviates reach the upper limits attained by white subjects. Although the incidence of superior cases is much lower among Negroes than whites, a phenomenon which might well be accounted for by differential environmental factors, we may conclude that race per se (at least as it is represented in the American Negro) is not a limiting factor in psychometric intelligence.

The abstract mental tests that contribute to psychometric intelligence do not measure the factors of personality and motivation that largely determine success in life. The findings of studies of gifted children, especially those of Terman, Hollingworth, and Witty, indicate that the highly gifted child usually fulfils his early promise. But not always. Failure among the gifted is also frequent.

The data of this article bring into sharp focus the limitations that our society places on the development of the highly gifted Negro. These superior deviates are nurtured in a culture in which racial inferiority of the Negro is a basic assumption. Consequently, they will typically experience throughout their lives educational, social, and occupational restrictions and must inevitably affect motivation and achievement. The unanswered question relative to the influence of this factor on the adult achievement of superior Negroes is a problem for future investigators to solve.

12 *The Influence of Race of the Experimenter and Instructions Upon the Expression of Hostility[1] by Negro Boys*

IRWIN KATZ, JAMES M. ROBINSON, EDGAR G. EPPS, & PATRICIA WALY

In this paper we encounter a systematic attempt to examine the role of relatively subtle psychological testing factors in the performance of Black youngsters. This is a signicant effort because it comes to grips with the problem of the whole psychological testing process in order to see if race, per se, interacts with psychological testing in such a way as to produce unusual or undesirable effects on the subjects' test scores. This is one way in which researchers have attempted to better understand the factors related to observed racial differences in psychological testing programs. However, such studies as these do not necessarily show that psychological tests are completely biased or meaningless, but rather that a number of quite complex factors, which need to be carefully considered and evaluated, are in operation while one is taking a psychological test. Specifically, this study shows that the race of the test administrator and the type of instructions used interact significantly with these youngsters' test performance and with their expression of hostility. The authors further consider the role that the suppression of aroused hostility may play in the test performance of Negro boys.

INTRODUCTION

It was recently demonstrated that the efficiency of Southern Negro college students on a verbal task can be influenced by both the race of the experimenter and the evaluate significance of the task. Katz, Roberts and Robinson (1963) found that when digit-symbol substitution was presented as a test of eye-hand coordination, Negro subjects scored higher with a

SOURCE. Reprinted from *The Journal of Social Issues*, 1964, XX, 2, 54–59, with permission of The Society for the Psychological Study of Social Issues.

[1] This research was carried out under Contract Nonr 285(24) between the Office of Naval Research and New York University.

107

white administrator than they did with a Negro administrator. But when the same task was described as an intelligence test, there was marked impairment of performance with the white tester, while subjects who were tested by the Negro experimenter showed a slight improvement. The present study deals with the effect of these experimental conditions upon the arousal and expression of hostility.

There is reason to believe that emotional conflict involving the need to control hostility may have a disruptive influence on the performance of Negro students when their intelligence is evaluated by a white person. Sarason et al. (1960) have described the test-anxious child, whether Negro or white, as one who typically reacts with strong unconscious hostility to the adult tester, whom he believes will in some way pass judgment on his adequacy. The hostility is not openly expressed, but instead is turned inward against the self in the form of self-derogatory attitudes, which strengthen the child's expectation of failure and desire to escape from the situation. Thus, he is distracted from the task before him by fear of failure and an impulse to escape.

A number of studies support the view of blocking of aggressive impulses as detrimental to intellectual efficiency. Lit (1956), Kimball (1953), and Harris (1961) found that scholastic underachievement was associated with difficulty in expressing aggression openly. Rosenwald (1961) reported that students who gave relatively few aggressive responses on a projective test suffered greater impairment in solving anagrams after a hostility induction than did students who had shown less inhibition on the projective test. Goldman, Horwitz and Lee (1954) demonstrated experimentally that the degree to which hostility against an instigator was blocked from expression determined the amount of disruption on three cognitive tasks.

With respect to Negroes, it is known that segregation engenders a feeling of intellectual inadequacy (cf. Dreger and Miller's, 1960, review of empirical evidence), hence they should be prone to experience test situations as threatening. Hostility would tend to arise against the adult authority figure from whom an unfavorable evaluation was expected. The Negro student's hostility might perhaps be stronger against a white tester than against a Negro tester, since the former might be expected to compare him invidiously with members of the advantaged white group. However, previous research suggests that aggressive impulses against a white person will usually be strongly inhibited (Yarrow, 1958; Winslow and Brainerd, 1950; Karon, 1958). There is also evidence (Berkowitz, 1962) that when there are strong restraints operating against openly aggressive behavior, even its expression on projective tests will be blocked to some extent.

In the present experiment, hostile expression was measured by means of a questionnaire that was disguised as a concept formation test. Negro students at a segregated high school in the South were given the questionnaire by either a Negro or a white experimenter, with instructions that described it either neutrally or as an intelligence test. Then scores were compared with those obtained previously by the same subjects in an informal, all-Negro setting. It was predicted that when neutral instructions were used, levels of hostile expression in the Negro-tester and white-tester groups would remain the same, but when intelligence test instructions were used, hostility scores would *increase* under a Negro experimenter and *decrease* when the experimenter was white.

METHOD

SUBJECTS AND PROCEDURES. The subjects were 72 male students at a Negro high school and junior high school in Nashville. They ranged in age from 13 to 18 years. Volunteers for the experiment were recruited in classrooms with an offer of one dollar for participating for an hour in a research project. The study was done on two successive days. The first day all subjects met after school in a large room and were administered the hostility scale by the assistant principal of the school. They were told that the purpose of the questionnaire was to aid in evaluation of a proposed new method for teaching vocabulary. Afterwards, they were given their assignments for the following day. For the second session the entire sample was divided into four groups of equal size. Each group was tested by either a white or a Negro adult stranger, with instructions that described the task as either an intelligence test or a research instrument. The two testers worked simultaneously in different rooms, and ran the two instructional conditions in quick succession, to prevent subject contamination. Both experimenters introduced themselves as psychologists from local universities (Fisk and Vanderbilt) and gave oral instructions.

The neutral instructions stated in part:

"Yesterday you did some vocabulary items. Today you will do a slightly different version of this task for me. It is *not* a test. I am doing research on the meaning of certain words in American speech. To a psychologist, the meaning of a word refers to how it is used by people who speak the language. So I want you to show me how you use these words. Your answers will not be shown to your teachers. Yesterday you had a practice warm-up. It will not be scored. Today's answers are the ones that count. So answer what you think is correct today."

The intelligence test instructions were in part:

"Yesterday you were given a vocabulary test. Today you will do a slightly different version of this test for me. I am interested in this vocabulary test because it will show me how intelligent you are. I am doing research on mental ability, and I want to see how bright you boys are at ——————— School. This test will show your knowledge of words, your ability to recognize abstract concepts, and your general intelligence. It will show whether you could succeed in college, or in your chosen field of work. But your individual scores will *not* be shown to your teachers. They will be used only for research on intelligence. Yesterday you had a practice warm-up . . . (rest of instructions same as neutral conditions)."

After the instructions were given, a hostility questionnaire was administered which was the same as the one used the previous day, except that the items were arranged differently.

THE HOSTILITY SCALE. The instrument used to measure hostile expression was based on a test that had been developed by Ehrlich (1961) to study the influence of aggressive dispositions on concept formation in Northern white adolescent boys. Our test had 58 items, each consisting of four words, with instructions to "circle the word that does not belong with the others." Twenty-nine items contained only nonaggressive concepts; elimination of a particular word resulted in a better concept than did elimination of any other word, e.g.: TUNNEL, BRIDGE, FERRY, TOLL. In the remaining 29 items, one word had an aggressive meaning, one was nonaggressive, and two were ambiguous, e.g.: HOMERUN, HIT, BASH, STRIKE. Here the subject could select an aggressive concept by eliminating HOMERUN, or a nonaggressive concept by dropping BASH. Out of a total of 58 items in our test, 47 were taken from Ehrlich's 84-item test. He found scores on his test to be related to ratings of overt aggression, as well as to hostility scores on a TAT-like projective test. The present version evolved from a preliminary tryout of the original instrument on a sample of Southern Negro college students, under neutral instructions. Items which did not appear to be suitable were dropped, and some new ones were added.

A subject's hostility score consisted of the total number of critical items in which he had included the aggression word, regardless of whether he had used the correct concept. In addition, a score indicative of the level of intellectual functioning was obtained by totalling the number of correct concepts attained on neutral items, and on aggression items. To study the effect of the experimental conditions, change scores were obtained by subtracting each subject's scores on the pretest from his scores on the post test.

RESULTS AND DISCUSSION

The main findings of the experiment are presented in Table 1. It can be seen that there was a significant interaction effect of the two variables,

Race of Tester and Test vs. Neutral Instruction, on changes in hostility scores from the previous day $(p < .025)$. The group means reveal that in the Neutral condition the change scores of subjects who had a white administrator were only slightly different from those of subjects who had a Negro administrator. But when test instructions were used, the White Tester group expressed *less* hostility than previously, while the Negro Tester group showed an *increase* in hostile expression. This difference between groups was significant $(p < .01)$. Thus the experimental prediction was supported.

There were no significant effects of the experimental conditions on changes in the number of correct concepts attained on neutral items, on aggression items, or on all items combined. Within each of the four experimental groups, there were no correlations between the various measures of conceptual accuracy and hostility change scores. Finally, several items in a post-experimental questionnaire, which were intended to elicit information about the subject's emotional state and perception of the situation, failed to reveal any group differences.

Our interpretation of the results in Table 1 is that both task administrators instigated hostility in subjects when they announced that they were testing intelligence; when the experimenter was Negro, students revealed their annoyance by forming aggressive concepts, but when he was white the need to control hostile feelings resulted in avoidance of aggressive

TABLE 1

Analysis of Variance and Group Means for Effects of Race of Tester and Instructions on Hostility Change Scores

	df	MS	F
Race of Tester	1	29.39	2.10
Instructions	1	.89	.64
Race × Instruc.	1	88.89	6.34**
Error (within)	68	14.01	

	Group Means Instructions		
Race of Tester	Test	Neutral	Difference
White	−2.11	−0.11	2.00
Negro	1.39	−1.06	2.45*
Difference	3.50***	.95	

Note.—N = 18 for all groups.

* $p < .07$.

** $p < .025$.

*** $p < .01$.

words. The latter finding is reminiscent of a study by Clark (1955) in which arousal of the sex drive in white male college students brought about a *reduction* in the manifest sex imagery of their TAT responses. This view of the data is of course inferential, since all that is actually known about the White Tester-Test Instructions group is that their hostility scores *declined* from pretest levels. There is no direct evidence of increased emotional conflict in this condition. Assuming that our interpretation is correct, the results suggest that inhibited hostility may have contributed to the behavioral impairment that Katz, Roberts and Robinson observed in Negroes who were tested intellectually by a white experimenter. Why then were there no effects in the present experiment on conceptual accuracy? Our belief is that the task was not an appropriate one for revealing the disruptive effects of emotional conflict. It has none of the usual features of tasks on which impairment has been found to occur under stress. For example, it was not speeded, and it did not involve complex learning, coordination of responses, or problem solving.

Finally, the results provide a methodological critique of previous research on Negro personality which did not take into account possible effects of the race of the investigator on subjects' responses. For example, the bulk of studies on Negro aggression that were reviewed by Dreger and Miller (1960) apparently were done entirely by whites.

References

Berkowitz, L. *Aggression, a social psychological analysis.* New York: McGraw-Hill, 1962.

Clark, R. A. The effects of sexual motivation on phantasy. In D. C. McClelland (Ed.), *Studies in motivation.* New York: Appleton-Century-Crofts, 1955, pp. 44–57.

Dreger, R. M., and Miller, K. S. Comparative psychological studies of Negroes and whites in the United States. *Psychol. Bull.,* 1960, **57**, 361–402.

Ehrlich, M. *The selective role of aggression in concept formation.* Unpublished doctoral thesis. New York University, 1961.

Goldman, M., Horwitz, M., and Lee, F. J. Alternative classroom standards concerning management of hostility and effects on student learning. ONR Technical Report, 1954.

Harris, I. *Emotional blocks to learning.* Glencoe: Free Press, 1961.

Karon, B. P. *The Negro personality.* New York: Springer, 1958.

Katz, I., Roberts, O. S., and Robinson, J. M. Effects of difficulty, race of administrator, and instructions on Negro digit-symbol performance. ONR Technical Report, 1963.

Kimball, Barbara. Sentence-completion technique in a study of scholastic under-achievement. *J. consult. Psychol.*, 1952, **16**, 353–358.

Lit, J. *Formal and content factors of projective tests in relation to academic achievement.* Unpublished doctoral thesis. Temple Univer., 1956.

Rosenwald, G. The assessment of anxiety in psychological experiments. *J. abnorm. soc. Psychol.*, 1961, **63**, 666–673.

Sarason, S. B., Davidson, K. S., Lighthall, F. F., Waite, R. R., and Ruebush, B. K. *Anxiety in elementary school children.* New York: John Wiley, 1960.

Winslow, C. N., and Brainerd, J. E. A comparison of the reaction of whites and Negroes to frustration as measured by the Rosenzweig Picture-Frustration Test. *Amer. Psychologist*, 1950, **5**, 297. (abstract)

Yarrow, Marian R. (Issue editor) Interpersonal dynamics in a desegregation process. *J. soc. Issues*, 1958, **14**, Whole No. 1.

13 A Study of the Wechsler-Bellevue Verbal Scores of Negro and White Males[1]

JAMES S. PETERS, II
Bureau Chief, Bureau of Vocational Rehabilitation, Connecticut State Department of Education

Dr. Peters very carefully examines differences in Verbal Intelligence between Black and white World War II veterans, and finds the white group scoring significantly higher than the Black. This difference holds for both normal and retarded subgroups of the two populations. The value of this particular paper lies in the author's detailed analysis of the results, and the explanations developed to explain the observed differences in the groups. The paper touches on many of the questions related to the concept of racial differences in intellectual ability, and has an excellent bibliography of related research and writing.

INTRODUCTION

A review of the literature from 1939 up to 1952 reveals that the Wechsler-Bellevue Scale (Form I) has gained widespread application in clinics and institutions for the measurement of intelligence and psychodiagnostic purposes. The population of these installations usuallly consists of both Negro and white patients, and the Wechsler is frequently administered routinely to both without regard for possible normative differences. During the several years of professional experience which the writer has had in using the scale with both Negroes and whites, he has never been ques-

SOURCE. Reprinted from *The Journal of Negro Education*, 1960, **29**, 7–16, with permission of the author and the publisher.

  [1] An abstract of a thesis completed at the Illinois Institute of Technology, with cases from the Vocational Advisement and Guidance Section, Veterans Administration Regional Office, Chicago, Illinois, under the direction of Dr. M. H. Groves, June 1952. The views expressed herein are not necessarily those of the Veterans Administration Office of Vocational Rehabilitation and Education. The writer gives his sincere thanks to Mr. C. Harold McCully, Director Counseling Service for Vocational Rehabilitation of the Veterans Administration, for securing VA approval for publishing this paper.

tioned as to the validity of the obtained I.Q.'s of the former unless it was for some pathological condition. Wechsler gives reasons why his norms cannot be used on the colored population of the United States.

"We have omitted the colored population from our first standardization because we did not feel that norms derived by mixing the populations could be interpreted without special provisions and reservations." (53, p. 107)

Wechsler's reasons for eliminating the colored population from his norm groups are in keeping with common standardization practices. The major difference is that he was willing to face the situation from the start which is proof enough that testing the Negro was recognized as a problem in 1944, the year the manual was published. In a further section, Wechsler stated:

"We eliminated the colored vs. white factor by admitting at the outset that our norms cannot be used for the colored population of the United States."

In practice, however, there is usually a tendency to ignore Wechsler's statement. Therefore, there arises the problem of ascertaining the possible differences between white and Negro groups on the Wechsler, and of determining the direction of such possible differences. In the event there are statistically significant differences between Negroes and whites on the various subtests of the verbal scale of the Wechsler, it would be important to be aware of these differences when interpreting results obtained from Negroes. In our study, we were primarily concerned with the factor of education and the effect which it had upon the scores made by Negroes and whites. The cultural factor is of secondary importance.

Negroes, as a group, are on a lower educational and cultural level than whites. Therefore, any conclusions made concerning their intelligence are questionable when based upon measurements using norms established on whites. Canady (5, p. 569), in discussing the methodology and interpretations of Negro-white mental testing, states that,

"It is significant, that almost without exception, all measurements of the Negro have been made with tests standardized chiefly on northern, urban whites."

He points out methodologically the unscientific nature of such an approach due to dissimilarity of educational background and experience of the two groups. He says (5, p. 560): "We violate not only the original aim of mental testers, but also the basic assumption of the intelligence test method. We wish to test Canady's contention in one area—educational background."

Three investigations making a research project of this nature necessary are those of MacPhee, Wright and Cummings (41) on the "Performance of Mentally Sub-normal Rural Southern Negroes on the Verbal Scale of the Bellevue Intelligence Examination." Machover's doctoral thesis (39) on "Performance of Negro and white Criminals on the Bellevue Adult Intelligence Scale," and Davidson, Robert, McNeil, Segal and Silverman's (13) study entitled, "Negro and white Differences on Form I of the Wechsler-Bellevue Scale." An analysis of the data of the first study showed that the verbal scale yielded discriminating scores. However, the investigators say:

"It cannot be inferred, of course, that the score or I.Q.'s received on a scale by these educationally destitute Negroes have the same implications with regard to native intelligence as do corresponding scores received by whites, for, as a group, rural southern Negroes differ radically in cultural, as well as racial background from white subjects of Wechsler's standardization groups." (41, p. 329).

In the second study, the white and Negro groups were roughly equivalent in gross cultural status but there were differences in subtest scores favoring whites and Negroes. In terms of unweighted means scores, the white group was superior in Arithmetic and Digit Symbol, while the Negro group was superior in Similarities and Picture arrangement. The difference in Arithmetic, however, was the only one which was statistically significant and arithmetic achievement is an educational variable.

Results of the third study revealed that the Negro group of psychoneurotic patients showed a significantly lower score than the white group on the arithmetic subtest. This is the only verbal subtest on which the difference in scores was significant. The mean, verbal, performance, and full scale I.Q.'s of the Negro group of psychoneurotic patients shows significantly lower scores than those of the white group.

In practice, there is usually a tendency to ignore the educational background of the Negro subject when the Wechsler-Bellevue Scale is used. This is a tendency which should not continue if psychometrists, psychologists or others interested in the true intellectual potentiality of Negro subjects are to be objective. Of the Wechsler Scale, Lorge (38, p. 490), says:

"The tests will reflect variation in educational opportunities. In tests of Information, of Arithmetic and even Comprehension, the environment and educational background of the person undoubtedly influences his test score."

Now there arises the problem of ascertaining the possible existence of statistically significant differences between white and Negro groups on the Wechsler-Bellevue Scale, and of providing a rationale for such possible differences. If there are statistically significant differences between Negroes and whites on the various aspects of the scale, it would be important to be aware of these differences when interpreting the results. It is the purpose of this study to compare the performance of white males with that of Negro males on the Wechsler-Bellevue Verbal Scale (Vocabulary excluded) and to investigate the possibility of consistent Negro-white differences due to the lack of equal educational opportunities for Negroes.

EXPERIMENTAL DESIGN

The following experimental design was formulated. Two hundred subjects were selected from among the thousands of male veterans who reported for vocational and educational guidance, over a period of five years, to the Veterans Administration Regional Office, Chicago, Illinois. All of the files were examined and those containing results of Wechsler-Bellevue testing were chosen for the study. Only verbal I.Q.'s and subtest scores (minus vocabulary) were used. Subtest scores used in the differential analysis were those of Information, Comprehension, Arithmetic and Similarities.

The subjects were divided into two major groups of one hundred Negroes and one hundred whites. The two major groups were further divided into educationally-retarded and educationally-normal groups of fifty each. Subjects who had not completed the equivalent of a grade school education (eight years of schooling) were placed in the educationally-retarded group. The other subjects made up the educationally-normal group of fifty Negroes and fifty whites. Subjects who had completed grade school or who had received, in addition, some high school training constituted this group.

This study employs the method of matched pairs. The white and Negro subjects were matched in terms of school grade completed, age, and Digit Span subtest score. The Digit Span subtest was used as a control variable because according to Wechsler (53, p. 83):

"As a test of general intelligence, it is among the poorest. Memory span, whether for digits forward or digits backward, generally correlates very poorly with all other tests of intelligence. ($r = .51$ with total minus the test). Rote memory contributes less to the individual's capacities than do other skills."

The findings of Davidson *et al.* (13), and Machover (39) support Wechsler's results. The following were observed rigorously:

1. All of the subjects were administered the Wechsler-Bellevue Scale by professional psychometrists with somewhat similar training and who had several years of experience in testing both white and Negro subjects. The testing rooms were designed for individual testing of a diagnostic nature.

2. The test results were checked for errors in scoring by the supervising psychologist (psychometrist).

3. Final grouping of the subjects into four sub-groups of fifty each came after checking of scores and the matching of pairs.

4. No effort was made to discriminate among subjects on the basis of any pathological condition or clinical syndrome. Subjects who were too sick for educational or vocational advisement and guidance were referred to the mental hygiene clinic or medical clinic in the regional office.

5. All subjects who had attained a grade level beyond the thirteenth year were excluded from the study.

Of the fifty members of each sample, the mean age of the Negro retarded group was 27.8 years, and of both the Negro and of the white normal groups was 23.8. The mean level of educational achievement was 6.9 grades for the retarded Negro group and 7.6 for the retarded white group. The mean level of educational achievement for the normal group was 10.8 for the Negroes and 10.9 for the whites.

The Verbal I.Q. and the mean weighted score of four of the verbal scale subtests (Information, Comprehension, Arithmetic, Similarities) were calculated for all four groups. The vocabulary subtest was excluded because it was found that in many instances it had not been administered. The Digit Span subtest was used as one of our control variables. The difference between Negro and white mean weighted subtest scores and intelligence quotients were tested by means of the t-test.

RESULTS

The following results were obtained:

1. Insofar as the mean verbal subtests weighted scores are concerned, the Negro groups, retarded and normal, show significantly lower scores on Information ($t = 3.82$ for the former and 3.25 for the latter) and arithmetic ($t = 3.09$ for the former and 2.46 for the latter) than the white groups. On the Similarities test the Negro retarded groups shows a significantly lower score ($t = 2.64$). There are no statistically significant differences between Negro and white retarded groups on the Comprehension subtest. The table also shows the coefficients of correlation for the subtest scores and I.Q.'s of the two groups. The only significant correlations are those of

r = .354 (Arithmetic or normal groups), r = .663 (I.Q.'s of retarded groups).

2. The mean verbal scale I.Q.'s of the Negro retarded and normal groups are significantly lower than those of white groups with whom they were matched (t = 4.11 for the former and 2.21 for the latter).

3. On the basis of the differences found, it is therefore concluded that: insofar as the mean verbal subtests weighted scores are concerned, the Negro retarded groups show significantly lower scores than the normal whites on Information (t = 6.00), Comprehension (t = 3.02), Arithmetic (t = 3.46) and Similarities (t = 3.99) students. The white retarded group does not show scores that are significantly lower than those of the Negro normal group on any of the four subjects.

4. The mean Verbal Scale I.Q.'s of the Negro retarded group is significantly lower than those of the normal white group (t = 5.19). The mean verbal I.Q.'s of the retarded white group is not significantly lower than those of the normal Negro group.

IMPLICATIONS

Before we can offer an adequate rationale to explain the significantly poorer showing of the Negro groups on the various subtests of the Wechsler Verbal Scale, we must examine two related problems: (1) The psychological functions involved in and purportedly measured by the Information, Arithmetic and Similarities subtests, and (2) the psychological make-up, largely culturally determined attitudes of the Negro toward tests.

According to Wechsler's examiners in the field during the standardization of his test (53, p. 80), the Information subtest, "Presupposes a normal or average opportunity to receive verbal information. It is a poor test for those deprived of such opportunity as well as for those who have a foreign language handicap." As for the Arithmetical reasoning test, Wechsler (53, p. 82) noted: "While the influence of education on the individual's ability to answer arithmetical problems lessens the value of the test as a measure of adult intelligence, the effect of the interrelation between the two factors is not entirely negative."

According to Wechsler the Similarities test contains a great amount of "g." These three tests, as reported by Wechsler, are among the best of his battery for they correlate highly with the total scale (Information .67, Arithmetic .63, and Similarities .73). Many of Wechsler's examiners reported that they were sometimes able to diagnose educational abilities on the basis of scores obtained on these three tests alone. They reported that the combined scores of Information and Arithmetic tests frequently furnished an accurate estimate of the subjects' scholastic achievement.

The fact that Negroes, as a group, are deprived of basic environmental opportunities raises some doubt as to their ability to make scores comparable to those of whites on tests that are educationally and culturally loaded, as for example, tests of Information and Arithmetic. Ordinarily, whites have an advanced start on Negroes in these two areas. Therefore, whatever potentiality is present, initially, the Negro is seldom able to catch up. This places the Negro group at a disadvantage when an attempt is made to predict his behavior in terms of his measured general intelligence.

It is well known that existing tests favor city children from middle-class homes even in the case of whites. This point has been well illustrated by Wellman (54, pp. 108–112). Lower-class children seem to be particularly handicapped on certain test items. If this is true of the white child, it has as much or more significance when it is applied to the Negro child because of the large number of lower-class Negroes. Let us take the item of speed for example. Lower-class people in general, and the Negro in particular, are not given to doing things in a hurry. Their tempo of life does not demand constant practice in performing swiftly. The fact that the speed of Negroes, for example, is slower than that of whites on timed tests, is probably due to the fact that Negroes, on a whole, in our society, have little incentive to do things rapidly. Perhaps, they do not possess what Davis (14, pp. 207–211) might call "the middle-class anxiety to get things done." The reason that Negroes do not exhibit much of this socialized and actually adaptive anxiety may be that the possibilities for achievement for Negroes in our society are distinctly limited to fewer economic and social opportunities. A realization of this factor may result in a lower level of aspiration in the Negro as compared to whites of equal age and education such as presented in our study. This in turn, may be reflected not only in the urban Negro's culture but also in his orientation toward tasks of any nature which he confronts. One possible explanation as advanced by Davidson et al. (13, p. 491) is that the more passive adjustment of the Negro to his social environment prevents him from concentrating actively on his problems. The lack of motivation depends on the particular cultural role that he is called upon to fulfill. This may, in addition, be a reflection of possible differences in standards of an academic nature required of Negro and white children in schools.

The difference in Verbal I.Q.'s of the Negro and white groups, like the difference in Information and Arithmetic, may be a reflection of educational and cultural opportunities. Wellman (54, pp. 108–112) says that in order to evaluate the influence of opportunities in general we should consider some outstanding findings, as reviewed briefly here.

(1) Foster children, if placed in early infancy in adoptive homes which generally are above average in socio-economic status and in other respects, are at least average or above average I.Q. when measured at the school ages. Usually their true parents are so characterized that it seems reasonably certain that the children would have tested considerably lower had they remained with their true parents. The foster homes represent better opportunities for them.

(2) There is some evidence that children whose mothers are feeble-minded decrease in I.Q. with age so long as they remain under the mother's care. One study made on this point showed that the younger children tested about as low as their mothers. This trend was checked, however, when the children were removed and placed under better circumstances. Gains were found at all ages.

(3) Negro children transferred from the South to the North have been found to be brighter than those of the same age who spent more time in the South. These findings illustrate three things important to our study: (a) The need for realizing that what a person has learned is a function of opportunity for learning as well as of capacity for learning; (b) that when educational opportunities are limited, the I.Q., along with other measures, is affected, and, (c) that there is hope for learning (and for change in I.Q.) among the less privileged groups in our society.

The results of this study indicate that factors of education and motivation should be taken into consideration when interpreting the performance of Negroes on the Wechsler Verbal Scale. This should be done with an awareness of the culturally restricted background from which the Negro has come, no matter how high his educational achievement. In a scatter analysis or other diagnostic procedures, Information and Arithmetic subtest (and Similarities with retarded groups) scores should be utilized with awareness of their possible altered significance for the Negro population.

SUMMARY AND CONCLUSION

The Verbal Scale of the Wechsler-Bellevue examination was given to two hundred Negro and white veterans of World War II, who reported to a large Veterans Administration Guidance Center for Vocational testing. These veterans were divided into two major groups of one hundred Negroes and one hundred whites. These major groups were further divided into an educationally normal group of white and Negroes, and an educationally retarded group of whites and Negroes. Each group was composed of fifty white or Negro subjects on the basis of educational attainment. Negro and white subjects were matched almost equally for age, education, and Digit Span subtest score. The variable factors not controlled in this study were the cultural and biological Standard errors of the differences between the means of educationally comparable Negro and white groups on four subtests and I.Q.'s of the Wechsler Verbal Scale were calculated and tested for the method of "t" for differences that were statistically significant.

The following conclusions may be drawn from the analysis of results.

1. Statistically, normal Negro and white veterans of approximately the same age and educational level show significant difference on the Information and Arithmetic subtests of the Wechsler-Bellevue Verbal Scale in favor of the whites. For educationally retarded Negroes, when compared with whites of the same age and education, there are differences on tests of Information, Arithmetic, and Similarities.

2. Negro and white veterans of approximately the same age and educational level, show a statistically significant difference in I.Q. on the Wechsler-Bellevue Verbal Scale.

3. The differences on the two subtests and I.Q.'s found in the present study favor the white groups, and it may be inferred that their superior cultural and educational opportunities contribute greatly to these differences.

4. A wider investigation using a similar experimental design with two groups of subjects similar in age, education and race, but different clinically or pathologically should aid in our acceptance or rejection of the need for a culture free test for subcultural groups such as Davis (14) and others advocate.

Bibliography

1. Alper, T. G., and Boring, E. G. "Intelligence Test of Northern and Southern White and Negro Recruits in 1918." *Journal of Abnormal Psychology*, 39: 471–457, 1944.

2. Anastasia, A., and Foley, J. P., Jr. *Differential Psychology*, New York: The Macmillan Co., 1949.

3. Buros, D. K. *The Third Mental Measurement Yearbook*, New Brunswick, N. J.: Rutgers Univ. Press, 1949.

4. Canady, H. G. The Problem of equating the Environment of Negro-White

Groups for Intelligence Testing in Comparative Studies. *Journal of Social Psychology,* 17: 3–5, 1943.

5. ————. The Methodology and Interpretation of Negro-White Mental Testing. *School and Society,* 55: 569–575, 1943.

6. Chearow, E. J., Wasika, P. M., and Remitz, A. H. A Psychometric Evaluation of Aged White Males. *Geriatrics,* 4: 169–177, 1949.

7. Clarke, D. P. Stanford-Binet Scale "L" Response Patterns in Matched Racial Groups. *Journal of Negro Education,* 10: 23–238, 1941.

8. Cotzin, M. and Gallagher, J. J. Validity of Short Forms of the Wechsler-Bellevue Scale for Mental Defectives. *Journal of Consulting Psychology,* 13: 357–365, 1949.

9. Cronbach, L. J. *Essentials of Psychological Testing.* New York: Harper and Brothers, 1949.

10. Cummings, S. B., Jr., Macphee, H. M., and Wright, H. F. A Rapid Method of Estimating the I.Q.'s of Subnormal White Adults. *Journal of Psychology,* 21: 81–89, 1946.

11. Cutts, R. A., and O'Kelley, M. T. "Effect of Hospitalization on the Wechsler-Bellevue Subtest Scores by Mental Defectives." *American Journal of Mental Deficiency,* 51: 391–393, 1947.

12. Cutts, R. A. and Sloan, W. "Test Patterns of Adjusted Defectives on the Wechsler-Bellevue Test." *Journal of Mental Deficiency,* 50: 98–101, 1945.

13. Davidson, K. S., Robert, G. G., McNeil, E. B., Segal, S. F., and Silverman, H. "A Preliminary Study of Negro and White Differences on Form I of the Wechsler-Bellevue Scale," *Journal of Consulting Psychology,* 14: 6, 489–492, 1950.

14. Davis, A. *Social Class Influences upon Learning.* Cambridge, Mass.: Harvard University Press, 1949.

15. Derner, G. F., Aborn, M., and Canter, A. H. "The Reliability of the Wechsler-Bellevue Subtests and Scales." *Journal of Consulting Psychology,* 14: 6, 489–492, 172–179, 1950.

16. Erickson, R. W. "On Special Training Unit Performance as an Index of Negro Ability." *Journal of Abnormal and Social Psychology,* 41: 481, 1946.

17. Estes, S. G. "Deviations of Wechsler-Bellevue Subtest Scores from Vocabulary Level in Superior Adults." *Journal of Abnormal and Social Psychology,* 41: 226–228, 1946.

18. Franklin, J. C. "Discriminative Value and Patterns of the Wechsler-Bellevue Scales in the Examination of Delinquent Negro Boys." *Educational and Psychological Measurement,* 5: 71–85, 1945.

19. Garret, H. E. "Negro-White Differences in Mental Ability in the United States." *Scientific Monthly,* N. G., 65: 329–333, 1947.

20. Gibby, R. G. "A Preliminary Survey of Certain Aspects of Form II of the Wechsler-Bellevue Scale as Compared to Form I." *Journal of Clinical Psychology,* 5: 165–169, 1949.

21. Glaser, N. M. "A Study of the Intelligence of Immigrants." *American Psychologist*, 4: 241, 1949. (Abstract).

22. Goldfarb, W. "Adolescent Performance in the Wechsler-Bellevue Intelligence Scales and the Revised Stanford d-Binet Examination, Form L." *Journal Educational Psychology*, 35: 503–507, 1944.

23. Gothberg, L. "A Comparative Study of the Stanford-Binet Old Form Test and Wechsler-Bellevue, Verbal Performance and Full Scale, as Shown in the Results of Unselected Employees." *American Journal of Mental Deficiency*, 5: 414–418, 1949.

24. Groves, M. H. "Some Relationship Between Certain Types of Mental Aberration and the Abilities Measured by the Wechsler-Bellevue Scale." Unpublished Ph.D. dissertation, The University of Chicago, 1950, chapter 5, 105–108.

25. Hamister, R. "The Test-Retest Reliability of the Wechsler-Bellevue Intelligence Test for a Neuropsychiatric Population." *Journal of Consulting Psychology*, 13: 39–43, 1949.

26. Guertin, W. R. "Mental Growth in Pseudo-Feeblemindedness." *Journal of Clinical Psychology*, 5: 414–418, 1949.

27. Hebb, D. D., and Morton, N. W. "Note on the Measurement of Adult Intelligence." *Journal of General Psychology*, 30: 217–223, 1944.

28. Hodgeon, G. "An Analysis of Subtests in the Wechsler-Bellevue Verbal Scale Administered to 139 Delinquent Mexican Boys." *American Psychologist*, 3: 343, 1948. (Abstract).

29. Jenkins, M. D. "A Socio-Psychological Study of Negro Children of Superior Intelligence." *Journal of Negro Education*, 5: 175–190, 1936.

30. Jennings, H. S., *et al. Scientific Aspects of the Race Problem.* The Catholic University of America Press, Washington, D. C.: Longmans, Green & Co., 1941.

31. *Journal of Negro Education*: Yearbook Number III. "The Physical and Mental Abilities of the American Negro." Washington, D. C. Department of Education, Howard University, July, 1934.

32. Klineberg, O. (ed.) *Characteristics of the American Negro*, New York: Harper, 1944.

33. Klineberg, O. *Race Differences*, New York: Harper, 1935.

34. Kutash, S. B. "A Comparison of the Wechsler-Bellevue and Revised Stanford-Binet Scale for Adult Defective Delinquents." *Psychiatric Quarterly*, 19: 677–685, 1945.

35. Levine, J., and Blackburn, A. B. "Intelligence Test Scores of Newly Blinded Soldiers." *Journal of Consulting Psychology*, 14: 311–315, 1950.

36. Lewinski, R. J. "Discriminative Value of the Subtests of the Bellevue Verbal Scale in the Examination of Naval Recruits." *Journal of General Psychology*, 1944.

37. Lewinski, R. J. "Illiteracy." Nov. Med. Bull., Washington, D. C., 42, 150–154.

38. Lorge, I. "Schooling Makes a Difference." Teachers College Record, 46: 483–492, 1945.

39. Machover, S. "Cultural and Racial Variations in Patterns of Intellect: Performance of Negro and White Criminals on Bellevue Adult Intelligence Scale." Teachers College Contributions to Education, 1943, No. 875, 5, 80–91.

40. Madonick, M. J., and Solomon, M. "The Wechsler-Bellevue Scale in Individuals Past Sixty." Geriatrics, 2: 3440, 1947.

41. MacPhee, H. M., Wright, H. F., Cummings, S. B., Jr. The Performance of Mentally Subnormal Rural Southern Negroes on the Verbal Scale of the Bellevue Intelligence Examination. Journal of Social Psychology, 25: 217–229, 1947.

42. Marlow, A. H. "What Intelligence Tests Mean." Journal of General Psychology, 31: 85–93, 1944.

43. McGraw, M. B. "A Comparative Study of a Group of Southern White and Negro Infants." Genetic Psychology Monography, 10: 1–105, 1931.

44. Pastore, N. "A Comment on Psychological Differences Among Races." School and Society, 63: 1626, 1946.

45. Porteus, S. D. "Racial Groups Differences in Mentality." Tabul. Biol., Hagg, 18: 6615, 1939.

46. Price, J. St. Clair. "Negro-White Differences in General Intelligence." Journal of Negro Education, 3: 424–452, 1934.

47. Rabin, A. J. "The Use of the Wechsler-Bellevue Scale with Normal and Abnormal Persons." Psychological Bulletin, 42: 410–422, 1945.

48. Rabin, A. J., and Guertin, W. H. "Research with the Wechsler-Bellevue Test: 1945–50." Psychological Bulletin, 48: 211–248, 1951.

49. Rapport, D. "Detecting the Feebleminded Registrant," Bulletin of the Menninger Clinic, 5: 146–149, 1941.

50. Ruch, F. L. Psychology and Life. Chicago: Scott, Foresman & Co. 3rd Ed., 1949.

51. Sartain, A. O. "A Comparison of the New Revised Stanford-Binet, The Bellevue Scale, and Certain Group Tests of Intelligence." Journal of Social Psychology, 23: 237–239, 1946.

52. Watson, R. T. "The Use of the Wechsler Scales": A Supplement. Psychological Bulletin, 43: 61–68, 1946.

53. Wechsler, D. The Measurement of Adult Intelligence. Baltimore: The Williams and Wilkins Co., 1944.

54. Wellman, B. L. "Some Misconceptions About Intelligence." Children's Education, 21: 108–112, 1944.

55. Witty, P. "Reply to Mr. Erickson," Journal of Abnormal Social Psychology, 41: 482–485, 1946.

14 Growth and Development XI: Descriptive Analysis of the Backgrounds of 76 Negro Children Whose Scores Are Above or Below Average on the Merrill-Palmer Scale of Mental Tests at Three Years of Age[1][2]

CARRELL P. HORTON & E. PERRY CRUMP
Department of Pediatrics, Meharry Medical College

This paper examines possible relationships between family background factors and Negro children's performance on an intelligence test much in the tradition of Canady (1937, this volume) and Jenkins (1948, this volume), since the authors are concerned with intraracial factors and ignore interracial comparisons. Their study suggests that the performance of 3-year-old Negro children on the Merrill-Palmer Test is related to the same type of factors as with white children: socioeconomic status, education of parents, parents' marital status, and number of siblings. Another significant aspect of this study is the comparison of above- and below-average children in order to see if they exhibit differing characteristics, a comparable approach to that ultilized by Jenkins and Randall (1948, this volume) in their study of Negro college students.

A. THE PROBLEM

The psychological development of infants and young children, as measured by test performance, has been scientifically explored from almost every conceivable viewpoint. Investigators have studied the reliability and validity of specific tests, and of juvenile testing in general; factors associated with test performance have been evaluated; and age-level norms have been established. Escalona and Rapaport (5) state that, ". . . psychological testing of children meets a variety of needs arising in medical,

SOURCE. Reprinted from the *Journal of Genetic Psychology*, 1962, **100**, 255–265, with permission of the senior author and The Journal Press.

[1] Received in the Editorial Office on April 25, 1960.

[2] This investigation was supported by a research grant [No. RG-3761 (CE)] from the National Institutes of Health, Public Health Services.

psychiatric or educational practice. By means of an analysis of the different degrees of retardation and acceleration of development, and of the specific nature of atypical forms of mental functioning, testing may help to differentiate between the manifestations of congenital mental deficiency, of specific disabilities, and of various types of maladjustment." Test results are used currently in a variety of situations to make far-reaching decisions about a child's capacities and adjustment.

Racial background is one of the factors which is almost uniformly considered to be related to test performance. Bakwin *et al.* (2) state that, "On practically all tests Negroes are inferior to white children as a whole." Yet the tests by which Negro children are evaluated are standardized, almost without exception, on white children; and it has been pointed out that in order for test results to be reliable and valid, the subject ". . . must be representative of the populations used originally in standardizing the test in regard to age, sex, educational level, and cultural background" (2).

This investigation was undertaken to analyze descriptively some of the background characteristics of a group of three-year-old Negro children whose scores on the Merrill-Palmer Scale of Mental Tests indicate above or below average performance. Another report will discuss intra-test performance among the same group.

Age three was chosen for two major reasons:

1. There is general agreement among persons in the field of infant testing (see, for example, Layman (7) and Baer (1)) that developmental status during the early part of life is not very highly associated with measurable intelligence in later years. Further, Baer (1) states that, "After the age of three years, mental growth becomes relatively stable so that it is possible to predict a child's capacities for the school years."

2. The third birthday marked the first exposure of the children studied to the Merrill-Palmer test, which eliminated any possibility of practice effects, although the Gesell Developmental Schedules had previously been administered to all of the subjects.

Factors chosen for consideration include those attributes in family and home background which might be expected to bear some relation to developmental progress, for which data are available, and are as follows:

Characteristics of the Child	*Family Characteristics*
Sex	Socio-Economic Status
Birth Weight	Education of Parents
Height and Weight at 36 months	Employment Status of Mother
	Number of Siblings
	Marital Status of Parents
	Occupation of Father

B. METHODS AND MATERIALS

Data for this study are drawn from a larger longitudinal study of factors influencing the growth and development of Negro infants and children from birth through five years of age (4). As part of the major study, the participating children are given developmental tests at 6-month intervals, after 24 months of age. The children included in this report represent that portion of the total group who: (a) reported for a 36-months evaluation between December, 1956, and September, 1959; and (b) whose corresponding scores on the Merrill-Palmer Scale of Mental Tests are considered superior or inferior according to test norms. All children were in good physical condition at the time of the test.

Measurement and/or evaluation of the majority of the background characteristics being considered has already been explained in previous publications in this series. It was, however, necessary to obtain an up-to-date count of the number of children in the family. This was obtained by asking the parent when the child was brought in for the 36-months evaluation.

1. Test Administration

All tests were administered in one of the psychological testing rooms of the Department of Pediatrics of Hubbard Hospital, by one of two persons professionally trained in the administration of psychological tests. In most instances, only the examiner and the child were present in the testing room. On rare occasions the presence of the person who accompanied the child was permitted, when necessary to obtain cooperation. No coaching was allowed. All tests were given within one month of the third birthday, with the scoring adjusted to the exact chronological age.

2. Test Evaluation

Standards for delineating children whose performances are considered superior or inferior are based on the percentile classifications used by Stutsman (8). Accordingly, the following divisions were used:

Percentile rank	Classification
1–4	Very inferior
5–19	Inferior
20–79	Average
80–94	Superior
95–99	Very superior

These percentile classifications are derived from score values resulting from the test, and are used for evaluating performance on the Merrill-Palmer as Intelligence Quotients are used for other tests.

C. RESULTS

There were 209 Merrill-Palmer tests administered and scored at the three-year level between December, 1956, and September, 1959. Of this total, 76 (36.4 per cent) received percentile scores of 1–19 or 80–99. The specific breakdown for each of the four classifications with which we are concerned, is shown in Table 1.

TABLE 1

Percentile Distribution of 209 Negro Children on the Merrill-Palmer Scale of Mental Tests at Age Three

Percentile	Total Cases		Extreme Groups	
	Number	Per Cent	Number	Per Cent
95–99	5	2.4	5	6.6
80–94	5	2.4	5	6.6
20–79	133	63.6	—	—
5–19	58	27.8	58	76.3
1–4	8	3.8	8	10.5
Total	209	100.0	76	100.0

There is an overwhelming preponderance of children in the "Inferior" category (76.3 per cent). Thus this group represents more than ¾ of those with superior and inferior scores, and equals 27.8 per cent of the total sample. Conversely, there are far fewer children in the superior range than would normally be expected.

D. CHARACTERISTICS OF THE CHILD

1. Sex

Beth Wellman (9), in a study of the intelligence of preschool children as measured by the Merrill-Palmer test, found that girls tended to receive higher scores than boys. No such clarity of results is apparent here. Table 2 presents the numerical distribution of the extreme groups by sex.

TABLE 2

Distribution of 76 Negro Children Whose Performance Was Above or Below
Average on the Merrill-Palmer Scale of Mental Tests at 36 Months, by Sex

| | Sex of Child | | |
Test Group	Male	Female	Total
Very superior	1	4	5
Superior	3	2	5
Inferior	34	24	58
Very inferior	4	4	8
Total	42	34	76

When the groups are combined into "Superior" and "Inferior," there are
proportionately more girls in the superior range and more boys in the inferior range, but the differences are slight.

2. *Birth Weight*

It has long been recognized that the development of premature infants
is slower than that of full-term infants, but the difference in developmental
rates is not generally expected to persist after the first year of life (2). In
the present study, children who were premature at birth were found in
all categories, except the "Superior" group. The only boy in the "Very
Superior" group was premature at birth. Among the "Inferior" and the
"Very Inferior," there were, respectively, 10 and two children who were
born prematurely.

3. *Physical Measurements at 36 Months*

There was very little difference in the mean height and weight of the
76 children being studied, at 36 months, according to Merrill-Palmer test
group. (See Table 3.)

Katz (6) found relationships between I.Q. and height and weight for
girls during the period from three to five years, but not for boys. He stated
that this variation in results could not be accounted for ". . . on the basis
of differential selection of the sex groups, greater variability of the girls, or
differences in the relative maturity of the two sexes." In the present study,
differences in mean height and weight among the four groups are very
slight, although there was a progressive increase in average height and
weight among the boys from "Very Inferior" to "Superior"; and it has already been pointed out that the only boy in the "Very Superior" group
was premature at birth, which may explain his smaller weight and stature.

TABLE 3
Comparative Statistics on Height and Weight at 36 Months, by Merrill-Palmer Test Group and Sex of Child

Height and Weight at 36 Months	Merrill-Palmer Test Group							
	Male Children				Female Children			
	Very Inferior	Inferior	Superior	Very Superior	Very Inferior	Inferior	Superior	Very Superior
Height								
(No.) (Cm.)	4	34	3	1	4	23	2	3
Mean	92.6	94.8	96.4	93.0	93.4	94.1	93.5	97.9
SD	2.6	3.6	0.9	—	4.0	3.7	0.5	2.1
Weight								
(No.) (Lbs.)	4	34	3	1	4	24	2	4
Mean	30.0	31.1	32.9	30.3	31.9	30.0	31.9	32.0
SD	1.6	3.4	1.4	—	2.7	2.9	1.9	2.9

E. FAMILY CHARACTERISTICS

1. *Socio-Economic Status*

The Socio-Economic Index used here divides study families into four broad groups from I (Low) to IV (High). Only the 58 children whose scores are rated "Inferior" cover the entire range. For both the "Superior" and "Very Superior" children, the socio-economic backgrounds ranged only from Groups II to IV, and for those children rated "Very Inferior," the highest socio-economic score fell into Group III. The small number of cases does not lend itself to statistical analysis, so that this report cannot be considered conclusive. It does, however, suggest that socio-economic differences *within* the Negro group may have some relation to test performance. Table 4 presents the composition of the four test groups by socio-economic group.

TABLE 4

Numerical Distribution of Socio-economic Status of Children Whose Performances Were Above or Below Average on the Merrill-Palmer Scale of Mental Tests at Age Three

Socio-economic Group	Merrill-Palmer Test Group			
	Very Inferior	Inferior	Superior	Very Superior
IV (High)	—	2	1	2
III	3	17	2	1
II	4	29	2	2
I (Low)	1	10	—	—
Total	8	58	5	5

2. *Education of Parents*

Among the children whose performance was rated "Very Inferior," no parent had completed college, and half of them had not completed eighth grade. Figures summarizing education of the parents are shown in Table 5.

A clear division exists between average education of parents whose children are in the below average range and those whose children are rated above average. Median education for fathers of the "Very Superior" children was 16 years (college graduate).

Variance analysis (using a 20 per cent sample of the "Inferior" group) indicates that there is some association between: (a) education of the mother and test performance of the child at 36 months; and (b) combined

TABLE 5

Comparative Statistics on Education of Parents, by Merrill-Palmer Test Group of Children at Age Three

Education of Parent (Highest Grade Completed)	Merrill-Palmer Test Group							
	Very Inferior		Inferior		Superior		Very Superior	
	Mother	Father	Mother	Father	Mother	Father	Mother	Father
Range	6–12	5–14	0–16	5–16	10–16	8–16	8–16	8–16
Mean	9.1	8.2	9.4	9.7	12.0	12.0	12.0	10.0
SD	2.4	3.2	2.9	2.9	3.1	3.6	5.6	7.4
Median	9.0	7.5	10.1	10.3	13.0	13.0	14.0	16.0
Number	8	6	58	45	5	5	5	5

education of parents and child's performance; but father's education alone had no significant relation to the factor being considered.

3. *Employment Status of Mother*

Theoretically, the presence or absence of the mother in the home might be expected to have some influence on the development of the preschool child. The direction and nature of the influence would, however, vary depending on the type of arrangements made for the child's care. This information was not available for the present study, so that in the case of mothers who work, it is not known whether or not their children received nursery care or remained in the home. In any event, it was found that proportionately fewer of the mothers of the "Very Inferior" children were habitually employed (three out of eight), while proportionately more of the mothers of "Inferior" children (58.6 per cent) held jobs. For mothers of children in each above average group, two out of five had full-time jobs. Thus no clear relation is seen between mother's employment status and development of the child at age three.

4. *Number of Siblings*

Table 6 presents comparative figures on the number of siblings in the families of the children in the four test groups.[3]

TABLE 6

Comparative Statistics on Number of Siblings, by Merrill-Palmer Test Group

Number of Siblings	Merrill-Palmer Test Group			
	Very Inferior	Inferior	Superior	Very Superior
Range	0–5	0–6	1–3	1–7
Mean	2.3	2.5	1.6	2.6
SD	1.4	2.2	0.8	2.3
Median	1.0	2.8	1.0	1.0
Number	6	39	5	5

Sibling influence on development could conceivably be exerted in either direction. It might be constructed to mean that a child would perhaps develop faster in the presence of older siblings, or might, on the other hand, retrogress in the presence of younger siblings. It would also be expected that the larger the number of siblings, the less time there would be to devote to each child, thereby either promoting independent development or

---

[3] This information was not available for all of the children.

retarding development as sponsored by parents. In this study, none of the children in the above average groups were "only" children, although there were relatively minor differences in the average number of siblings among the four groups. Detailed examination suggests, however, that there is a distinct trend for the number of siblings to be less among the above average children. Figures presented in Table 6 are skewed considerably for the "Very Superior" children by the presence of one child with seven siblings, while one had three siblings, and the remaining three each had only one sister or brother.

5. *Marital Status of Parents*

The parents of all children in the superior range were legally married, while one parent of a "Very Inferior" child was unmarried. Seventy-nine and three-tenths per cent of the parents of children rated "Inferior" were married. In all cases where parents were unmarried, the children had been born out of wedlock, as opposed to marriages disrupted by divorce, death or separation.

6. *Occupation of Father*

The range of father's occupations among the study group was fairly wide, with one exception. Using an adaptation of the occupational classification developed by the Bureau of the Census,[4] no father of a child who was rated "Very Inferior" (where this information was available) was employed above the "Semi-skilled" capacity. Among the fathers of the "Very Superior" children, in contrast, two fathers were members of professions, while two were unskilled workers, and the remaining one was a student in a professional school. Variance analysis failed to reveal any significant association between occupation of the father and development of the child.

F. SUMMARY AND CONCLUSIONS

This study was proposed to analyze descriptively some of the background characteristics of 76 Negro children who exhibited above or below average performance on the Merrill-Palmer Scale of Mental Tests at 36 months of age. The small number of cases precludes the possibility of drawing concrete conclusions, but several trends were apparent.

There was little indication that physical characteristics of the child were related to this development at age three. On the other hand, certain family characteristics which were studied did suggest some association with test performance, notably socio-economic status, education of parents, parents'

[4] See Appendix.

marital status, and number of siblings. For the most part, these factors have long been recognized as affecting test performance of white children (3); but when speaking of the performance of Negro children, there has been a tendency to speak in terms of the group as a whole, disregarding the possibility of intra-group variations similar to those which exist among white children. Results of this study would suggest that the performance of Negro children at age three is subject to the same environmental factors which affect the performance of white children. There is, of course, no contention that environmental background alone can determine any child's development, as is evident by the heterogeneity in the backgrounds of children whose performances were in the superior range. Much of the impetus for development undoubtedly comes from factors which cannot be quantified, in addition to native endowment.

Several factors which may be strongly related to test performance were not considered here because of the unavailability of data. The extent of nursery school attendance, in particular, would have been valuable. Nevertheless, the differences which were apparent in the backgrounds of the four groups of children lend credence to the postulation that racial origin alone is not enough to allow valid generalizations about children's test performances. Since such performances cover a wide range of intra-group variability and are accompanied by more or less corresponding variations in background, any reference to differences based exclusively upon race probably should not receive more than minimum consideration.

APPENDIX

Classification Used in Rating Parents' Occupations

Classification Number*	Classification
0	Unskilled workers (except farm)
1	Farm laborer or farm foreman
2	Domestic service workers
3	Other service workers
4	Protective service workers
5	Semi-skilled workers
6	Skilled workers
7	Clerical workers
8	Proprietary (officials and managers, excluding farm)
9	Professionals and semi-professionals

* This number was used in socio-economic scoring.

References

1. Baer, P. E. Evaluation of intelligence in children. *Postgrad. Med.*, 1958, **23**, 285–291.
2. Bakwin, R. M., Weider, A., and Bakwin, H. Mental testing in children. *J. Pediat.*, 1948, **33**, 384–394.
3. Bayley, N., and Jones, H. E. Environmental correlates of mental and motor development: a cumulative study from infancy to six years. *Child Devel.*, 1937, **8**, 329–341.
4. Crump, E. P., Horton, C., Masuoka, J., and Ryan, D. Growth and development I. Relation of birth weight in Negro infants to sex, maternal age, parity, prenatal care, and socioeconomic status. *J. Pediat.*, 1957, **51**, 678–697.
5. Escalona, S. K., and Rapaport, D. Testing of children: intelligence and emotional adjustment. *Bull. Menninger Clin.*, 1944, **8**, 205–210.
6. Katz, E. Relationship of IQ to height and weight from three to five years. *J. Genet. Psychol.*, 1940, **57**, 65–82.
7. Layman, E. M. Psychological testing of infants and preschool children. *Clin. Proc. Child. Hosp.*, Washington, 1955, **11**, 126–136.
8. Stutsman, R. Mental Measurement of Preschool Children. Yonkers-on-Hudson, New York: World Book, 1948.
9. Wellman, B. L. The intelligence of preschool children as measured by the Merrill-Palmer Scale of Performance Tests. *Univ. Iowa Studies, Studies in Child Welfare*, 1938, XV, 1–150.

15 Longitudinal Performance of Negro American Children at Five and Ten Years on the Stanford-Binet[1]

S. O. ROBERTS[2]
Fisk University

E. P. CRUMPS,[3] ANN E. DICKERSON,[3] & CARRELL P. HORTON[3]
Meharry Medical College

The significance of this paper lies in the fact that it is a *longitudinal study,* in which the same persons are observed and evaluated over a period of years. This is an important research technique and, although an expensive and large-scale undertaking, results in significant information regarding the development of physical, psychological, and social processes. Perhaps the most widely known longitudinal study is that of the Fels Institute in Yellow Springs, Ohio. Most striking of the findings regarding these Black youngsters is that between the ages of 5 and 10 they have (1) declined about an overall year in mental age, (2) declined in average IQ from 98 for boys and 99 for girls to 88 and 84 respectively, and (3) when from broken homes the observed declines have been even more pronounced.

Many descriptive studies have been done such as those reported by Shuey (1958) that show that *the performance* of Negro American samples

SOURCE. Unpublished manuscript, 1965, reprinted with the permission of the senior author.

[1] This study is part of a longitudinal investigation, which was supported in part from a research grant, R-126(R), from the Children's Bureau Welfare Administration, Department of Health, Education, and Welfare to Fisk University; and from RG3761(CE) and several others, National Institutes of Health, U.S. Public Health Service to Meharry Medical College.

[2] S. O. Roberts, Professor and Chairman Department of Psychology, Fisk.

[3] E. P. Crump, Professor and Chairman Department of Pediatrics, Meharry.

[3] A. E. Dickerson, Psychologist, Department of Pediatrics, Meharry.

[3] C. P. Horton, Statistical Analyst, Department of Pediatrics, Meharry.

138

is typically lower than that observed in white samples. While probably not expressing the full extent of their interest, Kennedy and his associates (1963) have gone so far as to set forth elaborate *separate norms* based upon the administration of the Stanford-Binet to 1800 Negro American elementary school children in five (5) southeastern states. However, Anastasi (1958) has pointed out the need for studies that go beyond description into the causes or associated factors of the observed differences. It would appear, in the face of rapid social and educational changes, that this more difficult path is the one that is more likely to be productive of constructive courses of interpretation and effective action. One such avenue is through the careful observation of a sample over extended periods of time with careful documentation of those factors considered most likely to be relevant to the physical and psychological development of the members of that group.

While several such studies are now current (as for example, Deutsch and Brown, 1964), to the authors' knowledge the oldest and most comprehensive investigation of this kind for a group of Negro American infants and children is that described by Crump and Horton (1961). This study was begun in December 1953 with mothers, obtained through the Hubbard Hospital maternity clinic and through private referral, until over 800 subjects were included (by December, 1958) in this early phase. The overall concern was with the physical and psychological development of their children from before birth until 5 years of age. Among the many kinds of measurements taken, were the administrations of the abbreviated Stanford-Binet Intelligence Scale at four (4) years and at five (5) years.

STATEMENT OF THE PROBLEM

During 1963–1964, with the assistance of a Children's Bureau grant, the senior author and the Meharry investigators began the extension of the study of these children beyond their fifth birthday. A total of over 300 children were considered to be available from the earlier phase and the present report concerns primarily the comparison of the results of the administration of the Stanford-Binet (Form L-M) to the oldest group (which averaged 10 years of age at the time of testing) with their previous results at age 5. The major aim was to examine these results in relation to factors presumed to affect their outcome. (See Roberts, 1950; Roberts and Balloch, 1952a; Roberts and Robinson, 1952b.)

METHOD

Subjects

Out of the larger group referred to above, 72 children had Stanford-Binet at 4 and/or 5 and at 10 years. Sixty-nine (69) had results at both 5 and 10 years and it is with these that the present report will mainly concern itself. There were 37 males and 32 females.

Data and Procedure

The subjects ere given the Stanford-Binet (Form L, abbreviated scale) within 30 days of their fifth (5th) birthday and the Stanford-Binet (Form L-M, abbreviated scale) within 6 months of their tenth (10th) birthday. The examiners at 10 had no knowledge of the earlier results. Uniformity was provided in that the same person was responsible for the overall testing at each age.

Data were also available or obtained regarding family pattern, socioeconomic background, etc. at each age. The test data were analyzed, by sex, according to standard procedures and they were also viewed in relation to selected background material. Other circumstances, that were considered pertinent to test performance, were examined qualitatively.

RESULTS

Both quantitative and qualitative results are summarized below.

A.   *Quantitative.* The major quantitative ones are presented in Table 1. The statistics at 4 years are included for their interest and for such contribution as they may make to the principal findings. From these results, the following statements may be drawn:

TABLE 1

Summary of Principal Statistical Results

A. Means and Standard Deviations of IQ Scores at 4, 5, and 10 Years, by Sex

Sex	Males			Females			
Age	4	5	10	4	5	10	10*
N	30	37	37	27	32	32	35*
M	98.2	95.6	88.4	98.8	94.3	84.5	83.8
SD	17.7	17.5	21.4	15.6	13.2	15.4	14.6

* At age 10, three girls had earlier IQ's at 4 years, but not at 5 years.

B. Correlations Between IQ Scores at 4, 5, and 10, by Sex

	Males	N	r's	Females	N	r's
(1)	4 vs 5	30	.821		24	.680
(2)	4 vs 10	30	.718		27	.536
(3)	5 vs 10	37	.660		32	.618

C. Mean IQ Scores by Head of "Household" Occupational Group at 5 and 10 Years, by Sex

Males	Unskilled and Unemployed		Service		Semi-skilled and Above	
	5 Years	10 Years	5 Years	10 Years	5 Years	10 Years
N	12		12		10	
M	100.3	85.3	90.7	87.2	96.9	94.6
SD	12.3	11.9	15.7	20.8	23.0	29.7
Females						
N	10		10		12	
M	93.4	85.4	89.0	80.3	99.5	87.2
SD	10.3	14.4	15.0	11.8	11.8	15.6

D. 1 Mean IQ Scores at 5 Years, by Known Marital Status of the Family at 5 Years, by Sex

	Males*			Females		
	Broken	Step-parent	Intact	Broken	Step-parent	Intact
N	5	—	29	9	—	23
M	94.2	—	96.2	82.6	—	98.9
SD	13.2	—	18.0	12.8	—	10.1

* Family status lacking for 3 boys at 5 years, hence not included at 10 years.

D. 2 Mean IQ Scores at 10 Years, by Present Marital Status of the Family, by Sex

	Males			Females		
	Broken	Step-parent	Intact	Broken	Step-parent	Intact
N	8	3	23	12	3	17
M	81.4	87.0	92.4	80.8	82.7	87.4
SD	8.6	21.6	24.8	14.0	13.7	14.3

E. Mean IQ Scores by "Intact" or "Broken" Family Pattern at *Both* 5 and 10 Years, by Sex

		Intact		Broken	
		M	F	M	F
Five years	N	23	16	3	7
	M	96.3	98.4	99.7	85.1
	SD	19.7	9.5	6.3	13.2
Ten years	N	23	16	3	7
	M	92.4	88.3	75.0	76.4
	SD	24.8	14.2	8.5	12.0

1. *Changes between 5 and 10 years.* Mean IQ scores were in the general range summarized by Kennedy and others (1963). However, over the five (5) years, males changed from 96 to 88, while females changed from 94 to 84. In both instances the decreases were found to be statistically significant. However, there should be borne in mind that the tests are somewhat different despite the strong case Terman and Merrill (1960) make for the comparability of the 1937 and 1960 versions of the Stanford-Binet.

2. *Correlations between 5 and 10 years.* While the correlations over the five (5) years were higher for the males than for the females, they are generally comparable to those reported by Bloom (1964) for roughly similar periods.

3. *Relation of socio-economic status.* From Table 1-C it may be observed that there were 66 subjects for whom a socio-economic designation was possible. Using three (3) broad groupings it was found that boys from the "unskilled and unemployed" group changed most—15 points. Girls changed by 8, 9, and 12 points going from "unskilled" to "service" to "semi-skilled and above" groups, respectively. Thus, all socio-economic groups were found to be subject to a decreasing change, with boys from the "service" and "semi-skilled" groups being least affected (2–3 IQ points).

4. *Relation of "family pattern."* From Table 1-D.1 and -D.2 it may be seen that children in "intact" families (parents married and together) have an advantage over those in "broken" homes (conditions other than married) or those with a step-parent and this is true both at 5 and 10 years. However, the difference was statistically significant, only at 5 years and for girls.

5. *Effect of a continued family pattern.* Table 1-E reveals that a continued family pattern of "broken-ness" had not only an immediate but possibly a serious cumulating effect. However, since the cases are few in the instance of the "broken" group, these results are only tentative. (See Deutsch and Brown, 1964.)

B. *Qualitative Observations.* In order to provide a broader perspective for the preceding results, a detailed examination was made of selected cases.

1. *Extreme Changes.* Extreme changes of more than one and one-half standard deviations were found for ten children. Only two of these extreme changes (both boys) were increases in IQ scores between the ages of five and ten (one subject changed from "above average" to "very superior" in classification while the other moved from the lower end of the average distribution to its upper range). Individual performances of the subjects at both age levels were

analyzed to determine, if possible, if a certain pattern of response was responsible for failure.

Examination of the results at age ten, of those whose scores declined the most, revealed that their basal levels were almost evenly distributed at years VI, VII, and VIII. Little difference in the difficulty of the items at year VII was observed; however, they seemed to have slightly less difficulty with "repeating digits." Two of the four girls failed to "copy a diamond" successfully. "Similarities" and "comprehension" appeared to present more difficult at year VII than similar tasks at year VIII. At the latter level the "verbal absurdities" task was an outstanding failure. The easiest task for the group, who reached the nine-year-old tasks, appeared to be "making change," the others seemed to be of comparable difficulty. A majority of the subjects had attained their ceiling at the year X level. However, all of those who had some success at that level failed the "vocabulary" task.

Response of these subjects to the California Test of Personality indicated some divergence in their adjustment. The subjects had a median percentile rank of 39 in the area of Personal Adjustment while their Social Adjustment was at a median percentile rank of 54. Their Total Adjustment was within the average range, median percentile rank of 45.

2. *Relationship to changes in family patterns.* In an earlier section reference was made to the general relation of family pattern at 5 and 10 years and the effect of a continued family pattern for the five year period. However, there were two other types.

   (a) *From "intact" to "broken."* In thisc case, five (5) boys, whose homes were "intact" at five years were living in "broken" homes at 10 years. These boys suffered a loss of 9 points in IQ, while five (5) girls, in similar circumstances, lost 14 points.

   (b) *From "broken" to "intact."* Two (2) boys in this category lost 14 points, while (2) girls gained 4 points.

These results for changes in family pattern support, in general, the previous findings. However, in this instance, the small numbers of cases can only be suggestive of the effects of these changes in family patterns.

DISCUSSION

A basic question concerns the representativeness of the group studied. Examination of other sources suggests that the children are slightly above the general Negro American community in socio-economic status (which is partly due more to improvement over the years than to selection alone). In terms of overall ability, grade placement, and marital status of the mother, they are about the same as the general community. (See Ryan et al. 1960.)

Despite different tests, examiners, etc. it appears that these children have suffered some loss—*about an overall year of mental age.* This fact is in keeping with cross-sectional studies of the same phenomena, but an effort is made and will be continued to give a more inclusive picture of the factors that are considered to be associated with the deficit.

While no thesis is advanced that all differences in performance of this ethnic minority can be traced to observable environmental or experiential factors yet, insofar as such factors are relevant, the aim is to explore them fully for such increased understanding as they may provide. (See Pettigrew, 1964.)

CONCLUSIONS

The following summary statements and conclusions may be made concerning all of the foregoing:

1. Results of tests administered to 72 Negro American children in a cooperative Fisk-Meharry longitudinal study at the ages of four, five, and ten show a consistent decline from mean IQ's of 98 and 99 for boys and girls, respectively, at four years to 88 and 84, at ten years. The decline between 5 and 10 years for both males and females was statistically significant. Almost one-third of the subjects had decreases in their IQ scores greater than would be expected on the basis of chance deviation.

   a. Examination of the results of the subjects who exhibited the greatest decline in scores revealed that they had more difficulty with those tasks involving verbal skills. The mean score of these children on the California Test of Personality also indicated some difficulty in the area of Personal Adjustment.

2. Boys in the "lowest" economic group declined most in their mean IQ over the five-year period. Girls in the "highest" economic group showed a greater decline than girls in the other groups.

3. Analysis of the data in relation to the subjects' family patterns revealed that those boys and girls in "broken" homes at age ten had definitely lower mean IQ's than the other children. The results also suggest that change from "intact" to "broken" homes is associated with the overall decline in IQ, but there is little evidence that change of a reverse nature in the family pattern can counteract this trend.

4. Thus, the data would seem to indicate that decline in IQ score with

increasing age may be related to low socio-economic status including unstable and unfavorable family patterns.

5. Further investigation will be made to determine other environmental or experiential factors that may be related to these longitudinal differences in intelligence test performance.

References

Anastasi, Anne. *Differential psychology.* (3rd ed.) New York: Macmillan, 1958.

Anastasi, Anne. *Psychological testing.* (2nd ed.) New York: Macmillan, 1961.

Bloom, B. S. *Stability and change in human characteristics.* New York: John Wiley, 1964.

Crump, E. P., and Horton, Carrell P. Growth and development in Negro infants and children. *The Journal-Lancet,* 1961, **81**, 507–517. (Summary of some 11 of their studies.)

Deutsch, M., and Brown, B. Social influences in Negro-white intelligence differences. *J. soc. Issues,* 1964, **20**, 24–35.

Grossack, M. M. (Ed.) *Mental health and segregation.* New York: Springer, 1963.

Kagan, J. American longitudinal research on psychological development. *Child Developm.* 1964, **35**, 1–32. (Summary of 10 different studies.)

Kennedy, W. A., Van DeRiet, V., and White, J. C., Jr. A normative sample of intelligence and achievement of Negro elementary school children in the southeastern United States. *Monogr. Soc. Res. Child. Developm.,* 1963, **28**, No. 6 (Ser No. 90).

Pettigrew, T. F. *A profile of the Negro American.* Princeton, N. J.: D. Van Nostrand, 1964.

Roberts, S. O. Socio-economic status and performance over a four-year period on the ACE of Negro college women from the "North" and "South." *Amer. Psychologist,* 1950, **5**, 295 (abstract).

Roberts, S. O., and Balloch, J. C. Socio-economic status, sex, and race differences in performance of ten-year-olds on the SRA Primary Mental Abilities. Paper read at Midwest, Psychol. Assoc., Cleveland, Ohio, April, 1952 (a).

Roberts, S. O., and Robinson, J. M., Jr. Inter-correlations of the Primary Mental Abilities Tests for ten-year-olds by socio-economic status, sex, and race. *Amer. Psychologist,* 1952, **7**, 304 (abstract). (b)

Ryan, Donnalda K., Horton, Carrell P., and Crump, E. P. Participation in a longitudinal study of Negro infants and children. *Publ. Hlth. Reps.,* 1960, **75**, 1085–1091.

Shuey, Audrey M. *The testing of Negro intelligence.* Lynchburg, Va.: J. P. Bell, 1958.

Terman, L. M., and Merrill, Maud A. *Stanford-Binet Intelligence Scale.* Boston: Houghton Mifflin, 1960.

16 Performance of Negro American Children Ages 7–10 on the Stanford-Binet by Selected Background Factors[1]

S. O. ROBERTS[2]
Fisk University

ANN E. DICKERSON,[3] & CARRELL P. HORTON[3]
Meharry Medical College

This paper further draws upon the wealth of available data from the Fisk-Meharry longitudinal study, and deals with the relationship between test performance and personal background factors. Specifically the authors find relationships between test performance and the mother's marital status and also her educational level. In addition, such environmental factors appear to interact more significantly at ages nine and ten than at seven or eight. They also feel that the intellectual development and stability of minority group and disadvantaged children would benefit from action directed toward stabilizing the total family situation at as early an age as possible. This paper, together with the previous paper by Roberts and his associates, suggests the crucial role that the home situation plays in children's ability to perform on psychological tests and also their ability to withstand the negative effects of disadvantaged environments. It further suggests the role that personal and social factors may play in a variety of behaviors.

At one time, there was great interest in what the senior author (Roberts, 1950) referred to as "static," in contrast to *"analytic,"* studies of group

SOURCE. Unpublished manuscript, 1966, reprinted with permission of the senior author.

[1] This study is part of a longitudinal investigation, which was supported in part from a research grant, R-126(R), from the Children's Bureau, Welfare Administration, Department of Health, Education, and Welfare to Fisk University; and from RG3761(CE) and several others, National Institutes of Health, U. S. Public Health Service to Meharry Medical College.

[2] S. O. Roberts, Professor and Chairman, Department of Psychology, Fisk.

[3] Ann E. Dickerson, Psychologist, Department of Pediatrics, Meharry.

[3] Carrell P. Horton, Statistical Analyst, Department of Pediatrics, Meharry.

differences, wherein some test was applied to two different ethnic, class, or other groups—sometimes not too carefully defined nor chosen. The results were then published very often with an explanation based on "heredity" or else a cultural hypothesis was advanced to account for the same.[4] For instance, when Kennedy and his associates (1963), after reporting a mean Stanford-Binet IQ of 81 for 1800 Negro American children in grades 1–6 in the southeastern United States, seriously proposed separate norms for this ethnic group, one wonders if this is not an echo of the "static" orientation. Incidentally, Schaefer (1965) has questioned some of Kennedy's results as artifacts of sampling. One also wonders about Shuey (1966), (who reports that, between 1945 and 1964, the average IQ's of Negro American and white children were 82 and 96, respectively) when she concludes on the basis of the materials reviewed by her, that "all taken together, inevitably point to the presence of native differences between Negroes and whites as determined by intelligence tests." Rather than pointing to differences, the analytic type of investigation seeks to determine the causes or correlates of observed differences.[5] Two factors that have been employed a great deal are (a) marital status of the family, and (b) educational level of the parents (usually the mother). For example, the Moynihan Report (1965) gave too much emphasis, in the views of some, to the marital factor among Negro Americans, and the latest U. S. Department of Labor Bulletin, *The Negroes in the United States* (1966) has sought to emphasize positive forces which are beginning to operate. Herzog (1966) has also reviewed the matter of family stability. In addition, many studies have explored the role of education of parents or combinations of other environmental and personality factors in such research as that reported by Kagan and Moss (1962), Deutsch and Brown (1964), and Chilman (1966)—all searching for a better understanding of children.

As a specific illustration of this latter approach, Roberts and colleagues (1965) found a *decrease in IQ* amounting to *one year of mental age* between ages 5 and 10 years for 72 Negro American subjects (members of a larger Fisk-Meharry longitudinal study of children from birth to adolescence in cooperation with Crump of Meharry).[6] The data seemed to indicate that the decline in IQ at ten may be a consequence of "low socio-

[4] Anastasi (1958) reviews in depth the methodological problems and issues of the interpretation of "race differences."

[5] A related example is the matter of mental retardation, where continued research has substantially reduced simple genetic explanations of this observed phenomenon.

[6] E. P. Crump, Professor and Chairman, Department of Pediatrics, Meharry, and Principal Investigator for the series of studies carried out at Meharry Medical College with these children.

economic status, including unstable and unfavorable family patterns" for many children. However, the investigators saw the need for further study to discover whether these environmental factors were influencing or were associated with intelligence test performance for the whole group.

STATEMENT OF PROBLEM

The objective of the present study was to examine the results of the administration of the Stanford-Binet, Form L-M, (abbreviated scale) to groups of Negro American children at ages seven through ten in relation to the marital status of the family and the mothers' educational level in an effort to see how these circumstances may relate to the children's performance on this measure of ability.[7]

METHOD

Subjects

The subjects were 281 children divided as follows according to age and sex:

Age	Boys	Girls	Total
7 years	16	33	49
8 years	42	37	79
9 years	30	43	73
10 years	42	38	80
Total	130	151	281

Data and Procedure

The abbreviated scale of the Stanford-Binet (Form L-M) was administered to all the children, during 1964 and 1965, by four examiners under comparable conditions. Background information was obtained in interviews with the mothers of the subjects; but, in a few instances the "mother substitute" was interviewed.

All data were analyzed according to standard statistical procedures and separately for boys and girls in terms of (a) age of child, (b) family marital status, and (c) educational level of the mother.

---

[7] See Wechsler (1966) in defense of the much maligned and besieged IQ as an "intelligent test."

RESULTS

General

Table 1 presents the findings by sex, age, marital status of the family, and mothers' education, from which the results, presented below, may be determined.

Initial analysis by means of the chi-square test, revealed no association between two of the independent variables—marital status (two groups) and educational level (three groups) for either sex.

SEX. The over-all mean IQ's for boys and girls included in the groups were found to be 86.0 and 86.8, respectively, with S. D.'s of 17.1 and 14.8.

AGE. Age at time of testing did not appear to be related to the mean IQ of boys; although, a small consistent decline in mean IQ with increase in age was found for the girls. Girls' mean IQ at ages seven and eight was 88.4, but at age ten they had a mean IQ of 84.4. The largest mean difference for boys occurred between ages seven and nine with mean IQ's of 88.4 and 82.4, respectively, while their mean IQ at age ten was 87.8.

Marital Situation

The data were also analyzed in terms of whether the child lived in a family where the parents were "married" (i.e., both parents married and living together—in some instances there was a step-parent instead) or in families *other than "married"* (hereafter called "other").

The mean IQ's of both boys and girls of 87.0 and 88.3, respectively, in the "married" situation were higher than those found for the boys and girls living in "other" families, where the IQ's were 82.2 and 83.5, respectively.

BOYS. The difference between the two groups of boys approached, but did not reach statistical significance at the .05 level. Also, boys living in situations classified as other than married showed the greatest variation in mean IQ with age. Their mean IQ at age seven was 94.5 while at age nine and ten they had mean IQ's of 75.0 and 78.0, respectively, which were significantly lower than those found for boys living in "married" families at these later age levels. The mean IQ's of the "married" boys increased with age from 82.5 at seven to 90.8 for the ten year group.

GIRLS. On the other hand, the difference in mean IQ's for the two groups of girls was statistically significant and the difference was consistently found at each age level. Both groups of girls showed variations in mean IQ of 4.4 points between ages seven and ten similar to that for the total group. Mean IQ for girls from "other" homes was fairly stable around 83.5 between seven and ten, while the mean IQ for girls in "married" families decreased from 89.4 at seven to 85.0 for the ten year group.

TABLE 1
Summary Statistics on Intelligence Quotients of 281 Negro American Children by Sex and Age of Child, and by Marital Status and Educational Level of the Mother

	Males						Females					
	"Married"			"Other"			"Married"			"Other"		
Age and Statistics*	"Low" 8th Gr. or less	"Middle" 9th–12th Grade	"College" 1–4 yrs. or more	"Low" 8th Gr. or less	"Middle" 9th–12th Grade	"College" 1–4 yrs. or more	"Low" 8th Gr. or less	"Middle" 9th–12th Grade	"College" 1–4 yrs. or more	"Low" 8th Gr. or less	"Middle" 9th–12th Grade	"College" 1–4 yrs. or more
7 years												
Mean	82.88	82.5	122.5	102.5	92.5	92.5	82.5	90.3	95.0	—	77.7	92.5
N	3	7	1	1	3	1	4	18	2	0	4	5
8 years												
Mean	84.2	79.8	96.9	95.0	91.7	67.5	83.9	89.5	99.5	—	81.2	97.5
N	6	19	8	2	6	1	7	15	5	0	8	2
9 years												
Mean	80.8	89.2	87.5	95.0	70.6	72.5	91.1	85.8	92.5	85.0	82.0	75.0
N	3	9	6	2	8	2	7	17	6	2	9	2
10 years												
Mean	84.2	88.1	112.5	76.7	82.5	72.5	80.0	86.8	87.5	74.2	85.0	92.5
N	3	25	4	6	3	1	6	13	3	3	12	1
Total												
Mean	83.2	85.0	98.6	85.7	82.0	75.5	84.8	88.2	94.1	78.5	82.4	90.0
S D	9.4	15.8	7.0	12.4	17.0	10.9	14.8	15.7	12.1	16.1	11.0	17.8
N	15	60	19	11	20	5	24	63	16	5	33	10

* All statistical values were computed from grouped data.

Educational Level of Mother

Mothers were divided, on the basis of highest school grade completed, into three groups—"low" (8th grade or less), "middle" (9th–12th grades), and "college" (one or more years of college).

The difference in mean IQ between all children whose mothers were in the "low" group and those whose mothers were in the "college" group was statistically significant for both the boys and the girls. Mean IQ's for the boys were 84.3 in the "low" group, 84.2 in the "middle" group and 93.8 in the "college" group. Girls, in the same categories, had mean IQ's of 83.7, 86.2, and 92.5, respectively.

BOYS. While there was a general trend for mean IQ to be higher as the educational level of the mother increased, the trend was not consistent for both sexes at each age level. The only completely consistent relationship in IQ of boys by education of mother was found at the ten-year level where an increase in mean IQ was found to be associated with an increase in mother's educational level; although, the differences were not statistically significant. Lowest mean IQ of the three groups of boys was found in the "middle" group at all ages except ten. However, the mean IQ of the "college" group was higher than that of the "low" group at all age levels except nine.

GIRLS. The mean IQ of girls rose consistently with educational level of the mother at all ages except at nine years, where the highest mean IQ was found in the lowest educational group.

Marital Status and Education

BOYS. The relationship between educational level of the mother and IQ was not clearly defined for boys in the "married" or "other" groups. Mean IQ increased with mother's educational level in the "married" group at age ten only. The mean IQ of the "college" group of "married" boys was significantly higher than that found for the "low" group of "married" boys at all age levels. No consistent relationship was found at any age level for boys from "other" homes; however, the numbers were rather small and there were only single cases in each of the age x "college" cells.

GIRLS. When IQ's of girls were considered according to the educational level of the mother, within the categories of "married" and "other," higher mean IQ's were found for girls living under "married" conditions at all three educational levels. This was also true at each age level analyzed except for the "college" group at age ten, where there was only one girl in the "other" x "college" cell. Finally, a positive relationship between educational level of the mother and mean IQ was observed for girls in both the "married" and "other" groups at all age levels except at nine years.

DISCUSSION

Age at the time of testing does not appear to be related to the mean IQ of boys but may be associated with a decline in the performance of girls. However, the type of home situation, of which the children are a part, seems to be related to their performance as they grow older with the "married" condition being more favorable. The data also indicated that the proportion of boys and girls living under "other" conditions is higher at age nine for boys (40 percent) and at age ten for girly (42 percent) than at other age levels where the proportion approximates that for the group as a whole (30 percent). The relationship between mother's educational level and mean IQ was also more apparent at ages nine and ten. There was present, though, a general trend for mean IQ to be higher as the educational level of the mother increased. This relationship was not consistent among boys when divided according to "married" and "other" families, but it was evident for girls. Last, when the performances of boys and girls in the "married" and in the "other" groups were compared on the basis of the educational level of the mother there was a tendency for mean IQ to be higher in the "married" group, particularly for the older age groups of nine and ten and in the two upper educational groups.

CONCLUSIONS

1. Age does not appear to be a significant factor in the Stanford-Binet performance of Negro American children from ages 7 through 10; however, marital status of the mother and her educational level exhibit important relationships to the children's performance.

2. These environmental factors appear to be more crucial at ages nine and ten than at the younger age levels of seven and eight.

3. Finally, the above conclusions suggest that the intellectual development of minority and disadvantaged children would benefit from action directed toward stabilizing their total family situation at an early age.

References

Anastasi, Anne. *Differential psychology.* (3rd ed.) New York: Macmillan, 1958.

Chilman, Catherine S. *Growing up poor.* Washington, D. C.: U. S. Dept. of Health, Education, and Welfare—Welfare Administration, Division of Research, 1966.

Crump, E. P., and Horton, Carrell P. Growth and development in Negro infants and children. *The Journal-Lancet,* 1961, **81,** 507–517. (Summary of some 11 of their studies.)

Deutsch, M., and Brown, B. Social influences in Negro-white intelligence differences. *J. soc. Issues,* 1964, **20,** 24–35.

Herzog, Elizabeth. Is there a "breakdown" of the Negro family? *Social Work,* January 1966, 1–8.

(Moynihan, D. P. The Moynihan Report) U. S. Department of Labor. *The Negro family: the case for national action.* Washington, D. C.: U. S. Government Printing Office, 1965.

Kennedy, W. A., Van De Riet, V., and White, J. C., Jr. A normative sample of intelligence and achievement of Negro elementary school children in the southeastern United States. *Monogr. Soc. Res. Child Developm.,* 1963, **28,** No. 6 (Ser. No. 90).

Roberts, S. O. Some mental and emotional health needs of Negro children and youth. *J. Negro Education,* 1950, **19,** 351–362.

Roberts, S. O., Crump, E. P., Dickerson, Ann E., and Horton, Carrell P. Longitudinal performance of Negro American children at five and ten years on the Stanford-Binet. *Amer. Psychologist,* 1965, **20,** 524. (Abstract)

Schaefer, E. S. Does the sampling method produce the negative correlation of mean IQ with age reported by Kennedy, Van De Riet, and White? *Child Development,* 1965, **36,** 257–259.

Shuey, Audrey M. *The testing of Negro intelligence.* (2nd ed.) New York: Social Science Press, 1966.

Terman, L. M., and Merrill, Maud A. *Stanford-Binet Intelligence Scale.* Boston: Houghton-Mifflin, 1960.

U. S. Department of Labor. *The Negroes in the United States.* Washington, D. C.: U. S. Government Printing Office, 1966.

U. S. Office of Education. U. S. Department of Health, Education, and Welfare. *Equality of educational opportunity.* Harold Howe II, (Ed.). Washington, D. C.: U. S. Government Printing Office, 1966.

Wechsler, David. The IQ is an intelligent test. *The New York Times Magazine,* June 26, 1966, pp. 12–13, 63–66.

17 *A Letter from the South*

WILLIAM F. BRAZZIEL
Virginia State College

"A Letter from the South" is a deeply personal and thoughtful reply to an
article written by Dr. Arthur Jensen (*Harvard Educational Review,* 1969)
which had developed the notion that the races did differ in intelligence
and that Blacks were, in some respects, possibly genetically inferior to
whites. However carefully or skillfully Dr. Jensen might have presented
his ideas, they were bound to generate a storm of critical protest, and
Dr. Brazziel's reply is remarkably restrained. Dr. Brazziel summarizes the
many factors that could be utilized to account for the bulk of the observed
differences in intelligence—all of them environmental. This is a difficult
and extremely sensitive issue: whether or not to attempt to explain *any*
observed difference in terms of racial-genetic structures. The "Letter"
expresses great chagrin at Jensen's giving the racists further ammunition
with which to belabor Black people, and attempts to develop what the
author feels to be a more balanced and meaningful presentation of the
racial intelligence issue. The reader should carefully review the many
sources devoted to this most difficult and complex topic in order to understand the position developed by Dr. Jensen as well as the extremely
thoughtful and comprehensive reply by Dr. Brazziel.

Sirs:

Thirteen years ago plaintiffs brought suit in Federal District Court to
integrate the Louisiana public schools. The main argument of the defense
attorneys and the superintendent of public instruction was that "white
teachers could not understand the Nigra mind" and, therefore, would not
be able to teach them effectively in integrated classrooms. The defense
quoted heavily from the theories of white intellectual supremacy as
expounded by Henry Garrett and Audrey Shuey.

Last week, a scant five days after Arthur Jensen made headlines in

SOURCE. Brazziel, W. F., "A Letter from the South," *Harvard Educational Review,*
39, Winter 1969, 348–356. Copyright © 1969 by President and Fellows of Harvard
College.

154

Virginia papers regarding inferiority of black people as measured by IQ tests, defense attorneys and their expert witnesses fought a suit in Federal District Court to integrate Greensville and Caroline County schools. Their main argument was that "white teachers could not understand the Nigra mind" and that the Nigra children should be admitted to the white schools on the basis of standardized tests. Those who failed to make a certain score would be assigned to all black remedial schools where "teachers who understood them could work with them." The defense in this case quoted heavily from the theories of white intellectual supremacy as expounded by Arthur Jensen.

It will help not one bit for Jensen or the HER editorial board to protest that they did not intend for Jensen's article to be used in this way. For in addition to superiority in performing conceptual cluster tricks on test sheets, the hard line segregationist is also vastly superior in his ability to bury qualifying phrases and demurrers and in his ability to distort and slant facts and batter his undereducated clientele into a complete state of hysteria where race is concerned.

Jensen and the HER editorial board will modestly admit that they have superior intellects and I am sure they realized the consequences of their actions. Questions now arise as to why they decided to raise this issue, in this way, and at this time.

Fortunately, doubts about the ability of black and yellow people to master war, finance, science and technology are waning rapidly in both white and black minds. The imprecision of standardized testing is now clear to most literate people and the criminal use to which they are put in schools is also becoming clearer. Black history has made people aware that white people did *not* give America such things as the stoplight, the shoe last, heart operations and sugar refining but that black people did this. That John Smith did not develop corn and tobacco but learned to grow these crops from the Indians. And the beat goes on. People are now witnessing with their very eyes the fact of black youth finally given a half of a chance at education and jobs and being able to make exotic formulas for bombs and napalm as well as anyone else. As a result of all of this, I think the present set-to might be the last go-round for white supremacy psychological theory.

I would hope the Jensenites could alter their stance and approach and try to bring some good out of this situation after all. They might work their way out of ethnic learning styles by broadening their research to include all ethnic groups. We have some rather learned men in our area who believe that English-Americans are atop the pyramid of abstract learning abilities with Welsh, German, French, Belgian, Norwegian, Swiss, Finnish, Danish and Swedish occupying the next nine rungs in the order listed. After the top ten have been given their just due, these gentlemen give a smattering of attention to the rest of Europe and proceed to ignore the rest of the world. The Jensenites might try to clear this up in some way. They might even look into intra-group differences within the top ten. I would suspect that many would be found and that it would be healthy to make this known at professional meetings, in the journals and in the news media.

We also have a religious wing in this group who suspect that English-American children who are brought up in Southern Baptist churches perceive things differently and might really deserve the top spot upon the pyramid. Southern-English-American-Episcopalians regard these assertions with a great deal of amusement. But who really knows? We all will if the ethnic learning line of research is extended logically to include every possible ethnic, regional and religious stock.

Also in the status research vein, we need research on the effects of racism and caste status on learning. The Jensenites can provide this by following Robert Coles and others around in Mississippi and South Carolina to study the parasitic worm and starvation situation among black children. Autopsies of a few who died might yield valuable evidence on the brain damages wrought by malnourishment. The team could change themselves into black people a la John Griffin and run the hostility gauntlet as they tried to find some information in the local library. Or the hilarity gauntlet as they made application for a professional or skilled job. They could fly as black men to Boston or Oakland and make the same applications to the craft union nearest the airport. Or they could try to get a tenured appointment in the Harvard Graduate School of Education, or a spot on the HER editorial board, or simply a rank higher than assistant professor among the 7,000 member Harvard faculty.

The Jensenites could give the same black injections to their children, enroll them in a different school and record what happens to them. Children learn efficiently if listening, reading, discussion, peer-group interaction, library resources and teacher-pupil interaction are all used efficiently. The investigators might be very interested in the change in quality in the last four areas for their now black off-spring and to see who is to blame and how the situation can be improved. To add a spicy dimension, low IQ scores could be substituted in the transfer folders.

Creation of multi-ethnic and multi-racial tests would also be a method of bringing some good out of the situation. If the only way to make *exactly* the same score on test items is to be of the same race, economic class, ethnic stock, and religious persuasion as the committee that developed the instrument, then we either must make intensive efforts to inter-marry, re-distribute income and institute religious purges and programs in this country or we must try to integrate more multi-racial and multi-ethnic material into the instruments. Said in the words of Dr. Nathan Wright, the Newark black power theorist, we must try to "dehonkify" the instruments.

Or we might decide that making *exactly* the same score is not important for all races and religions and come up with an Ethnic Success Quotient for tests based on validation studies of all of the hypenated groups we are going to study. Under such a system a Richmond born, Episcopalian, of English stock, from a family with an income of $12,000 would be declared below average if his Binet score was below 120. A score of 100 would relegate him to success quotient oblivion as a low normal. The Beaufort County, S. C. black children with worms might have a success quotient of 90 based on performance of adults from this sort of situation who somehow scrambled up the ladder. A black 100 score in this county would indicate a ESQ of potential genius.

Finally, in this vein, the Jensenites might make their most important contribution if they could somehow join with Earl Schaefer of the National Institutes of Health and others at the Universities of Florida, Western Michigan, etc. who are fastening on early infant stimulation and teaching as the key to agility on standardized tests. (The problem, of course, may be in getting the Schaeferites to join with the Jensenites given the Klan types who have embraced the latter as their own.) Schaefer has already published some fine results of efforts with black children. The logic here is simple and very much in the vein of Cronbach's rebuttal to the Jensen paper, i.e., if you want black kids to think like white kids, imprint this type of thinking habit early (5 days to 2 years of age) with simple thinking, concept cluster tasks. White teachers can enable black parents to learn how. White disadvantaged children are being imprinted in the same manner in some studies. Ethnic and religious backgrounds have not been treated as yet. There might be a problem or two here regarding people who might want to imprint their children with their own brand of thinking or who have deep affection and preference for certain racial, ethnic or religious ways of thinking. Other parents might not want the new imprints to attend their schools on an integrated basis or live in their neighborhoods and play in their recreation centers. Something in the imprinting would thus be lost in this sort of forced isolation. But I am certain these reservations can be swept aside in the name of psychological research and the cognitive homogenizing process can progress.

Now for a closer look at some of Jensen's theories about black IQ. To begin, I received a form letter from Jensen in response to a request for clarification of his *real* stand on the implications of racial genetic inferiority that seemed to shine through the somewhat hazy statements of conclusion of his paper at the AERA, implications which the press quickly translated into flat statements of white intellectual supremacy. His article was based on this paper and gave the same impression to the press. (See Joseph Alsop, *Washington Post*, March 11; *Virginian-Pilot*, March 12: "Yet there is no use being mealy-mouthed about it. Dr. Jensen is really saying that in *addition* to the handicaps wickedly imposed by prejudice and discrimination, the average black American begins the race of life with a detectable genetic handicap").

Jensen's letter was addressed to the *Berkeley Daily Gazette* which he feels misinterpreted his position. The following are excerpts from the letter:

"Obvious differences in inborn mental ability 'between races'—these are a reporter's words. They certainly are not mine. The quotation marks, attributing this phrase to me, are therefore wrong. Furthermore, the statement is quite indefensible. The complex *causes* of objectively measurable differences in mental abilities among individuals or between different socioeconomic and racial groups are not at all 'obvious.'

"Although my study of the existing evidence has led me to the position that intelligence differences among individuals, social classes, and racial groups are conditioned by both genetic and environmental factors, the estimation of the relative contributions of these influences is a problem of great technical and practical difficulty for researchers in behavioral genetics, and the research so far has been inadequate as a basis for definitive conclusions about racial differences in intelligence."

Jensen's treatment of the racial aspects of IQ in his article comes to the same point of inconclusiveness. It is very, very unfortunate that he, or the editors, failed to include a clear statement to this effect. Truth squad operations such as this letter and the rebuttals by psychologists in the HER Spring issue will never get read.

Jensen's second error in my estimation was to lean heavily on the Coleman Report for data on black inferiority. This report has been heavily criticized for inaccuracy. The most notable criticism is contained in the Winter, 1968 issue of the Journal of Human Resources in an article by Bowles and Levin. Sampling procedures, lack of cooperation by big school systems, failures to match black-white sample by curriculums, over-reliance on administrators' contentions that black-white facilities were indeed separate but equal (black parents in Eutaw, Alabama must have thought the research team had been smoking pot when they read the conclusions of the report) and crudeness of statistical measures were all analyzed as weaknesses which, when added to the fact that the study was made in pre-ESEA days, relegated it to the status of a 737 page, million dollar pilot study. On page 292 of the report, the authors state similar disclaimers, especially regarding the precautions necessary in interpreting their statistics.

In regarding as law this report's conclusions that the average black kid can get no further than a 9th grade operating level after 12 years of public school, Jensen ignores completely (or is unaware of) the record being compiled by the JOBS program of the National Alliance for Businessmen. These gentlemen take black drop-outs, place them on the job half-time and in reading and math classes half-time; they produce a two-year gain on tests every six weeks.

Jensen's major error, I believe, was his inconsistency in following a definite line of reasoning regarding the separation of gene linkage and pre-postnatal ravages of protein malnutrition. The latter is the most intensively researched thesis these days with NIH teams leading the way. Jensen did not even mention this line of research which (together with research in infant stimulation) I believe has answers for 42% mental retardation found in low-low (Jensen's level V) income black children and a lot of the other differences. In a half-starved brain like these kids have, how are we to really know if high or low IQ genes were linked? Jensen did not tell us how.

Jensen calls compensatory education a failure. So did reporters of the *Washington Post* who in turn received and printed a report by the ESEA staff of the Virginia Department of Education calling their allegations inaccurate and stating that they had hard data to back their claims. In response to a request for same, I received tables for statewide pre-post testing of 10,200 pupils in 15 school districts for 1967–68. The data show average month's increase in grade equivalency per month of 1.06 of instruction or an average overgain in achievement of more than a half a year per pupil as a result of compensatory education. Children scoring in the lowest decile had decreased from 41% to 28%. In the second quartile the number jumped from 8% to 16% and the drop-out rate had decreased by 63%. The officials noted that age-grade decrement had been scotched and that they believe that they had convincing evidence that their Title I program was a success. And this from one of the more conservative states in the Union and one with a record of slow starts in educational innovations. School people, it seems, are just now learning how to run compensatory programs. Or really try to. The first report to the President of the National Advisory Council on Disadvantaged Children noted this reluctance to really plan and implement on the part of many school systems. They quoted one superintendent who stated flatly that "it was useless and a waste of money to teach those jigs anything." Let us all hope he has since initiated a good program and that he doesn't read Jensen's article.

In drawing conclusions from 200–300 comparative studies of black-white IQ, Jensen failed to consider that all of the pre-1948 studies and most of the post-'48 studies failed to give attention to the deprivation axioms made popular by the University of Chicago group (Davis, Eels, et al.) and until recently almost no psychometrists gave attention to the fact that white examiners in a black classroom are, in many, many cases, getting an invalid test performance. Their color, voice, manner, gestures turn many kids off, and they refuse to try. *This phenomenon is growing in intensity and must be dealt with.* How are you going to have a valid test session with kids who read in black papers and magazines that white researchers are sending their kids to Harvard by over-studying the black communities with federal grants? Or with kids who received a leaflet from a community group blasting tests as an "unfair tool of colonialists who control the black community"?

I believe that Jensen is wrong and I hope he does not do too much damage. I believe the HER editorial board should publish the rebuttals in the same issue with future attacks on the Negro. Rumors abound that attacks on the Negro church are planned. This will scotch the sensationalism of the press caused by the lag in time between issues. Indeed, the rebuttals will never be read by reporters, much less printed.

Jensen failed to take into consideration the black infant mortality rate as a factor in black infant supremacy on the motoric area of the Bayley Scales. This rate is three times that of white infants. Black kids must literally undergo a survival of the fittest test to be born, once conceived, and to stay alive.

Jensen has a serious contradiction in his analysis of tests and studies of black IQ. After offering half a dozen or so studies to document his thesis that black kids don't do as well on IQ tests as white kids, Jensen closes his paper by stating that IQ tests fail to measure the full potential of black kids.

Jensen failed to consider the 1969 report of the Research and Evaluation Branch of Project Head Start in writing off Head Start gains as transitory. According to this report of several studies of the maintenance of gains, the investigators concluded that the gains were maintained when the children were enrolled in first grades or kindergartens in middle-class schools. Edmund Gordon of Teachers College and John McDavid of Miami led the team which wrote this report.

Jensen, like other psychologists, is completely incapable of un-raveling what would have to be un-raveled in order to separate genetic from environmental influences where American black and white people are concerned, to wit:

1. If 90% of the black people in America have ancestors that include

white people, how can we tell when black genes or white genes make for a wrong mark on a test score sheet?

2. If a large per cent of white people have black ancestors, who are they? Are their samples controlled for this factor? Which genes, black or white, make for right marks on a test score sheet?

3. How can we parse out the effects of brain damage, brain stunting (due to malnutrition) and lack of early stimulation? Which accounts for a wrong mark on the test score sheet?

4. How can we parse and measure the degree of access and *welcome* of black people to cultural learnings?

5. How can we parse and measure the interest in and acceptance of the white "way of life" by black mothers and children? One can't get good scores on a "way of life" test like IQ unless one lives and accepts this life fully.

6. How can we develop indices which show comparability of school strengths, weaknesses and emphases? The school assessment study by Tyler's group is just getting underway over loud cries from many school people.

Jensen failed to consider the learning styles of black parents and the origins of these learning styles when he made white-black comparisons on associative and problem-solving learning. If you go to many rural schools in the south today, you will find the associative type of learning proceeding as it has for many, many years—*for both races*. This is the learning heritage of most big city black parents. They pass this style on to the kids early and it shows up in test profiles. If conceptual learning is viewed as a gradual acculturation process and offered early in school careers, these kids can be made to think. Jensen's exhortations to teachers to rely completely on associative learning might preclude this ever becoming a reality, however. Before any more articles are published, I think Jensen should do more work in the area of black history, demography and culture and that he should try to get into the area of racism and isolation and the big role they play in differences. There really is merit in his actually taking the black injections and getting first-hand information. He would only have to be a black man for two months.

Jensen's "g factor," the main basis of his claims for white supremacy, cannot be accepted as the mysterious phenomenon he postulates. Even little children now know from their television science that if something really exists, scientists will isolate it and measure it—especially before making serious conclusions about it.

I believe Jensen made two good points. One is that IQ tests don't show the full learning potential of kids who are poor and black. I was happy to learn that he had invented a test which does a better job. We should all buy it. He should make millions. The other is that intensive instruction rather than "cultural enrichment" is necessary to make these kids learn if they are locked in neighborhood schools. Unlike Jensen, I believe that they can proceed from associative learning to abstract reasoning if the instruction gradually brings them to this point. And even with this, I believe black kids will continue to think and score test items differently until full equality is achieved. Black kids screen out much of the curriculum and perceive the rest differently. Consider perceptions of Tarzan and the British Empire, for examples. Of course some black nationalists feel that it is a blessing that black people don't think like white people. As long as they can handle modern technology, make war, manipulate stocks, etc., I don't guess it really matters.

I believe the most potent strategy in the end will prove to be a combination of early stimulation and imprinting, and integrated schools with teachers who are free of racial and social class prejudices. IQ tests will also be eliminated from the schools. This is the strategy on which Neil Sullivan based his cross-bussing operations for the Berkeley schools. This may account for some of Jensen's concerns and reservations and perhaps, for his article. Pettigrew and others presented evidence in their work for the Civil Rights Commission that the earlier black children were placed in integrated schools, the closer they came to white norms on achievements tests. In turn, the white children came closer to perfection in their social learnings while losing no ground in test proficiency. The black children pick up the mysteries of Jensen's "g-factor" through association, I suppose, while the white children pick up the mysteries of "soul."

Bibliography for Part III

Anastasi, A. Intelligence and family size. *Psychological Bulletin*, 1956, **53**, 187–209.

Bayley, N. Behavioral correlates of mental growth: birth to thirty-six years. *American Psychologist*, 1968, **23**, 1 17.

Bloom, B. S. *Stability and Change in Human Characteristics*. New York: Wiley, 1964.

Burt, C. Class difference in general intelligence: III. *British Journal of Statistical Psychology*, 1959, **12**, 15–33.

Burt, C. Is intelligence distributed normally? *British Journal of Statistical Psychology*, 1963, **16**, 175–190.

Burt, C. British tests show today's IQ rate down. *Los Angeles Times*, Sunday, February 22, 1970, p. 9, in reference to *Irish Journal of Education* article.

Carlson, Hilding B., and Henderson, Norman. The intelligence of American children of Mexican parentage. *Journal of Abnormal and Social Psychology*, 1950, **45**, 544–551.

Cattell, R. B. The multiple abstract variance analysis equations and solutions: for nature-nurture research on continuous variables. *Psychological Review*, 1960, **67**, 353–372.

Dobzhansky, T. Genetic differences between people cannot be ignored. *Scientific Research*, 1968, **3**, 32–33. (a)

Dustman, R. E., and Beck, E. C. The visually evoked potential in twins. *Electroencephalic Clinical Neuro-Physiology*, 1965, **19**, 570–575.

Eells, Kenneth, et al. *Intelligence and Cultural Differences*. Chicago: University of Chicago Press, 1951.

Ferron, O. The test performance of "coloured" children. *Educational Research*, 1965, **8**, 42–57.

Fishman, Joshua. Guidelines for testing minority group children. *The Journal of Social Issues* (April, 1964), **20**, 129–145.

Fuller, J. L., and Thompson, W. R. *Behavior Genetics*. New York: Wiley, 1960.

Goodenough, F. L. New evidence on environmental influence on intelligence. *Yearbook of Natural Social Studies Education*, 1940, **39**, Part I, 307–365.

Guilford, J. P. *The Nature of Human Intelligence*. New York: McGraw-Hill, 1967.

Hansen, C. F. The scholastic performances of Negro and white pupils in the integrated public schools of the District of Columbia. *Harvard Educational Review*, 1960, **30**, 216–236.

Harris, Albert J., and Lovinger, Robert J. Some longitudinal data on IQ changes in the intelligence of Negro adolescents. The City University of New York, 1965, mimeographed.

Heber, R., Dever, R., and Conry, J. The influence of environmental and genetic variables on intellectual development. In H. J. Prehm, L. A. Hamerlynck, and J. E. Crosson (Eds.), *Behavioral Research in Mental Retardation*. Eugene, Oregon: University of Oregon Press, 1968.

Higgens, C., and Sivers, Cathryne M. A comparison of the Stanford-Binet and the Colored Raven Progressive Matrices IQ's for children with low socioeconomic status. *Journal of Consulting Psychology*, 1958, **22**, 465-468.

Honzik, M. P. Developmental studies of parent-child resemblance in intelligence. *Child Development*, 1957, **28**, 215–228.

Huntley, R. M. C. Heritability of intelligence. In J. E. Meade and A. S. Parker (Eds.), *Genetic and Environmental Factors in Human Ability*. New York: Plenum Press, 1966. Pp. 201–218.

Kennedy, W. A., Van De Riet, V., and White, J. C., Jr. A normative sample of intelligence and achievement of Negro elementary school children in the Southeastern United States. *Monograph on Social Research and Child Development*, 1963, **28**, No. 6.

Klineberg, Otto. Negro-white differences in intelligence test performance: a new look at an old problem. *American Psychologist* (April, 1963).

Lee, Everett S. Negro intelligence and selective migration: a Philadelphia test of Klineberg's hypothesis. *American Sociological Review* (April, 1951), **16**, 227–233.

McCord, William M., and Demerath, Nicholas J. Negro versus white intelligence: a continuing controversy. *Harvard Educational Review* (Spring, 1958), **28**, 120–135.

McQueen, Robert, and Church, Browning. The intelligence and educational achievement of a matched sample of white and Negro students. *School and Society* (September, 1960), **88**, 327–329.

Medical World News. Using speed of brain waves to test IQ. 1968, **9**, 26.

Osborne, R. T. Racial differences in mental growth and school achievement: a longitudinal study. *Psychological Reports*, 1960, **7**, 233–239.

Passamanick, B., and Knobloch, Hilda. Early language behavior in Negro children and the testing of intelligence. *Journal of Abnormal and Social Psychology*, 1955, **50**, 401–402.

Reymert, M. L., and Hinton, R. T., Jr. The effect of a change to a relatively superior environment upon the IQs of one hundred children. *Yearbook of Natural Social Studies Education*, 1940, **39**, (I), 255–268.

Semler, Ira, and Iscoe, Ira. Structure of intelligence in Negro and white children. *Journal of Educational Psychology*, 1966, **57**, 326–336.

Shuey, A. M. *The Testing of Negro Intelligence.* (2nd ed.) New York: Social Science Press, 1966.

Thompson, W. R. The inheritance and development of intelligence. *Res. Pub. Assn. Nerv. Ment. Dis.,* 1954, 33, 209–331.

Vane, Julia R. Relation of early school achievement to high school achievement when race, intelligence and socioeconomic factors are equated. *Psychology in the Schools,* 1966, 3, 124–129.

PART IV

Higher Education

Since the Civil War the role of higher education in furthering the development and growth of Black Americans has been pivotal because it has always been assumed that higher education would guarantee eventual and lasting equality.

The selections presented here begin with Professor Canady's excellent analysis of the unique needs of Negro students in college, which he wrote in 1937, and then cover a range of significant issues in higher education. Harleston (1965), Green and Farquhar (1965), and Bayton and Lewis (1967) examine the more general issues involved, while Jenkins and Randall (1948) focus their attention on selected and unselected Negro college students. Dr. Atchison (1968) discusses high and low anxiety students, Dr. Froe (1968) presents a comparative study of disadvantaged Negro college freshmen, Drs. Williams and Cole (1969) discuss Southern Negro students, and Dr. Ladd (1965) analyzes some of the perceptions and attitudes of Black students at Harvard University. Finally, Dr. Green (1968) discusses some of the admissions problems related to the recruiting of Black students as well as the special, on-campus needs of high-risk students.

18 Adapting Education to the Abilities, Needs and Interests of Negro College Students[1]

HERMAN G. CANADY
West Virgina State College

This early classic by Dr. Herman G. Canady examines the many problems associated with adapting education to the needs, abilities, and interests of Negro college students, and the understanding of more than 30 years has not invalidated the major points as they were originally stated. Professor Canady develops the notion that there are actually two major needs, the study and guidance of students as early as their secondary school years, and also the organization of school curricula and programs to meet the needs of individual students. Although ideas such as these are an integral part of very contemporary thinking in educational circles, that they were developed clearly and forcefully by a Black psychologist working in the South prior to World War II is a remarkable compliment to this most distinguished American psychologist.

Slowly but surely the conviction is gradually gaining ground in educational circles that comparisons by means of psychological and educational tests within a "race"[2] is much more meaningful than between "races." In other words, for practical purposes, knowledge of "intra-racial" differences is of much more importance than determination of "inter-racial" differences.[3] Even if it is eventually proven that whites are inferior to Negroes, or that whites are superior to Negroes, or even that both "races" are equal, *what of it?* Negro children must still be educated and their education must be suitable to the abilities, interests and needs

SOURCE. Reprinted from *School and Society*, 1937, **46**, 437–439, with permission of the author and the publisher.

[1] An address delivered before the National Association of Teachers in Colored Schools, Philadelphia, Pa., July 30, 1937.

[2] M. J. Herskovits, *American Mercury*, 2: 207–210, 1924.

[3] See Herman G. Canady, West Virginia State College Bulletin, Series 23, No. 2, 1936.

of every child whom the parents send to our schools. The Negro child needs not to be shown that he is superior, inferior or equal to the white child. No! No! He needs education or, perhaps, as Dr. Judd would put it, he needs to be taught to be a better reader.[4]

Modern education declares that no educational institution can be efficient and really successful unless its curricula, its methods and its organization take into consideration, in a proper and adequate manner, the countless individual differences found among people. Wilkins[5] says:

"No two students bring to college the same background, the same experience, the same achievement in knowledge; and no two students face the same future of work and leisure. We have no right to do less than study with utmost care each individual prospect and plan the individual curriculum in accordance with the results of that study."

DEFINITION OF THE PROBLEM

Adjusting education to the abilities, needs and interests of individual students involves two coordinated programs: (1) the study and guidance of students, which should begin at least early in the secondary school period; (2) the organization of college curriculum, instruction and administration with the primary purpose of serving the needs of the individual.

(1) *The Study and Guidance of Students*

A fundamental change in the American college program, based upon the recognition of individual differences, began when educators became interested in the development of the intellectual life of each student rather than the monstrous size of their colleges. There have been some comments suggesting that Negro institutions of higher learning, even at this late date, are not showing intimate concern for student problems and are diverting their time and energies to raising money and developing their institutions into larger colleges or into universities. Thompson, editor of the *Journal of Negro Education*, after pointing out the expansion of the physical plants of Negro colleges and universities, remarks, "It is strange, however, that little or no attention has been given to the most important factor in the whole scheme of Negro education, namely, the student."[6] Mays, dean of the School of Religion at Howard University, interviewed 1,714 students, distributed in 22 colleges for Negro youth,

[4] Charles H. Judd, *Journal of Negro Education,* 5: 517–520, July, 1936.
[5] E. H. Wilkins, "The Changing College," p. 364. University of Chicago Press, 1927.
[6] Charles H. Thompson, *Journal of Negro Education,* 2: 26, January, 1933.

concerning their vocational plans. On the basis of these data he says, "This study suggests that practically nothing is being done in Negro high schools and colleges to aid Negro students in an intelligent choice of an occupation."[7]

These comments by keen responsible men insinuate that in Negro institutions of higher education the student becomes the forgotten man, and that one is perfectly justified in applying to student life in these institutions the slogan of a widely advertised brand of bread, "Untouched by human hands." This should not be; why, the very breadth and complexity of collegiate education call for a thorough study of the individual student.

There came to the attention of a certain superintendent of schools recently a boy who, when upon the visit of a supervisor was asked by his teacher to answer what she considered a simple question, replied, "Search me, lady!"

While he did not know it, or so intended it, there was a lesson in this boy's answer, "Search me." That is exactly our task with every student, a searching investigation and study of his whole personality to discover his assets, his liabilities, his dislikes, his determining circumstance and the means of awakening him to his own possibilities and the happiness that life may hold for him as a result of his development.

If education is to be adjusted to individual differences or to the needs of each student, the methods for discovering the differences and for understanding students must be generally known and widely used. The steps which the college may take to get necessary information concerning individual differences and student needs may be conceived as including:[8]

(1) A general testing program before or at school entrance, with standardized objective achievement tests in all the fields in which instruction is regularly given, such as English, language, history, mathematics, chemistry, et cetera; with the inclusion of a standardized psychological or aptitude test and such tests as the Strong Vocational Interests Blank and Bernreuter Personality Record Scales. As reliable devices for measuring non-intellectual traits are developed, they too should be used.

(2) The maintenance of cumulative records for every college student, beginning at least early in the secondary school period, which will give accurate, objective information about his abilities, his interests, his plans for the future and his achievement in various types of school work, as well as factual notes on such items as family and community relationships,

---

[7] Benjamin E. Mays, *The Crisis*, 37: 408–410, December, 1930.

[8] See *The Educational Record Supplement*, July, 1928, No. 8. Published by The American Council on Education, Washington, D. C.

study conditions, physical and mental health, unusual accomplishments and anything else which will help the college see the student as a whole *developing* person.

(3) An essential feature of this phase of the work would be, of course, the development of a guidance program. An adequate conception of guidance makes it a part of every teacher's work—not merely the function of a specialized personnel officer or selected counselors. One thing seems clear, intelligent guidance must of neccessity rest more and more on a continuous and more accurate study of the interests, capacities and achievements of each individual student, and less on mass characteristics.

This is an ambitious program, and it will take *money*. It is not easy or cheap, however, to plan a program designed to reestablish the ancient principle that education is a personal affair. Let me say here and now that Negro colleges have not so far begun to face the money costs of the program which looks toward the conservation and preservation of human resources through personal guidance of students.

(2) *Organization of College Curriculum, Instruction and Administration*

Thus far we have concerned ourselves with the problem relating directly to the students. When their salient needs are ascertained and understood, our next problem will be that of the organization of the college curriculum, instruction and administration with the primary purpose of administering to these needs and enhancing the welfare of individual students.

Colleges and universities that have developed carefully planned educational programs after a study of the students' needs, the instructional procedures, materials available and the environmental influences report satisfactory improvements in their educational offerings and performances. A recently published year-book of the National Society for the Study of Education[9] made available to the public material collected and organized by the American Association of University Women on current changes and experiments in liberal-arts education at the college level. It as reported that there were then (1932) going on in American colleges and universities 128 *outstanding* changes and experiments to improve college teaching. Many of these experiments were designed to transform education in a given college from a monotonous lock-step leveling process of mass instruction into diversified educational procedures adapted to individual students. The various measures may be classified under three categories, namely (1) care and direction of

[9] G. M. Whipple, editor, "Changes and Experiments in Liberal Arts Education," National Society for the Study of Education, Thirty-first Year-Book, Part 2.

students, (2) curriculum and instruction, (3) organization and administration.

It will be illuminating to set forth a few of the subjects included under the last two measures mentioned:

(a) *Curriculum and Instruction.* (1) Variation in student load; (2) unit assignment; (3) honor courses; (4) comprehensive examinations; (5) tutorial work; (6) class size and efficiency of instruction; (7) survey and orientation courses; (8) undergraduates *vs.* graduate courses; (9) non-credit courses; (10) independent study; (11) ability grouping.

(b) *Organization and Administration.* (1) Upper and lower divisions; (2) special studies of the cost of instruction; (3) research provisions; (4) special studies of aims and objectives; (5) student participation in government; (6) tuition and scholarship systems.

All this activity indicates that at least some of the white colleges are alive to their responsibility to develop a practical program to provide for individual differences. Negro colleges, as a whole, seem to have become resigned to being victims of circumstances, and to lack vision and initiative to overcome impediments and create a new program. The result is a mechanized and dehumanized school system lacking in character, dependent upon tradition, regulation and system, lagging from ten to twenty years behind the educational procession and satisfied with mediocre achievement.

In their endeavor to work out a program to provide for individual variations, Negro educators often compare their present procedures with the measures employed at the University of Chicago, Columbia, Wisconsin, Harvard, Swarthmore and other outstanding colleges and universities. They fail to see that each college presents specific problems, in many respects unique; for there are striking differences in intellectual efficiency, in interests and in needs not only between individuals, but rather distinct differences between schools and communities and between students coming from different economic and social groups.

No educator should expect to find somewhere ready-made a program of provisions for individual differences adapted to his particular school. Such a program must be the product of the intelligent use of data derived from research and scientific planning and experimentation with the local situation in mind. "If wishes were horses, beggars would ride," but they are not. The beggar must find a horse if he would ride, and the ideal of adjusting education to the abilities, needs and interests of individual students requires due consideration, in a given school, to a large number of variables, such as size of school, social and economic group served, financial support, type of training which the college offers and others too numerous to mention, in the development of a program which will make theory effective. Our educators and the faculties may get suggestions for their programs from what other colleges are doing to solve the problems presented by the ever-widening variation in the needs and abilities of students, but they can hardly get a program.

SUMMARY

I have attempted to say that the job of our educators is that of finding out what the needs of Negro boys and girls are, and then ascertaining what these needs mean in terms of the curriculum, instruction, administration and aspiration of individual students. Never let it be said that when called upon to solve the educational problems of any boy or girl we threw up our hands and cried, "It can't be done," "This student doesn't ant to learn," "He can't learn," "He doesn't belong in college." There is no such student. Every Negro boy or girl who is now enrolled in our colleges belongs there, and there is something we can do for every one of them if we but have the determination.

19 *Higher Education for the Negro*

BERNARD W. HARLESTON[1]

This article contains a rather pointed and candid look at higher education for Negroes. The paper also examines both the nature and quality of the predominantly Negro colleges in America, and presents certain of Dr. Harleston's expectations for their future growth and development. The paper echoes many of Dr. Canady's (1937, this collection) earlier sentiments regarding higher education for Negroes, but is developed from the perspective of recent research and thinking in the area.

For the large majority of college-bound Negro students, the procedures and decisions in making applications to colleges are in certain respects relatively simple. In the first place, they are spared the anguish over whether to apply to a Big Ten school, an Ivy League college, a Seven Sisters college, a small New England college, or a somewhat larger private university on the West Coast. Such choices simply do not exist for these students. Second, Negro students escape the trauma of college boards and selection by college-board scores. In general, the colleges which at present exist as real alternatives for them either do not require college boards or do not use them as a final selection device.

But the Negro students have to struggle with a more fundamental problem: they have to gain confidence—in the face of considerable evidence to the contrary—that higher education will open up for them economic opportunities which will provide security, social mobility, and a greater sense of personal worth. Some of the most promising Negro

SOURCE. Reprinted from *The Atlantic Monthly*, 1965, 139–144, with permission of the author and publisher. Copyright © 1965, by The Atlantic Monthly Company, Boston, Mass.

[1] A graduate of Howard University, with a Ph.D. from the University of Rochester, Bernard Harleston is an associate professor of psychology at Tufts University. He is chairman of the faculty committee on Negro education, and served as director of the Pre-College Center at Tufts, where eleven Negroes from Mississippi and twelve Negroes and sixteen white high school seniors from Massachusetts lived and studied together.

students decide quite early in their schooling that such a belief is without validity and reject completely the idea of continuing their education. For many of those who enter college, this struggle with self-doubt accounts in part for the fact that seven out of ten Negro students who enroll in Negro institutions drop out before graduation.

Negro institutions educate the majority of Negro students who go to college. Of the 123 Negro colleges and universities in the United States, 119 are located in the 17 Southeastern states and the District of Columbia. Thus, most Negro students pursue their higher education in what is geographically a very narrow area of the country, an area that has not been noted for intellectual enlightenment or educational innovations. There is both irony and tragedy in this situation. The irony is that the doors to higher education for Negroes should swing open most widely in states with the greatest prejudice toward the Negro and with a strong belief that Negroes cannot profit from higher education. The tragedy is that the educational opportunities which many of these institutions offer are so limited in range and depth that what they call higher education is at best a cruel hoax, a hoax that really was started long before, in the segregated kindergartens of our towns and cities. The origins of inferior education—poor and inexperienced teaching, insufficient books, and inadequate facilities—have their roots there.

Few of the Negro institutions have reached or can hope to reach full educational maturity. I mean by maturity an able and intellectually curious faculty and student body, adequate library resources and laboratory and classroom facilities, and an intellectual climate committed to academic freedom and intellectual integrity. Many Negro institutions lack the facilities and budget for an ambitious curriculum. The curricula lack diversity and show an imbalance in favor of the humanities over the natural and social sciences, since the cost of maintaining laboratory facilities for natural science courses far exceeds the financial resources of many of these institutions. Finally, there is little evidence of a healthy respect for academic freedom. In many Negro institutions the abilities of both students and faculty members are circumvented, and in effect, unchallenged, by an incentive system in which conformity is rewarded and individualism is rejected or punished.

Few of these Negro educators ever achieve publication. In part, this is due to the lack of research facilities and the absence of institutional support for creative work; in part, it is due to the lack of preparation by many of the faculty for independent and original work. But there are other considerations also. These institutions have no traditions that encourage involvement in scholarly activities. Since one's peers are not involved in research, there is neither motivation to engage in scholarly effort nor observable rewards for so engaging. Further, there is little intellectual gratification from sharing one's ideas or views. Thus, despite the intensive and dedicated teaching in Negro institutions—and there is considerable evidence of both—the majority of them impose, directly and indirectly, constraints and limitations on their teachers which become insurmountable barriers in the pursuit of academic and intellectual excellence.

From the point of view of the needs of the students, the educational opportunities in most Negro institutions are at best limited. To be fair, many students in these institutions are stimulated and even strained by the demands and challenges which confront them. There is, also, a long list of distinguished Negro Americans, not to mention the African leaders, whose liberal arts education was obtained at one of the Negro institutions. But the fact that the large majority of Negro students have to attend Negro institutions is significant in itself and raises serious questions about the implications of the limited educational opportunities.

In the first place, intellectual talent is wasted by a program of protracted mediocrity in which ordinary college-level study is impossible. Many of the male students who drop out of Negro institutions cite the lack of challenge as one of their reasons for leaving. Again, the range of available models with whom the student can identify, and whose intellectual behavior and commitment can serve as a guide, is narrow and lacks diversity. Many of the great and distinguished teachers in the colleges and universities of this country have been judged to be great because they were inspiring teachers and because they had attributes that caused them to be appreciated as models. But as the *Carnegie Corporation Quarterly* recently observed, "Negro academics have been cut off from the opportunity to develop a strong sense of professionalism, of kinship with their colleagues in their own disciplines, of being effective participants in the entire academic adventure—of seeing themselves as biologists or historians or physicists rather than solely as teachers."

The effects of the relative absence of models in Negro institutions are evident in the occupational and professional choices of the students. In 1962–1963, more than half of all the degrees granted by eighty-five Negro institutions were degrees in education. Very few degrees were taken in the arts, philosophy, English, business, and engineering. This heavy disproportion occurs not only because Negroes are attracted to teaching per se; it also reflects the employment opportunities—the kind of security —that have been available to the college-educated Negro. Many companies and businesses which are now eager to add Negro personnel to their staffs are surprised indeed to discover that there are few Negroes who are qualified and who do not need intensive on-the-job training. There have been no models to support and reinforce certain occupational aspirations; furthermore, many occupational choices simply have not been open to Negroes. Whitney M. Young, Jr., of the National Urban League, recently observed that "when job opportunities in some fields are opened, everybody wants the superior Negro. We get calls for accountants who should have the qualifications of Ralph Bunche and for secretaries who can type 180 words a minute and look like Lena Horne. We run out of people pretty rapidly."

This interdependence of educational experience and job opportunity accounts in large measure for the current widespread concern about the inequality of educational opportunities for Negroes. It is a concern driven to the surface by the explosive protests over job discrimination, and to a lesser degree, by the racial imbalance in the elementary schools. At the psychological level these protest demonstrations have dramatized the frustration and the despair that second-class education and constricted and limited employment opportunities produce. Insistently they raise the question, Can our society continue to lose a significant amount of creative, intellectual, and productive talent because a sizable segment of the population is forced to reach maturity under conditions of cultural deprivation?

In response to this question, a number of colleges have rapidly developed programs to improve and increase educational opportunities for Negro students. Oberlin, Yale, Hampton, Berkeley, Tufts, Wisconsin, Howard, Carnegie Tech, Brown, Michigan, Reed, Cornell, and Dartmouth are only a few of the colleges that are engaged in specific efforts. The programs are directed to one of three goals: strengthening Negro institutions, identifying and supporting promising Negro candidates for college admission, and strengthening the pre-college background of potentially able students.

In an effort to strengthen Negro institutions, several Northern universities—Brown, Cornell, Michigan, and Wisconsin—have "adopted" or formed "sister" relationships with Negro institutions. Brown's relationship is with Tougaloo College in Tougaloo, Mississippi. Cornell's is with Hampton Institute in Virginia. Michigan's is with Tuskegee Institute in Alabama. Wisconsin has a multiple relationship involving Texas Southern, North Carolina Agricultural and Technical, and North Carolina College. The development of these formal relationships is an outgrowth of the far older tradition of student exchanges between white and Negro institutions. For some time past, colleges like Wellesley, Yale, Denison, and Smith have participated in student exchanges with Negro institutions such as Howard University and Fisk University. The new programs, however, are more ambitious: they provide for faculty and student exchanges, consultations on curriculum development, advisory conferences on administrative procedures, and the possibility of joint participation in research projects. In addition, there is the opportunity for faculty members from the Negro institutions to take refresher courses or participate in short-term institutes and workshops of a professional nature at the sister university.

The attractive features in such arrangements are obvious: the wide variety of people participating and encouraging interaction at all levels, the increasing depth of the students' experiences, and the conscious effort to upgrade the faculty. The University of Wisconsin stated it fairly when it said that "this exchange will benefit both the southern institutions and the University of Wisconsin. Fresh viewpoints will be brought to our campus, as well as good doctoral candidates. The education of our own faculty and student body through exposure to a completely new set of problems will be of lasting effect."

Yet, there are serious limitations which are equally obvious. The faculty and student exchanges are episodic, providing only short-term and intermittent contact. In addition, there is the very real danger that a superior-subordinate relationship will develop between the Northern and Southern institution. For example, if the participants from the Negro institution take undergraduate and graduate courses at the Northern university while the Northern participants at the Negro institution engage primarily in teaching, then a superior-subordinate relationship will have been established. There are other more tenuous aspects. For example, Brown University recently announced that a pilot effort would be undertaken at Tougaloo College in which the students would be taught Standard American English as if it were a foreign language. Brown officials explained that "the language problem is central to the academic deficiencies of many college students," and that regional language habits that vary significantly from standard English impose severe social and classroom handicaps. But the Negro students involved are aware of a difference and a condescension which breeds resentment.

Without setting up formal relationships, several colleges have held summer institutes for teachers from Negro colleges to give them an opportunity to study the latest developments in their fields and new methods of teaching them. During the summer of 1964, Indiana University offered an institute in English. Carnegie Tech, Princeton, North Carolina College, and the University of Wisconsin offered institutes in history, physics, biology, and mathematics, respectively. Ten institutes were offered in the summer of 1965, including one in business administration at New York University, one in economics at Wayne State, and one in psychology at the University of Michigan.

A second major approach has concentrated on seeking out and admitting promising Negro students to predominantly non-Negro institutions. With the cooperation of groups like the National Merit Scholarship Corporation and the National Scholarship Service and Fund for Negro Students (NSSFNS), several colleges, among them Amherst, Williams, Vassar, Harvard, Radcliffe, and Roosevelt College, are admitting and offering financial support to more Negro candidates. Also, some colleges have made tours of Negro institutions in search of promising students.

These efforts of non-Negro colleges to enroll more Negro students have been bitterly criticized by some Negro educators. In the first place, most of the universities have been seeking out only those Negro students for whom the probability of success is quite good. These institutions operate under the paternalistic shibboleth that it is unfair to encourage Negroes to enroll unless we know they can make it, for a failure would be psychologically harmful and would do them a grave disservice.

In addition to being unduly protective, this view virtually guarantees that only a very small percentage of Negro students will be admitted, for they have to be selected on the basis of test scores, rank in class, and other criteria that have been correlated with success in college. Unfortunately, these criteria are prescribed for a middle-class urban population. It is doubtful that they apply in the same way to applicants from other cultural backgrounds. In a recent study of the performance by Negro students who were aided by NSSFNS in their efforts to enter non-Negro colleges, Professors Kenneth Clarke and Laurence Plotkin found that the dropout rate was less than one quarter the national average dropout rate. While the academic performance of these students was not exceptional, their achievements were far greater than what would have been predicted by such indices as college-board scores, family income, and educational background. The authors concluded that their determination to graduate and to achieve a measure of economic success accounted for their successful performance. Our present selection tests do not measure these motivational forces.

A second criticism, in truth a corollary of the first, is that universities and colleges have been raiding the Negro institutions of their most outstanding students. In a candid denunciation of such tactics, Dr. Rufus Clement, president of Atlanta University, recently said that when these universities take the best students, they leave the Negro institutions without an academic cream of the crop and without able and effective leaders for the student body.

The real challenge that confronts the non-Negro universities is to seek out and invest in risk students, students who show promise and potential but whose academic background and cultural experiences do not fit within the middle-class pattern of most undergraduates. The present conservative and selective course that most institutions are following will not meet this challenge. Our colleges and universities must develop long-range programs of financial, academic, and consultative support for large numbers of these students so that many more Negroes can have access to first-class liberal arts education.

The most recently developed support for higher education for Negroes is the pre-college study program. These programs, as they have been developed by schools like Tufts, Oberlin, Princeton, and Dartmouth, have two aims: to strengthen the academic background for college, and to motivate students to aspire to a college education. The details of the programs vary with the participating schools, but in general, the programs of summer study focus on all aspects of English and mathematics. In most instances the emphasis is on both remedial work and new explorations in these disciplines. In addition to the academic work, the students participate in cultural and athletic activities.

The participating students come from the eighth to the twelfth grade, in most cases from local schools. Thus in the Princeton Summer Study Program of 1964, forty boys (thirty-three of them Negroes) who lived within a seventy-five-mile radius of Princeton University were selected. Programs sponsored the same summer by Oberlin, Berkeley, and Carnegie Tech similarly drew from local residents.

On the other hand, some colleges have developed their programs so that students from diverse geographical, cultural, and racial backgrounds can be brought together. In the Summer Study Center which Tufts University sponsored this year, thirty-nine students who had just completed the eleventh grade spent six weeks on the Tufts campus at no personal expense in a program of academic, cultural, and social activities. Eleven Negro students in the program came from Mississippi, and twelve Negro students and sixteen white students came from the Greater Boston area. The academic program consisted of an intense course in mathematics; an intense course in English, including writing, literature, and rhetoric; a seminar titled "Man's Expanding Perimeter," in which the students examined the meaning of man in contemporary society; and visits to the various departments and laboratories of the university. Students attended four theater presentations, made trips and tours in and around Boston, had a weekend at a camp in western Massachusetts, participated in organized sports, and went on weekly picnics. Each student was selected because he showed ability to do college work. The long-term effects and the contributions of this experience to the success of these students in college remain to be revealed. But it is certainly clear that programs like this can both strengthen educational backgrounds and devise methods for identifying promising students.

Dartmouth has developed a pre-college program which is unique in its emphasis on preparing boys for preparatory school. The rationale is that academic and cultural enrichment come only when the disadvantaged youth is removed from his usual environment. The Dartmouth program, called A Better Chance (ABC), was started in the summer of 1964 and consists of eight weeks of study in English and communications and mathematics. Emphasis is also placed upon social learning, athletics, and cultural events. In the first year of the program, fifty-five disadvantaged ninth- and tenth-grade boys participated (forty-four of them Negroes). Forty-nine entered a preparatory school in the fall. Project ABC is administered in association with the Independent Schools Talent Search Program, which selects the boys and obtains the necessary contingent admission to one of the sixty-three participating preparatory schools. In 1965 Mount Holyoke introduced a comparable program for girls.

The development of pre-college programs has not been limited to non-Negro institutions. Hampton Institute has sponsored a pre-college program whose goal is to reduce the percentage of failures among college freshmen and to help students toward a successful transition from high school to college. The Hampton program is well attended by Negroes from many states, only a few of whom then enroll at Hampton. However, this program is not designed for, nor does it tend to attract, culturally or economically disadvantaged students.

Perhaps the most ambitious program of pre-college study has been developed by Educational Services, Incorporated, with the support of the Carnegie Corporation. Under the direction of Dr. Herman Branson, chairman of the department of physics at Howard University, ESI has set up pre-college campuses in six cities: Howard University (Washington, D. C.), Texas Southern University (Houston), Morehouse College (Atlanta), Fisk University (Nashville), Dillard University (New Orleans), and Webster College (St. Louis). Each center enrolled two hundred high school seniors from low-income families, both Negro and white, for Saturday classes in English and mathematics and an intensive eight-week summer session, plus programs of cultural and athletic events. ESI has developed special curriculum materials for strengthening the verbal and quantitative skills of the students.

While all these efforts have opened up new avenues, they seem unlikely to effect much more than the surface aspects of the basic problem of disparities in access to higher education. None of the programs gets directly at the risk student, or involves the colleges in investments in students for whom the prognosis is in fact quite poor. Many of the pre-college programs select their students on the basis of test scores and other traditional indices of ability. Yet the largest pool of Negro students consists of youths, and in particular, male youths, who are of average or better IQ but who do not excel on any of the traditional selection devices. To reach these students and hold out to them the promise of an opportunity to continue their education requires a more extensive commitment of energy, money, and other resources than the colleges have been willing to make. And it also is likely to involve far more frustration, for many of these students will fail to respond successfully. But education has in the past traditionally involved, and even courted, risks of various sorts. Many of these risks—such as the experimental programs at Antioch and Goddard—have become the basis for outstanding educational advances. We all know individuals who as beginning students were slow starters but who blossomed into distinguished scholars and statesmen.

In business, in politics, in the professions, in the technological fields, and even in the military services, the college degree is essential, and colleges prepare the manpower for the large majority of the vital tasks in our society. But they have been unable or unwilling to exercise boldly and creatively the power and influence on our social systems that would match their responsibility. There are some indications that this is changing. For example, the president of Yale University recently proposed that colleges like Yale develop training programs for the Peace Corps that would be available to the student during his undergraduate career.

In that same spirit I should like to propose that colleges and universities sponsor the operation of an Educational Service Training Corps, a formal program of training for service to primary and secondary education. The Educational Service Training Corps would be to education what the Reserve Officers Training Corps is to the military services. The Educational Service Training Corps would not train professional teachers or interfere with an undergraduate majoring in education or preparing for teaching. Rather, the Educational Service Training Corps would create a corps of aides who would work in deprived areas. Through lectures, field trips, and seminars, the program of the Educational Service Training Corps would give training that would permit the students after graduation to take college-sponsored and supervised jobs in these areas. They would work for the kind of educational and social reform which would bring to an end the social, political, and cultural alienation so evident in our major cities.

As we reach for more and more Negro students, the question of what will happen to Negro institutions will become critical. As I see it, the concept of the Negro institution is an anachronism which today lacks validity and social relevance. As centers of learning, Negro institutions, like Negro education itself, must be integrated into the larger context of higher education. They must be representative of the full range of educational experiences, opportunities, and commitments.

Clearly, not all the existing Negro institutions can hope to meet these criteria. Many should be vigorously assisted in their efforts to attract able students of *all races*. Howard University in Washington, D. C., a distinguished university which is rapidly becoming truly integrated, is perhaps the most outstanding example of this kind of development. Other former Negro institutions, such as Bluefield State College and West Virginia State, have already been transformed into interracial colleges. Schools like Hampton Institute and Lincoln University are actively seeking out non-Negro students. Certain other institutions should be either closed or radically changed. In supporting them, state and local officials effectively cut the Negro student off from the access to the more mature and sophisticated white institutions.

Some of the present four-year Negro colleges should be converted to strong integrated junior colleges. In many respects the junior college is a brilliant feature of American higher education. It nurtures the late bloomer who in a four-year liberal arts college might well be destroyed by the experiences of the first two years. Further, it helps many students to find themselves—to experiment with course offerings and the processes of learning without the pressure of having to decide immediately on an area of concentration. The junior college frequently attracts as teachers able people who are interested only in teaching and wish to avoid the pressures of research and publishing. Finally, the junior college offers an opportunity for older people to resume their education in a challenging setting.

Still others of the existing Negro institutions should be converted to pre-college centers which are sponsored by established white and Negro institutions and perhaps supported by federal funds. For a long time to come young men and women will show the scars of cultural deprivation, social and economic impoverishment, and racial imbalance. At present we deny these individuals an adequate chance to catch up and move on to a college education. Yet many white students whose parents can afford it are sent to select schools where they "bone up" on how to get into college and how to survive in the classroom. Should not all students have the opportunity of college-oriented preparation? The widespread development of pre-college centers would offer to the deserving Negro student a similar opportunity to prepare and compete for college admission and to hold his own in any course of study.

To a far greater extent than ever before, the problems and issues in Negro education bear directly upon the fate of higher education in general. The pressures for greater access by Negroes to higher education will rapidly increase as the squeeze resulting from economic barriers to mobility and social improvement increases. The response of the white institutions to these pressures will have to be decisive, for a considerably larger number of Negroes—not all of them potential Phi Beta Kappa students—will be demanding a college education. Boldness rather than caution and conservatism must guide the policies of non-Negro institutions in providing education for more Negro students. For example, they will have to go far beyond their current, no-risk policy of seeking out the top 12 percent of the Negro candidates for admission. They should admit candidates from the top 35 percent or 40 percent of Negro students. To do this is to accept the risk of academic failure on the part of some of these students. But with that hazard comes a challenge—to bend the resources of a university to the needs and aspirations of Negro students who have not been (and often cannot be) adequately prepared for a college education. To ignore the Negro's inequality of condition is to make meaningless his equality of opportunity.

20 Reflections and Suggestions for Further Study Concerning the Higher Education of Negroes[1]

JAMES A. BAYTON
Professor of Psychology

HAROLD O. LEWIS
Professor of Psychology

THE JOURNAL OF NEGRO EDUCATION EDITORIAL COMMITTEE
Howard University

This article relates closely to those of Canady (1937, this collection) and Harleston (1965, this collection) in that it develops an excellent historical perspective from which to view the predominantly Negro college, while at the same time offering a most realistic analysis of the problems associated with the higher education of Negroes. The paper constitutes a candid appraisal of both Negro college students and particularly Negro colleges. In addition, a relatively functional theoretical statement of the interaction between Negroes and higher education is developed that furnishes a useful framework within which to visualize problems as well as solutions.

The concern for improving the provisions for the higher education of Negroes has grown through the years. Various Howard University faculty members have engaged in discussions (perhaps dialogues) on the issues and problems involved. Emerging from their discussions are certain observations, questions and conclusions. The April 1967 Conference on "The Higher Education of Negro Americans: Prospects and Programs" provided an opportunity for added stimulation and challenge. Out of this

SOURCE. Reprinted from *The Journal of Negro Education*, 1967, **36**, 3, 286–294, with permission of the senior author and the publisher.

[1] Part I of this paper was prepared by Professor Bayton, Parts II and III by Professor Lewis, and Part IV by the *Journal of Negro Education* Editorial Committee.

experience communication has continued among us. In this chapter we share with our readers some of our concerns.

I

More attention needs to be given to establishing a broad perspective within which the specific problems associated with the higher education of Negroes could be placed in context. The most pressing problems in this area will never be understood in terms of their fullest implications unless placed in this broad perspective. We need first to look to higher education in the general American scene and then to appraise the higher education of Negroes within that context.

What are the goals of higher education in America? There seem to be two essential objectives: (1) to develop those capacities, attitudes, and motivations which will facilitate the individual's efforts to attain maximal personal achievement and (2) to develop those capacities, attitudes, and motivations which will make the individual sensitive to the fact that he must strive to make maximal social contributions. These personal achievements and social contributions are to be made within the context of contemporary vocational and socio-cultural life. The individual who has been seriously involved in the best that higher education has to offer would be expected to be able to capitalize upon the best that American life has to offer and, at the same time, to contribute to changing those aspects of American life which represent deficiencies in the system.

Institutions of higher education can be expected to vary in the quality of programs they make available to their students. Some institutions of higher learning provide programs of very high quality. Still other institutions provide programs of very low quality. On the other side of the equation, students approach higher education with great variance in what they can bring to the programs available. The following types can be identified:

1. Students with a high degree of personal capacity and motivation combined with a background of superior educational-socio-cultural experience.

2. Students who, although they have completed elementary and high school, do not have the native capacity to benefit from any sound program of higher education.

3. Students with the requisite native ability to benefit from sound or superior programs of higher education but whose educational-socio-cultural backgrounds have left them deficient in the capacities needed to make substantial progress in such programs.

Given the fact of differences in quality of higher educational programs and the fact of differences in quality of students approaching the higher educational system, several types of "mix" should be avoided:

1. Students with capacities, attitudes, motivations and backgrounds giving them the potential for utilizing the best that higher education can offer enrolling in programs that are much beneath their potential. Students of this type will most likely tend to make a considerable degree of progress in later life, even though they went to a college somewhat beneath their potential. The agonizing question will always be how much better might they have done if they had been exposed to the quality of higher education really suited to them.

2. Students who lack the native ability to profit from a sound program of higher education enrolling in such a program. If the program is in fact sound, these people cannot benefit from it.

3. Students with a high degree of native ability but serious educational handicaps enrolling in a sound program of higher education without some realistic effort being made to correct their deficiencies. Again, if the program is in fact sound, these students, without correction of their difficulties, would be expected to fail in making the best of the opportunity presented.

4. Students with serious educational handicaps enrolling in what are actually very low-level programs of higher education. Such graduates of such programs will live in "fool's paradise," unprepared to compete or to capitalize upon the American possibilities available to bona fide products of the real higher educational system.

What does all of this have to do with the higher education of Negroes? We need, once again, to look at the two sides of the equation—programs of higher education available to Negro students and the Negro students themselves. The first reality to face is that the American system of racial segregation and discrimination produces a tremendous proportion of Negro high school graduates who fall into Type 3 cited above—students with a high degree of native ability but serious educational handicaps. The most critical problem facing the higher education of Negroes centers upon this group (primarily because of its size).

The majority of Negro colleges should be striving to provide sound programs of higher education coupled with realistic efforts at remediation for the large proportion of their applicants who will need this. This is, of course, much easier said than done. One of the most critical problems facing higher education today is the development of techniques for identifying those persons with educational-socio-cultural handicaps who have sufficient native capacity to profit from remediation and then to move on to a sound higher educational program. Another critical problem is devising realistic remedial programs for these individuals, once they have been identified. Research efforts in these directions need to be intensified. Even so, these colleges will have to face up to the problems of how large a proportion of their functions can be devoted to remedial programs and still leave them able to provide a sound program of higher education.

There should be, however, some Negro colleges with the primary purpose of providing higher quality education for students with the highest potential for benefiting from such a program. These colleges will be competing more and more with "white" colleges in making all-out efforts to recruit such students. What with the relatively limited supply of such students available and the competition to enroll them, it is doubtful whether more than four or five Negro colleges, at best, could concentrate on this highest level quality of program. Even so, they would need special funding in order to provide the staff and facilities for relatively small student bodies.

Any Negro college *sincerely* pursuing this type of quality program (everyone is for excellence) will have to decide that it will be necessary to keep remedial work to a minimum. Each should provide some type of remedial work for students with very high potential but educational handicaps (once they can be reliably identified). But one can question whether a really high-quality program of higher education can be achieved when any substantial proportion of the entering students have woefully inadequate backgrounds.

One of the major pitfalls in discussing the higher education of Negroes comes from the sincere effort on the part of Negro colleges to do something to off-set the terrible effects of the prior educational experience of so many of their students. It is a hard thing to say but a large proportion of the students approaching these colleges are so handicapped that they will not be able to respond to remediation and then proceed on to a sound program of higher education. The correction for this situation is re-doubled efforts to see that the localities from which these students typically come are forced to provide the quality of lower education they should receive. There is just so far that the colleges can go to "re-make" individuals harmed by local educational systems deficient in just about every respect.

II

We are handicapped by our lack of knowledge and by our failure to investigate with objectivity or depth the problems that demand solutions.

The gaps in our knowledge are tragic in their implications and the abstractions employed will remain dubious and readily challengeable until more substantial research is undertaken and completed.

The experience of the historian will substantiate this conclusion. Historiography seems to fluctuate between subservience to the general—to a search for cycles, patterns of civilizations, and stages—and the interrelated particular, which represents, supposedly, a refusal to generalize from specific events and facts. When scholarship lacks a sound empirical foundation in detailed monographic research, its practitioners rely upon a high level of historical abstraction. In the early period of investigation in economic history, for example, Bücher, Gras, Marx, Roscher and others resorted to the classificatory system of stages. The next generation of economic historians (Lipson, Heaton and Clapham) professed a strong dissent against these abstractions, directing their energies into empirical investigation. It is significant to note W. W. Rostow's reversion to the stage-by-stage approach in his *Stages of Economic Growth* (1960)—a reversion forced upon him by the dearth of information about economic development in the new stages.

Currently most historians, who have at last learned to live with the social and behavioral sciences and with a journal devoted to contemporary history, accept with strong reservations such abstractions as "Africa Emergent" or "Third World." These historians agree that these abstractions represent conceptually justifiable attempts to convey some meaning to a complexity of facts and events. Finally, students of the past believe that they serve some constructive purpose in generalizing about the "uses and abuses" of abstractions in contemporary affairs. In a recently published study, Robert C. Stalmaker has observed:[2]

1. Abstractions may obscure rather than clearly describe a movement or institution. For example, the Renaissance and the Reformation have been described as ". . . the set of words with which we obscure the revolution or transition from the medieval to the modern state system."[3]

2. Social critics must exercise extreme care to avoid becoming prisoners of their abstractions—in believing that they have validity above and beyond the set of circumstances they originally conceptualized.

3. Abstractions are nevertheless of essential pragmatic significance since ". . . one can use such terms without committing oneself to a precise determination."[4] It is in this sense, for example, that the concept "revolu-

[2] Robert C. Stalmaker, "Events, Periods, and Institutions in Historians' Language," *History and Theory*, I (1967), 159–179.

[3] George Pettee, "Typology and Process" in Carl J. Friedrich (ed.), *Revolution* (New York: Atherton Press, 1967), p. 24.

[4] Stalmaker, *op. cit.*, p. 166.

tion" may be applied to the Civil Rights Movement. As long as no effort is made to reach a consensus as to its chronological dimensions and as to the degree of social transformation which is involved, it is an essential idiom by which analysis proceeds. Studies of the process of revolution do warn against identifying ". . . as revolutionary every profound change, in any sphere of civilization, which is produced suddenly, without sanction of law, and accompanied by outbursts of passion and violence."[5]

In his approach to the topic at hand, the social analyst is confronted with another aspect of the dilemma of conceptualization. For purposes of sharper perspective he feels constrained to remove, substantially, the institution from its total cultural setting. The distortions and misconceptions that result from this myopic approach are recognized, but it is believed that the disadvantages of this method are far outweighed by the analytical advantages derived from such abstracting. This, I assume, is the explanation for the dichotomy in treatment by some authorities on higher education between expositions about colleges and universities in the United States as a general phenomenon and expositions dealing specifically with "predominantly" Negro colleges and universities. Three significant works by influential specialists in the field treat higher education in the United States in approximately 1600 pages which contain only scattered explicit statements about Negro colleges and universities.[6] Most of the Conference papers, however, do assert that the problems of these institutions and their solution are a responsibility of the "Great Society" as a whole.

But perhaps what is required to resolve the dilemma about perspective is a broad examination of the most frequently employed term used to characterize our Conference problem, i.e., "The Predominantly Negro Colleges and Universities." As employed by Earl J. McGrath, it appears to apply "to those institutions in which Negro students comprise from 50 to 100 per cent of the full-time enrollments."[7] If one wishes to evaluate these same 123 colleges and universities by application of the concept of power (How organized? By whom exercised? And for what purposes?) the perspective must be broadened to include external factors. Power is hardly exercised by Negroes on the 51 campuses under State, county or municipal control. The influence of externally centered power

[5] Paul Schrecker, "Revolution as a Problem in the Philosophy of History" in Carl J. Friedrich (ed.), op. cit., p. 36.

[6] Logan Wilson, Emerging Patterns in American Higher Education (Washington, D. C.: American Council on Education, 1965); Nevitt Sanford, op. cit., "The Contemporary University: U.S.A.," Daedalus (Fall 1964).

[7] Earl J. McGrath, The Predominantly Negro Colleges and Universities in Transition (New York: Teachers College, Columbia University, 1965), p. 12.

upon such publicly controlled schools has, on occasion, assumed awesome proportions. Experiences at Alabama State, Tennessee A & I, Albany State, and Southern University in the early 1960s do not require repeating. The recently announced proposal by the North Carolina Board of Education to raise the "Scholastic Aptitude Test" score to 750 exemplifies another dimension of the threat of external power to these colleges and universities. If implemented this policy would, by reliable estimates, exclude 50 per cent of the Negro students in schools under the Board's jurisdiction.[8] To suggest that the above considerations would require a substition of "predominantly white" for "predominantly Negro" would serve no purpose other than to stress again the need for perspective derived from rigorous examination of the history of Negro colleges and universities. Some writers have suggested a more accurate appellation—the historically Negro college and university.

Certainly, neither the crisis which threatens the autonomy and integrity of higher education, nor the selective process by which the crisis subjects certain types of universities to severer stresses has any direct connection with the racial composition of the student body, faculty or administration of a particular college or university involved. Here again, a dichotomized perspective will not suffice.

The exigencies of a highly structured and computerized society have imposed problem-solving and subsidized research responsibilities upon the universities and some colleges. Foundations and government, dictating the terms and content, have become a "centrifugal force" shifting the center of power beyond the confines of the campus; simultaneously the residue of power within is shifting to research coordinators and budget officers.[9] Academic entrepreneurs, oblivious to the Berkeley experience, sometime teachers, reject the belief that ". . . research is for the purpose of enlivening their teaching and not necessarily solving problems posed by others . . . ." Here is a situation which provoked one observer to enquire: "Are Our Universities Schools?"[10] The campus-centered agency for general and applied research symbolizes the encroachment and must accept a large share of the responsibility for the deterioration of the educative function of universities which have allowed them wide latitude on the campuses.[11]

---

[8] Wm. P. Fidler, "Academic Freedom in the South Today," *AAUP Bulletin,* LI (Dec. 1965), 413–421; and Robert L. Green, "Why the Push to 'Upgrade' Negro Colleges?," *Southern Education Report,* III (July–August 1967), 23–26.

[9] W. Allen Wallis, "Forces in University Organization," *Daedalus* (Fall 1964), pp. 1078–79.

[10] Henry C. Johnson, "Are Our Universities Schools?," *Harvard Educational Review,* XXXV (Spring 1965), 165–177.

[11] *Ibid.,* p. 172.

The dangers inherent in a parochial approach to the problems of higher education are revealed with frightening clarity in this situation. Published materials dealing with this acute crisis ignore the Negro colleges and universities although foundation and government funds are exercising a growing influence on Negro campuses. If a challenge to the existence of a vital institution is to be met with any reasonable degree of effectiveness, all ramifications of the challenge must be clearly grasped and understood. Perhaps the impact of external encroachment upon certain Negro colleges and universities may assume a different form from that already comprehended. A broad comparative study of the "centrifugal" and "centripetal" forces," mentioned above, might produce common denominators aligning "Negro" universities with Harvard, Berkeley, and Chicago while "Negro" colleges might from this perspective be aligned with Amherst, Williams, and Antioch. The distinction would be based upon the relative effects of these pressures upon universities as opposed to colleges.

The relationship between "Negro" universities and colleges and the "top-rated" universities must be reassessed. For the "best" universities, the ones presumed to have a monopoly upon quality education are the very schools whose educational capabilities have deteriorated under the crushing impact of crisis. Professor Pettigrew has punctured the mystique surrounding them by stating that "an input-output 'value added' analysis of predominantly Negro colleges might well reveal a greater contribution to the final graduate product than many prestigious, predominantly white institutions."[12] One does not have to be a chauvinist to suggest that the faculties of "Negro" colleges and universities may make constructive contributions both to their own problems and to the resolution of the nationally oriented crisis in which higher education is enmeshed. The search for solutions must involve all educational institutions and must proceed on a clearly delineated reciprocal basis.

One wonders whether the "Negro" school's immediate task of combatting inadequate secondary preparation requires as many special programs as have evolved belatedly from foundation and government subsidy. The real key to the educational problems of "Negro" colleges and universities is money: money in amounts at the disposal of the "great" colleges and universities; money to provide freshman "tutorials," small classes, fewer lecture courses, and all of the other plans outlined in the "Muscatine Report" (On Berkeley).

III

Recent events serve to reawaken the interest in examining the administrative organization of higher educational institutions in the nation.

[12] Thomas F. Pettigrew, "A Social-Psychological View of the Predominantly Negro College," *Journal of Negro Education* XXXVI (1967).

Amidst the welter of controversy about the aims of higher education and its role in contemporary society, one indefeasible fact provides guidance in the investigation of structure in colleges and universities. That fact is the positive correlation between the excellence of universities on the one hand and the broad participation of faculties in academic affairs on the other.[13] This is an inextricable integrant of academic freedom; for academic freedom includes not only the personal prerogatives of writing and speaking in free and professionally responsible terms but also means rights and authority associated with the community of scholars. The excellent universities, therefore, are those which have guaranteed the full measure of academic freedom to their faculties, and through this guarantee have attracted and retained distinguished professors through whose efforts in scholarship and teaching excellent students have been attracted and enriched. Specifically, professors in the "prestigious" universities and colleges participate in the governance through control over curriculum, appointments, promotions and dismissals of colleagues; their influence over academic affairs extends from the department through the college and university levels. Evidence of a re-awakening of faculty concern about academic freedom in the universities where professional interests had been distracted by internal and external forces, mentioned above, is the most hopeful omen of a recapture of the spirit and content of quality education. Academic freedom has been extended to embrace serious concern with student rights. This is clearly evident in the widely endorsed "Statement on Government of Colleges and Universities," buttressed by a charter of student liberties formulated by five national campus-oriented organizations.[14]

Throughout the limited material on the structure of Negro colleges and universities runs a disturbing theme of paternalism. McGrath speaks of "the dominant, if not patriarchal, role of the president" as a long existing problem.[15] But apart from a trenchant indictment by the editor of the *Journal of Negro Education,* few Negro professional educators have expressed concern about the structural defects of their institutions.[16] At a time when faculty autonomy grew as an issue in white schools, Kelly Miller, W. E. B. Dubois, and others were preoccupied with displacing white presidents of such schools as Fisk, Hampton and Howard, and

[13] Robert M. MacIver, *Academic Freedom* (New York: Columbia University Press, 1955), p. 72.

[14] Reprint from *AAUP Bulletin* (Winter 1966) and *Washington Post,* July 21, 1967.

[15] McGrath, *op. cit.*, p. 123.

[16] Charles H. Thompson, "A 'New Deal' in the Administration of Negro Colleges?," *Journal of Negro Education,* VI (Oct. 1937), 589–591.

with increasing the number of Negro faculty members.[17] In a study peripheral to this question, "Problems of Faculty Morale," Daniel C. Thompson discovered that 50 teachers associated with 30 Negro schools were critical of "dictatorial" presidents; only about one-half of the deans and 13 per cent of heads of departments with whom he was in contact exercised any influence upon policy.[18] The most devastating attack, "Cowards from the Colleges," was written by Langston Hughes for the *Crisis* in 1934. His experiences were derived from visits to more than 50 schools and colleges where he was shocked by the ". . . docile dignity of the meek professors and well paid presidents." He concluded that from institutions where academic freedom and race consciousness were unknown "the race's emancipation will never come through its intellectuals."[19] Since these words were written some Negro colleges and universities have begun to follow the national trend toward faculty participation in college and university government.

It is difficult to see how Negro institutions of higher education can ignore historical experience. No matter what the focus of the educational program may be, distinguished achievement will prove a frustrating illusion unless faculty and students share in governance. There are of course the democratically oriented elements of motivation, morale and recruitment of able students and faculty. But perhaps the intangibles flowing from a democratic structure are as important as the structure itself. The esteem in which students and professors are held is high where professors are not considered as employees and the students are not viewed as suppliants; or where statutes are enriched by the tradition that a university is indeed an association of scholars and students.

Broader participation by students and professors in the governance of Negro colleges and universities should facilitate responses to the challenge of social reform and revolutionary militancy. Historically, universities have never, alone, been effective instruments of social change. But the Negro intellectuals must play a role in formulating new ideologies which meet the challenge of frustration and poverty-inspired militancy and the canons of rationality.

IV

The Conference gave encouragement to the *Journal* staff and supplied suggestions for further studies. One member of the faculty committee

[17] *Crisis*, XXXVI (Feb. 1929), 43–44; XL (Aug. 1933), 175–177; and XIII (Aug. 1946), 234–236.
[18] Daniel C. Thompson, "Problems of Faculty Morale," *Journal of Negro Education*, XXIX (Winter 1960), 43.
[19] Langston Hughes, "Cowards from the Colleges," *Crisis*, XLI (Aug. 1934), 226–228.

felt that much time was spent in discussing "instant" or "either-or" solutions to the problems. There was an impression of controversy and of airing unsupported opinion. It could be argued that what appeared to be controversy actually reflected several facets of a very complex problem. Practically all views expressed had a certain validity for some particular aspect of the general problem.

Another faculty member suggested a series of investigations that would include facets of administration and organization of the historically Negro college, comparative studies of institutions in the varying roles of serving diversified, similar, or differing populations, or as agents of change, or in meeting the needs of a changing society. He recommended a publication such as *Power, Presidents, and Professors,* a study of changes in structure and function at the University of North Carolina, as an example of a useful and challenging model for future work.

Some of our consultants and colleagues from other institutions have indicated the need for longitudinal studies, clinical investigations and intensive work on Negro family histories and the communities in which they have lived. As a result of the activities of civil rights organizations, the black power movement, Federal programs, or newer developments in employment, industry, etc., new approaches and re-thinking must characterize the next steps in this field.

There has been a call for providing more emphasis upon learning and for improving conditions under which students learn and faculty members teach. Researchers are concerned about the appropriate use of standardized tests with minority groups and with determining the best predictors of college success for the non-white population.

Several programs have been proposed and many have been tried at both predominantly white and predominantly Negro institutions. Questions have been raised about these programs, their effectiveness, the methods of evaluation and their implementation.

In looking back over previous yearbooks, we note the persistence of certain problems associated with the higher education of Negroes. In the initial chapter of the 1933 Yearbook of the *Journal,* the editor wrote:

"Our analysis revealed at least three general problems that the Negro college must solve immediately. *First,* it was observed that the socioeconomic status of the Negro college student creates a problem which deserves more attention than has been given to it previously. *Second,* it was pointed out that the supply of adequately-trained teachers in Negro colleges needs to be increased considerably; and, in view of the isolation of the Negro college, some special effort must be made to keep Negro college teachers in contact with the changing currents of thought in their particular fields, as well as in the field of education in general. *Third,* it has been indicated that the program of the Negro college needs to be reorganized either in content or emphasis, or both, to insure the production of intelligent leadership for the Negro masses—an objective which it fails to realize at the present time."[20]

These same observations seem pertinent in 1967. Efforts have been made, nevertheless, to effect improvements. Our 1966 Yearbook reported some recent efforts. The supplementary section of this volume includes some additional papers and information that may be suggestive of new approaches and procedures.

[20] Chas. H. Thompson, "Introduction: The Problem of Negro Higher Education," *Journal of Negro Education* II (Summer 1933), 270–271.

21 *Differential Characteristics of Superior and Unselected Negro College Students*[1]

MARTIN D. JENKINS & CONSTANCE M. RANDALL
Department of Education, Howard University

This paper carefully examines the differences between a group of superior and a group of unselected Negro college students in order to enumerate some of the background factors related to superior performance. The work is also of interest in that it is a survey study in which the authors were attempting to demonstrate significant differences between the groups in which they were interested. This is a comparable scientific approach to the *Experimental Group-Control Group* design discussed earlier with the exception that here we are concerned with differences between two separate groups, the one superior to the other in academic achievement. Care should be taken in examining the various tables because they contain a wealth of information concerning the students that were surveyed. The authors discuss the many background factors that serve to distinguish superior from unselected Negro college students.

A. THE PROBLEM

The present study has its origin in one of the studies of the National Survey of Higher Education of Negroes, conducted by the United States Office of Education during 1940–41 (8, Ch. 5). The survey study, which included as subjects 5,578 freshmen and seniors in 48 Negro institutions of higher education, is without question the most comprehensive study of Negro college students which has been made.

Among the principal findings of the survey study were the following: that, in general, freshmen and seniors in institutions of higher education of Negroes attain low rank on standardized psychological and achieve-

SOURCE. Reprinted from *The Journal of Social Psychology*, 1948, **27**, 187–202, with permission of the senior author and The Journal Press.
[1] Received in the Editorial Office on March 15, 1947.

198

ment tests; that students score throughout the range of these tests, the best exceeding the 99th percentile of the test norms; that when group medians are considered, males are superior to females in test performance; that students are drawn predominantly from homes of low socio-economic and educational level; that students are recruited largely from southern, urban, public, segregated elementary and secondary schools; that there is a significant relationship between test performance and such factors as parental occupation, place of previous schooling, and type of college attended. These survey findings were derived from an analysis of the total group performance; no attempt was made to examine, in any detail, characteristics of subgroups within the sample. Often the information gained from study of deviating cases is fully as important as that gained from study of typicals. Certainly in the present instance, where the typical test performance falls so far below the national norm, study of the superior deviates seems especially important, since these cases may serve to illuminate the causes for the generally poor performance of the larger group. We are concerned here, consequently, with an examination of the characteristics of the upper deviates in psychometric intelligence and achievement.

Specifically, the problem of the present study is as follows: What differences in background factors exist between a superior group and an unselected group of Negro college students?

Previous studies of superior students (1, 5, 15, 16, 19, 20), of Negro college students (2, 3, 4, 8, 10, 12, 13), and of gifted children (9, 11, 14, 21, 22) have all found a relationship between superior psychometric intelligence and various social and educational background factors. The studies concerned with Negro populations have revealed that Negro groups conform to the same general pattern as white groups in this respect.

On the basis of the findings of previous studies we should expect to find that the superior students in this study emanated from substantially higher socio-economic and educational strata than an unselected group of Negro college students.

B. SOURCES OF DATA AND PROCEDURE

The primary data are those of the National Survey study (8, Ch. 5) and consist of the test performance and certain personal data of 4,032 freshmen in 23 colleges and 1,546 seniors in 45 colleges. These subjects, all of whom are Negro students, constitute a strictly representative sample of freshmen and seniors in attendance at racially segregated institutions of higher education in the United States. The following tests were administered: *American Council on Education Psychological Examination,* 1940 Form (Freshmen); *Coöperative General Culture Test, Form P* (seniors); *Cooperative English Test C-2, Reading Comprehensive* (freshmen and seniors); and the *Test of General Knowledge of the Negro* (freshmen and seniors). An inquiry form, designed to elicit information relative to the familial, social, economic, and educational background of the subjects was also administered to both freshmen and seniors.

The present study consists of a statistical comparison of "superior" freshmen and seniors with "survey" freshmen and seniors on selected items. The superior freshmen are the upper 4 per cent of the survey freshman population on the basis of performance on the *American Council on Education Psychological Examination.* The superior seniors are the upper 5 per cent of the survey senior population on the basis of performance on the *General Culture Test.* It is to be observed that the superior freshmen and seniors are also members of the survey groups.

C. FINDINGS

1. *Test Performance*

Differences in the test performance of the survey and superior groups are shown on Table 1. The median score of the superior seniors on the

TABLE 1

Differences in Test Performance Superior and Survey Groups $\dfrac{D}{(PE_{diff.})}$

	N		Md.		Q		$\dfrac{D}{PE_{diff.}}$
	Survey Group	Superior Group	Survey Group	Superior Group	Survey Group	Superior Group	
General Culture							
Test (Seniors)	1,482	78	90.1	235	40.5	15.3	87
ACE Psychological Examination							
(Freshmen)	3,684	159	56	117	18	3.2	358
Reading Comprehension							
(Seniors)	1,496	77	50.1	68.3	6.3	4.0	35
(Freshmen)	3,187	129	42.5	59.8	5.2	5.8	34
Knowledge of Negro							
(Seniors)	1,469	77	52	66.6	9.0	6.6	19
(Freshmen)	3,050	131	37	47.8	7.0	5.3	17

General Culture Test is 235. This score, which falls at the 88th percentile of the test norms, is 78 percentile points above the median score of the survey seniors.[2]

The $\dfrac{D}{PE_{diff.}}$ of 87 indicates complete reliability of the difference between the two medians.[3] The median score of the superior freshmen on the American Council of Education Psychological Examination is 117, which falls at the 68th percentile of the test norms and 64 percentiles points above the median score of the survey freshmen. The $\dfrac{D}{PE_{diff.}}$ is 358.

The upper limits attained by the groups on these two tests is of some significance. On the *General Culture Test* 2.3 per cent of the survey seniors and 42 per cent of the superior seniors score at or above the 90th percentile of the sophomore test norms. On the *A.C.E. Psychological Examination,* .5 per cent of the survey freshmen and 15 per cent of the superior freshmen score at or above the 90th percentile of the test norms. Further, in both the freshman and senior distributions there are cases above the 99th percentile of the test norms. The percentages of cases found at these high levels is, of course, much smaller than that expected in a group of representative American college students. Nevertheless, the very existence of these cases is of great importance in that they prove that race, *per se*, is not a delimiting factor in the abilities measured by the tests.

In the two other tests, which were administered, both to freshmen and seniors, the superior groups are likewise reliably superior to the survey groups. On the *Reading Comprehension Test* the superior senior median score is 68.3; this score is at the 83rd percentile of the test norms and is 63 percentile points above the median of the survey seniors. The median score of the superior freshmen on this test is 59.8, the 55th percentile and 50 percentile points above the survey freshman group. The $\dfrac{D}{PE_{diff.}}$ for the

[2] The percentile comparisons for seniors are based on the sophomore test norms for the *General Culture Test* and the freshman test norms for the *Reading Comprehension Test.*

[3] Where the ratio $\dfrac{D}{PE_{diff.}}$ is greater than 4.0 the obtained difference regarded as statistically significant. The probable error of the difference between two medians is formed by the formula

$$PE_{diff.} = \sqrt{PE^2_{(md\ 1)} + PE^2_{(md\ 2)}}$$

Attention is called to the fact that since the members of the superior groups are also included in the survey groups the actual differences between the superior and non-superior groups are somewhat greater than those found throughout this study.

senior groups is 35 and for the freshmen groups 34. On the test of *General Knowledge of the Negro* the $\frac{D}{PE_{diff.}}$ is 19 for the senior groups and 17 for the freshman groups. There were no previous norms available for this test.

It is seen, then, that the superior groups excel the survey groups not only on the selecting instruments but on tests of reading and general information as well. The differences are significant at a very high level, of course, due to the method used in selecting the superior groups.

2. *Familial Factors*

Presented in this section are differences between the superior and survey groups in a number of familial items. In each instance the differences found are in accord with the hypothesis and they have high statistical reliability.

A. INCOME OF PARENTS (Table 2).[4] The students in the superior groups

TABLE 2

Differences in Background Items Between Superior and Survey Groups $\dfrac{D}{PE_{diff.}}$

			Md.		Q		$\dfrac{D}{PE_{diff.}}$
	Survey Group	Superior Group	Survey Group	Superior Group	Survey Group	Superior Group	
Income of Parents							
Seniors (Annual)	1,195	66	$1,046	$1,457	433	550	4.7
Freshmen (Monthly)	3,770	153	$ 71	$ 126	38	40	12.2
Number of Siblings							
(Freshmen)	3,332	147	3.7	2.2	2.1	1.8	8.8
Chronological Age							
Seniors	1,482	78	22.5	21.6	1.3	1.25	3.7
Freshmen	4,024	159	19.1	18.8	1.0	0.8	5.0

tend to have significantly higher familial incomes than students in the survey groups. The median reported income of parents of the senior group is $1,457 per year and of parents of the survey group $1,046. The $\frac{D}{PE_{diff.}}$ is 4.7. The median reported monthly income of the parents of the superior freshmen is $126 per month and of parents of the survey freshman $71 per month. The $\frac{D}{PE_{diff.}}$ is 12.2. Perhaps the most striking fact

[4] Current incomes are in general much higher than in 1940 when the original data were collected.

revealed by these data is the decidedly low income of the parents of both survey and superior groups. In general, even the superior Negro college students come from homes which can hardly afford the luxury of a college education for their children.

B. OCCUPATIONAL STATUS OF PARENTS. Parents in the high status occupations contribute a disproportionately large share of the superior groups. A majority of the members of the superior groups, however, are recruited from occupational groupings below the professional and business levels. It is to be seen in Table 3 that among the superior freshmen the following groupings contribute more than their expected number of subjects: Business (3.7), clerical and government service (2.8), professional (1.8), and interestingly enough, semi-skilled labor (1.3). On the other hand, the following groupings contribute less than their expected number of subjects: Personal and domestic service (.22), farming (.54), unskilled labor (.61) and skilled labor (.73). What these proportions mean is seen, for example, in the following comparison: in an equal population of subjects drawn from parents in the business grouping and in the personal and domestic service grouping, the former would contribute about 17 times as many subjects (3.7:.22) as the latter. These proportionate contributions should not divert attention from the fact that, in the aggregate, the largest *number* of superior students are drawn from the lower occupational levels. Sixty-one per cent of the superior freshmen and 54 per cent of the superior seniors are drawn from occupations below the professional and business level.

We have used chi-square (χ^2) throughout to test the reliability of the differences between the survey and superior groups in those cases where the data are assembled in non-quantitative categories.[5] For the occupational grouping of fathers of freshmen $\chi^2 = 115.12$. (Here there are seven degrees of freedom and a χ^2 of 18.475 would show significance at the 1 per cent level). We may infer with confidence that the observed differences are completely reliable.

The occupational level of the senior groups is quite similar to that of the freshmen and consequently will not be analyzed here in detail. Although the obtained X^2 of 28.74, which is significant at the 1 per cent level is probably not altogether accurate because of the small frequencies within the categories, there is no question but that the differences between the superior and survey groups at this point are reliable.

[5] $\chi^2 = \dfrac{(o - e)^2}{e}$ where o = the observed frequency and e = the expected frequency.[e] *Cf.* (6, pp. 239 ff.).

TABLE 3
Differences Between Superior and Survey Groups in Familial Background Items (χ^2)

Items	Survey Group N	Per Cent	Superior Group (N)	Number Expected in Superior Group	Proportion of Expectancy*	$\dfrac{(o-e)^2}{e}$	χ^2
Occupational Groupings of Fathers (Seniors)	1,435	100.0	72				28.74
Professional	272	19.0	26	13.7	1.90	1.10	
Business	114	7.9	7	5.7	1.22	.30	
Clerical	92	6.4	7	4.6	1.52	1.25	
Skilled	249	17.4	11	12.5	.88	1.80	
Personal and Domestic	245	17.1	2	12.3	.16	.86	
Farming	238	16.6	9	12.0	.75	.75	
Semi-Skilled	78	5.4	7	3.9	1.8	2.46	
Unskilled	147	10.2	3	7.3	.41	2.53	
Occupational Grouping of Fathers (Freshmen)	3,758	100.0	155				115.1
Professional	454	12.1	32	18.8	1.8	9.26	
Business	184	4.9	28	7.6	3.7	54.74	
Clerical	190	5.0	22	7.8	2.8	25.90	
Skilled	630	16.8	19	26.0	.73	1.50	
Personal and Domestic	758	20.2	7	31.3	.22	12.46	
Farming	763	20.3	17	31.5	.54	6.66	
Semi-Skilled	381	10.1	20	15.7	1.3	1.15	
Unskilled	398	10.6	10	16.3	.61	2.45	

Table 3 (*Continued*)

Items	Survey Group N	Survey Group Per Cent	Superior Group (N)	Number Expected in Superior Group	Proportion of Expectancy*	$\dfrac{(o-e)^2}{e}$	χ^2
Education of Fathers (Freshmen)	3,823	100.0	151				60.3
Elementary School only	1,979	51.7	41	78.1	.53	17.62	
High School, Grades 9–12	1,056	27.6	46	41.7	1.10	.44	
College 1–4 years	559	14.6	39	22.0	1.77	13.14	
Graduate or Professional	229	5.9	25	8.9	2.80	29.10	
Education of Mothers (Freshmen)	3,922	100.0	149				31.3
Elementary School only	1,592	40.5	35	60.3	.58	10.6	
High School, Grades 9–12	1,429	36.4	53	54.2	.97	0	
College, 1–4 years	799	20.3	53	30.2	1.75	16.3	
Graduate or Professional	102	2.6	8	3.9	2.1	4.4	

* Proportion of expectancy $= \dfrac{o}{e}$ where o = number of cases in the superior group and e = number of cases expected in the superior groups on the basis of the proportion in the survey group.

C. EDUCATIONAL STATUS OF PARENTS. Parents of high educational status contribute a disproportionately large share of the superior group. A majority of members of the superior groups, however, come from homes in which the parents themselves have not attended college. The median father of the superior group has had approximately 4 years more of schooling than the median father of the survey group; for the mothers the difference in medians is about three years. Shown in Table 3 are distributions of the educational levels attained by the parents of the survey and superior freshmen. The highest proportion of expectancy is shown by the parents who have had graduate or professional training (2.80 for fathers and 2.05 for mothers), and the lowest by the parents who have had less than eight years of formal schooling (.53 for fathers and .58 for mothers). It is to be noted, however, that among the superior freshmen 57 per cent of the fathers and 60 per cent of the mothers had not reached the college level.

These differences have high statistical reliability. χ^2 for education of fathers is 60.3, and for the education of mothers 31.3. Both of these are significant at the 1 per cent level (with three degrees of freedom a χ^2 of 11.34 would show significance at the 1 per cent level).

D. NUMBER OF SIBLINGS. Members of the superior groups are drawn from smaller families than members of the survey group. Thirteen per cent of the superior freshmen and 5 per cent of the survey freshmen are "only" children. In each group, however, there are families in which there are 10 or more children. As shown in Table 2 the median survey freshman has 3.7 siblings and the median superior freshman 2.2 siblings. (Since the subjects themselves are not included in these figures the median number of children in the families would be 4.7 and 3.2 respectively.) The $\dfrac{D}{PE_{diff.}}$ of 8.8 indicates that the difference is statistically reliable.

3. Educational Background Factors

Discussed in this section are differences between the superior and survey groups in several items of educational background. Here again, the differences found are in accord with the hypothesis and in most instances they have high statistical reliability.

A. GEOGRAPHIC LOCATION OF ELEMENTARY AND SECONDARY SCHOOLS AT-TENDED.[6] Among both freshmen and seniors the students who attended

---

[6] Attention is drawn here to the significance of this item especially as it relates to Negro students. There are distinct differences in the average quality of the schools attended by Negroes in the northern and southern states. On every objective criterion, such as per capita expenditures, teacher salaries, length of school term, teacher load,

northern elementary and secondary schools provide a disproportionately large share of the superior groups. This tendency is especially marked among the freshmen where an actual majority are products of these schools.

The data relative to the location of the elementary and secondary school attendance of the freshman and senior groups are presented in Table 4. In each instance the northern schools contribute more than their expected share to the superior groups, the proportion of expectancy ranging from 3.6 for place of elementary education of freshmen, to 1.9 for place of elementary schooling of seniors. The border-state schools likewise contribute more than their expectancy in each instance, ranging from 2.3 for place of secondary schooling of seniors (the only instance in which the border-state students are superior to the northern students) to 1.1 for place of elementary schooling of freshmen. The southern schools consistently contribute less than their share of expectancy ranging from .57 for place of elementary schooling of seniors to .30 for place of elementary schooling of freshmen.

The observed differences are highly reliable in each instance, and all are significant at the 1 per cent level. The χ^2 values are as follows: Place of secondary schooling of freshmen, 224.2; place of elementary schooling of freshmen, 195.8; place of elementary schooling of seniors, 33.8; place of secondary schooling of seniors 23.9. (With two degrees of freedom characteristic of all these distributions, χ^2 value of 9.21 is required for significance at the 1 per cent level.)

B. TYPE OF SECONDARY SCHOOL ATTENDED. Among both freshmen and seniors, students who had attended schools not segregated by race contribute a disproportionately large share of the superior groups; the racially segregated schools, however, contribute a larger number of cases due to the fact that the survey group is composed largely of products of these schools. As may be seen in Table 4 the products of non-segregated schools furnish 2.1 their expected share among seniors and 6.1 among freshmen. The χ^2 values of 18.31 and 195.5 respectively, are significant at

etc., the average southern school at both the elementary and secondary levels, is greatly inferior to the average northern school. The border state schools (i.e., the northern tier of southern states, including the District of Columbia) are in general superior to the southern schools and inferior to northern schools. This difference in facilities is reflected in the achievement of students. Among the survey group, for example, northern students were, *on the average*, superior to border-state students who were in turn superior to southern students. The extent of these differences is revealed by the fact that among the survey groups, less than 4 per cent of the southern rural freshmen exceeded the median of the northern freshmen! *Cf.* (8, pp. 59–61).

TABLE 4

Differences Between Superior and Survey Groups in Educational Background Items (χ^2)

Items	Survey Group N	Survey Group Per Cent	Superior Group (N)	Number Expected in Superior Group	Proportion of Superior Group Expectancy	$\dfrac{(o-e)^2}{e}$	χ^2
Place of Elementary School							
Attendance (Seniors)	1,474	100.0	74				33.78
Northern States	244	17	24	12.6	1.9	10.32	
Southern States	1,054	71	30	52.5	.57	9.64	
Border States	176	12	20	8.9	2.3	13.82	
Place of Elementary School							
Attendance (Freshmen)	3,180	100.0	157				195.8
Northern States	520	16	87	25.1	3.5	152.7	
Southern States	2,040	64	35	100.5	.35	42.7	
Border States	620	20	35	31.4	1.1	0.4	
Place of Secondary School							
Attendance (Seniors)	1,465	100.0	74				23.90
Northern States	252	17	29	12.6	2.5	2.13	
Southern States	1,041	71	27	52.6	.56	12.45	
Border States	172	12	18	8.9	1.5	9.32	
Place of Secondary School							
Attendance (Freshmen)	3,676	100.0	158				224.2
Northern States	590	16	91	25.3	3.6	170.6	
Southern States	2,424	66	31	104.3	.30	51.6	
Border States	662	18	36	28.4	1.3	2.0	

Table 4 (Continued)

Items	Survey Group N	Survey Group Per Cent	Superior Group (N)	Number Expected in Superior Group	Proportion of Expectancy	$\dfrac{(o-e)^2}{e}$	χ^2
Type of Secondary School (Seniors)	1,471	100.0	74				18.31
Segregated	1,247	83	47	61	.77	3.21	
Non-Segregated	224	17	27	13	2.1	15.10	
Type of Secondary School (Freshmen)	3,173	100.0	157				195.5
Segregated	2,684	85	71	133.5	1.88	29.3	
Non-Segregated	489	15	86	23.5	.27	166.2	
Type of Elementary School (Seniors)	1,474	100.0	76				5.9
Urban	1,220	83	71	63	1.1	1.0	
Rural	254	17	5	13	.38	4.9	
Type of Elementary School (Freshmen)	3,180	100.0	159				6.1
Urban	2,601	82	142	130	1.1	1.1	
Rural	579	18	17	29	.59	5.0	

the 1 per cent level. (With one degree of freedom, a χ^2 value of 6.63 is required for significance at the 1 per cent level.)

Members of the superior group, both proportionately and numerically, are drawn more largely from urban than rural schools. The data are presented in Table 4. Among both the seniors and freshmen the urban group contributes 1.1 times its expectancy. This index for the students who had attended rural schools is .38 for seniors and .59 for freshmen. The χ^2 values of 5.9 for seniors and 6.1 for freshmen are significant at the 2 per cent level. (A χ^2 value of 6.63 is required for significance at the 1 per cent level.)

4. Chronological Age and Sex Ratio

A. CHRONOLOGICAL AGE. The typical superior student is somewhat younger than the typical unselected college student. The median ages of the superior and survey seniors (Table 2) are 21.6 and 22.5 years, respectively, and of the superior and survey freshmen 18.8 and 19.1 respectively. The age difference between the senior groups is fully reliable $\dfrac{D}{PE_{diff.}} = 5.0$ while the difference between the freshman groups does not quite meet the test of statistical reliability $\dfrac{D}{PE_{diff.}} = 3.66$.

B. SEX RATIO. There are proportionately more males than females in the superior groups than in the survey groups. In both the senior and freshman survey groups the sex distribution is 43 per cent male, 57 per cent female. In the superior senior group, however, males constitute 50 per cent of the total and in the superior freshman group they are 67 per cent of the total. Thus, the true sex ratios (i.e., the ratio in a population drawn from an equal number of males and females) are 1.3:1 for the superior senior group and 2.6:1 for the superior freshman group.

The difference between the survey and superior groups is statistically reliable in the case of freshmen ($\chi^2 = 36.3$, significant at the 1 per cent level), but unreliable in the case of the seniors ($\chi^2 = 1.58$, significant at the 30 per cent level).

C. TYPE OF COLLEGE ATTENDED. There is a distinct tendency for the better colleges (i.e., those which rank high in the median performance of students on standardized examinations) to attract more superior freshmen and to produce more superior seniors than the poorer colleges. It is particularly noticeable that the poorer colleges infrequently produce superior seniors. Of the 45 colleges from which the survey seniors were drawn, only 21 contributed cases to the superior group. Eighteen of these 21 institutions are at or above the median of the distribution of the institutions on the basis of performance of students on standardized examinations and only three are below the median. The freshmen were drawn from 23 colleges; 16 of these institutions contributed cases to the superior group. The seven colleges which did not contribute cases to the superior group were all poorer colleges (as defined above).

5. Sex Differences in Test Performance

In both the survey and superior groups the males are, in general, superior to the females in test performance although, in the superior groups these differences are not statistically reliable. As may be seen in Table 5, in the survey groups the males are distinctly superior to the females on the *General Culture Test*, the *American Council on Education Psychological Examination*, and the *Test of General Knowledge of the Negro*, and slightly superior on the *Reading Comprehension Test*. Among the superior groups the general pattern of the test performance of the males and females is the same as in the survey group, except that in *Reading Comprehension* the females are superior to the males; none of the differences in this series, however, is statistically significant. One other significant fact revealed in Table 5 is that the females, throughout, reveal less variability than the males.

D. DISCUSSION

The findings of this study of Negro college students, relative to the relationship of social and educational background factors to performance on intelligence and achievement tests, are consistent with, and serve to verify the findings of, previous studies concerned with this problem.

The major conclusion to be derived from the findings of the present study is that Negro college students selected on the basis of their superior psychometric intelligence and test achievement, differ significantly from unselected college students in important social and educational background items. By this we mean that students who come from superior elementary and secondary schools and whose parents are of high educational, occupational, and economic level are much more likely to reveal superior ability at the college level than are students not so characterized. Yet there is an equally important conclusion, namely, that these cultural background factors are by no means altogether crucial, since, numerically superior Negro college students are drawn predominantly from homes of relatively low educational, occupational, and economic level and, to a large extent, from sub-average elementary and secondary schools. To indicate that differences in environmental factors are not the only determinants of differences in scholastic performance is not, however, to

TABLE 5

Sex Differences in Test Performance in Survey and Superior Groups

Item	Survey Group				Survey Group			
	N	$Md.$	Q	$PE_{diff.}$	N	$Md.$	Q	$\dfrac{D}{PE_{diff.}}$
General Culture (Seniors)								
Male	653	96.8	39.6	4.3	39	237.5	22.2	2.9
Female	846	86.0	37.5		39	231.8	13.5	
Reading Comprehension (Seniors)								
Male	644	50.2	6.6	.24	38	67.3	4.5	2.3*
Female	852	50.1	5.9		39	69.4	3.4	
Knowledge of Negro (Senior)								
Male	638	55.2	8.8	8.5	39	69.8	9.3	3.8
Female	831	50.4	8.4		38	63.7	5.6	
ACE Psychological Examination (Freshmen)								
Male	1,611	163.0	19.5	15.8	106	117.7	9.4	1.1
Female	2,073	51.0	164.0		53	116.3	5.2	
Reading Comprehension (Freshmen)								
Male	1,287	43.0	5.7	3.3	89	57.9	6.3	1.0*
Female	1,900	42.2	4.8		39	58.7	5.1	
Knowledge of Negro (Freshmen)								
Male	1,242	40.0	7.0	12.4	91	48.9	6.8	.76
Female	1,808	36.0	7.0		40	47.9	6.2	

* Difference favors females.

deny the significance of environment in the development of the individual. These conclusions are consistent with the view, held by almost all psychologists, that heredity sets the limits of development and that environmental factors determine the level of development within these limits.

Although, in this study, causal relationships have not, of course, been demonstrated, the most likely inference to be drawn is that psychometric intelligence and scholastic achievement tend to fluctuate with environment; that is, poor environment depresses and good environment raises the level of performance. In light of this conclusion we may reiterate the trite statement that racial comparisons between white and Negroes with respect to psychometric intelligence and scholastic achievement are apt to prove misleading in the absence of control of the educational and social background factors.

It may be pointed out further that our findings at this point help to illuminate the causes of the low test performance of the unselected Negro college population. The characteristics significantly associated with superior performance-high educational level of parents, superior schools, etc., are the exact reverse of the characteristics of the unselected Negro college population, which comes from homes of low educational level, from poor schools etc. It can readily be predicted, therefore, that a population so characterized will reveal low average performance on intelligence and achievement tests.

Finally, the findings serve to emphasize the importance of giving attention to the variability of a group as well as to its central tendency. The population of Negro college students from which our superior groups was drawn reveals low median performance on intelligence and achievement tests. There may be a tendency, consequently, to conclude that Negro college students have lower psychometric intelligence and scholastic ability than white college students and that their educational needs are different from those of other American college students. As a matter of fact, many Negro college students have superior ability, and significantly enough, some are found in the highest one per cent of test norms. These data serve to support the generalization that one should never think of differences in terms of *race* but rather in terms of *individual* variation.

References

1. Applesby, F. L. A study of American Rhodes Scholars. *J. Hered.*, 1939, **30**, 493–495.
2. Caliver, A. A Background Study of Negro College Students. U. S. Office

of Education, Bulletin No. 8. Washington: Government Printing Office, 1933.

3. Davenport, R. K. Background study of a Negro freshman population. *J. Negro Educ.*, 1939, **8**, 186–197.

4. Davis, T. E. A study of Fisk freshmen from 1928–1930. *J. Negro Educ.*, 1933, **2**, 477–483.

5. Eckert, R. E. Analyzing the superior college student. *Sch. & Soc.*, 1935, **41**, 69–72.

6. Edwards, A. L. Statistical Analysis. New York: Rhinehart, 1946.

7. Garrett, H. E. Statistics in Psychology and Education. New York: Longmans, Green, 1932.

8. *General Studies of Colleges for Negroes* (Volume II of the National Survey of the Higher Education of Negroes). U. S. Office of Education Miscel. No. 6, Vol. II. Washington: Government Printing Office, 1942.

9. Hollingsworth, L. S. Gifted Children: Their Nature and Nurture. New York: Macmillan, 1926.

10. Jenkins, M. D., and Phillips, M. V. The characteristics of Negro College students who score at or above the 90th percentile on the ACE Psychological Examination. (In preparation for publication.)

11. Jenkins, M. D. A. socio-psychological study of Negro children of superior intelligence. *J. Negro Educ.*, 1936, **5**, 175–190.

12. Johnson, C. S. The Negro College Graduate. Chapel Hill: Univ. North Carolina Press, 1936.

13. Johnson, J. H. Graduates of Northern High Schools as Students at a Southern Negro College. *J. Negro Educ.*, 1933, **2**, 484–486.

14. Lewis, W. D. Comparative study of personalities, interests, and home background of gifted children of superior and inferior educational achievement. *J. Gen. Psychol.*, 1941, **59**, 207–218.

15. Moore, M. A Study of Young High School Graduates. New York: Bureau of Publications, Teachers College, Columbia University, 1931.

16. Portenier, L. Aspects of socio-economic status which differentiate university students. *J. Appl. Psychol.*, 1938, **22**, 261–270.

17. Posey, T. E. Socio-economic background of freshmen at West Virginia State College. *J. Negro Educ.*, 1933, **2**, 466–476.

18. Randall, M. Differential characteristics of superior and unselected Negro college students. Unpublished Master's Thesis, Howard University, Washington, D. C., 1944.

19. Speight, H. E. Who is the superior student? *Sch. & Soc.*, 1938, **48**, 545–549.

20. Struit, D. B. Differential characteristics of superior and inferior students. *Sch. & Soc.*, 1937, **46**, 733–776.

21. Terman, L. M., *et al.* Genetic Studies of Genius: Vol. I, Mental and Physical Traits of a Thousand Gifted Children. Stanford University: Stanford Univ. Press, 1925.

22. Witty, P. A. A Study of One Hundred Gifted Children. Univ. Kansas Bull. Educ., 1930, No. 13.

22 Negro Academic Motivation and Scholastic Achievement[1]

ROBERT L. GREEN & WILLIAM W. FARQUHAR
College of Education, Michigan State University

This brief article examines the relationship between Negro academic motivation and scholastic achievement, and the references cited are particularly worthwhile for the student interested in this very complex problem. In view of the fact that the authors were unable to demonstrate a significant relationship between aptitude and achievement for Negro males, a highly unusual result, the article suggests some significant areas for further study and research.

Separate samples of 233 Negro and 515 Caucasian high school students of both sexes, randomly selected to represent a wide range of socioeconomic environments, were tested as to verbal aptitude, academic achievement, and academic motivation. Except for Negro males, both samples obtained significant correlations between verbal aptitude and achievement. The Negro males showed no such relationship between aptitude and achievement, but academic-motivation tests (the M scales) correlated significantly with achievement for all groups of interest.

Recent studies have indicated that the typical Negro student fails to achieve as well (Boykin, 1955; Bullock, 1950), drops out of school more frequently (Conant, 1961), and demonstrates a lower need for achievement than his Caucasian counterpart (Lott & Lott, 1963). Many edu-

SOURCE. Green, R. L. and Farquhar, W., "Negro Academic Motivation and Scholastic Achievement," *Journal of Educational Psychology*, **LVI**, 1965, 241–243. Copyright 1965, by The American Psychological Association and reproduced by permission.

[1] Based in part on the first-named author's doctoral dissertation submitted to Michigan State University, December 7, 1962.

cators assert that the school achievement (grade-point average) of both groups is related to achievement motivation and academic aptitude.

Norton (1959) found that the total Differential Aptitude Test (DAT) correlated significantly with science-achievement scores of white ninth-grade males and females. Jacobs (1959) found that the DAT Verbal Reasoning correlated significantly with grade-point average (GPA) for senior high school males and females.

Additional studies (Bennett, Seashore, & Wesman, 1959) have demonstrated that cognitive and personality factors correlate with achievement for Caucasian students. However, few have attempted to explore the relationship between the latter factors and achievement for Negro student populations.

The purpose of the present study was to investigate the relationship of personality and cognitive factors with academic achievement (GPA) for eleventh-grade Negro and white students of both sexes.

METHOD

Subjects

The Negro sample consisted of 104 males and 129 females selected from two Detroit-area high schools with a total eleventh-grade school enrollment of 700 students. The schools were selected a priori in order to represent a full range of socioeconomic environments.

The Caucasian sample, tested by the second author, consisted of 254 males and 261 females randomly selected from a population of 4,200 eleventh-grade students from nine high schools in eight Michigan cities.[2]

Measures

Three measures were gathered on both samples:

1. Michigan State M Scales—a theoretically based objective measure of academic motivation. The M scales consist of four subtests which were designed to assess the following motivational components: (a) the need for academic achievement (Generalized Situational Choice Inventory), (b) academic self-concept (Word Rating List), (c) occupational aspirations (Preferred Job Characteristics Scale), and (d) academic personality factors (Human Traits Inventory). The total scale contains 139 male and 136 female items.

2. Aptitude Measure—the verbal score of the School and College

[2] For a full description of the sample-selection procedure and the development of the Michigan State M scales, see Office of Education Cooperative Research Project No. 846.

Ability Test (SCAT) and the Verbal Reasoning score of the DAT were obtained from the school records of the Negro and Caucasian students, respectively.[3]

3. School Achievement (GPA)—each student's GPA was computed using ninth- and tenth-grade subjects. Only academic subjects were included, that is, those requiring homework.

RESULTS

The correlations between achievement (GPA) and aptitude for both races and sexes are shown in Table 1. As indicated in this table, there is

TABLE 1

Correlations Between Aptitude and M-scale Subtests with Grade-Point Average as a Function of Race and Sex

Sample		Aptitude and M-Scale Subtests Correlated with Grade-Point Average					
Race and Sex	Verbal Aptitude	GSCI	HTI	PJCS	WRL	M Total	N
Negro							
Male	−.01	.26*	.14	.30*	.36*	.37*	104
Female	.25*	.46*	.40*	.34*	.64*	.55*	129
White							
Male	.62*	.50*	.42*	.32*	.51*	.50*	254
Female	.21*	.21*	.29*	.18*	.34*	.43*	261

Note.—Abbreviations used: GSCI, Generalized Situational Choice Inventory; PJCS, Preferred Job Characteristics Scale. The variability of verbal aptitude and the HTI subtest for the Negro Male sample did not exceed the variability of the other subtests.

* $p < .05$.

no correlation between verbal aptitude and achievement (GPA) for Negro males despite the significant correlation between verbal aptitude and GPA for Negro females. All motivation subtests—except the male Human Traits Inventory (HTI)—correlate significantly with achievement for both Negro males and females. The self-concept—Word Rating List (WRL)—is the best single prediction of achievement for the Negro sample.

[3] Both the SCAT and DAT Verbal tests correlate comparably with the American Council on Education (ACE) Linguistic test. SCAT Verbal and ACE Linguistic = .89, DAT Verbal and ACE Linguistic = .84 females, .74 males.

Both verbal aptitude and the motivation scales correlate significantly with achievement for the white male and white female samples. The best single predictor of achievement is for the white male sample, verbal aptitude (.62) and, for white females, the self-concept (WRL) scale (.34). The M-scale total correlates significantly with achievement for all groups.

DISCUSSION

The most important finding of the study was the lack of correlation between aptitude and achievement ($-.01$) for Negro males. This finding is noteworthy in light of the correlation between aptitude and GPA (.64) for white males. The relationship between aptitude and achievement for Negro males must be qualified as pertaining to a northern urban educational system. It may be hypothesized that in a rural southern segregated educational system, verbal aptitude might again be a significant predictor for Negro males because, in most segregated educational systems, those scoring high on aptitude tests would be given priority on the typically meager educational facilities. Thus, in a segregated system verbal-aptitude results may become a self-fulfilling prophecy. However, in our northern sample, educational opportunity was available in sufficient abundance to reach a reasonably wide range of youngsters, irrespective of aptitude.

Among the subtests of the M scales, the self-concept scale (WRL) is the best predictor of achievement for Negro males (.36) and females (.64) and white females (.34). This finding is supported by the recent research of Payne and Farquhar (1962) and indicates the strong relationship between the students' self-perception and school achievement.

For the Negro males, the M scales appear to be more valid predictors of achievement than verbal aptitude. This finding has implications for school administrators and counselors since scores on aptitude tests are often used in making student educational-vocational decisions. Because verbal aptitude was shown to be a poor predictor of achievement for the Negro male students of this sample, critical examination should be given to the validity of the SCAT Verbal and other verbal-aptitude measures before making decisions concerning Negro students solely on verbal measures.

The finding that verbal aptitude was a significant predictor of achievement for Negro females in contrast to Negro males should be more fully explored.

Obviously, cross validation of these correlations is needed. Furthermore, the value of the M scales in estimating achievement for this sample of Negro students emphasizes the relationship between nonintellectual factors and school performance. It may well be that many Negro students (especially males) are being graded on other than academic performance (e.g., social desirability). Future studies employing other forms of standard achievement tests are needed to isolate the pertinent factors which determine school achievement of this minority group.

References

Bennett, G. K., Seashore, H. G., and Wesman, A. G. *Differential Aptitude Test Manual.* (3rd ed.) New York: Psychological Corporation, 1959.

Boykin, L. L. The reading performance of Negro college students. *Journal of Negro Education,* 1955, **24**, 435–441.

Bullock, H. A. A comparison of the academic achievements of white and Negro high school graduates. *Journal of Educational Research,* 1950, **44**, 179–192.

Conant, J. B. *Slums and suburbs.* New York: McGraw-Hill, 1961.

Jacobs, J. M. Aptitude and achievement measures in predicting high school academic success. *Personnel and Guidance Journal,* 1959, **37**, 334–341.

Lott, Bernice E., and Lott, A. J. *Negro and white youth; a psychological study in a border-state community.* New York: Holt, Rinehart & Winston, 1963.

Norton, D. P. The relationship of study habits and other measures to achievement in ninth grade general science. *Journal of Experimental Education,* 1959, **27**, 211–217.

Payne, D. A., and Farquhar, W. W. The dimensions of an objective measure of academic self-concept. *Journal of Educational Psychology,* 1962, **53**, 187–192.

23 Scholastic Attitudes of Southern Negro Students

ROBERT L. WILLIAMS
University of Tennessee

SPURGEON COLE
East Carolina University

In this paper the authors examine the scholastic attitudes of Southern Negro students in order to assess some of the effects of segregation and integration on their feelings toward school. Drs. Williams and Cole conclude that most Negroes have poorer academic morale than the whites in integrated schools, have less affinity for the school setting, and discuss the implications of this in their ability to achieve significantly.

It has generally been assumed that a segregated academic milieu often produces in the Negro child apathy and antagonism toward education. Kardiner and Ovesey (5, p. 72) have described the atmosphere in segregated Negro schools as one of unparalled boredom: "It is difficult to conceive of a more hopeless and dispirited group than a high school class of Negro adolescent girls; nor a more bored and resentful group than a high school class of Negro boys." Kardiner and Ovesey propose three dominant reasons for the Negro's resistance to education: (a) failure to see relevance of education to vocational oportunities, (b) necessity to work part-time, and (c) competition of street life.

Part of the Negro's antipathy toward education can also be attributed to the impoverishment of his learning experiences in the pre-school years. Deutsch (4, p. 163) suggests that "the lower-class child enters the school situation so poorly prepared to produce what the school demands that initial failures are almost inevitable, and the school experience becomes negatively rather than positively reinforced." An additional factor that

SOURCE. Reprinted from *The Journal of Negro Education*, 1969, 38, 1, 74–77, with permission of the author and the publisher.

contributes to the academic demise of Negro students is the deficiency of scholastic opportunities in segregated schools. Some contend that the training of Negro teachers in the South typically has not been comparable to that of Caucasians and that facilities, equipment, books, etc., in Negro schools are woefully inadequate.

Despite the widespread assumption that Negro students possess extremely negative academic attitudes, an examination of the psychological literature reveals a paucity of empirical studies related to this issue. Another accepted generalization is that integration of schools will produce in Negro students a more positive academic orientation. This assumption also lacks empirical confirmation. In fact, several studies (3, 6, 8) indicate that Negro morale is higher in segregated settings than in an integrated milieu. St. John (6) failed to obtain any relationship between degree of segregation and educational vocational aspirations of Negro high school students. However, Boyd (1) found that Negro students in nonsegregated elementary schools had higher levels of aspiration than a concomitant group of white Ss. The effect of desegregation on academic morale undoubtedly depends on the quality of the integrated experience. Physical integration per se will solve few problems for Negroes. If the integrated climate is fraught with hostility, ridicule, and failure (3), it is not surprising that academic morale would be diminished.

The present study was undertaken to provide an empirical assessment of the academic attitudes of Negro students in segregated and integrated schools and to compare the academic orientations of these Negro Ss with those of Caucasian students from the same geographic areas.

METHOD

Subjects

The Ss were selected from rural and urban areas in the deep South. The sample was comprised mainly of 11th grade students chosen at random from the various types of academic settings: 73 Negro Ss from totally segregated schools, 18 Negro Ss from at least partially integrated schools, and 124 Caucasians from both segregated and integrated settings. The Ns for the groups were generally analogous to the distribution of these Ss within the total student population. All the integrated Negro students had been in desegregated academic settings for at least one year. In most instances these students had a choice between attending integrated schools or remaining in segregated settings.

Instrument and Procedure

The California Study Methods Survey (2) was administered to all Ss at the termination of the academic year. The California Study Methods Survey (CSMS) is a standardized instrument which provides three basic measures of academic orientation: (a) attitudes toward school, (b) mechanics of study, and (c) planning and system. The 60-item attitudes toward school scale relates to student affinity for academic experiences, his satisfaction or dissatisfaction with school. Mechanics of study is a 60-item measure of the mechanical aspects of study such as approaches to learning new subject matter, techniques for retention of material, and reviewing for tests. The 30-item planning and system scale assesses "the student's estimate of the extent to which he budgets his study time properly and the degree of care and deliberation he exercises in performing his academic tasks" (2, p. 3).

RESULTS

The mechanics of study and planning and system scales yielded significant differences between the groups, whereas the attitudes toward school scale did not. On the mechanics of study dimension the segregated and integrated Negro Ss were statistically equivalent, but the integrated Negro students were significantly below the Caucasians ($p < .02$). In contrast, on the planning and system scale the integrated Negro and Caucasian students did not differ, however, both obtained significantly lower scores than the segregated Negroes ($p < .02$).

In addition to the statistically significant differences, a close examination of the results revealed other relevant trends (see Table 1): (a) the integrated Negro Ss obtained the lowest mean score on each of the three dimensions, (b) the rank order of the groups on the first two scales was Caucasians, segregated Negroes, and integrated Negroes, and (c) the means for the integrated Negroes were consistently one standard deviation or more below the corresponding normative mean.

TABLE 1

Mean T Scores for Academic Groups

	Attitudes toward School	Mechanics of Study	Planning and System
Segregated Negroes	44.205	40.123	47.973
Integrated Negroes	42.167	36.167	41.500
Caucasians	46.516	42.911	42.976

DISCUSSION

The present study suggests that Southern Negro students have poorer academic morale in recently integrated schools than in segregated institutions and that Negroes generally have less affinity for scholastic pursuits than Caucasians in the same geographic regions. The latter finding is quite consistent with the tenor of thinking expressed in the psychological literature; however, the former is somewhat incongruous with the assumed efficacy of academic integration. Inasmuch as this study is not longitudinal in nature, the data do not delineate the etiology of the integrated students' academic apathy. Many of these Ss or their parents had made the decision to attend an integrated rather than a segregated school. Would students with the least proclivity toward academic progress be the most likely to choose an integrated setting? It seems reasonable to assume that the more confident, highly motivated students would be the first to enter a desegregated school.

What was the caliber of experience for these Negro children in integrated schools? The classes were generally conducted in a competitive fashion and grades were assigned primarily on the basis of class standing. The Negro students were frequently identified by their Caucasian teachers as being dull and unable to compete academically with white students. The excruciating deprivation in the Negro culture undoubtedly does produce academic limitations, but many Caucasian teachers initially expect Negro students to be obtuse and consequently treat them as intellectually inferior. It has therefore been virtually impossible for a Negro student to excel in the predominantly white Southern classroom. The segregated school, while having egregious deficiencies, usually does afford equitable evaluation of the Negro child's academic work.

In general, how are Negro students in desegregated Southern schools treated by Caucasian teachers and students? Chesler's survey (3) of the experiences of Negro children in recently integrated Southern schools presents an ignominious picture. Negro students describe humiliating discrimination in the integrated environs and considerable resentment from fellow Negroes within their own communities. Another recent investigation (8) indicates that even prior to integration, Negroes are very apprehensive about attending desegregated schools. Two of the greatest fears pertain to white peer acceptance and the fairness of Caucasian teachers. Inasmuch as Negro students are already sensitized to these possibilities, the slighest evidence of discrimination may be keenly felt by them.

The present study suggests that physical integration per se will not instantly remediate the scholastic apathy produced by years of second-rate opportunities. Periods of basic social reform can be extremely painful. New opportunities create new problems, new responsibilities, and new questions about self-adequacy. With time, much of the early conflict experienced by the Negro in integrated settings will likely be eliminated. However, the attitudes of Caucasian teachers and students can markedly accelerate or impede the adjustment of Negro students to desegregation. An atmosphere of mutual respect in which students are evaluated on an individual rather than a competitive basis offers the greatest likelihood for successful adjustment.

In interpreting the findings of this study, two limitations must be considered. One is the sample size for the integrated group. Because of the dearth of integration in the geographic region from which the Ss were selected random sampling produced a much smaller N for the integrated than for the other groups. With a small N there is greater likelihood that the sample is not representative of the total population of Southern Negro students in desegregated settings. Another factor is the pattern of scores obtained by the Caucasian Ss. The Caucasian means were also well below the normative means; in fact, on the planning and system scale the Caucasian students obtained scores significantly below those of the segregated Negroes. Consequently, part of the apathy manifested by Negro students can be attributed to the general sociological-educational impoverishment of the geographic area rather than racial discrimination per se.

Bibliography

1. Boyd, G. F. "The Levels of Aspiration of White and Negro Children in a Non-segregated Elementary School," *Journal of Social Psychology*, 36: 191–196, 1952.

2. Carter, H. D. *California Study Methods Survey: Manual*. Los Angeles: California Test Bureau, 1958.

3. Chesler, M. A. *In Their Own Words: A Student Appraisal of What Happened After School Desegregation*. Atlanta: Southern Regional Council, 1967.

4. Deutsch, M. "The Disadvantaged Child and the Learning Process," in A. H. Passow (ed.) *Education in Depressed Areas*, 163–180. New York: Columbia University, 1965.

5. Kardiner, A., and Ovesey, L. *The Mark of Oppression: Explorations in the Personality of the American Negro*. Cleveland: The World Publishing Company, 1962.

6. Pugh, R. W. "A Comparative Study of the Adjustment of Negro Students

in Mixed and Separate High Schools," *Journal of Negro Education*, 12: 607–616, 1943.

7.   St. John, N. H. "The Effect of Segregation on the Aspirations of Negro Youth," *Harvard Educational Review*, 36(3):284–294, 1966.

8.   Williams, R. L. "Cognitive and Affective Components of Southern Negro Students' Attitude toward Academic Integration," *Journal of Social Psychology*, in press.

24 Relationships Between Some Intellectual and Nonintellectual Factors of High Anxiety and Low Anxiety Negro College Students

CALVIN O. ATCHISON
Assistant Graduate Dean, Tennessee A. and I. State University

This exploratory attempt to enumerate certain characteristics related to high and low anxiety Negro college students further adds to the existing body of data on superior students. The paper furnishes normative data relevant to Manifest Anxiety Scale Scores, Incomplete Sentences Blank, I.Q. and G.P.A. Perhaps the explanation for the lack of correlation between I.Q. and other measures may be the restricted range of intelligence. Dr. Atchison concludes that his findings do not agree with those of other researchers (see his references regarding these), since his data were derived from Negro college students.

The Taylor Manifest Anxiety Scale has received wide popularity as a tool for the experimental investigation of conditioning and learning. Seigman (10) notes contradictory results in his review of studies using the Taylor scale as a correlate of thinking and learning. Wesley (14) found that college subjects who had high Manifest Anxiety Scale scores did consistently better on concept formation and abstract tasks than subjects with a low Manifest Anxiety Scale scores; whereas, Matarazzo *et al.* (4) used college students as Ss and failed to find a significant relationship between Manifest Anxiety Scale scores and performance on the Comprehension, Vocabulary, and Similarities of the Wechsler Bellevue. There is evidence to indicate that anxiety is not always a disruptive force in thinking and problem solving; in some cases it may serve as a facilitating

SOURCE. Reprinted from *The Journal of Negro Education*, 1968, **37**, 2, 174–178, with permission of the author and the publisher.

factor. It has been reported that Ss who scored high on the Manifest Anxiety Scale have been found to perform relatively better on simple tasks (6, 13) and relatively more poorly on complex tasks (1, 7, 11) than Ss who scored low.

If scores on the Taylor Scale suggest general drive level, and if variations in drive affect task performance, the psychological factor of individual differences in individuals and in groups might determine whether anxiety will function as a disruptive or as an energizing function. In spite of the recent increased interest in investigating anxiety through a variety of activities and with many different populations, no one has turned attention to a population of Negro college students. This study is primarily concerned with some intellectual and nonintellectual correlates with anxiety in Negro college students. More exactly, the study involves a comparison of relationships between intellectual and nonintellectual factors of high anxiety and low anxiety groups.

PROCEDURE

One hundred sixty sophomores enrolled in educational psychology at Tennessee A. & I. State University were administered the Taylor Manifest Anxiety Scale, the Rotter Incomplete Sentence Blank, and the Otis Quick Scoring Test of Mental Ability. Cumulative grade point averages were obtained from the Office of Admissions and Records. The 51 Ss scoring from zero to 11 on the Manifest Anxiety Scale were arbitrarily designated as low Manifest Anxiety Scale scores, and 42 Ss scoring 17 and above were arbitrarily designated as high anxiety scores.

The Incomplete Sentence Blank was administered to determine an index of adjustment according to the degree of conflict expressed in sentences. Grade point averages were used as a measure of achievement and the Otis Quick Scoring Test was used to obtain the intelligence quotient. Data were analyzed to determine the relationships between anxiety and other variables under investigation for the separate groups, and low anxiety and high anxiety groups were compared to determine if there were statistical differences in the nonintellectual and intellectual factors under investigation.

RESULTS

The correlations obtained from the study are reported in Table 1. The results show that level of anxiety tended to be positively related to both intellectual and nonintellectual factors for both the low anxiety and high anxiety groups, though not significantly related to any of the factors

TABLE 1

Correlations Between Intellectual and Nonintellectual Factors of Low Anxiety and High Anxiety College Students

Variables Correlated	r	SEr	Level of Significance
Low Anxiety Group (N = 51)			
MAS and IQ	.13	.14	NS
MAS and ISB	.17	.14	NS
MAS and GPA	.25	.13	.05
IQ and GPA	.19	.14	NS
IQ and ISB	.29	.12	.05
ISB and GPA	.35	.12	.05
High Anxiety Group (N = 42)			
MAS and IQ	.09	.15	NS
MAS and ISB	.21	.15	NS
MAS and GPA	.06	.16	NS
IQ and GPA	.18	.15	NS
IQ and ISB	.06	.16	NS
ISB and GPA	.16	.15	NS

under investigation for the high anxiety group. The significant positive relationship (.05) between anxiety and grade point average for the low anxiety group may be explained in terms of the narrow range of grade point averages noted in the low anxiety group. The correlation between Manifest Anxiety Scale scores and grade point average for the low anxiety group (r = .25 − .13) was significant at the .05 confidence level. Likewise there were significant relationships (.05 confidence level) between grade point average and Incomplete Sentence Blank, as well as intelligence quotient and Incomplete Sentence Blank.

A comparison of the factors under investigation for the two groups is shown in Table 2. There was a significant difference (.05 confidence level) between low anxiety and high anxiety groups in intelligence quotient in favor of the low anxiety group. Likewise, there was a statisti-

TABLE 2

Comparison of Low Anxiety and High Anxiety Groups

Variables	Means		SDs		Mean Diff.	t	Level of Significance
	LA	HA	LA	HA			
GPA	2.22	2.22	.45	.83			
IQ	103.41	99.14	10.20	8.94	4.27	2.11	.05
ISB	121.91	137.40	11.30	15.20	15.20	2.84	.01

cal difference (.01 confidence level) between the groups in degree of conflict as expressed by the Incomplete Sentence Blank. The high anxiety group expressed more conflict in adjustment.

DISCUSSION

In general, the findings of this study yielded correlations between nonintellectual and intellectual factors of low anxiety and high anxiety groups that are all positive but insignificant except for Manifest Anxiety Scale and grade point average, intelligence quotient and Incomplete Sentence Blank, and grade point average and Incomplete Sentence Blank for the low anxiety group. These findings failed to support the findings of Kerrick (3), Grice (2), and Spielberger and Katzenmeyer (12), but tend to support those of Schulz and Calvin (9), Sarason (8), and Mayzner (5). Several possibilities may be offered as explanation for contradictory results found in similar studies using college students as Ss. Among the extraneous variables which have not been offered are different racial and socio-economic groups and differences in the universities and student bodies themselves.

The correlations obtained with the low anxiety group are significant in that they tend to show a higher relationship than those of the high anxiety group. Although all correlations are positive, differences are noted in the two groups as revealed by the mean score in Table II. The finding of significant relationships between variables on the low anxiety group leads, of course, to two possible interpretations. The obtained results could simply be due to the differences noted in intelligence and adjustment of the two groups. However, the factor of adjustment and intelligence quotient had no influence on achievement in terms of grade point averages of the two groups. A further possible influence might be that high anxiety Ss with greater conflicts in adjustment have, to some extent, repressed general intellectual drives but have been able to maintain the same level of academic performance as low anxiety Ss who were better adjusted and measured higher on an intelligence test.

The results of this study seem to indicate that the Taylor scale is confounded with intelligence, conflicts in adjustment, and grade point averages for low anxiety Negro college Ss. Significant differences in adjustment and intelligence along with low but significant positive relationship between Manifest Anxiety Scale scores and grade point average, intelligence quotient and Incomplete Sentence Blank, and Incomplete Sentence Blank and grade point average further complicate the findings.

It is impossible to make unequivocal interpretations of these findings since they may be due to the group studied and the college setting. Con-

clusions should be restricted to the population under study until further
evidence is obtained on similar groups in comparable institutions.

SUMMARY

One hundred sixty-four college sophomores at Tennessee A. & I. State
University were administered the Manifest Anxiety Scale developed by
Taylor. They were split into three groups on the basis of scores earned on
the scale. Only the extreme groups were used for this study. The low
score group consisted of 51 Ss with scores from zero to 11. The high score
group consisted of 42 Ss with scores above 16. All Ss were administered
the Rotter Incomplete Sentence Blank and the Otis Quick Scoring Test
of Mental Ability. Grade point averages were obtained from the Office of
Admissions and Records. Findings from the study yielded correlations
between nonintellectual factors of low anxiety and high anxiety groups
that were all positive but insignificant except for Manifest Anxiety Scale
and grade point average, intelligence quotient and Incomplete Sentence
Blank, and grade point average and Incomplete Sentence Blank for the
low anxiety group. The findings do not agree with many studies using
college students as Ss. Results may be peculiar to the racial group used
and the setting for the study.

References

1. Farber, I. W., and Spence, Kenneth W. "Complex Learning and Condi-
    tioning as a Function of Anxiety," *Journal of Experimental Psychology,*
    1953, 45:120-125.

2. Grice, G. R. "Discrimination Reaction Time as a Function of Anxiety and
    Intelligence," *Journal of Abnormal and Social Psychology,* 1955, 50:71–74.

3. Kerrick, Jean S. "Some Correlates of the Taylor Manifest Anxiety Scale,"
    Journal of Abnormal and Social Psychology, 1955, 50:75–77.

4. Matarazzo, J. D., Ulett, G. S., Saslow, G., and Guze, S. B. "The Relation-
    ship Between Anxiety Level and Several Measures of Intelligence," *Jour-
    nal of Consulting Psychology,* 1954, 18:201–205.

5. Mayzner, Mark S. Jr., Sersen, E., and Tresselt, M. M. "The Taylor Mani-
    fest Anxiety Scale and Intelligence," *Journal of Consulting Psychology,*
    1955, 19:401–403.

6. Montague, E. K. "The Role of Anxiety in Serial Rote Learning," *Journal
    of Experimental Psychology,* 1953, 46:91–96.

7. Raymond, C. "Anxiety and Task as Determiners of Verbal Performance,"
    Journal of Experimental Psychology, 1953, 46:120–125.

8. Sarason, Irwin G. "The Relationship of Anxiety and Lack of Defensiveness to Intellectual Performance," *Journal of Consulting Psychology*, 1956, 20.

9. Schulz, R. E., and Calvin, A. D. "A Failure to Replicate the Findings of a Negro Correlation Between Manifest Anxiety and ACE Scores," *Journal of Consulting Psychology*, 1955, 19:223–224.

10. Seigman, Aron W. "The Effect of Manifest Anxiety of a Concept Formation Task, a Nondirected Learning Task, and on Timed and Untimed Intelligence Tests," *Journal of Consulting Psychology*, 68:671.

11. Sinha, Durgan and Singh, Tripat Raj. "Manifest Anxiety and Performance on Problem Solving Tasks," *Journal of Consulting Psychology*, 1959, 23:469.

12. Spielberger, Charles D., and Katzenmeyer, William G. "Manifest Anxiety, Intelligence, and College Grades," *Journal of Consulting Psychology*, 1959, 23:278.

13. Taylor, Janet A., and Chapman, J. P. "Paired-Associate Learning as Related to Anxiety," *American Journal of Psychology*, 1955, 68:671.

14. Wesley, Elizabeth L. "Perseverative Behavior in a Concept-Formation Task as a Function of Manifest Anxiety and Rigidity," *Journal of Abnormal and Social Psychology*, 1953, 48:129–134.

25 A Comparative Study of a Population of "Disadvantaged" College Freshmen

OTIS D. FROE
Director, Research and Evaluation, Morgan State College

Dr. Froe presents a detailed and lengthy characterization of a group of Black, "disadvantaged" college freshmen who enrolled at Morgan State College. From his research he derives some implications for educational planning that deserve serious consideration. It is interesting to compare the results of this survey to the earlier study by Herman G. Canady (1937, this collection) because their conclusions and recommendations are so similar. Dr. Froe's paper should be carefully studied in view of the fact that it contains such an abundance of data on Negro college freshmen.

The purpose of this survey-type study was to collect information that will facilitate a systematic description (largely noncognitive) of a population of college freshmen (predominantly Negro) usually described as "culturally disadvantaged," and to compare this profile with that of a population of freshmen enrolled in predominantly white higher institutions. The variables included in the description represent important considerations in any overall planning by a college as it relates to maximizing the growth and development of its students.

The hypothesis underlying this survey is that higher institutions enrolling students largely from sub-cultures which represent social, educational and economic disadvantages must deviate in many respects, from plans made by colleges enrolling students having experienced, prior to college, a fuller participation in the broader American Culture. Students enrolled in predominantly Negro higher institutions have experienced severe restrictions in terms of participation in the broader American Culture. This restricted cultural participation requires a "compensatory" type of planning which will remove or minimize the gaps between the advantaged and disadvantaged student populations.

SOURCE. Reprinted from *The Journal of Negro Education*, 1968, 37, 4, 370–382, with permission of the author and the publisher.

The backgrounds, aspirations, and attitudes of college students are important factors for consideration in planning experiences aimed at modifying the behaviors of students. These nonintellective factors are as important as the more cognitive factors which usually receive disproportionate emphasis in planning. This survey is largely concerned with these noncognitive variables. Many of these variables can be effectively and constructively manipulated in changing the behaviors of students in the attainment of objectives common to many of our institutions of higher education.

The present study is based on the fall, 1967 freshman class enrolled at Morgan State College (a predominantly Negro college), and freshmen enrolled, for the same period, in several higher institutions with predominantly white enrollments. In both populations, the survey questionnaire was administered to new freshmen prior to the beginning of classes. Included in the institutions with predominantly white enrollments were state universities, state colleges, private universities, independent coeducational colleges, women's colleges, and technical institutes. These institutions are located in the East, in the Mid-West, in the South, and in the Far-West. Morgan State College is a Maryland state controlled college. The population for Morgan State College consisted of approximately 600 new freshmen, and the population in the other institutions consisted of over twelve thousand freshmen.

Fifty-seven per cent of the Morgan freshmen were women; forty-three per cent were male. A similar analysis by sex for the other institutions (hereafter referred to as the "other population") was 61 per cent men and 39 per cent women.

Roughly two thirds of the students from both populations were attending institutions in the state where their homes are located. Thirty-five per cent of Morgan freshmen live at home and commute to college, as against 16 per cent of the freshmen in the other institutions. Over half (52%) of Morgan freshmen reported parents as main source of financial support. This percentage is 65 for the other freshmen. Seven per cent of Morgan freshmen and 10 per cent of the other population indicated scholarships to be their main source of support (24% Morgan freshmen; 29% other freshmen actually had scholarships). Fifty-four per cent Morgan freshmen sought to obtain part-time employment during the freshmen year as against 70 per cent of freshmen in the other institutions.

EDUCATIONAL AND VOCATIONAL ORIENTATIONS

By and large, both groups of entering freshmen seem to have more or less definite educational plans. The percentages indicating that they had made a decision about a major field of study were 96 and 90 for Morgan freshmen and for the other freshmen population respectively. Typically, for both populations, this decision had been made two or three years back. For both populations, high school teachers were most often held to be the persons who were most influential in major field choice—more often more influential than either parent. About two thirds of both populations indicated that their parents strongly approved of their choice of major. About one fourth of the Morgan students and one third of the other freshmen reported difficulty in choosing a major. For both groups, the choice was usually made from among two or three possible fields.

Expectation of study beyond the baccalaureate degree was not uncommon. Seventy per cent of Morgan freshmen and 60 per cent of freshmen in the other colleges reported expectations of graduate or professional schooling. Twenty-nine per cent of Morgan freshmen reported that they would "definitely" attend a graduate or professional school. Forty-two per cent indicated that attendance at graduate school was a probability. These same percentages for the freshmen in other colleges were 23 and 37 respectively. Ten per cent of Morgan freshmen envisioned one year of graduate work; 20 per cent planned for two years. These same percentages for other colleges were 17 and 18 respectively. In both populations, roughly one in four hoped to work for a doctoral degree. Also, for both groups, graduate work most often began to be considered late in high school. Twenty-one per cent of Morgan freshmen were "very certain" about attaining the Ph.D. degree. Only 12 per cent of the other freshmen were as certain about attaining this degree.

A surprisingly large proportion of the samples seem to be settled about their occupational future. Ninety-three per cent of Morgan freshmen and 85 per cent of the other freshmen indicated having already made a career or vocational decision. The three sources of job satisfaction judged to be most important to Morgan students were: opportunity to be helpful to others, useful to society (40%); opportunity to use ones special abilities and talent (19%); opportunity to work with people rather than with things (12%). Another source of job satisfaction for Morgan students was "stable, secure future." The three sources of job satisfaction judged to be most important for other freshmen were: opportunity to be helpful to others, useful to society (26%); opportunity to use one's special abilities and talents (24%); a stable, secure future (13%). Seven per cent of Morgan freshmen indicated "Prospects of an above average income" to be the most important source of job statisfaction.

An indication of the relative interest in six general career areas among the students surveyed is provided by the responses to an inquiry about their preferences for certain careers. These responses are indicated in Table 1.

About one fourth of the Morgan freshmen women and about one half

TABLE 1

Preferences Expressed for Certain Career Areas

Career Area	Morgan Freshmen %	Other Freshmen %
An academic life (teaching, research, other scholarly work)	43	22
A business life	8	12
A professional life (doctor, lawyer, engineer, etc.)	18	24
A life of a trained technician or craftsman	2	2
A life centering around some aspect of the creative arts	3	4
A life centering around a home and a family	12	21
Other	3	4
Have not given sufficient thought to this matter to say	10	11

of the freshmen women in the other colleges view their future primarily in terms of marriage and family. Responses to an additional question made clear that of the freshmen women who envisaged a career, a vast majority also envisaged a family.

The sample of freshmen in both populations reported wide interest in becoming involved in college extracurricular activities with more than 70 per cent hoping to participate in student government, school spirit, and athletic activities. Eighty per cent of Morgan freshmen and 64 per cent of other freshmen hoped to participate in activities of religious organizations. About two thirds of both populations hoped to participate in avocational groups. Intended participations in other activities for Morgan freshmen and other freshmen were respectively as follows: journalistic activities 43 per cent—42 per cent; literary activities 51 per cent—39 per cent; musical activities 42 per cent—32 per cent; political activities 50 per cent—40 per cent; service extracurricular activities 62 per cent—40 per cent. Roughly half (44% Morgan freshmen, and 48% other freshmen) planned to join a fraternity or sorority.

Several questions regarding instructional preferences were included in the questionnaire. Thirty-eight per cent of Morgan freshmen and 42 per cent of other freshmen admitted disliking "assignments requiring original research"; 60 per cent Morgan freshmen and 55 per cent other freshmen preferred "mostly assigned work" over "mostly independent"; over 70 per cent Morgan freshmen and 60 per cent other freshmen preferred objective to essay examinations; and 35 per cent Morgan freshmen as against 44 per cent other freshmen preferred instruction through lectures over instruction through class discussion.

In describing student populations, sociologists have described four college student types—the vocational, the academic, the collegiate, and the nonconformist. In an attempt to research this typology, the four statements below were included in the questionnaire along with instructions to the student to indicate which one of the four "most accurately" described his own philosophy of higher education. The percentages of students in each of the two populations choosing each of the four philosophies are also given below, following each description.

PHILOSOPHY A. This philosophy emphasizes education essentially as preparation for an occupational future. Social or purely intellectual phases of campus life are relatively less important, although certainly not ignored. Concern with extracurricular activities and college traditions is relatively small. Persons holding this philosophy are usually quite committed to particular fields of study and are in college primarily to obtain training for careers in their chosen fields. (Morgan freshmen—37%; other freshmen—27%.)

PHILOSOPHY B. This philosophy, while it does not ignore career preparation, assigns greatest importance to scholarly pursuit of knowledge and understanding wherever the pursuit may lead. This philosophy entails serious involvement in course work or independent study *beyond* the minimum required. Social life and organized extracurricular activities are relatively unimportant. Thus, while other aspects of college life are not to be forsaken, this philosophy attaches greatest importance to interest in ideas, pursuit of knowledge, and cultivation of the intellect. (Morgan freshmen—26%; other freshmen—19%.)

PHILOSOPHY C. This philosophy holds that besides occupational training and/or scholarly endeavor an important part of college life exists outside the classroom, laboratory, and library. Extracurricular activities, living-group functions, athletics, social life, rewarding friendships, and loyalty to college traditions are important elements in one's college experience and necessary to the cultivation of the well-rounded person. Thus, while not excluding academic activities, this philosophy emphasizes the importance of the extracurricular side of college side. (Morgan freshmen —35%; other freshmen—51%.)

PHILOSOPHY D. This is a philosophy held by the student who either consciously rejects commonly held value orientations in favor of his own, or who has not really decided what is to be valued and is in a sense searching for meaning in life. There is often deep involvement with ideas and art forms both in the classroom and in sources (often highly original and individualistic) in the wider society. There is little interest in business or professional careers; in fact, there may be a definite rejection to this kind of aspiration. Many facets of the college—organized extracurricular activities, athletics, traditions, the college administration—are ignored or viewed with disdain. In short, this philosophy may emphasize individualistic interests and styles, concern for personal identity and, often, contempt for many aspects of organized society. (Morgan freshmen—3%; other freshmen—4%.)

SECONDARY SCHOOL ACTIVITIES AND PERCEPTIONS

Ninety-five per cent of Morgan freshmen as against 78 per cent of the other freshmen surveyed had attended public high schools; less than one per cent (0.3) of Morgan freshmen as against 3 per cent of other freshmen attended independent secondary schools; and 3 per cent of Morgan freshmen as against 16 per cent other freshmen came from Catholic secondary schools. (These proportions, of course, reflect the nature of the sample of colleges.)

Over 40 per cent of Morgan freshmen and 56 per cent of other freshmen estimated that they had graduated within the top one-fifth of their classes. Median estimated overall secondary school grade-point average for Morgan freshmen was a C plus while that for other freshmen was a straight B. Fifty-one per cent of Morgan freshmen as against 61 per cent of other freshmen reported receiving at least one academic honor.

Certain perceptions of various secondary school courses were given. For both groups, the median reported daily homework during the senior year amounted to two hours per day. The great majority of freshmen in both groups (over 80%) attached either "quite a bit" or "a great deal" of importance to grades. Three out of ten Morgan students and almost four out of ten other freshmen, however, indicated that they had learned little in high school about how to study.

Generally speaking, the sample of freshmen had participated extensively in high school extracurricular activities. Forty-six per cent of Morgan freshmen and 35 per cent of other freshmen had held an "important" student government office; two out of three Morgan freshmen had held at least one "minor" office while three out of four other freshmen had held such an office. Participation in voluntary organization outside of high school amounted to the following (sexes combined): church groups—Morgan freshmen 59 per cent, other freshmen 53 per cent; Scouts—Morgan freshmen 22 per cent, other freshmen 26 per cent; the "Y"—23 per cent Morgan freshmen, 19 per cent other freshmen; a social fraternity or sorority—Morgan freshmen 27 per cent, other freshmen 15 per cent.

FAMILY BACKGROUND

Sixty-five per cent of the sample of Morgan freshmen and 84 per cent of other freshmen reported both parents to be at home. For 18 per cent of Morgan freshmen and 7 per cent of other freshmen, parents were either separated or divorced. For 14 per cent of Morgan freshmen and 7 per cent of other freshmen one or both parents were deceased.

Seventeen per cent of Morgan freshmen as against 28 per cent of other freshmen reported that their father works "for himself." Fathers of 40 per cent of Morgan freshmen and 21 per cent of other freshmen are trade union members. Over 20 per cent of Morgan freshmen as against 53 per cent of other freshmen reported that their mothers had been gainfully employed during their (the students) lifetime. Nearly one half (46%) Morgan freshmen as against 36 per cent other freshmen reported their mother to be salaried at the time of the survey. A breakdown of parents occupation is given in Table 2 below.

TABLE 2

Occupation of Parents

	Father		Mother	
Occupation	Morgan Freshmen	Other Freshmen	Morgan Freshmen	Other Freshmen
	%	%	%	%
Blue collar	75	33	40	16
Lower white collar	10	37	17	27
Professional	10	28	10	10
Or not gainfully employed	5	2	33	47

The median estimated annual family income from all sources before taxes was about $4500 for Morgan freshmen as against $8500 for other freshmen. Twenty-nine per cent of Morgan freshmen and 7 per cent of other freshmen estimated family income to be less than $4000, 2.4 per cent Morgan freshmen and 11 per cent other freshmen estimated it to be over $20,000. Over 70 per cent of the freshmen from both populations considered their families' economic position to be higher now than it was 10 years ago; 12 per cent of Morgan freshmen and 15 per cent of other freshmen indicated it to be about the same, and 12 per cent of

Morgan freshmen as against 10 per cent of the other freshmen estimated it to be lower.

An inquiry concerning the formal education attained by parents was made. Although economic and educational levels of parents are strongly related to a specific college, the combined data, nonetheless, seemed to attest to the generally extensive entry into higher education of students from lower socioeconomic backgrounds. With three out of four of the Morgan fathers represented employed at the blue collar level, the fact of increasing democratization in higher education would seem to be unmistakable. With the other freshmen, one in three of the fathers represented were employed at the blue collar level.

The questionnaire inquired into the religious preferences of students in both populations. Three fourths of the students in both samples reported having "an adequate personal philosophy or religious faith which serves as a guide for personal conduct." The remainder indicated either that they did not have such a philosophy, or that they were uncertain.

PERSONAL ATTITUDES

The questionnaire contained five groups of questions designed to assess five attitude or personality dimensions. These qualities may be referred to as (1) independence-dependence in relation to parents and family, (2) independence-dependence in relation to peers, (3) political liberalism-conservatism, (4) social conscience, and (5) cultural sophistication.

At a very general level it appears that most entering freshmen (with an average age of eighteen) view themselves as (still) closely tied to their parents and family. Over seventy per cent of the freshmen in both samples affirmed (1) "the importance of satisfying parental wishes," (2) the likelihood of *not* "becoming so absorbed in some activity that they lose interest in the family," (3) that "a person should consider the needs of his family as more important than his own needs," and (4) that "members of (your) family should hold fairly similar religious beliefs."

With regard to peer independence-dependence, two very general and related conclusions seem warranted. First, most entering freshmen attach considerable significance to the inter-personal side of college life. Second, freshmen behavior would appear to be in a substantial degree influenced by the behavior of student associates. In answering the question, "how important to you personally is the inter-personal side of college life—the opportunity to form and maintain close friendships with other students?," 35 per cent of the sample of Morgan freshmen and 47 per cent of the sample of other freshmen indicated "very important," and 47 per cent of Morgan freshmen and 40 per cent of other freshmen indicated "fairly important." Over 50 per cent Morgan freshmen and over 60 per cent of other freshmen reported (1) pursuing "leisure time and recreational activities" "almost always" or "usually" with a group of friends, and (2) "definitely no" or "it is unlikely" to the possibility of becoming "so absorbed in some activity that you would not need close friends." Between 50 and 60 per cent of the freshmen in both populations responded negatively to questions about (1) maintaining "a point of view despite other students losing patience (with you)" and (2) doing "things in your own way and without regard for what other students around you may think."

The twelve "liberalish" items consisted of one straight-forward question about political orientation and eleven "position-statements" on political-social issues about which the student could agree or disagree. Fifty-six per cent of the sample of Morgan freshmen and 54 per cent of the sample of other freshmen chose to identify themselves as "fairly" or "very liberal."

Social conscience is the label given to a block of questions which inquired about the degree of *concern* over social injustice in what might be called "institutional wrongdoing in American society." Because these items are likely to be particularly susceptible to a "socially desirable" response bias, absolute response patterns are somewhat difficult to interpret.

The relative extent of concern about various problems or conditions, however, may be of some interest. Seventy-four per cent of Morgan freshmen as against 70 per cent of the freshmen in the twenty-two other colleges (predominantly white) reported being "mildly" or "highly" concerned about lynchings. Over 70 per cent of the freshmen in both populations expressed mild or high concern about the increasing number of illegitimate births. Sixty-two per cent of Morgan freshmen as against 75 per cent of other freshmen expressed mild or high concern about union leader dishonesty. Forty-nine per cent of Morgan freshmen as against 67 per cent of the freshmen in the other colleges expressed high or mild concern about business ethics such as price fixing. Forty-seven per cent of Morgan freshmen as against 65 per cent of the other freshmen expressed mild or high concern about graft in government. Two thirds of the freshmen in both populations expressed mild or high concern about poverty in the U.S.A. Sixty-seven per cent of Morgan freshmen as against 61 per cent of the other freshmen expressed high or mild concern about the lesser opportunity for nonwhite Anglo-Saxon Protestant. Fifty-two per cent of Morgan freshmen as against 63 per cent of the other freshmen expressed high or mild concern about growing materialism and moral breakdown. Two thirds of the freshmen in both populations expressed high or mild concern about the availability of obscene literature to children. Approximately 60 per cent of the freshmen in both populations were concerned about the rise in juvenile crime. Seventy-five per cent of the Morgan freshmen as against 58 per cent of the other freshmen were concerned about the plight of nonaffluent elderly people. Nearly half of the Morgan freshmen as against 24 per cent of the other freshmen believed the decision to atom-bomb Hiroshima was wrong. The position of both populations on some political and social issues is summarized in Table 3.

TABLE 3

Position on Some Political—Social Issues

| | Per Cent Agreeing or Strongly Agreeing | |
Issue	Morgan Freshmen	Other Freshmen
Government intensify efforts to provide universal medical care	85	66
Excuse conscientious objectors from military service	56	53
Legislative committees *not* investigate political beliefs of college faculty	56	51
Abolition of capital punishment	57	46
Idea of interracial marriage	83	25
Police hampered by necessity for search warrant	47	36
Prohibition of peaceable assembly for persons disagreeing with our form of government	42	39
Labor unions: More harm than good	33	58
Liberty and justice not possible in socialist countries	58	63
Welfare state as destroying individual initiative	51	71
Democracy as fundamentally dependent on free business enterprise	77	86

The final group of questions was used to assess certain facets of what might be called cultural sophistication, the gist of which is sensibility to ideas in art form. Selected responses to items in this area are reviewed here. Twenty-four per cent of Morgan freshmen indicated "no interest whatsoever" in modern art. Thirty-nine per cent of the other population checked this same category to indicate interest in modern art. Seventeen per cent of Morgan freshmen said that they were "quite interested" in modern art, as against 11 per cent for other population. The percentage of Morgan freshmen who indicated that they were "very much interested" in modern art was double that of the other population. These percentages were 10 and 5 respectively. The percentages of freshmen indicating that they received varying degrees of pleasure from classical music were about the same for both populations. In answer to the inquiry concerning the number of books (not textbooks) owned by the informants, 35 per cent of Morgan freshmen and 26 per cent of other freshmen indicated that they owned less than ten volumes. Twelve per cent of Morgan freshmen owned from 31 to 74 books as against 20 per cent for the other freshmen. The frequency patterns with which both populations attended "serious evening lectures" were very similar. About half of both populations (52% Morgan—53% other) checked the "not at all" category to indicate frequency of attendance at these serious evening lectures. Thirty-five per cent of Morgan freshmen indicated that they attended "once or twice" during the last year. For the other population, this per cent was thirty. Also, the "knowledge" of both populations concerning the history of paintings was very similar for both populations—ranging from about half in both populations who indicated that they know "almost nothing" about such history to three per cent in both populations who indicated that they knew "a good deal" about the history of painting. In response to other inquiries concerning cultural sophistication—enjoyment of poetry, personal reaction to works of art, reaction to plays of Shakespeare, etc.—the two populations appeared to be quite similar. A summary of these responses, along with comments relating to their reliability, is presented later in a discussion of four other personality type scales.

A final part of the survey was concerned with the difference of the two populations along five personality dimensions. Also, an overall index of family socio-economic status (FSSI—Family Social Status Index) was obtained from each respondent by summing responses to select items in the questionnaire (these results are summarized in Table 4). Personality is here used in a broad, rather inclusive sense. A brief description of the variables measured by these experimental scales follows. *Family Independence* refers to general autonomy in relation to one's parents and parental family—freedom from family authority. Students with high scores tend to perceive themselves as coming from families that are not closely united, as not being "close" to their parents, as not consulting with parents about important personal matters, as not being concerned about living up to parental expectations and the like. *Peer Independence*, in a similar sense, means freedom from peer authority. Students with high scores on this scale tend not to seek close friends, not to be concerned about how their behavior appears to their acquaintances, not to consult with peers about important personal matters and the like. *Liberalism* refers to a liberal-conservative political-economic-social value dimen-

TABLE 4

Scores of Morgan and "Other" Freshmen on Five Personality-Type Scales
and on Family Socio-economic Index

	Morgan Freshmen			Other Freshmen			t Ratio Scale
Scale	N	Mean	S.D.	N	Mean	S.D.	Means
Family Independence	563	22.36	5.29	12,709	24.35	5.57	8.8
Peer Independence	585	27.43	4.24	12,814	27.27	4.36	0.9†
Liberalism	574	31.19	4.00	12,574	27.68	4.69	20.2
Social Conscience	584	34.12	5.66	12,687	33.02	5.66	4.5
Cultural Sophistication	585	25.44	5.00	12,685	24.83	5.74	2.9
Family Social Status Scale (FSSI)	486	24.93 (23.93)*	11.53	11,940	42.11 (34.11)*	12.33	19.0

* Scores in parentheses (means) for FSSI scale = computations after deletion of ethnic background data.

† Difference in means not statistically significant; all other differences are significant at .01 level.

sion. The nucleus of this variable is a preference either for an ideology of change or for an ideology of preservation; both ideologies are supported in behalf of some conception of the "good society." *Social Conscience* is defined as moral concern about perceived social injustice and what might be called "institutional wrongdoing." Students with high scores, for example, are concerned about poverty, illegitimacy, juvenile crime, graft in government, and the like. Low scores indicate a lack of concern. The *Cultural Sophistication* variable has been defined earlier in this report. In addition, some of the responses to items making up this scale were also discussed. Table 4 summarizes the findings relative to these five scales and the overall index for family socio-economic status.

It is revealed, in Table 4, that only on one of the five scales (Peer Independence) is there no significant difference in the mean scores for the two populations. On three of these scales (Liberalism, Social Conscience, and Cultural Sophistication) the Morgan freshmen have higher mean scores than the combined "other" population. On the first two of these three scores these results are somewhat to be expected. The high scores on the liberalism variable are probably accounted for by the fact that these students, largely from impoverished backgrounds, are expressing preference for an ideology of change in terms of a perceived concept of a better society—sympathetic with welfare statism, organized labor, abolishment of capital punishment, academic freedom for teachers, and the like. There is the expression of anxiety and frustration concerning the gap between the pronouncements of the larger formal American Culture and the sub-culture in which these students have had most participation. Likewise, the social conscience variable is likely the expression of concern over the many "wrongdoings," the many "social injustices" inherent in the larger American Culture—a concern about poverty, crime, unethical business practices, graft in government and the like. There is some question concerning the reliability of the responses of Morgan freshmen to the items making up the Cultural Sophistication scale. Although the "other" combined population represents largely an unselect population in terms of "knowledgeability about institutions and ideas and works of art . . . about the Great Society, its history and culture," here, giving the "right" or expected answers to the items on this scale is probably a means by which these disadvantaged students identify with the larger American Culture in which their active participation has been severely restricted.

SOME EDUCATIONAL IMPLICATIONS

The rationale for this study is the belief that the typical measures (tests of academic potential and high school grades) used by rather nonselective type higher institutions in program planning and in predicting student achievement are insufficient in that they overlook other important variables involving student potential and needs. Establishing goals and planning the total college experience must take into consideration the fact that the student population is characterized by differential levels of academic potential (academic readiness) and many configurations of attitudes, personality patterns, interests, and goals. Since students differ on almost any characteristic one might examine, and since in many publicly supported higher institutions differential selection and rejection of students can be used only mildly, if at all, one recourse remaining is that of differential planning. If goals considered worthy by the institution are to be attained, then in many areas must the college remodel its socio-psychological climates. Many of these higher institutions will admit to the need for differential planning in the area of the academic curriculum (the formal academic culture), but ignore other areas of the college climate in their active planning. Manipulation of the academic culture is likely to prove futile if the other college sub-cultures are not involved in this planning. While difficult to manipulate, the *affective* domain is to be involved along with the *intellective* domain. The many sub-cultures existing on any one college campus must be considered not as being highly visible or easily distinguishable but as fluid systems of norms and values which flow into one another. No doubt, many of those behaviors of students thought to be unalterable can be manipulated toward desired ends. Our knowledge of student characteristics and the complex college culture has value and must be applied to the extra-class experiences as well as to the teaching process. This information can be employed in total program planning to learn what student traits, for example, can be exploited to facilitate the student's learning and to establish some goals for his personal development. In the present survey, for example, it was found that the largest proportion of Morgan freshmen entering a liberal arts college classified themselves as "vocational." This is certainly a predictable and reasonable orientation for youth of a minority which historically has had to settle for a rather different opportunity structure. However, if a college's students are largely vocationally oriented why not couch more initial college experiences in practical terms, then lead them to more idealistic considerations? This will not be easy, and cannot be accomplished by mere exposure to those ideas and concepts identified with the idealistic. The "need systems" of these students must be altered if we consider the goal of *living effectively* in our culture to be important along with the goal of *earning a living*. If, for example, as indicated in the present study, the typical Morgan freshman is a somewhat dependent person, why not accept this and begin with more structured experiences but lead him to more independence in a rational, well planned, integrated set of steps. In institutions of higher education in which socio-economic and intellective democratization is becoming more and more a fact, student financial aids programs (work programs), for example, can be used to supplement the educative experience rather than to dilute it. Such utilization of this work experience is embodied in cooperative work-study program arrangements found on many campuses. Perhaps, there should be radical increases in the number of such arrangements found on college campuses.

Student counseling services on college campuses must become an integral part in the master planning for student growth and development. Counselors can no longer be content as remedial and corrective agencies —they must become skillful architects in the planning process. This is not to say that individual and group counseling at several professional levels will not be needed, but the role of the counselor must become more involved in basic planning of the total college experience. He will still need to help students work out satisfactory solutions to the many problems which are likely to influence learning and development. Educationally deprived students will still suffer from the many fears and anxieties which are inherent in the process of coping with the larger American Culture in which they have restricted participation and thus have developed few of the skills of behaviors needed in this coping process.

One final illustration of implications for planning is shown in a statistic from this present study. It was indicated that the per cent of Morgan freshmen who live at home and commute to the college is over twice that of the other freshmen. These percentages for Morgan and other freshmen were 35 and 16 respectively. If the college setting is to serve somewhat as a "model" in the process of modifying student behavior toward certain ends, then, perhaps, college planning should arrange for a longer and more intensified exposure to this desired model while minimizing the exposures to the many undesirable models to be found in the many off-campus sub-cultures in which these students participate. One aspect of intensifying the exposure to our desired model might be smaller class size arrangements whereby the college teacher as a model can exert a greater influence on students—increasing the opportunity for inter-personal relations. Also, planning must give some attention to other physical arrangements and activities which will attract students to the desired setting at more frequent intervals and for longer periods of time. These activities and arrangements must be those that will facilitate a high level of interaction between student and models.

No attempt has been made to point up all of the implications of the foregoing data on students. These few examples are used to emphasize the point of view that if we are to plan effectively for a diverse population of college students, we must know what they are like in the first place. This knowledge must be of a comprehensive nature. Also, the sheer accumulation of information is not enough. The implications that these data have for planning must be thoroughly studied and understood.

26 Some Impressions of Fair Harvard's Blacks[1]

FLORENCE SHELTON LADD

This article constitutes a rather broad attempt to analyze in depth what it very personally meant to 15 Black men to be students at Harvard University. Experimentally, it is somewhat typical of depth interviewing within the survey method technique. Dr. Ladd presents some very interesting information regarding the men's reasons for accepting Harvard, their social lives, their analyses of Harvard's opinion of themselves, their family and social backgrounds, as well as their opinions regarding the nature and frequency of racially motivated experiences while they were students.

In a previous paper[2] I attempted to characterize the social network of some of the Negro students who attended Harvard College in the late nineteen forties and early fifties, and to capture their reminiscences about the sweet and bitter aspects of their college experiences, many of which seemed very much influenced by their being Negro. Theirs was a small, motley brotherhood based primarily on skin color and perhaps on some aspects of a shared culture. Beyond that, they seemed to share little else in terms of intellectual interests and style of life. Had they been fellow-students at a Negro college, it is likely that most of them would not have known each other, so divergent were their lives. The common experience they shared through being the few blacks at Harvard in their time forged a strong bond that linked them even after their college years. Because of what they discovered at Harvard about themselves and about

SOURCE. Reprinted from *Harvard Journal of Negro Affairs*, 1965, **2**, 13–26, with permission of the author and the publisher.

[1] I am indebted to Ulysses G. Shelton, Jr. '53 for an introduction to some of the experiences of Harvard men who are Negro. I also wish to thank Mary Belenky for her coding the data and suggesting interpretations which helped clarify some issues.

[2] Shelton, Florence C. "Conversations with Some Harvard Blacks." Unpublished manuscript, 1962.

their relative positions in the social and economic structure of the United States, the inevitable theme of all their informal reunions was what they learned about being black while they were in college. On the occasions when I witnessed those reunions, I considered their conversations important accounts of their personal histories and commentaries on the social history of the "type" they represented, the Ivy League Negro.[3] Their accounts of what Harvard was like for them a decade or so ago raised some questions about what the Negro students there recently and presently are learning about themselves with respect to race.

During the past decade, there have been a number of national and international developments which have had personal significance for most Negroes in America. The impact of those events has been felt most profoundly by the current generation of college students, black and white. One suspects that the experiences of Negro College Students in many quarters today are quite different from those of Negro students of a decade or more ago. Regrettably, comparable accounts are rarely available and comparisons with regard to race-related experiences probably would not be very meaningful anyway, since there have been changes influencing the position and presence of Negroes in American colleges and universities. In the Ivy League colleges, as well as in other colleges outside of the South, there has been a marked increase in the number of Negro students now in attendance. Furthermore, the appearance of Negroes in faculty and administrative positions has provided students with evidence of the possibility of academic careers for Negroes in outstanding colleges and universities.

In undertaking this study, it was my hope to elicit expressions of what it meant socially and psychologically to be a Negro at Harvard College from students matriculating there during 1963–64. From the viewpoint of the social history of the College, it seems important to document some aspects of their experiences. Their non-Negro fellow students perhaps from time to time wonder about the nature of the college experience when felt beneath a darker skin. The faculty and administration of Harvard College and of other colleges are displaying a growing interest in contributing more effectively to the self-realization of students with marginal positions and minority group status in their college communities and in society in general. Other Negro students in college situations comparable to the situations Harvard presents are interested in knowing about the

[3] For recent autobiographical accounts by Negroes who attended Ivy League Colleges, see W. M. Kelley, "The Ivy League Negro," *Esquire Magazine*, August, 1963; and M. W. Davis, "A View from Further South in the Ivy League: A Negro Goes to Yale," *Esquire Magazine*, April, 1964 (reprinted, *Harvard Journal of Negro Affairs*, Vol. 1, No. 1).

view from Harvard Square. Finally, students attending colleges quite different from the Ivy League schools are somewhat curious about what they might be gaining or missing by virtue of their circumstances. To these readers, this paper attempts to bring some fragments of the personal experiences of a few Negro Americans attending Harvard College, highlighting the racial dimensions of their experiences.

Of the fifteen young men invited[4] to participate in the study, seven are members of the class of '66, four represent the class of '65, and three the class of '64. Only one member of the class of '67 was interviewed. It was my feeling that the impressions of freshmen were of limited value to the study.

In several respects the group was probably indistinguishable from many of their college contemporaries. They were concentrating in government, social relations, history, English, mathematics, engineering, biology and philosophy. Their extra-curricular activities included participation in varsity football, lacrosse, and track, as well as an assortment of intra-mural sports as players or managers. One was affiliated with *The Harvard Crimson,* another with Harvard's radio station. Among them were Young Republicans, Young Democrats, and a member of the Young Socialist Club; members of the Wesley Foundation, Harvard Christian Fellowship, Hillel, and the Newman Club. Some were hospital volunteers. One was associated with the Chess Club and one with the Camera Club. Two had been elected to their house committees; another also ran but had lost. Some were involved in activities of the Student Non-violent Coordinating Committee and the Northern Student Movement. A few listed ROTC among their activities. A few added that they worked in dining halls or one of the University's libraries. A few others had occasional jobs.

---

[4] First students who were active members of AAAAS were interviewed. After the interview each was asked to identify other students characterized by these descriptions: (a) those who are highly unlikely to become affiliated with AAAAS and have no connections with civil rights groups; (b) those who are not active members of AAAAS and/or civil rights groups but sometimes attend meetings or participate in their activities. The first description consistently elicited the same names. Those students were interviewed. Those mentioned most frequently in response to the second description were sought for interview purposes, also. Consequently, the opinions and experiences reported here are those of students who might be regarded as "types." The procedure for selection of subjects was not intended to yield a representative sample.

Questions other than those mentioned in the text were asked during the interview. A copy of the interview schedule is available upon request. The author interviewed all subjects. She was not affiliated with Harvard University at the time.

A few interviews with black Africans who were students at Harvard made it evident that their experiences were not comparable to those of black Americans. For this reason the former were not included in the study.

Participation in some other activities, however, makes this group racially distinguishable. Some were affiliated with the Association of African and Afro-American Students which then was becoming established at Harvard. Two said they were affiliated with the all-black Boston Action Group. A few were members of a Negro fraternity.

Nearly half of the students in this group were southern-born. The rest were born in border states, in the mid-West and North West. Many of them had grown up in the places where they were born although almost half had been transplanted from southern and border state communities to mid-Western and West Coast cities and towns. For the most part, they had attended public schools. Three, however, had prepared for Harvard at eminent New England preparatory schools. These three are sons of men employed in professional or semi-professional occupations—a lawyer, an elementary school principal, and a career U. S. government employee. The rest, those educated in public schools, gave as their father's occupations the following: university professor, tavern operator, engineer, public accountant, and tailor. Three worked as truck drivers, two as physicians, and two as semi-skilled laborers. Their own occupational aspirations are in these areas: law (the choice of five of the students), teaching, diplomatic service, medicine, the ministry, engineering, and social science. Two are preparing for careers in social change organizations, one in the Peace Corps, and the other in a civil rights organization. None was making the occupational choice his father had made.

Since they had considered other colleges and other colleges had considered them, each student was asked why he had chosen Harvard and then was asked why Harvard had chosen him. Their reasons were straight forward. Most frequently, as one might expect, they mentioned Harvard's tradition of academic excellence, the challenge it presented, and the glory it promised. One seemed keenly aware of the prestige-value of being a Harvard man. The scholarship aid and other forms of financial assistance offered by Harvard influenced the choice of some. One student said that he was pleased that Harvard had not offered him an athletic scholarship as some other colleges had. He acknowledged an outstanding athletic record in high school, but it was important to him to enter college on academic terms. He wanted to feel that he was being supported for his scholastic merit rather than for his athletic abilities. Other factors which influenced the selection of some were being near Boston and near colleges with women students. One student chose Harvard because it meant being a long way from his home town while another made the choice to be near his.

For some the decision to come to Harvard was an easy one. A student with an impressive preparatory school record said he had applied to

Harvard and Yale only and that Harvard was his first choice. For others the decision required much deliberation. During the period of decision-making it sometimes was the insistence and the encouragement of interested relatives, teachers or friends that influenced the choice. One student was considering a small New England college. Another initially had decided upon a predominantly Negro college in part because many of his friends would be in attendance there. A recruiting Harvard alumnus, however, turned this student's sights toward Cambridge. Of those interviewed, four had been recruited by individuals or organizations assisting Harvard in its effort to include more Negroes in the College.

Their responses to the question, "Why do you think Harvard chose you?" required considerably more self-evaluative reflection than their fluent listing of factors which determined their own choices. This question elicited from some explanations that revealed a kind of self-abasement or, more euphemistically, modesty, which I judged to be influenced more by their personal perspective than by objective evidence. Others seemed proud of their scholastic achievements and personal attributes and were confident that in choosing them Harvard had chosen wisely and well. The latter noted that their grades were very good or outstanding, that they had performed well on the College Boards, that they had excellent recommendations from former teachers, that they were well-rounded students with records which showed successful participation in several areas of school life, and that they seemed highly motivated to undertake academic projects independently. These things, they felt, qualified them for the privilege of becoming Harvard men. Those who seemed modest or even self-abasing attributed their selection primarily to external circumstances rather than personal qualifications. For example, three mentioned their geographic origin as a critical determining factor in their selection. Several, even some who had expressed a relatively high degree of self-confidence or self-esteem, felt the fact they were Negro had positively influenced their selection. It was expressed usually as one of several factors which contributed to the student's individuality. In the opinion of some, being Negro also served to help the college meet its diversity criteria. A few thought race *per se* was of critical significance with regard to their selection. "I like to think it's because I was one of the qualified applicants but I guess they were trying to get some Negro students" was one such explanation.

One wonders about the social and psychological experiences of a student who feels that the standards which most of the other students had to meet were not applied to him and perhaps to a few more like him.[5] He

---

[5] Included in this group are non-Negro students who feel their being selected

feels instead that because of present social and educational conditions it was expedient for this college (and some others) to make available to him a princely education that otherwise might have been out of reach. Just now his race makes him a needed commodity—he comes in an attractively wrapped package. What if the times, the circumstances had been different? Does this question evoke in him dreams of more satisfying experiences of what college might have been had he gone elsewhere? Or does it evoke a nightmarish sequence of very unsatisfactory college experiences hardly comparable to all to the intellectual and personal pleasures he has found in his life at Cambridge? More important, how does what he views as his second-class studentship influence his own feelings of personal worth and the manner in which he presents himself to others? How does it modify his academic expectations and his future aspirations and performance? Do the advantages of an excellent education perceived in these terms outweigh the disadvantages? If this view represents a misperception on the part of some students, how might those students be detected and their misperceptions corrected by interested and responsible persons in the college? I have stated that only a few felt that their race was a critical factor in their selection. They are, in many ways, a precious few. If they deserved the opportunity, they also deserve the attention needed to help them maximize the opportunity and what it might offer.

And how might the college provide that special attention without accentuating their feeling that they are special cases? Or worse, without appearing to be condescending or—God forbid—paternalistic? Such is the dilemma of the college.[6] Most abhorrent to this group of students was the occasional feeling that they were once more victims of paternalism, children of another Great White Father—sometimes in the role of dean, instructor, tutor, and most painful of all, classmate and peer. Associated with it was their distrust and disdain for the attitudes which they referred to as white liberalism. Their statements expressed the constant wariness that some feel whenever they enter a situation in the college context which includes an untested white person with whom they must interact. (How frequent such encounters must be!) A poignant

---

depended upon factors other than scholastic performance, College Board scores or other evidence of academic potential. The relationship between students' explanations of their being accepted by a college and their performance in college should be explored.

[6] This is not solely Harvard's dilemma. At the moment this is a concern of a number of institutions which have sought students whose possibilities for success might be enhanced by assistance extended in a manner that does not embarrass or offend the student.

example of such vigilance was offered by the student who said "I'm always on the lookout for the so-called liberal—someone stretching *down* a helping hand." He added that the "someone" usually is a fellow-student. Other students—four or five in all—indicated their resentment of relationships which were marked by patronizing or condescending acts or signs of excessive interest or concern.

They were annoyed by those whom they describe as bending over backwards to please them, to help them or to assure them of their good intentions. To one who participated in intramural baseball it meant that he sometimes was given what he regarded as an unfair advantage. He felt he was a mediocre player. He said that his teammates, however, "always assumed I was good enough to start when I played." He could not decide whether they were being "nice" to him because he is Negro or whether they expected him to perform well on the playing field because he is Negro.

There were fewer references to perceptions of paternalism or white liberalism on the part of faculty members, deans and other administrative personnel. But contacts with them are less frequent. Besides, such claims would need thorough exploration since the roles themselves embody some behavior which even more objectively might be characterized as paternalistic. As we shall see below, an act or attitude which may be dismissed as paternalistic if expressed by a peer, is entirely appropriate and acceptable when a faculty member or administrator is the source.

Direct inquiry was made about differential treatment which was felt to be race-related. The students were asked to discuss both positive and negative instances of discrimination, that is, discrimination toward them and against them. One student reported that he was not aware of differential treatment of any kind. The rest were able to recall instances of differential treatment—a few citing only positive instances, a few recalling only negative ones. The others, nearly half the group, related some episodes which gave evidence of discrimination in their favor as well as episodes involving discrimination against them. Reported instances of positive or favorable discrimination occurred in contacts with faculty members and administrative personnel only. For example, one student attributes his receiving additional financial assistance to his being Negro. Another said he was admitted to one seminar because of his race. One student stated that, when talking with some instructors, he sensed that they made a special effort to establish rapport; he felt they made the effort because he was Negro.

Aside from several references to an ROTC instructor who seemed to display consistently anti-Negro sentiments, accounts of negative discrimination involved other students only. Most of the incidents were related to their participation in social activities. Some statements about the nature of the discrimination revealed the complexity of the situation. A student from a blue-collar background presented this view: "Socially I'm discriminated against. I'm just not in. I'm just not part of the white world. A white guy from a working class background must feel more in. Lots of them study a lot . . . they don't seem to make friends . . . don't become part of a larger group. They, too, might be discriminated against in social things." An observation from another angle was offered by a prep school graduate for whom the most salient form of discrimination is his exclusion from the group of young Harvard men present at social gatherings of "people in the social register, wealthy New England aristocrats." He described their "polite brush-off." He mentioned exclusion from final clubs on racial grounds as another example of the kind of discrimination that is important to him. Still another variety of discrimination was alluded to by a student from a Southern working class family. He asserted that "some Negroes here seem to have lost their identity . . . they act as if they want to be a part of the other race. They don't associate, they don't speak." He added that they had resisted his attempts to become acquainted and had rejected the overtures of others as well.

With respect to their social orientation, racially-speaking, these students seem to fall into three fairly distinct groups. This is not at all surprising in view of the selection of students who were interviewed. (See footnote 4.) There are two students whose social contacts are with white students almost exclusively. One stated that he is "more comfortable in the white world." A review of their educational histories suggests a plausible explanation for their orientation. Both had attended preparatory schools and probably had maintained contacts with other students from their respective schools. It is also likely that they are more familiar with the forms for initiating relationships with others of similar scholastic backgrounds, a condition which markedly reduces the number of students, white and Negro, whom they are likely to regard as socially accessible. In their cases, social class seems to be a prime factor influencing their friendships and acquaintances.

Another group of students described a rather varied social life with respect to race and social class. They described most of the collegiate parties they attend as "racially mixed"; however, each reported that occasionally he is the sole Negro at a party and occasionally also attends all-Negro gatherings. There is no evidence that the racial composition of the group differentially influences their satisfaction with the occasions.

The orientation of the majority of those interviewed is toward a predominantly black social world. A few implied that they have made a conscious effort to include a number of other Negroes at Harvard among their friends and consciously, too, they have discouraged or have been indifferent to "invitations to become acquainted" extended by whites. For example, after his freshman year, one student began to feel that he wanted to be in the company of other Negro students more often. He arranged to spend more and more time with them by refusing invitations from friends he had made in his preparatory school. For others it rarely required deliberate strategy, at least not on their part. According to one student, an athlete, the parties he attends usually are all-black. He said that only the "very liberal whites" had invited him; he had never been invited to a party by a "jock" or a "WASP." For this group, a Negro fraternity with an undergraduate chapter in Boston was one entree into local Negro social activities. A few had independently established contacts with other young people in Negro communities in the Boston area.

Parties were mentioned most frequently as entertaining occasions. Other entertainment interests included motion pictures, theater, football games, card playing, dinner dates, and live performances of jazz and classical music. (It is impossible to estimate the frequency of participation in such activities on the basis of the data available.) One student made a point of saying that he is definitely against going to a play or opera since it is a "sign of accepting the white man's values." He said that he was not reared in a culture in which you take a girl to see a play.

A number of different attitudes were expressed when the racial aspect of their dating was discussed. For the most part, their dates were with girls attending colleges in the Boston area.

One student expressed his skepticism about the motives of the white girls he dates. For him a date with a white girl often presents some "distressing" moments when he finds himself asking, "Are you sincerely interested in me? Are you so ineffectual that you can only feel secure with me? Or are you just trying to be nice?"

A less self-conscious reply from another student began with his saying, "I date whom I please. I like pretty girls, interesting girls." He stated further that he does not consider dating along racial lines unless he is "out to prove something." A few students simply stated that they date white girls more frequently than they date Negro girls. One explained that he does not attend social gatherings where he would have opportunities to meet Negro girls. Another, who estimated that he dates about twice as many white girls as Negro girls, added that his parents disapprove of interracial dating. He expects to marry a Negro girl. Availability is a factor which influences his current dating pattern or in his words, "It's easier to date a white girl than a Negro girl at Radcliffe. There's more competition for the Negro girls."

Those who reported dating Negro girls exclusively or more frequently sometimes had arrived at the decision "to date black" after what must have been agonizing hours of social analysis and self-examination. A few talked about it as if it were a kind of conversion. During their freshman years they had dated white girls most of the time but then an incident or insight changed the course of their dating. Others presented it as if they consciously had formulated a statement of policy. A student from Tennessee who decided to date "mostly black" offered his reasons for it in this way: "I feel I can't separate my present life from my future. Blacks are the people I have to live among and whites are those whose attitudes I want to change. . . . Dating a white girl is like an excursion. It's not a relationship I would try to sustain." He had stated explicitly what the expressions of others had implied: The racial pattern of their dating in particular and of their relationships with other students in general is determined to a considerable extent by where they are from and where they expect to go, socio-economically as well as geographically.

Interracial dating as well as other relationships involving white students heightened an awareness of what some called their "negritude." A sophomore remarked that he felt he was enveloped in an atmosphere which compelled him to accentuate his "soul qualities." He found himself insisting that he preferred "soul music" and "soul food" although he rarely found them really pleasurable. It was as if he felt he was in a cathedral to high WASP culture . . . fair Harvard . . . and from time to time he had an uncontrollable urge to do or say something that would seem terribly blasphemous. His own interpretation of it was that he wanted to show that he is not ashamed of some traditions associated with Negro Americans. It might also be taken as a sign of his coming to terms with some aspects of his being Negro, at least in his present setting.

Struggles with the recognition of racial identity and the acceptance or rejection of a Negro identity were reflected in many of the students' statements. In response to a question about how he had changed since coming to Harvard one student asserted, "I've become more Negro." He said that he was not aware of cultural differences before coming to Harvard, an observation he shared with others from the South where their contacts with members of other ethnic and racial groups were limited. What he had discovered were some customs and mores unique to his sub-culture. Aware of his racially ambiguous physiognomy, another student said that now he does not like being mistaken for "something else," that is, he has come to want to be recognized as Negro. One of the students from the South wondered if he was "missing a feeling of identity with the Negro" by having infrequent contacts with Negroes outside the

258 The Psychological Consequences of Being a Black American

College and finding many of the Negroes he met at Harvard an unfamiliar breed. He wondered if he perhaps should have gone to an all-Negro college.

In the opinion of another student, the personal decisions that one must make about the "relevance of his negritude to his way of life" are of utmost importance to the future lives of Negroes now at Harvard. His being Negro seemed central to what he described as his "current identity crisis."[7] There was one student who felt "no need to come to terms with a racial identity." He commented, "I've been telling myself the important concern is to be an individual, a personality, a human being." He said that he avoids people who approach him "in a limited way—too narrow for my identity." He also stated that he avoids relationships "predicated on blackness." "It allows you to filter yourself through only one lens," he declared. These responses suggest the extent of variability of the reactions to racial identity as a personal issue.

Student life at Harvard College, it seems, affords many opportunities for diverse experiences which bring into focus different facets of oneself such as one's racial identity. Under such circumstances varied resolutions of the problems presented might be expected.

A final question intended to elicit an over-all evaluation of their days at Harvard was posed in these terms: "Would you send a son of yours to Harvard?"[8] Each answered "yes"; and their saying yes said also that they were satisfied generally with their lives at Harvard. The reasons given for their affirmative responses to the question pertained to the quality of the education offered, which perhaps is what they value most about their experience. The advantages of such an education are thought to off-set the disadvantageous aspects of this collegiate venture.

One can only speculate about what the lives of these Harvard men will be like when their sons are of college age. Indeed, what will their lives be like a decade from now? It is suggested that those who associate mainly with other Negro students attending the College do so because they share similar backgrounds, similar interests and similar goals. It seems likely that they will maintain some of these relationships after

---

[7] A number of the students spoke of experiencing an "identity crisis" in a way which indicated that the concept had become a part of the undergraduate vernacular.

[8] Only two said that they would want daughters of theirs to attend Radcliffe. Those who were opposed to the idea indicated that they disapprove of intellectual competitiveness in women and of other signs of "defeminization" they feel Radcliffe students display. One student explained that he objected because the position of the Negro female in an integrated college is very different from that of a male. "A fellow has a chance to go out and seek things. A girl has to wait. It would make dating difficult for her."

their college years. Others have indicated clearly that their friendships and affiliations are only slightly or perhaps not at all determined by their racial backgrounds. A choice of this nature is available to them at Harvard. The circumstances prevailing ten or fifteen years ago which contributed to the formation of a self-conscious clique of blacks no longer exist at Harvard. The change can be attributed in part to the increase in the number of Negro students attending the College in recent years. It has meant including a more diverse group of Negroes in the College population, too. Other aspects of the current social revolution are continually changing the status and situation of Negroes at Harvard. It was pointed out that the situations and statements related in this presentation characterize the Harvard experienced by those who were students in 1963–64. It may not seem valid to the members of the Class of '69 because there have been many important changes since then.

It is regrettable that the scope of this inquiry did not permit a more intensive exploration of the movement related to social change, particularly the civil rights movement. The nature and extent of the students' participation in this movement would be of considerable interest.[9] Their varied reactions to the organization of AAAAS were inventoried; however, it seems more appropriate to report them in another context. Frequent references to the freedom they have found at Harvard, both academic and personal, are not included in this account. Harvard freedom (i.e., the sense of freedom some students experienced) is widely recognized; but does this freedom have deeper, more personal significance for those who feel their freedom is limited in some quarters? This, too, might have been investigated.

Ideally, the total population or at least a probability sample of a sizable number of the Negroes attending the College might be surveyed for the purpose of establishing a basis for some definitive statements about this group of students and providing information which might influence college policies with consequences particularly relevant to them. An examination of the relationships among demographic variables, indices of academic potential and performance and students' attitudes toward aspects of their college experiences seems warranted. A comparison with white students at Harvard of similar educational and socio-economic backgrounds would reveal some of the differences related partially or entirely to race. One might consider an Ivy League-wide study of this type. Recruitment programs are bringing more Negro students to these

[9] Opinions about involvement in civil rights activities which were expressed by some of the Negro students at Columbia College appeared in "Six Undergraduates Speak Out," *Columbia College Today*, 1964, *12*, 32–33.

and other colleges, however, the current emphasis on research projects involving the disadvantaged dictates a low research priority for Negroes attending Ivy League schools. Still, an exploration of several dimensions of their experiences and their prospects seems in order.

This report attempts to convey some impressions of only a small group of students. It is my hope, however, that these impressions have revealed some aspects of the college situations of some Negro Harvard men whose experiences may have gone unrecorded or even unrecognized.

27 The Black Quest for Higher Education: An Admissions Dilemma

ROBERT L. GREEN[1]

Dr. Green discusses the variety of issues related to admitting increased numbers of Black students to colleges and universities in terms of modifying existing admissions criteria. He suggests that such characteristics as motivation and attitude together with the usual measures of intellectual ability be considered when selecting students for admission, and shows that with proper tutorial and counseling services such "high-risk" students can achieve very well.

During the past academic year, black students on major college campuses have demanded that institutions of higher learning admit greater numbers of minority youth. This demand has raised serious questions regarding the traditional admissions criteria established by these institutions. As a means of increasing the relevance of the university and of making higher education available to a larger and more representative portion of our society, admissions officers should assess admissions criteria which take into account motivational and attitudinal, as well as the usual intellectual, characteristics of the individual. Colleges and universities that have revised their admissions criteria have found that "high-risk" students can achieve successfully with proper tutorial and counseling services.

The so-called "Black Revolution" has finally reached major university campuses throughout the United States. During the past academic year

SOURCE. Green, R. L., "Black Quest for Higher Education: An Admission Dilemma," *The Personnel and Guidance Journal*, **47**, 1969, May. Copyright © 1969 by the American Personnel and Guidance Association and reproduced by permission.

[1] Robert L. Green is Associate Professor of Educational Psychology and Associate Director, Center for Urban Affairs, Michigan State University, East Lansing.

261

we have observed Black Student Alliances, United Students for Black Action, and similar groups organized on major white and black college campuses, demanding social reform and changes in academic objectives. These demands have focused primarily on the black students' thrust for a voice in the university decision-making process, curricular changes that reflect the contribution of black Americans, an increase in black faculty and black students, and, in one instance, an all-black residence hall (Black and White at Northwestern University, 1968).

The one demand that has perhaps caused the most concern among college administrators is that of enrolling greater numbers of minority youth. Black students were not aware of the fact that this demand, more than any other, has challenged structured admissions procedures of major universities throughout the country. The result has been the establishment of middle- and upper-socioeconomic student body populations which have formerly been essentially white. Black students who have, in the past, been able to complete their education at predominantly white institutions were not necessarily from middle- or upper-socioeconomic backgrounds, but were either themselves the recipients of an "abundant" high school curriculum or were able to do so because of an unusually effective educationally reinforcing home environment.

Universities have reacted differently to the important admissions question raised by black college students. Some universities have actually begun to recruit minority youth on a wide scale, waiving traditional admissions criteria, while others have attempted to recruit only a very small number of minority youth, selecting only the "cream of the crop" of black high school graduates, i.e., only those who meet the traditional criteria of major universities. Others have somewhat ignored or actively resisted any effort related to changing admissions criteria in order to admit black, Mexican-American, or other minority students. Those universities who have been most resistant to this new press have asserted that their role is not to "overcome" or "make up" for disadvantages that have been systematically built into the youngsters' prior educational background. The latter argument is also used by some high school, junior high, and elementary school administrators who frequently assert that the student's disadvantaging home background has produced his low educational achievement, and the school cannot be held responsible for its amelioration.

In light of new efforts that many universities are making to remove their "white only" student body image, what considerations are important for college admissions officers if the enrollment and subsequent success of minority youth at institutions of higher learning is to be realized?

TRADITIONAL ADMISSIONS CRITERIA

Many universities throughout the country utilize College Board Examinations, perhaps better known as the Scholastic Aptitude Test (SAT), and similar aptitude tests as major variables for predicting college success. As indicated in the 1967 College Entrance Examination Board bulletin, the SAT has five major sections—English Composition, Humanities, Mathematics, Natural Science, and Social Science. Scores for the five areas are reported on a standard score scale ranging from 200 to 800, with a mean of 500 and a standard deviation of 100. In many southern colleges the average combined SAT score earned by black students is about 550. The North Carolina Board of Higher Education recently considered a proposal to raise the SAT minimum score to 750 or higher for admission to Negro colleges in the state. This caused much concern throughout the state since this meant that the new cut-off score would eliminate more than 50 percent of the black college population in North Carolina (Green, 1967).

Since tests such as the SAT are viewed as important predictors by many scholars in the field of measurement and more importantly by college admissions officers in assessing a student's chance for college success, it is important to examine the predictive validity of such instruments.

A brief review of prediction studies will provide information regarding the usefulness of aptitude and intelligence tests in predicting college success. Boney (1966) used several aptitude and mental ability measures to predict high school grade point average (GPA) for 222 Negro male and female secondary students. Boney found that the predictor variables "yielded substantial correlations with high school grade point average" and stated that "it appears that Negro students are as predictable as other groups." The correlations between the Cooperative Ability Test total score and grade point average for Negro males was .66 and .70 for Negro females. The correlations between grade point average and the Differential Aptitude Test scores were as substantial.

A detailed analysis of a series of statistical reports by Stanley and Porter (1967) supports the position that academic aptitude tests predict college freshman GPA equally well for blacks and whites. Included in the review is an analysis of statistical reports from the university system of Georgia for which a preliminary study had been made by Hills (1964). Hills' data contrasting three predominantly Negro colleges with the Georgia Institute of Technology, a predominantly white college, suggest that the SAT-verbal (SAT-V) and SAT-mathematic (SAT-M) predict freshman grades equally well for these two college groups. Stanley and Porter also refer to McKelpin's study (1965) at the North Carolina College at Durham, a predominantly black college in which the SAT-V and SAT-M predictive validities for black college students were "as high as those usually reported for college freshmen . . . ." In an extension of a study by Biaggio and Stanley (1964), Stanley and Porter (1967) conclude that

"In view of the detailed analysis of the Georgia data and several related studies, it seems likely that SAT-type test scores are about as correlationally valid for Negroes competing with Negroes and taught chiefly by Negroes as they are for non-Negroes competing chiefly with non-Negroes and taught chiefly by non-Negroes."

Stanley and Porter further state that "prediction may be approximately equal for the races within integrated colleges." They cite Cleary's research (1966) as additional data which indicates that SAT-type tests are as predictively valid for non-whites as they are for whites. Cleary studied three integrated colleges to determine if the SAT was predictively biased against non-white students. Again, college GPA was the criterion variable. In two of the three colleges assessed, the SAT was as predictively valid for Negroes as it was for whites. In one college, the SAT overpredicted for blacks.

In a post-dictive study, Munday (1965) found "that grades for socially disadvantaged students are generally as predictive as grades for other students using standardized measures of academic ability." Munday correlated high school grades and scores on the American College Test with college grades. Although he does not indicate the college level at which the correlations were obtained, the article suggests that total college GPA was the criterion. The multiple R's obtained "by averaging the GPA predictions made by the optimal weighting of tests and those made by optimally weighting high school grades" ranged from .52 to .66. Munday's study concludes that "if such tests [SAT, etc.] are culture-bound, as seems likely, this feature does not appear to detract from their usefulness as predictors of academic success."

However, Green and Farquhar (1965), found later that there was essentially no relationship (−.01 correlation) between the secondary grades (GPA) of black male high school students and their verbal scores on the School and College Ability Test. The correlation between the two variables was significantly higher (.25) for black females on the same study. It was found that a test of achievement motivation (Self-Concept of Academic Ability Scale) correlated slightly higher with high school grades than the verbal section of the SCAT (.36 for males and .64 for females). The −.01 correlation between high school grades and SCAT scores for black males is of interest. McKelpin (1965), cited earlier, suggests that high school GPA may be a poor criterion of school success for disadvantaged students, in that high school academic programs often adjust to environmental factors. In the case of disadvantaged students this adjustment may often "preclude proper emphasis on the development of intellectual potential for many students." McKelpin further states that "this would seem to account for the relatively low correlation between SAT and HSA that is often reported for these students" (p. 165).

Morse (1963) found that for a sample of eighth grade students the relationship between grade point average and measured intelligence was significantly lower among black students than among Caucasian students (.16 for black and .57 for white students). Morse also found that a Self-Concept of Academic Ability Scale was a better predictor of school achievement for both black and white students than IQ (.43 for Negroes and .61 for Caucasians). Morse states that the black student's self-perception "of his ability to succeed in school and his motivation to do so apparently provide a better basis for forecasting his school achievement than a measure of intelligence." Although Morse was predicting junior high school grades, and Boney (cited earlier) was predicting high school grades, these studies have implications for the prediction of college achievement, since high school GPA and college achievement (first-year GPA) are often highly related (Payne, Davidson, & Sloan, 1966).

This study by Payne, Davidson, and Sloan (1966) provides some further insights into prediction of academic success. In a study of 48 freshman students they found that the best of a set of predictors of average final work at the end of the first university year were high school grade point average ($r = .61$) and vocabulary ($r = .41$). The personality measure yielding a significant correlation (.43) with freshman grade point average was a "measure of the tendency not to repress incompleted tasks derived from Alper's Zeigarnik experiment." The most striking finding was that the predictors of freshman grade point average—high school GPA and vocabulary—were not significant predictors of average final examination marks at the end of the third university year.

Irvine (1966) has examined the prediction of college graduation from the university system of Georgia where several studies cited by Stanley and Porter were conducted. Irvine found that prediction of graduation through use of high school grade point average, SAT scores (math and verbal), number in class, and units of various subject matter courses could be made at about the .38 level of correlation. High school GPA alone correlated .34 with college graduation. However, Irvine did find a substantial multiple correlation (.59) between first-semester GPA and a combination of high school GPA and SAT verbal and math scores.

Lins, Abell, and Hutchins (1966), in a major study involving the entire entering freshman class at the University of Wisconsin in 1962, concluded that there is only a limited relationship between traditional aptitude tests such as the American College Testing Examination, the Scholastic Aptitude Test, the College Qualification Test, and first semester academic performance as reflected in GPA. The correlation between SAT total score and first semester GPA was .52 for males and .59 for females. Similar correlations were found between other aptitude measures and first-semester GPA. Lins concludes that none of the scores on the aptitude tests, as sole predictors of academic success, appear to have high predictive validity.

The above data is not conclusive regarding the validity of aptitude tests for predicting college success for a range of student body populations. It suggests that more research is needed, particularly in colleges that are integrated or are predominantly white with growing minority populations.

It is generally conceded that high school grade point average is the best single predictor of college grade point average, and that often a substantial amount of additional predictive power can be achieved by forming a composite set of predictor variables. Additional variability may rest in more individual characteristics such as motivation, persistence, and self-perception. On the basis of recent data, university support programs may also be related to the college success of minority youth.

PROGRAMS FOR "HIGH-RISK" STUDENTS

Edgerton's survey (1968) indicates that universities who have recently inaugurated programs for high-risk students are beginning to demonstrate that youngsters who did not meet traditional admissions criteria such as high SAT scores, "high" high school grades, as well as graduation from excellent academic programs, can still survive in college if proper tutorial or support services are made available to them.

Southern Illinois University's "support program" indicates that proper tutorial and counseling services will assist disadvantaged students in overcoming their educational deficits. On the basis of test scores and high school grade averages, Southern Illinois University's Counseling and Testing Office predicted at the beginning of their program in October of 1966 that the high-risk group (N = 100) would make average grades of 2.2 (a very low "D" on S.I.U.'s five-point grading system), that 24 students would fail to make a 2.0 (D) average, and that only one student would achieve a 3.0 (C) or better. But of the 74 students still in the program, 65 have made grade averages above the figure predicted for them. At the end of the first four quarters, 30 were at or above C level, including 10 who averaged 3.5 or better and two who averaged 4.0 (B) or higher. Only five were below 2.0.

Plaut (1966) stated that the University of California at Los Angeles, New York University, and Hofstra University were admitting students with weak academic credentials and providing them with special courses, counseling, summer academic programs, and a longer period in which to graduate. Plaut noted Clark and Plotkin's data on the black student at integrated colleges which indicated that success was possible for disadvantaged students. They studied five classes of the National Scholarship and Service Fund for Negro Students and found that "90 percent of the respondents from this very deprived group, and over two thirds of the whole group, received their bachelor's degree, against a national completion rate of less than 60 percent" (Plaut, 1966).

Similar programs for high-risk students at the University of California at Berkeley have accomplished equally good results. Of the 424 students to enter Berkeley's program, so far 74 (17 percent) have left, half of them for academic reasons. Of the 350 who remain, almost 70 percent are in good academic standing with grades of C or better. Of the 395 high-risk students at U.C.L.A., only 13 students have been dismissed for academic reasons. At least 25 other institutions of higher learning have had success with programs for high-risk students (Edgerton, 1968). Vocational and personal counseling, as well as academic tutorial assistance, are vital aspects of each of these programs.

These recent experiences with high-risk programs suggest that students with low test performance who lack the traditional university "dressings" can succeed in major four-year colleges. These experiences also indicate that many support-program characteristics may be more highly related to college success than was previously thought. This becomes especially important when viewed in light of the recent important national concern with providing blacks and other minority groups with an opportunity for higher education.

Predictors other than aptitude tests are important because the majority of disadvantaged black students who are educated in both urban and rural communities, North and South, have experienced grossly inadequate elementary and high school educations. The result has been that large numbers of blacks score below national norms on standardized achievement and aptitude tests. Bloom (1964) documents the fact that a deprived environment (home and school) in contrast to an abundant environment will seriously interfere with an individual's ability to perform well on academic aptitude and achievement tests. In essence, the low scores of many disadvantaged students on traditional aptitude and achievement tests result from a combination of non-academic environmental influences. Included are such factors as low teacher expectation, the press for excellence in athletics rather than in the classroom, and, in the case of many black students, grossly inadequate public school programs.

We should perhaps note here that among the other important aspects of one's past educational background that either facilitate or interfere with test performance is what measurement specialists refer to as "test-wiseness." There is evidence to support the point of view that many middle-class children are test-wise and that most children from very poor educational environments tend to be "test-blind." The writer can recall testing a group of black youngsters in a large, midwestern, urban high school. While completing the verbal section of SCAT, many youngsters would complete the first five or six items and, if they found item seven to be a difficult one, they would spend the remaining part of the allotted time working on that one item, rather than completing the remaining part of the test and returning to the difficult item. Behavior such as this does not facilitate performance on a given test no matter what the ability of the student involved. Such factors as these can be taken into account in tutorial or college support services.

UNIVERSITY STANDARDS

An examination of admissions criteria raises the question of whether the standards of the university will be lowered by admitting low-income students who do not meet "normal" admissions standards. The experience of those schools which have initiated programs for high-risk students suggests that this fear is unfounded. However, the issue of lowering standards, since it seems to be a source of consternation to many university personnel, deserves further consideration.

At many large universities the dropout rate for freshman students approximates 30 percent. Edgerton (1968) stated that at the University of Wisconsin, where more than 5,000 freshmen enroll each September, more than 25 percent drop out or flunk out by the end of the first year. Michigan State University, where the freshman enrollment in the fall of 1967 was 7,279—one of the largest freshman classes in the nation—experienced a similar attrition rate.

On the basis of the high dropout rate for many of the major colleges and universities, it would seem that present academic standards are already too high. It could be that educators are masking their exclusion policies behind the statement that disadvantaged youth should not be placed in a situation where they will fail. (Medsker & Trent [1965] found that more middle-class children with low ability are admitted into college than lower-class children with high ability.) If standards are raised high enough, the university may find itself with a relatively small student body which academically is very bright, but in the process the university will have become irrelevant to the vast majority of society.

NEW ADMISSIONS CRITERIA

To increase the relevance of the university and to make higher education available to a larger and more representative portion of our society, what is needed is not a raising or even a lowering of standards, but instead the use of a *different* set of standards which takes into account motivational and attitudinal characteristics of the individual as well as the usual intellectual factor. Revised standards should take account of diverse previous educational experiences of the many black, Mexican-American, Puerto Rican, Indian, and disadvantaged white students who often come from educationally inferior backgrounds. Once these students have been admitted, special tutorial and other support services, such as educational and personal counseling, must be made available to them.

It is also important to distinguish between a more accurate set of admissions criteria and course work criteria. We may use a different set of standards to admit students, but they should not be provided a special curriculum, i.e., "a curriculum for the disadvantaged." They will still be asked to compete in the same classes with students admitted under normal standards. The major difference is that they will be given realistic and needed support services.

SUMMARY

If we are to make an impact on the present crisis confronting this nation in terms of poverty and racial discrimination along with educating the white community regarding its own racism, we must provide black and other minority students with an opportunity for higher education. If this is to be done, traditional admissions criteria (standardized aptitude tests and high school grades) must be carefully assessed. Although the studies completed to date suggest that aptitude tests predict college success equally well for white and non-white students, there is a need for further research in this area. Because of the disadvantaging school backgrounds of many black, Mexican-American, Puerto Rican, and low-income white students, these individuals will generally score below national norms on aptitude tests. But when admitted to college and given proper tutorial and counseling services (both personal and academic), their chances for success are greatly enhanced. Hopefully this new educational opportunity will allow black and other minority youth to assume greater leadership within our society. However, the foremost challenge to predominantly white institutions of higher learning is to evaluate carefully and to reconsider those admissions policies of many years' standing in order to provide *all* segments of our society with an opportunity to share in programs of higher education.

References

Biaggio, A. B., and Stanley, J. C. Prediction of freshman grades at southern state colleges. Paper read at IX Inter-American Congress of Psychology, Miami, Fla., December, 1964.

Black and white at Northwestern University. *Integrated Education*, 1968, 6 (3), 33–40.

Bloom, B. *Stability and change in human characteristics.* New York: Wiley, 1964.

Boney, J. D. Predicting the academic achievement of secondary school Negro students. *Personnel and Guidance Journal*, 1966, 44, 700–703.

Cleary, T. A. Test bias: Validity of the Scholastic Aptitude Test for Negro and white students in integrated colleges. *Educational Testing Service Research Bulletin*. Princeton, N. J.: Educational Testing Service, June, 1966.

Edgerton, J. *Higher education for "high risk" students.* Atlanta, Ga.: Southern Education Foundation, 1968.

Green, R. L. Why the push to upgrade Negro colleges? *Southern Education Report*, 1967, 3 (1), 23–27.

Green, R. L., and Farquhar, W. W. Negro academic motivation and scholastic achievement. *Journal of Educational Psychology*, 1965, 56, 241–243.

Hills, J. R. Prediction of college grades for all public colleges of a state. *Journal of Educational Measurement*, 1964, 1, 155–159.

Irvine, D. W. Multiple prediction of college graduation from pre-admission data. *Journal of Experimental Education*, 1966, 35 (1), 84–89.

Lins, J. L., Abell, A. P., and Hutchins, H. C. Relative usefulness in predicting academic success of the ACT, the SAT, and some other variables. *Journal of Experimental Education*, 1966, 35 (2), 1–29.

McKelpin, J. P. Some implications of the intellectual characteristics of freshmen. *Journal of Educational Measurement*, 1965, 2, 161–166.

Medsker, L., and Trent, J. W. *The influence of different types of public higher institutions on college attendance from varying socio-economic and ability levels.* Berkeley, Calif.: University of California, Center for the Study of Higher Education, 1965.

Morse, R. J. Self-concept of ability, significant others and school achievement of eighth-grade students: A comparative investigation of Negro and Caucasian students. Unpublished master's thesis, Michigan State University, 1963.

Munday, L. Predicting college grades in predominantly Negro colleges. *Journal of Educational Measurement,* 1965, *2,* 157–160.

Payne, R. W., Davidson, P. O., and Sloan, R. B. The prediction of academic success in university students: A pilot study. *Canadian Journal of Psychology,* 1966, *20* (1), 52–63.

Plaut, R. L. Plans for assisting Negro students to enter and to remain in college. *Journal of Negro Education,* 1966, *35* (4), 393–399.

Stanley, J., and Porter, A. Correlation of Scholastic Aptitude Test scores with college grades for Negroes versus whites. *Journal of Educational Measurement,* 1967, *4* (4), 199–218.

Bibliography for Part IV

Dansby, Pearl G., and Dansby, Wm. A. Authoritarianism, dogmatism, and the teaching profession. Presented at the annual Southeast Psychological Convention, March 1, 1969 (this collection).

Glenn, Norval D. Negro prestige criteria: a caste study in the bases of prestige. *American Journal of Sociology* (May, 1963), **68**, 645–657.

Jencks, Christopher, and Riesman, David. The American Negro college. *Harvard Educational Review* (Winter, 1967), **37**, 3–60.

Katz, Irwin. Academic motivation and equal educational opportunity. *Harvard Educational Review* (Winter, 1968), **38**, 57–65.

Katz, I., and Greenbaum, C. Effects of anxiety threat, and racial environment on task performance of Negro college students. *Journal of Abnormal Social Psychology*, 1963, **66**, 562–567.

Munday, Leo A. Predicting college grades in predominantly Negro colleges. *Journal of Educational Measurement* (December, 1965), **2**, 157–160.

National Scholarship Service and Fund for Negro Students. Annual report 1959–1960. New York: NSSFNS, 1960.

Plaut, R. L. *Blueprint for Talent Searching.* New York: National Scholarship Service and Fund for Negro Students, 1957.

Roberts, S. O., and Carr, L. Social action participation as related to selected variables for Negro American college students. *American Psychologist,* 1961, **16**, 898 (Abstract).

Searles, Ruth, and Williams, J. A. Negro college students' participation in sit-ins. *Social Forces,* 1962, **40**, 215–220.

Sims, V. M., and Patrick, J. R. Attitude toward the Negro of the Northern and Southern college students. *Journal of Social Psychology,* 1936, **7**, 192–204.

Stanley, Julian C., and Porter, Andrew C. Correlation of Scholastic Aptitude Test score with college grades for Negroes versus whites. *Journal of Educational Measurement* (Winter, 1967), **4**, 199–218.

Wayson, William W. Securing teachers for slum schools. *Integrated Education* (Feb.–Mar., 1966), **4**, 31–38.

Wilcox, Roger. Effects of context, Thorndike-Lorge frequency and race of subjects on continuous word association. *Psychological Reports,* 1968, **23**, 1255–1260.

Wilcox, Roger. Racial differences in Associative style. *Language and Speech* (England), 1971.

PART V

Educational Psychology

This series of papers constitutes an overall look at educational problems, techniques, principles, and careers and suggests the many possibilities available for further study and work in this crucial area of education. Dr. Jones (1966) reviews research related to special education teachers, while Drs. Dansby and Dansby (1969) examine the social-personality traits of teachers. Drs. Goff (1963) and Cameron (1966) present two fairly theoretical-research efforts in predicting and facilitating success in the learning environment. Finally, Dr. Cameron (1968) examines some nonintellectual correlates of academic achievement in order to clarify the role that such factors may play in learning.

28 Research on the Special Education Teacher and Special Education Teaching

REGINALD L. JONES[1]

Dr. Jones presents a general review of problems, personnel, and processes in special education. The paper concerns Blacks to the extent that they may also be exceptional children, i.e., gifted, retarded, blind, delinquent, hard of hearing, etc. The selection contains a very thoughtful review of the relevant research literature, and suggests considerable potential for further research. Now that increasing emphasis is being placed on the education and treatment of exceptional children, the paper could obviously serve as a source of stimulation for students interested in a meaningful and significant career devoted to working among Black exceptional children.

Research on the special education teacher and special education teaching was reviewed, and several unpublished studies reported. The need for systematic research programs in this area was highlighted. Such programs would (a) explore individually classes of variables that might have some usefulness in explaining attraction to special education teaching, (b) combine the most promising of these variables into a model which would maximize the explanatory power of the individual variables, and (c) test the predictive efficiency of the model using certain experimental techniques.

There is at present widespread concern about the shortage of special education teachers (Cruickshank and Johnson, 1958; President's Panel on Mental Retardation, 1962; Western Interstate Commission on Higher Education, 1960). The best estimates indicate a need for some 200,000

SOURCE. *Exceptional Children*, 251–257, Dec., 1966. Reprinted by permission of the author and The Council for Exceptional Children.

[1] Reginald L. Jones is Associate Professor, Department of Psychology, The Ohio State University, Columbus, Ohio.

teachers, 55,000 in the field of mental retardation alone. To adequately staff classrooms for the mentally retarded in the next decade, it has been estimated that 6,000 teachers must be added each year to the pool of already available specialists. It is highly unlikely that all needed teachers of the retarded or of other exceptionalities will be attracted, although increased funds for training do make it probable that relative numbers will increase. It does not appear feasible, from a practical standpoint, to subsidize all special education teachers needed. Clearly, alternative solutions must be explored.

A program of research inquiring into a variety of concerns related to special education teaching as a career field may be most fruitful in the long run. An exploration of such areas as the image of special education teaching and exceptional children held by high school students and others, the standing of special education in the occupational structure, the characteristics and satisfactions of practicing special education teachers, the occupational desires of adolescents and the extent to which these desires are perceived as being satisfied by special education teaching, the relative attractiveness of special education teaching compared to other fields, and the interactions among these and other variables would seem to contribute substantially to our understanding of the reasons why small numbers have been attracted to special education teaching.

OVERVIEW

There has been a paucity of research on the characteristics of special education teachers themselves and on the motivations underlying the choice of special education teaching as a career field. Some work (Gottfried and Jones, 1964) has been done on stated reasons for becoming a special education teacher. However, there appears to be little published research on the standing of special education teaching in the occupational structure (i.e., the relative attractiveness, prestige, etc. of special education teaching compared to other kinds of teaching or other occupations) or on the images of special education teachers held by presently employed or prospective candidates of this occupational area. A few studies (Billings, 1963; Guskin, 1963; Horowitz and Rees, 1962; Perrin, 1954) have been done on attitudes toward certain exceptionalities and on the correlates of such attitudes. The personality traits possessed by special education teachers have also been studied.

A variety of studies (Kilpatrick, Cummings, and Jennings, 1964; Super, Starishevsky, Matlin, and Jordan, 1963; Tiedeman and O'Hara, 1963) in closely related areas, as in occupational psychology, provides a number of suggestive leads bearing on our concerns here. However, except in one or two instances, these leads have not been pursued.

RESEARCH FINDINGS

EXPERIENCE. Lord and Wallace (1949) reported that the influence of friends and relatives, as well as actual contact with exceptional children, was related to the decision to become a special education teacher. These findings were confirmed by Gottfried and Jones (1964) and by Meyers (1964). It is well to note in the three studies just cited that, while there is some evidence that preteaching experience is related to a decision to teach exceptional children, such knowledge by itself does not advance theoretical formulations seeking to account for attraction to special education teaching. Unexplained are the reasons why some individuals having such experiences elect to work in other occupational areas or why some without such experiences elect to work in special education. As Gottfried and Jones (1963) note in their discussion of the experience variable:

"One could presume that not all observers of the handicapped neighbor would choose to enter a field involving work with handicapped. One could assume that only those observers whose psychological-motivational makeup made them sensitive to the stimulus situation (handicapped neighbor) were greatly affected. Some observers appropriately motivated would have entered the field whether or not they had a handicapped neighbor. The determination of the relative contribution of psychological need structure and situational structure to career choice requires considerable further investigation" (p. 14).

Johnson (1964) developed a comprehensive questionnaire designed to assess experience with the exceptional as a variable that might be predictive of attraction to special education teaching. The rationale of his investigation was that the length, time, and type of contact with the exceptional might have much greater explanatory usefulness than might knowledge only of whether the respondent had some kind of unspecified contact with an exceptional person. Unfortunately, Johnson was unable to procure a large enough sample of teachers of exceptional children to make a thorough analysis of his questionnaire. However, the instrument has been thoroughly pretested and is now available for use in studies in which experience or contact with the exceptional may be a variable.

PREFERENCES. Several studies (Badt, 1957; Jones and Gottfried, 1962; Meyers, 1964) of preferences for teaching exceptional children have been reported. These studies reveal that certain teaching specialties have greater attractiveness than do others; generally, specialities involving work with the emotionally maladjusted, the mentally gifted, and the mentally handicapped are rated highly attractive.

Three studies inquired into how preferences among various teaching specialties were interrelated. The first study (Jones and Gottfried, 1962), which compared only special education fields with themselves, identified several interest clusters. One cluster, bipolar in nature, consisted of interest in teaching the educable mentally retarded on the one hand and interest in teaching the mentally gifted on the other. A second bipolar cluster consisted of the hard of hearing and the partially seeing on one pole of the continuum and the severely mentally retarded on the other. A third cluster was composed of certain preferences for teaching deaf, blind, delinquent, and emotionally disturbed children. The subjects of the study were naive college students (of both sexes) in education.

Three methodological questions relating to the generality of the results have been raised: (a) The sexes were combined in undetermined proportions. Since there are sex differences in interest in the special education fields, any analysis combining the sexes runs the risk of yielding unclear results. (b) The population included subjects who were largely unfamiliar with the characteristics of exceptional children. Therefore, they may not have clearly understood what is involved in teaching such children. Hence, their responses could have been little more than random in nature. (c) The technique of cluster analysis is crude, with a certain subjectivity involved at critical points in the computational process.

These questions led to a second study, presently unpublished, designed to remedy the aforementioned problems: (a) only females were included as subjects; (b) experienced teachers (both in regular and special classes), students enrolled in special education, and students enrolled in regular education training programs served as subjects; and (c) the technique of factor analysis (principal components analysis, varimax rotation) was used in data analysis. The results revealed some overlap in the results of the study involving cluster analysis and the factor analytic study. The patterns of relationships were sharpened in the latter study.

A third and unpublished study of preferences identified patterns of interest related to preferences for teaching intellectually exceptional (gifted and retarded) and certain of the more common specialities (e.g., kindergarten, secondary English, or foreign languages). Factor analysis uncovered meaningful relationships among the variables. Also, there was considerable consistency in the patterns for four samples of subjects. Of special interest was a factor of preference for teaching educable mentally retarded children, found in all samples. This factor suggested that preferences for teaching the various levels of mentally retarded children (i.e., elementary, junior high school, and senior high school) were seen as belonging together and also different from other teaching specialities. A second factor of interest, usually bipolar in nature, consisted of the elementary teaching specialties on the one hand and the secondary specialties on the other, with the exception that teaching of the retarded at the secondary level never loaded on the secondary pole of the factor, while preferences for teaching elementary level retarded children did load on the elementary pole of the factor.

Why the concern about interrelationships among preferences in the special education teaching areas? Studies of preferences for special education teaching were undertaken following the assumption that, if interests in certain areas are closely related, there is the possibility that a common core of variables might explain attraction to these areas. If this should be the case, we need not study each area of exceptionality separately for purposes of isolating crucial variables. Much time and energy are saved, and a more powerful conceptual model is developed.

PERSONALITY. Several studies (Cawley, 1964; Garrison and Scott, 1961; Jones and Gottfried, 1966b) have been done on personality characteristics of presently employed teachers or prospective teachers of exceptional children. One methodological shortcoming of these investigations is their failure to use teachers of nonexceptional children or persons employed in other occupations as contrast subjects. Thus, while a given group of traits may be seen as characteristic of teachers of a given exceptionality, they may be in reality no different from those possessed by persons employed in a wide variety of seemingly diverse occupations.

In another unpublished study, Gottfried and Jones identified a number of personality variables differentiating satisfied from dissatisfied teachers of the educable mentally retarded. Satisfied teachers were found to score significantly higher on the teacher preference schedule subtests nondirective and preadult fixation and significantly lower on the orderliness subtest. The results could not be generalized to all teachers of the educable mentally retarded, since an analysis of variance indicated that level of satisfaction and teaching level (i.e., elementary or secondary) interact, often obscuring differences between satisfied and dissatisfied groups at each level.

Jones and Gottfried (1966a) explored psychological need variables for the purpose of differentiating persons expressing interest in or actually preparing for one area of special education from those interested in teaching in another. Again, a number of differentiating noncognitive variables were identified, many of which, on logical grounds, seem reasonable. Unfortunately, this study possesses the same methodological shortcoming

282 The Psychological Consequences of Being a Black American

mentioned previously: it presents no evidence supporting the view that the particular psychological needs identified as being related to a preference for teaching any one exceptionality are uniquely related to preferences for teaching that exceptionality.

Garrison and Scott (1961) identified certain psychological needs differentiating prospective teachers of the exceptional from those of others. A methodological shortcoming of this study is its lumping together of teachers of a variety of types of exceptional children. Certain evidence on preferences for teaching exceptional children (Cawley, 1964; Jones and Gottfried, 1962) suggests that entirely different factors may be operating in determining preferences for teaching one exceptionality as opposed to preferences for teaching another; exceptional children cannot be considered a single group.

Indeed, recent studies (Jones and Gottfried, 1965; Jones, Gottfried, and Owens, 1966; Semmel and Dickson, 1966) indicate that some differentiation among exceptional persons is made, depending upon the degree and kind of interpersonal contact required. Thus, one may accept any given exceptional person in one situation, but not in another. More to the point, Jones and Gottfried (1966b), using samples of teachers of exceptional and nonexceptional children, found rather clear agreement in the assignment of the degree of prestige enjoyed by the various specialties subsumed under special education.

The studies just cited suggest that special education teaching may attract persons having characteristics different from those in other occupational areas and also that some differentiation is made among exceptional children as individuals to be interacted with or to be taught.

PRESTIGE. Prestige was one variable which seemed to have usefulness in explaining attraction to special education teaching. To date two studies in this area have been completed. The first (Jones and Gottfried, 1966b) presented a comparison of the perceived prestige of certain special education teaching areas and regular class teaching. The results revealed that special education teaching carried higher prestige than regular class teaching and also that certain differential perceptions of prestige occurred among the various specialties subsumed under special education teaching; teachers of the blind, the gifted, the emotionally disturbed, and the severely mentally retarded were seen as possessing especially high standing.

The second study (Jones, 1966) presented data on the rated prestige (using a point scale) of certain special education areas compared to regular class teaching and a wide spectrum of other occupational specialties, using a high school population. The purpose of this study, consisting of over 200 subjects and 64 occupations, was to determine how certain special education areas compared with a full range of occupational areas, rather than regular class teaching only, in rated prestige. The results reported in the present paper consist of only 24 occupations and 50 subjects (25 boys and 25 girls in their junior or senior year of high school). The data of Table 1 reveal the overall perceptions of the prestige carried by a given specialty, and they also reveal the differential occupational perceptions of boys and girls. These perceptions are especially apparent

TABLE 1

Rated Prestige of Certain Special Education Teaching Specialties and Other Occupational Areas

Occupation	Combined Average Rating	Girls	Boys
College and University Teacher	8.06 (1)	8.40 (1)	7.78 (1)
Mayor of Large City	7.44 (2)	7.48 (2)	7.40 (2)
Architect	7.22 (3)	7.28 (3)	7.16 (3)
Airline Pilot	6.54 (4)	6.32 (12)	6.76 (4)
Junior College Teacher	6.48 (5)	6.56 (8)	6.40 (5.5)
Teacher of Severely Mentally Re-	6.48 (6)	7.20 (4.5)	5.76 (11)
tarded Newspaper Columnist	6.38 (7)	6.36 (10.5)	6.40 (5.5)
Teacher of Secondary School Edu-			
cable Mentally Retarded	6.32 (8)	7.01 (6)	5.64 (12)
Teacher of Secondary School Gifted	6.28 (9)	6.72 (7)	5.84 (9)
Teacher of Secondary School Science	6.24 (10)	6.36 (10.5)	6.12 (8)
Teacher of Secondary School English	5.97 (11)	6.40 (9)	5.44 (13)
Building Contractor	5.86 (12)	5.56 (14.5)	6.36 (7)
Teacher of Elementary School Gifted	5.84 (13)	6.28 (13)	5.40 (14)
Teacher of Elementary School			
Educable Mentally Retarded	5.68 (14)	7.20 (4.5)	4.16 (18.5)
Insurance Agent	5.45 (15)	5.14 (16)	5.80 (10)
Teacher of Elementary Grades 4–6	5.04 (16)	5.56 (14.5)	4.56 (16)
Teacher of Elementary Grades 1–3	4.88 (17)	5.00 (18)	4.76 (15)
Teacher of Nursery School and			
Kindergarten	4.62 (18)	5.12 (17)	4.12 (20)
Teacher of Secondary Home Eco-			
nomics (girls) and Industrial Arts			
(boys)	4.23 (19)	4.84 (19)	4.40 (17)
Plumber	3.96 (20)	3.76 (20)	4.16 (18.5)
Taxi Driver	3.60 (21)	3.08 (21.5)	3.04 (21)
Streetcar Motorman	2.76 (22)	3.08 (21.5)	2.22 (22)
Sharecropper	2.02 (23)	3.04 (23)	1.02 (23)
Shoe Shiner	1.19 (24)	1.06 (24)	1.32 (24)

Note: Rank order in parentheses.

where the teaching occupations are concerned. The teaching occupations in virtually all instances are rated lower in prestige by boys than by girls.

A MULTIVARIATE APPROACH.   Any understanding of the dynamics under-lying attraction to special education teaching will require consideration of a number of variables. To capture the richness of the interrelationships, it will be necessary to plan and conduct studies utilizing a multivariate approach. The study of single variables may be valuable in preliminary explorations. However, there is always the possibility that complex inter-actions underlie the phenomena under study. These interactions are not uncovered by the study of single variables in isolation.

The fruitfulness of the multivariate approach has been revealed in a study by Johnson (1964). The essential procedure of the Johnson experi-ment involved the building of hypothetical teaching situations which in-cluded elements of the work situation which a previous analysis had suggested to be promising. The elements included for study were (a) the label (e.g., educable mentally retarded), (b) prestige and salary, and (c) certain characteristics of the children to be taught (for example, their need for sympathetic understanding).

It was thus possible to build hypothetical job descriptions in which a variable was absent or present in varying degrees and in which each variable could be studied both singularly and in combination with others. In responding, the subject indicated the strength of his interest in the hypothetical positions by checking a nine point rating scale. Two of the hypothetical positions are presented below:

A position is offered to you to teach a group of educable mentally re-tarded children who have no special needs for sympathetic understanding. This is a position of average salary and prestige in the community.

I would   would not

9 | 8 | 7 | 6 | 5 | 4 | 3 | 2 | 1

like a position teaching this group of children under the circumstances cited above.

A position of above average salary and prestige is offered to you to teach a group of children who need considerable sympathetic understanding. This is a group of educable mentally retarded children.

I would   would not

9 | 8 | 7 | 6 | 5 | 4 | 3 | 2 | 1

like a position teaching this group of children under the circumstances cited above.

For any given exceptionality, 10 different hypothetical positions (including the variables in various combinations) were developed. It was thus possible, using analysis of variance techniques, to isolate the combinations of variables leading to greatest attraction to a given area of special education teaching. And by developing the same kinds of hypothetical situations describing the teaching of nonexceptional children as were used to describe the teaching of exceptional children, it was also possible to isolate aspects of special education teaching which serve to heighten or diminish its attractiveness compared to regular class teaching.

Data obtained on a small and select group of students revealed statistically significant differences in degree of interest in teaching exceptional and nonexceptional children related to prestige and salary and to certain psychological characteristics of the children to be taught. Where teaching of exceptional children was concerned, prestige and salary were not always critical variables. The study needs replication. The intent in this section has been merely to point out the need for a multivariate approach in the study of preferences for special education teaching and to indicate the work that has been undertaken using this approach.

SUMMARY

A three pronged research program has been suggested in this paper: (a) delineation of the status of certain areas of special education teaching as occupational areas, the images held of these areas and their practitioners, and the relationship of the images of special education teaching compared to the images of other occupations; (b) a delineation of the actual unique characteristics and experiences possessed by special education practitioners, as compared to persons in other occupational areas; and (c) a meshing of data obtained from the two analyses above, taking account of the interactions among variables where appropriate.

When put into proper long range perspective, the aim of a total research program would be to (a) explore individually classes of variables that might have some usefulness in explaining attraction to special education teaching, (b) combine the most promising of these variables into a model which would maximize the explanatory power of the individual variables, and (c) test the predictive efficiency of the model using certain experimental techniques. If certain crucial variables predictive of interest in special education teaching are identified with some precision, it should be possible (a) to include these variables in certain communications (e.g., films and written messages) to maximize interest in special education teaching, and (b) to predict the characteristics and backgrounds of individuals most likely to be attracted to this vocational area and hence receptive to the communication.

Data of the type presented in this paper represent only the first level of analysis in a multiphased research program. Once crucial variables are identified, it will be necessary to demonstrate their practical value, a step taken only recently (Meisgeier, 1965).

References

Badt, Margit I. Attitudes of university students toward exceptional children and special education. *Exceptional Children,* 1957, **23**, 286–290, 336.

Billings, Helen K. An exploratory study of the attitudes of noncrippled children toward crippled children in three selected elementary schools. *Journal of Experimental Education,* 1963, **31**, 381–387.

Cawley, J. F. Selected characteristics of individuals oriented toward mental retardation. Paper read at The Council for Exceptional Children, Chicago, April, 1964.

Cruickshank, W. M., and Johnson, G. O. *Education of exceptional children and youth.* Englewood Cliffs, New Jersey: Prentice Hall, 1958.

Garrison, K. C., and Scott, Mary H. A comparison of the personal needs of college students preparing to teach in different teaching areas. *Educational and Psychological Measurement,* 1961, **21**, 955–964.

Gottfried, N. W., and Jones, R. L. Some observations on background factors associated with career choices in the teaching of exceptional children. Paper read at The Council for Exceptional Children, Philadelphia, April, 1963.

Gottfried, N. W., and Jones, R. L. Career choice factors in special education. *Exceptional Children,* 1964, **30**, 218–223.

Guskin, S. L. Measuring the stereotype of the mental defective. *American Journal of Mental Deficiency,* 1963, **67**, 569–575.

Horowitz, Leola S., and Rees, Norma S. Attitudes and information about deafness. *Volta Review,* 1962, **64**, 180–189.

Johnson, M. R. An experimental investigation of some dimensions underlying preferences for teaching exceptional children. Unpublished master's thesis, Fisk University, 1964.

Jones, R. L. Special education teaching in the occupational structure: a factor analytic study. Paper read at The Council for Exceptional Children, Toronto, April, 1966.

Jones, R. L., and Gottfried, N. W. Preferences and configurations of interest in special class teaching. *Exceptional Children,* 1962, **28**, 371–377.

Jones, R. L., and Gottfried, N. W. The social distance of the exceptional. Paper read at American Psychological Association, Chicago, September, 1965.

Jones, R. L., and Gottfried, N. W. Psychological needs and preferences for teaching exceptional children. *Exceptional Children,* 1966, **32**, 313–321.(a)

Jones, R. L., and Gottfried, N. W. The prestige of special education teaching. *Exceptional Children,* 1966, **32**, 465–468.(b)

Jones, R. L., Gottfried, N. W., and Owens, Angela. The social distance of the exceptional: a study at the high school level. *Exceptional Children,* 1966, **32**, 551–556.

Kilpatrick, F. P., Cummings, M. C., and Jennings, M. K. *The image of the federal service.* Washington, D. C.: The Brookings Institution, 1964.

Lord, F. E., and Wallace, H. M. Recruitment of special education teachers. *Exceptional Children,* 1949, **15**, 171–173.

Meisgeier, C. The identification of successful teachers of mentally or physically handicapped children. *Exceptional Children,* 1965, **32**, 229–236.

Meyers, C. E. Realities in teacher recruitment. *Mental Retardation,* 1964, **2**, 42–46.

Perrin, Elinor H. The social position of the speech defective child. *Journal of Speech and Hearing Disorders,* 1954, **19**, 250–252.

President's Panel on Mental Retardation. *A proposed program for national action to combat mental retardation.* Washington, D. C.: US Government Printing Office, 1962.

Semmel, M. I., and Dickson, S. Connotative reactions of college students to disability labels. *Exceptional Children,* 1966, **32**, 443–450.

Super, D. E., Starishevsky, R., Matlin, N., and Jordan, J. P. *Career development: self concept theory.* New York: College Entrance Examination Board, 1963.

Tiedeman, D. V., and O'Hara, R. P. *Career development: choice and adjustment.* New York: College Entrance Examination Board, 1963.

Western Interstate Council on Higher Education. *Teachers of exceptional children for the west.* Boulder, Colorado: Author, 1960.

29 Authoritarianism, Dogmatism, and the Teaching Profession

PEARL MAYO DANSBY & WILLIAM A. DANSBY
Tennessee A. and I. State University, Nashville, Tennessee

This paper was a speech that Dr. Pearl Dansby and Dr. William Dansby delivered at the Southeastern Psychological Association meetings (1969) and deals with the personality traits of authoritarianism and dogmatism within members of the teaching profession. Interesting data are presented which differentiate Black and white student teachers, and certain of these differences are related to actual in-class effectiveness of performance. This work relates to Dr. Pearl Gore's paper in this volume (she is now Mrs. Dansby), and also to Dr. Taylor's paper regarding authoritarianism and ethnocentrism in Black college students.

What kinds of college students select the teaching profession as a career? The available data indicate that a female student is more likely to make this choice than a male and that a Black student is more likely to choose teaching than a white college student. A review of the research suggests a varied and sometimes conflicting picture of the personality characteristics of those entering the teaching profession. This research examines two personality variables and investigates their relationship not only to the choice of teaching as a profession for both Negro and white college students but to criteria of teaching effectiveness as well. The present study asks two related questions: (1) How accurate are the stereotypes of dogmatism and authoritarianism as personality traits of persons choosing teaching as a career?, and (2) is there a relationship between measured teaching effectiveness and the personality traits of dogmatism and authoritarianism?

Scales of Dogmatism (D-Scale) and Authoritarianism (F-Scale) were administered to college students at predominantly Negro and predominantly white schools. The racial differences in measured dogmatism and

SOURCE. Paper presented to the Southeastern Psychological Association, 1969 Annual Convention, New Orleans, and reprinted with permission of the senior author.

authoritarianism are presented in Table 1 which shows that both male and female college students scored significantly higher on measures of authoritarianism and dogmatism than did white college students. Sex differences in authoritarianism and dogmatism alluded to in other research were seen here only in the Negro college student sample. Negro females scored significantly higher on the D and F scales than did Negro males. It is interesting to note that the category of students scoring highest on dogmatism and authoritarianism were Negro females who represent the category of students most likely to choose teaching as a career, while the students lowest in measured dogmatism and authoritarianism were white male students, the group least likely to choose teaching as a career. The high authoritarianism and dogmatism score of the Negro female may be another related manifestation of the Negro matriarchal home setting.

College students engaged in student teaching were compared with other upperclassmen on measures of authoritarianism and dogmatism. In comparing those who were in student teaching with students preparing for other vocations, statistically significant differences were found in dogmatism scores, but no significant differences in authoritarianism scores. Table 2 shows that both Negro and white student teachers were less dogmatic than students in other fields.

No significant difference was found between the overall authoritarianism scores of student teacher and non-student teacher groups. In the small white male student teacher group the mean score was lower than that of the non-student teacher group. However, the Negro male student teacher tended to be more authoritarian than his upper-class counterpart. Contrary to public opinion the current results suggest that persons who choose teaching as a profession are no more authoritarian in personality makeup than those who do not. Furthermore, the results seem to show an above average degree of open mindedness in persons choosing teaching, as evidenced by the significantly lower dogmatism scores.

TABLE 1

A Comparison of Authoritarianism and Dogmatism Scores of Negro and White College Students

	D Scores	F Scores	N
Negro College Students			
Male	5.6	−1.06	50
Female	13.2	7.66	50
White College Students			
Male	− 4.72	−7.91	77
Female	.46	−8.56	33

TABLE 2

A Comparison of Authoritarianism and Dogmatism Scores of Student Teachers with Other College Students

	D Scores	F Scores	N
White Male Student Teachers	−30.16	−30.75	14
White Male Students that are not Student Teachers	− 4.62	− 7.91	77
White Female Student Teachers	−10.5	− 9.65	25
White Female Students that are not Student Teachers	.46	− 8.56	33
Negro Male Student Teachers	2.38	+13.91	43
Negro Male Students that are not Student Teachers	5.6	− 1.05	50
Negro Female Student Teachers	4.40	4.54	48
Negro Female Students that are not Student Teachers	13.2	7.66	50

The second author of this paper supervises college students engaged in practice teaching. A rating scale of student teacher performance is used by the university supervisor in conjunction with the regular classroom teacher. The rating scale has four areas of evaluation, with descriptive items for each area to be rated, and are: *Teaching Techniques*—with sub-areas such as (1) "Clearness of objectives," (2) "Ability to motivate students," and (3) "Provision for individual differences"; *Classroom Management*—with sub-areas such as (1) "Ability to maintain classroom discipline," (2) "Classroom efficiency in time and materials," and (3) "Care of physical condition of classroom"; *Professional Attitude*—with sub-areas as (1) "Professional interest in school," (2) "Respect for authority," and (3) "Cooperation and loyalty"; and *Personal and Social Qualities*—with sub-areas such as (1) "Self-confidence," (2) "Judgement," (3) "Initiative and leadership," and (4) "Dependability." All items are rated on a four point scale from 1 (Poor) to 4 (Outstanding).

Where the student teachers who scored low on both D and F scales were compared with those scoring very high and D and F, statistically significant differences were observed between professional attitude and personal and social qualities. A trend was found just short of significance for students scoring high on the D and F scales to receive higher evaluation than those who were below the mean on both scales, and no statistically significant difference was observed for classroom management. Low scorers on the D and F scales received a higher evaluation in professional attitude than high scorers at a statistically significant level (Chi square = 5.49, 2 df, p .025).

Low scorers on the D and F scales received a higher evaluation in personal and social qualities than high scorers at a statistically significant level (Chi square = 5.09, df = 2, p .025). The combined effect of the measures of dogmatism and authoritarianism was a significant predictor variable to independent evaluations of teacher effectiveness. It appears that open-minded non-authoritarian students are perceived as having more of the personal and social qualities and the professional attitudes desirable in teachers. There was a tendency, however, for close-minded authoritarian students to be perceived as more adept in teaching techniques. These results suggest the need for research that would specifically question the role that such personality traits may play in promoting more effective interaction between teachers and students in the learning setting.

30 Trait Identification as a Means of Predicting Academic Goal Attainment[1]

REGINA M. GOFF
Morgan State College, Baltimore, Maryland

This research examines certain personality and other differences between Black freshmen and senior university students. In terms of experimental design, studies such as this take what are thought to be very different groups of subjects and examine a variety of test responses of the two groups in order to specify the nature of the difference. Dr. Goff finds that personality factors, as such, inadequately predict scholastic performance, and reasonably suggests that many factors need to be considered in order to meaningfully predict success in college. She cautions us by observing that trait trends should not be ignored because of her finding that "self-doubt," "self-abasement," and "impulsiveness" would make a student vulnerable to outside influences, which in turn, would render such a student unable to cope with the college setting and predispose him to either failure or withdrawal.

It is the purpose of this study to consider the feasibility of using personality features as a basis for judgment in predicting academic goal attainment. Interest in the problem has led to intensive investigation (1, 2, 3) of behavior traits which aid in adaptive responses toward academic goals. The attempt hypothesizes the presence of distinctive forces in addition to intellect which are a priori to achievement. Conceptualized, the behavior of emotional energy described as traits is the force which presses toward response. Sthenic, or positive, emotion appears as personal warmth, outgoingness, and the individual is said to possess the trait of sociability. Asthenic, or negative, emotion appears as aggression, belliger-

SOURCE. Reprinted from the *Journal of Experimental Education*, 1963, 31, 3, 287–302 with permission of the author and Dembar Educational Research Services, Inc.

[1] This study was supported by a grant from the Faculty Research Fund of Morgan, Baltimore, Maryland.

ence, and the person is said to possess the trait of pugnacity. The assumption concerning the role of behavior features or traits poses inquiry.

A specific question may be stated as follows: Can the relevance or weight of traits in determining academic response be considered in isolation of the complex of mental life and its consequents?

It is assumed that the mind organizes its content, gives meaning to situations and determines which traits shall operate in adaptive response or in carrying out a course of action under conditions of the specified environment. Further, emotional energy, some of which is deeply embedded, has force potential which takes shape under the press of particular environmental stimulations different from the form which it would have taken in the absence of these stimulations. Finally, goal-reaching is the function of variables, dependent upon operation of selected traits which are anticipatory means to ends and which are in turn affected by psychic tendencies and experience.

To the end of examining the question raised and testing hypothesis, the following approach was used. Two measures were obtained on the graduating class and on some members of the freshman class of a liberal arts college. The college selected is a state institution, predominantly Negro, where admittance of graduates of high schools of the state is mandatory though some screening is achieved through use of aptitude and subject-matter tests. Freshmen reported in this study were assumed competent of meeting scholastic requirements of the college. Drop-outs due to finance are relatively few, due to work opportunities and financial aid arrangements. All of the subjects in the study are Negro. The instruments used were the California Personality Inventory and Harrower's Group Rorschach. The senior group consisted of 103 men and 86 women. The original freshman enrollment of this class approximated 600 students. Traditionally at this college, despite original intentions, two-thirds of the freshman group drop out prior to graduation with the smallest percentage of cases attributed to finance. Measures were obtained on the California Personality Inventory for 100 randomly selected freshman men and 100 freshman women. It is assumed that the sample will include potential drop-outs and that trait differentials which relate to motivation may be revealed in comparative examination of freshman and senior responses. Rorschach data were available on a smaller freshman population including 56 men and 25 women.

THE INSTRUMENTS

The California Personality Inventory purports to reveal characteristics of personality "specific to socially functioning individuals" with requisites among other things for academic success. The Inventory consists of 18 scales grouped in four classes or categories. Each category seeks to "emphasize some of the psychological and psychometric clusterings which exist among them." Of this number, 10 scales in three of the classes are reported which appear specific to academic intent and behavior. These are:

Class I.   Measures of poise, ascendancy and self-assurance. Scales selected: Dominance (Do) - identifies the "aggressive, confident --- persistent, planful individual."
Self-acceptance (Sa) - Assesses factors of independence in thought and action and a sense of personal worth.
Well-being (Wb) - Identifies individuals "relatively free from self-doubt and disillusionment - ambitious and productive."

Class II.   Measures of socialization. Scales selected: Responsibility (Re) - identifies the "planful, responsible --- conscientious person --- alert to ethical and moral issues."
Social maturity (So) - Indicates "degree of integrity and rectitude" inclusive of honesty, seriousness, conformity.
Self-control (Sc) - Assesses "adequacy of self-regulation," deliberateness, thoroughness, patience.
Community (Cm) - Indicates "the degree to which an individual's reactions and responses correspond to the modal (common) pattern established for the inventory."

Class III. Measures of achievement potential. Scales selected: Achievement via conformance (Ac) - "Identifies those factors of interest and motivation which facilitate achievement in any setting where conformance is a positive behavior."
Achievement via independence (Ai) - "Identifies those factors of interest and motivation which facilitate achievement in any setting where autonomy and independence are positive behaviors."
Intellectual efficiency (Ie) - Indicates "personal and intellectual efficiency which the individual has attained."

These scales were selected because components such as foresight, judgment, self-reliance, persistence, industry, effective intelligence and self-direction would appear to be relevant to pursuit of academic goals. Class IV, which includes scales measuring psychological-mindedness, flexibility, and femininity, was not used. It was felt that the aforementioned scales were perhaps most pertinent to the problem.

The study will be presented in the following manner. The question raised will be answered with appropriate data reference followed by conclusions and implications.

FINDINGS

Can the relevance or weight of traits in determining academic responses be considered in isolation of the complex of mental life and its consequents? Trait identification is based on the California Personality Inventory and is shown in Tables 1 and 2. Table 1 illustrates the mean scores

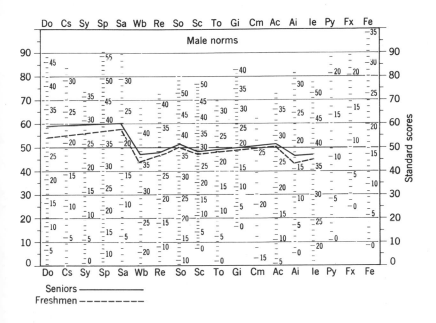

Seniors ———————
Freshmen — — — — — — — —

TABLE 1

Means Scores for Senior and Freshman Male Students on the California Personality Inventory

on each of the selected scales for freshman and senior male students. A most striking finding was the great similarity between the two groups. In some instances scores were practically identical. The greatest distance between means was found on the dominance scale with the seniors having a slightly higher mean of 31.3 compared with the freshman score of 28.9. The difference is not significant and the null hypothesis was accepted at the 0.7 level of probability.

Table 2 represents mean scores of freshman and senior women, where

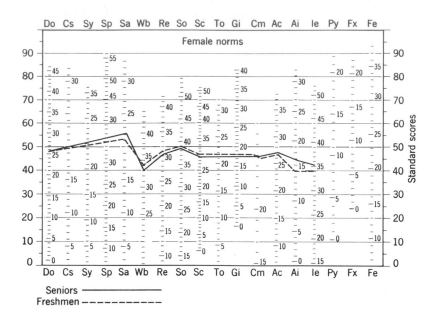

TABLE 2

Means Scores for Senior and Freshman Female Students on the California Personality Inventory

even closer similarity prevailed. The greatest distance between means in this instance was on the achievement via independence (Ai) scale with senior women having a mean of 16.75 and freshman women a score of 15.2 with no significant difference involved. The null hypothesis was accepted at the .05 level of probability.

By way of brief description, the profile for male students was characterized by a slight elevation of two of the three scales in the cluster concerned with poise, ascendancy and self-assurance, and a depression of scores in the area of achievement potential. Highest points were on the dominance and self-acceptance scales indicating uninhibited, aggressive, self-centered behavior with reflections of assurance and confidence. The lower point on the well-being scale, however, the third in this cluster, suggested that this behavior belied the presence of caution, disillusionment, and self-doubt. Conscientious effort and seriousness of purpose indicated on the socialization scale is tempered somewhat by impulsive, changeable, assertive behavior, some lack of control and interest in personal gain as revealed on the responsibility and self-control scales. The communality scale scores, however, indicate that this population does not depart from normal expectations in terms of reliability, adequacy in judg-ment, and realistic appraisal of situations and would contrast to a restless, imaginative group revealing more than expected by way of internal problems and conflicts.

Scores in the achievement potential group were among the lowest in the profile. In terms of these responses, mental capacity is best exercised in traditional, structured settings where creativity, flexibility, and in-dependence in thinking are not demands.

Significantly, the shape of the profile for women approximated that of male students and, if superimposed on the male profile, would show precise directional trends though scores were not as high. Women ranked lower than men on measures of poise, ascendancy, self-assurance, and intellectual efficiency. Men students were either slightly above or at the established norm (found on profile for college students in CPI Manual) on five characteristics out of nine, while women students were below on seven with, in the case of freshman women, two of the seven departing by one standard deviation below the norm.

According to these finds, sex was more related to personality differences than was academic classification.

TRAIT DIFFERENCES IN RELATION TO THE INTELLECTUAL FACTOR

An attempt was made to see if personality differences would occur between seniors and freshmen if the intelligence factor were held con-stant. To this end, selections were made of high and low scorers on the intellectual efficiency scale in each of the four groups; freshman and senior men and freshman and senior women. Means were then compared on the remaining traits as illustrated in Table 3.

TABLE 3

Mean Scores on Traits of Senior and Freshman Male and Female Students When the Intellectual Factor Was Held Constant

| Trait | Male | | | | Female | | | |
| | High | | Low | | High | | Low | |
	Sr.	Fr.	Sr.	Fr.	Sr.	Fr.	Sr.	Fr.
Do	32	34.2	29.5	27.5	45.1	30	25	24.1
Sa	24.6(25)	25.3	21.9(22)	21.1	23.0	22.1	21	20
Wb	38.2	38.4	32.7(33)	31.8(32)	38	39	30	31.2
Re	31.6(32)	31.2	26.7(27)	27.5	33.5	33.3	29	29.4
So	35.6	34.6(35)	34.2	32.7(33)	40	43.8(44)	34	37.4
Sc	31.0	28.8(29)	22.7(23)	24	35.2	38.1	24	26.4

Highest trait scores in all groups with the exception of high-scoring females were on socialization and well-being. Seven groups were thus undifferentiated among themselves and from the student population at large. High-scoring senior women were singularly high on the dominance trait though this, too, is among the cluster which includes well-being. All eight groups were lowest on self-acceptance.

A further comparison of these findings with those of the total population revealed a reversal in the case of two traits. In the total population, the mean on the self-acceptance scale was higher than that on the well-being scale. When high and low scores were isolated, in all instances the Sa score was lower than the Wb score. Intellect may be operative in one's assessment of his personal worth. The data suggest that individuals above or below the average range of mentality are probably more sensitive in comparing the self with others, less confident, and less accepting of the self than are individuals considered intellectually average. The higher score on the Wb scale suggests that feelings of well-being are not affected or lowered in instances where conscientious effort is made toward improvement.

Sex differences were less prominent when the intelligence factor was held constant. Academic classification, again, was not a decisive factor associated with the presence of specific traits.

RORSCHACH FINDINGS

Rorschach data supported CPI findings. These responses indicate that in the range of psychological experience: intellectual, emotional, inner, and social—in other words, in terms of cohesiveness—there was a normal pattern of expression representative of the average of the wider population. Table 4 shows that the mean for whole responses in all four groups was 4. The cut-off point for deviant or poor responses was 5.

Table 5 shows similarities in levels of proficiency among groups when numerical values 1–10 were attached to responses. Scores 1–4 were assigned responses representative of adequate intellectual functioning and inner resources for adjustment; ability to maintain a balance between

TABLE 4

Whole and Weighted Poor Responses on Rorschach

	Male		Female	
R	Sr.	Fresh.	Sr.	Fresh.
w	4.4	4.4	4.0	4.6
wp	9.12	11.3	9.4	13.5

TABLE 5

Rorschach Responses When Numerical Values Are Attached

| | Male | | | | Female | | | |
| | Senior | | Freshman | | Senior | | Freshman | |
Scores	No.	%	No.	%	No.	%	No.	%
1	293	12.0	97	12.4	207	10	152	12
2	654	25.4	210	27.0	570	27.5	352	27
3	463	18.0	135	17.2	361	17.4	175	13
4	89	3.0	25	3.1	87	4.2	34	3
5	3		3		1			
6	307	12.0	52	7.0	201	10.2	77	6
7	225	9.0	39	5.0	147	7.1	111	9
8	109	4.0	41	5.1	71	3.4	64	5
9	238	9.2	88	11.2	239	11.0	202	16.16
10	191	7.4	90	11.5	181	8.7	123	9
Total	2572	100	780	99.5	2065	99.5	1290	100

impulse and values; to delay immediate gratification in deference to long-range goals; to exercise qualities of empathy; and to achieve acceptance of self and harmony in one's social world. Senior and freshman male students had 58% and 60% of the responses, respectively, within this value range while senior and freshman women had 59% and 55%, respectively, in this category.

The low percentage of "1" responses is noticeable, assuming "1" to incorporate all functions of excellence. The range among groups is from 10% to 12% of the total responses. Concurring with intellectual potential scores on the CPI, the factor of cognition, creative organization of thought, is not highly developed.

PREDICTIVE PROPERTIES OF TRAITS

These findings bring the question raised into sharp focus. Given a set of traits which characterizes an individual or group, can reasonable expectations in response or predictions of academic success be made?

It would appear from the data, revealing great similarity between a group of freshmen (some of whom are potential drop-outs) and seniors who are prospective graduates, that personality features of themselves may not be adequate forecasts of academic goal attainment and that behavior traits might best be considered within the context of the total mental configuration of the individual. The following example is an illustration.

A particular freshman student of the population under consideration holds an original intention of completing requirements for graduation. The student has a great need for status acceptance. The campus environment may or may not be compatible to need satisfaction. If it is incompatible, the student may respond to substitute stimuli, in this instance probably a non-college group where aspiration levels are lower and status attainment less difficult. The same set of traits would be operative in the new response for there would exist no variation in motive. However, decreased interest in the academic setting might lead to eventual dropping out. A senior student with a similar trait profile may be observed to have reached stated goals. Incidentally, the illustration also suggests that, apart from personality features, consideration should be given to the place of academic goals in the value hierarchy of the individual, and further, that beyond trait identification, consideration should be given to the relationship of various levels of motivation and to the association process as it operates among energy systems.

The question of trait continuity also arises when predictions are attempted on the basis of trait assessment. A freshman student may identify so closely with an admired upper classman as to lose, at least temporarily, original characteristics. A trait appraisal of such a student at a particular point in time may actually be an evaluation of unrecognized developmental interferences. To some extent, profile similarities between upper and lower classmen shown in this study may be reflections of identification.

It would appear on the basis of the data and in terms of observed behavior that the search for traits which have predictive properties in relation to academic goals is questionable if considered in isolation of this wider context.

CONCLUSIONS

Findings on the California Personality Inventory and Harrower's Group Rorschach revealed no significant trait differences between freshmen and graduating seniors. Sex was more related to personality differences than was academic classification. When the intellectual factor was held constant, sex differences were less prominent.

Likenesses among independent groups as indicated by statistical means suggest a universality of traits and the subsequent assumption of modulation of individual uniqueness. In actuality, however, a wide variation in behavior and outcome exists with reference to stated goals. Likenesses may indicate a conscious effort on the part of the individual, at a partic-

ular point in time, to submerge personal tendencies in favor of the mass
prototype or "student image."

IMPLICATIONS

Test results are very useful in suggesting trends or making generalizations from mass data. However, because of the complexity of ego structure, the probing for distinctive features of individuals which may be
used in making sharp predictions is best served through intensive, plural-
istic investigation beyond trait identification.

Trait trends should not be ignored. For example, indications noted in
this study of self-doubt, self-abasement, and impulsiveness make for
vulnerability to substitute stimuli and possible abandonment of the student role. The employment of positive counter-stimuli would minimize,
if not offset, their presence and power. The data suggests further that
students in general would profit from help in the development of strong,
personal convictions which allay vacillation; sound, realistic personal
credos; and confidence in decisions bolstered by freedom to act or make
adaptive responses in accordance with positively oriented thinking. Guidance of this nature would direct attention to values of merit, increase
feelings of worth of self and acceptance of self, and augment the probability of consummation of intent in relation to academic goals.

References

1. Froe, O. *Non-Intellectual Factors Influencing Academic Achievement.* Unpublished study, Morgan College, Baltimore, Maryland.
2. Gough, H. G. "The Construction of a Personality Scale to Predict Scholastic
   Achievement," *Journal of Applied Psychology,* XXXVII (1953), pp. 361–
   366.
3. Gough, H. G. "Factors Relating to the Academic Achievement of High
   School Students," *Journal of Educational Psychology,* XL (1949), pp.
   65–78.

31 *The Effectiveness of Feedback in Teaching Principles of Educational Psychology*[1]

HOWARD K. CAMERON
Howard University

This paper reports the results of an experiment to examine the effectiveness of feedback in an Educational Psychology class. Psychologists have long seen the importance of feedback (i.e., information regarding one's own behavior or the results of what one does) in learning, and this research deals with the specific function of feedback in a particular course. The innovatively taught students achieved significantly better than control students, and also exhibited increased ability to relate the principles of Educational Psychology to teacher-pupil interaction. The implications of such research for teaching Black students is quite clear, and can be seen in the paper by Brazziel and Terrell (1962, this volume).

One of the persistent educational problems which plagues the classroom teacher is that of increasing the effectiveness of classroom instruction. Underlying this problem is the general realization that classroom teaching needs to be improved, and continuous efforts made by investigators to untangle the complex factors surrounding the phenomenon called "learning." So far, the learning theorists have amassed a considerable amount of data pertinent to this problem. However, due to the subjects used in most of their experiments (lower animals), and the absence of a learning situation simulating that of the usual academic classroom, the applicability of much of the theorists' data is often questioned. There exists an urgent need for psychologists to assess the practical application of many of our learning principles.

The primary purpose of this study was to determine the effect of feedback in learning principles of educational psychology. A basic question

SOURCE. Reprinted from the *Journal of Experimental Education*, 1966, 34, 3, 53–56 with permission of the author and Dembar Educational Research Services, Inx.

[1] This research is based on a dissertation completed in 1963 at Michigan State University; the data were collected in 1962 at a state university in Louisiana.

was: What will be the differential effect of systematically informing one group of students of the correctness and incorrectness of their classroom responses, and not providing such information for a control group?

RELATED RESEARCH

Among psychologists there is widespread acceptance of the principle that immediately provided feedback has a positive influence on learning and/or performance of students. According to Greenspoon and Foreman (5), immediate feedback is thought to reduce the possible interference which might result if the internal between response and feedback were of a longer duration. Chansky (3) states that the schedules and types of feedback students receive are significantly related to verbal learning. It has also been stated that feedback among or between students can lead to desirable changes in behavior in the same manner as feedback from the classroom instructor (6).

Skinner (8) believes that feedback is influential in controlling the probability of subsequent student behavior, and suggests various feedback schedules for specific learning conditions and objectives. Michael and Maccoby (7) summarize their data by stating that students who received feedback scored significantly higher on a test measuring knowledge of a film viewed than students who received no feedback. In reviewing experimental studies concerned with the influence of feedback in motor learning (under laboratory conditions) Bilodeau and Bilodeau (2) state:

"Studies of feedback of knowledge of results (KR) show it to be the strongest, most important variable controlling performance and learning. It has been shown repeatedly, as well as recently, that there is no improvement without KR, progressive improvement with it, and deterioration after its withdrawal. A number of studies show that performance is seriously disrupted or made impossible by lags in feedback of even less than 1.0 second. . . ."

Not only is it considered important to provide feedback for the responses of students, but several of the investigators above emphasize that if it is to be effective, it should immediately follow the response. These studies also indicate that the role of feedback depends on how frequently a given response receives feedback. In the study reported herein provisions will be made for ensuring the existence of frequent and immediate feedback for experimental subjects via the teaching technique and class size.

THE SAMPLE

Subjects for the study were students enrolled for a semester course in educational psychology. These students were randomly assigned to the experimental and control groups provided they possessed the following characteristics: (1) were between the ages of 17 and 21, (2) were classified as either sophomore or junior, and (3) were enrolling in their first course in psychology. The purpose of these restrictions was to rule out possible contaminating factors due to previous experiences of subjects.

The initial sample contained 72 students in the control group and 72 students in the experimental group. By the time the study was completed, this number had decreased to 61 students in the experimental group and 62 students in the control group. This reduction resulted from some students dropping the course and/or withdrawing from the university. All statistical analyses will be based upon data derived from the remaining 123 subjects.

EVALUATIVE MATERIALS EMPLOYED

Various measuring instruments were employed in the pre-experiment uniformity trial, and in testing treatment effects. The School and College Ability Test (SCAT) was used to test for significant differences in scholastic aptitude between the control and experimental groups prior to treatment. A revised version of the Minnesota Student Attitude Inventory (MSAI) was used to measure the variable of teaching method. Subjects in the experiments responded to MSAI items; their responses were interpreted as being indicative of the amount of feedback the instructor gave students during the instructional sessions.

The MSAI was compiled by Flanders (4) who has described the instrument in this manner:

"The MSAI is an attitude test which has shown a significant correlation in earlier studies with the teacher's pattern of influence. The test is made up of items that reflect the student's attitudes toward the teacher, the class activities, the teacher's system of rewards and punishments and their dependence on the teacher."

The Minnesota Teacher Attitude Inventory (MTAI) was employed to measure the differential effects of the treatment procedures on student perception of the role of teachers. It is believed that the viewpoints of students in the teacher preparation course should be affected by the teaching experiences they undergo. Finally, the Semester Examination, consisting of 100 multiple choice questions of an application nature, was used to measure achievement of the students.

PROCEDURES

The Ss in this experiment were randomly assigned to the control and experimental classes. An analysis of SCAT data showed no significant difference in the mean and variance test scores of the two treatment groups. The only instructor was the experimenter.

Two classes of experimental students (totaling 61) met for two 50-minute lectures each week. For the third class period the experimental Ss were divided into six classes of the following sizes: 8, 9, 10, 11, 12. The investigator followed the postulate of Thelen (9) that the frequency and amount of feedback received by each student could be better manipulated with this group arrangement than in the larger classes. The important idea here was not one of class size, but a question pertaining to what "happens" in the classroom situation regardless of class size. During the third class period of each week Anderson and Brewer's Integrative Technique of instruction was followed. (1) The basis of this instructional approach was to permit students to ask questions or to further explore subject matter covered during the two previous lectures. Oftentimes, the instructor asked students to further explain the practical application of textbook principles, and questions were asked to help focus the attention of students upon central points in the lectures and to help clarify student understanding. Most instructional emphasis was devoted to enticing students to participate in class discussions, and making sure that the responding student received immediate feedback from his classmates or the instructor.

The specific teacher behavior for the control subjects may be described as follows. The instructor discussed different psychological concepts throughout each 50-minute class period; he gave directions and criticized students, and justified his right to follow the pattern above on the basis of his authoritative position. Students were given very few opportunities to express verbally their conception of or reaction to ideas and psychological principles. Lectures were organized so that the same amount of subject matter was covered in both the experimental and control groups. In connection with this point, it should be stated that the latter endeavor necessitated a more thorough coverage of material in the control groups in some instances.

RESULTS

A crucial question in this study is that of the degree to which feedback was differentially provided for control and experimental Ss. To determine

TABLE 1

A Sample of MSAI Items Showing Significant Student Perception of Teacher-Pupil Relations

	Control Subjects (N = 62)			Experimental Subjects (N = 61)			Significant Chi Squares*
	Yes	No	Undecided	Yes	No	Undecided	
1. This teacher asks our opinion in planning work to be done.	36	12	14	48	3	10	7.77
2. This teacher keeps order with a firm and fair hand.	35	13	14	46	4	11	6.61
3. I get along exceptionally well with the teacher.	39	12	11	49	3	9	7.73
12. This teacher takes great care in making sure we understand our lesson.	38	8	16	50	3	8	6.57
24. This teacher wants to check our work to make sure we are on the right track.	32	15	15	43	4	14	8.01
27. This teacher helps us to get the most out of every class period.	35	13	14	49	4	8	8.73
28. The self control of this teacher is one of his greatest assets.	42	11	9	52	3	6	6.25
35. This teacher spends a lot of time letting us discuss psychology.	35	12	15	48	4	9	6.53
47. This class is noisy and fools around a lot.	45	3	14	37	15	9	9.86
52. This teacher makes very careful plans for each day's work.	49	4	9	37	14	10	7.28
60. This teacher likes to hear student's ideas.	29	17	16	44	5	12	10.19
62. Most of the students in this class like the instructor very much.	36	13	13	48	3	10	8.35

* All chi squares presented are significant at .05 level of confidence with 2 degrees of freedom.

the answer to this question each of the 62 items on the MSAI was weighted along the order of a Likert-type scale, and assigned points on the basis of its agreement or disagreement with the Integrative Technique (the feedback situation). For instance, consider item 12 in Table 1. If a student responded by "agreeing" his response was recorded as +1; if he "disagreed" −1 was recorded, and 0 value was assigned to an "undecided" response. A test for a significant difference between the experimental mean of 57.66 and the control mean of 51.65 on the MSAI indicates that the experimental Ss scored significantly higher. The resulting t-ratio of 2.35 is significant beyond the .05 level of confidence.

A chi square test was computed for control and experimental Ss on each of the MSAI items. In preparing the data for the chi square analyses, frequencies for each item were assigned to a 2 × 3 cell. There were 12 items on which experimental and control Ss differed significantly in their perception of the teacher-pupil relation. These 12 items are depicted in Table 1. The data in Table 1 show that the experimental Ss generally perceived the instructor as being more accepting and more "involved" in the teacher-pupil relationship; thereby providing a greater amount of feedback.

The reader will recall that it was predicted that students taught by different instructional techniques would differ significantly in their scores on the MTAI, a test designed to measure the type of teacher-pupil relations a prospective teacher might establish. As a group, the performance of all students on the MTAI yielded low scores when one compares their scores with norms for the test. The highest raw score obtained on the test was 60 (64th centile for college juniors), and the lowest raw score was −75 (below 1st centile for college juniors). The means for the experimental and control subjects are −1.35 (5th centile) and −15.85 (1st centile) respectively, for college junior-academic. The investigator is unable to offer a credible explanation for such low scores.

The raw data on the MTAI was coded in order to convert all numbers to positive figures; therefore a constant of 100 was added to the score of each student. Coded means of the experimental and control groups are 98.65 and 84.15 respectively. Analyses are presented with coded data in Table 2.

An examination of raw data on the final test reveals that the scores for experimental and control subjects are not very high. Sixty-two was the highest score made on the examination out of a possible high of 100. The scores for the experimental subjects range from 18 to 62; the control subjects had a range of scores from 20 to 59. Table 3 contains the statistical comparison of scores made by experimental and control subjects on the final examination.

TABLE 2

t-Test of Experimental and Control Subjects' Performance on MTAI

Treatment Groups	Mean Scores	F-Ratio	t-Ratio
Experimental Subjects	98.65	1.14	4.30*
Control Subjects	84.15		

* t-ratio is significant beyond the .005 level of significance with 121 degrees of freedom.

TABLE 3

t-Test Data for Subjects' Performance on Final Examination

Treatment Groups	Mean Scores	Standard Deviations	t-Ratio
Experimental Subjects	35.62	8.33	1.68*
Control Subjects	33.70	7.84	

* This difference is significant at the .05 level of confidence with 121 degrees of freedom.

SUMMARY

In this study dealing with the effect of feedback (given via Integrative Technique) on student learning and performance it was found that feedback did have a significant overall effect on test performance. The experimentally taught subjects scored significantly higher than the control subjects on an achievement examination designed to measure their ability to interpret and apply psychological principles to problematic situations. There exists additional support for feedback since similar results were obtained when the investigator tested for the effect integrative teaching might have on the probable type of teacher-pupil relations a prospective teacher might maintain. Integratively taught students appeared to possess a better understanding of how psychological principles should be used in teaching, and are more prone to establish positive teacher-pupil relations.

An explanation of why the experimental treatment was more effective might emphasize that feedback helps the student to avoid learning inappropriate responses and concepts (in the early stages of a learning experience) which may be difficult to extinguish later on. The early confirmation of a response seems to strengthen the probability that the response will be learned and retained as an aspect of student behavior.

References

1. Anderson, H., and Brewer, J. "Studies of Teachers' Classroom Personalities," *Applied Psychology Monographs*, No. 8 (1946).
2. Bilodeau, Edward, and Bilodeau, Ina. "Motor Skill Learning," *Annual Review of Psychology*, Volume 12 (Stanford, California: Stanford University Press, 1960), p. 250.
3. Chansky, Norman. "Learning: A Function of Schedule and Type of Feedback," *Psychological Reports*, 7 (1960), p. 362.
4. Flanders, Ned. *Teacher Influence, Pupil Attitudes, and Achievement, Final Report 1960*. Cooperative Research Project No. 397. United States Office of Education. Department of Health, Education and Welfare.
5. Greenspoon, J., and Foreman, S. "Effect of Delay of Knowledge of Results on Learning, A Motor Task," *Journal of Experimental Psychology*, 51 (1956), pp. 226–228.
6. Jenkins, David. "Feedback and Group Self-Evaluation," *Journal of Social Issues*, 4 (Spring, 1948), pp. 50–60.
7. Michael, D., and Maccoby, N. "Factors of Influencing Verbal Learning From Films Under Varying Conditions of Audience Participation," *Journal of Experimental Psychology* 46 (1953), p. 414.
8. Skinner, B. F. "Teaching Machines," *Science*, 128 (1958), pp. 969–977.
9. Thelen, Herbert. "Group Dynamics in Instruction: Principle of Least Group Size," *School Review*, 57 (1949), pp. 139–148.

32 Nonintellectual Correlates of Academic Achievement

HOWARD K. CAMERON
Associate Professor of Education, Howard University

Many efforts have been made to predict college grades from the nonintellectual characteristics of students, and Dr. Cameron has attempted to clarify relationships that may exist between academic self-concepts, achievement motivation, and grade point average for a group of Black college students. Although the study does present significant correlations between rated self-concepts and achievement motivation and also between tested college ability and grade point average, the hoped-for clarification of the relation between nonintellectual factors and grades failed to occur. Dr. Cameron reviews related research, and suggests areas requiring additional study.

There is increasing concern on the part of many educators about the questionable validity of so-called I.Q. tests in predicting the scholastic performance of culturally disadvantaged students. This concern, in some instances, is revealed in the form of harsh criticism or even the rejection of scholastic aptitude tests as acceptable measuring instruments for determining educational placement of disadvantaged children. Recent actions by the Board of Education in New York City,[1] and U. S. Appeals Court Judge J. Skelley Wright[2] in Washington, D. C. are exemplary cases.

The experiences with I.Q. or scholastic aptitude tests in academic settings have not been totally disappointing, however. In numerous instances test data have proven to be a valid predictor for "within" ethnic groups

SOURCE. Reprinted from the *Journal of Negro Education*, 1968, **37**, 3, 252–257 with permission of the author and the publisher.

[1] Arthur Hughson, "The Case for Intelligence Testing," *Phi Delta Kappan*, XLVI (Nov. 1964), 106.

[2] *Congressional Record, Proceedings and Debates of the 90th Congress*, First Session, Vol. 113, No. 98 (Washington, D. C.: Government Printing Office, 1967), pp. H7655–H7697.

academic performance, and for minority group children whose experiential background approximated that of the predominantly middle-class white group. Many of the criticisms of standardized aptitude tests have arisen mainly from the unprofessional and erroneous use of these tests to appraise the potential educational development of disadvantaged Negroes, Spanish-Americans, Indians and poor whites on the basis of middle-class norms. When employed in this manner aptitude test results (especially group tests) generally depict many disadvantaged children as possessing questionable potentiality for success in the academic situation. But the data from studies by Jensen *et al.* clearly indicate that many disadvantaged children with low I.Q. test scores perform at a normal rate on learning tasks.[3]

The task of employing an aptitude measure for predicting the academic success of the disadvantaged child is complicated because the sociocultural bases of current tests are not perceived as relevant and do not represent the sub-culture of many minority group children. When administering scholastic aptitude tests to these students one frequently observes not only poor motivation for taking these tests, but considerable anxiety, complicated by fears of failure. It is not difficult to discern that many of these students are poorly prepared to negotiate highly verbal and abstract tests by observing their different communication styles, expressed attitudes, work habits, low test motivation, and seemingly a lack of experiential background with test materials. Quite early in their formal education too many disadvantaged children appear to have been conditioned to expect failure on standardized aptitude tests. The recurring experiences of failure are said to account, in part, for these students' lower academic perception of self, limited range of occupational aspirations, and lower need to achieve when compared to middle-class whites.[4]

The many disappointing results experienced with scholastic aptitude tests, however, have caused some educators to look elsewhere for valid predictors of academic performance of various student groups. During the last several years professional attention has been increasingly focused upon assessing the validity of nonintellectual traits (measures of interests, self concept, achievement motivation, personal adjustment, etc.) as predictors of school success. The goal has been to find predictors more valid

[3] A. R. Jensen, C. C. Collins, and R. W. Vreeland, "A Multiple S-R Apparatus for Human Learning," *American Journal of Psychology*, LXXV (1962), 470–476; and A. R. Jensen, "Reply to Inquiries Concerning the Article on Early Learning," 1967. Mimeograph.

[4] M. Deutsch, "Minority Group and Class Status as Related to Social and Personality Factors in Achievement," *Society for Applied Anthropology Monograph* #2, 1960, pp. 1–32.

than aptitude scores alone, or variables which when combined with aptitude scores will result in a better multiple predictor of classroom performance.

Lewis *et al.* found that scores on selected scales of the Strong Vocational
Interest Blank for men (SVIB) significantly differentiate between engineering students who dropped-out and those who graduated from an
engineering program.[5] Similarly, Saddler concluded that students who
transferred from the engineering program tended to have different interest
profiles from those students who remained in engineering and graduated.[6]
A study of 783 gifted freshmen female students by Faunce also revealed
that measures of nonintellectual traits may serve as valid predictors of
academic performance. His analyses of M.M.P.I. data show that girls who
left college before graduating had less insight into their personality structures, greater difficulty in interpersonal relations, more problems with
impulse controls, and greater inner tensions. On the other hand, the college graduates were said to be more temperate, modest, self-confident,
had better ego strength and psychological integration, and were relatively
free from tension. Faunce concluded that even as freshmen these students
exhibited personality traits which later influenced their persistence in college.[7] Michael *et al.*, however, observed that scores on the M.M.P.I.,
Edwards Personal Preference Schedule, and Cattell's 16 P. F. Questionnaire lacked predictive validity for the academic performance of students
in a B.S. degree nursing program.[8]

There is increasing evidence that personality tests such as the California
Personality Inventory (C.P.I.) have predictive validity for academic
performance in mathematics,[9] creative writing[10] and architectural design-

[5] E. C. Lewis *et al.*, "Interests and Ability Correlates of Graduation and
Attrition in a College of Engineering," *American Educational Research Journal,* II
(1965), 63, 74.

[6] L. E. Saddler, "A Comparison of Students Remaining in an Engineering
Curriculum with Those Transferring from Engineering to Other Curricula,"
Microfilm Abstracts, IX (1950), 89–91.

[7] P. S. Faunce, "Personality Characteristics and Vocational Interests Related to
College Persistency of Academically Gifted Women," *Journal of Consulting
Psychology,* XV (1968), 31–40.

[8] W. B. Michael *et al.*, "The Predictive Validities of Selected Attitude and
Achievement Measures and Three Personality Inventories in Relation to Nursing
Training Criteria," *Educational and Psychological Measurement,* XXVI (1966),
1035–1040.

[9] R. I. Keimowitz, and H. L. Ansbacher, "Personality and Achievement in
Mathematics," *Journal of Individual Psychology,* XVI (1960), 84–87.

[10] F. Barron, *Creativity and Psychological Health* (New York: D. Van Nostrand
Co., 1963).

ing,[11] and significantly predicted those college students who later become dropouts.[12] Holland has reported that the C.P.I. yielded predictive validities significantly superior to S.A.T. scores for grade point averages of National Merit Scholarship winners.[13] Also, Gough *et al.*, data indicate that their C.P.I. regression equation proved to be a more valid predictor of performance in medical school than premedical scholastic achievement and scores from the Medical College Admission Test.[14] The equation components consisted of positive score weightings from the sociability, tolerance and cummunality scales, and negative weighting of the status scale. Students with high scores on their equation exhibited the traits of unselfishness, considerateness, informality, reasonableness, self-confidence, and forgiveness. Low scorers tended to be young men who were thankless, cold, prejudiced, fault-finding, and restless.

Beno Fricke has developed an Opinion Attitude and Interest Survey (O.A.I.S.) which is reported to greatly improve the predictive validity of scholastic aptitude measures for Negro college students.[15] Sub-test scores on Achiever Personality and Creative Personality scales of O.A.I.S. for 62 Negro students enrolled at University of Michigan correlated significantly (.47) with college grades when combined in a multiple regression equation with S.A.T. scores.

The study of Clark and Plotkin provided a motivational hypothesis to explain the significant lower dropout rate (33.4%) among 1,519 Negro students attending Northern integrated colleges as compared to a dropout rate of 40 per cent among the larger group of white college students.[16] This finding gains significance when one observes that the group of Negro students had significantly lower S.A.T. scores and lower socioeconomic status than their white counterparts. These investigators reasoned the Negro students felt that they had to complete college; to drop out would

[11] D. W. MacKinnon, "The Personality Correlates of Creativity: A Study of American Architects," in H. Nielsen (ed.), *Proceedings of the XIV International Congress of Applied Psychology,* 1962, pp. 11–39.

[12] M. Maxwell, "An Analysis of the CPI and the ACE Psychological Tests as Predictors of Success in Different College Curricula," *American Psychologist,* XV (1960), 425.

[13] J. L. Holland, "The Prediction of College Grades from CPI and SAT," *Journal of Educational Psychology,* L (1950), 135–142.

[14] Harrison Gough, and Wallace Hall, "Prediction of Performance in Medical School from CPI," *Journal of Applied Psychology,* XLVIII (1964), 218–226.

[15] Benno Fricke, *The OAIS Handbook* (Ann Arbor, Michigan: OAIS Testing Program, 1965), pp. 279–280.

[16] K. B. Clark, and L. Plotkin, "The Negro Student at Integrated Colleges," (New York: National Scholarship Service and Fund for Negro Students, 1963).

have relegated them back to the nonspecialized labor force where Negroes are usually insured the permanence of low status. The alternative to college graduation was perceived in terms of lower pay and status, greater unemployment, and under-utilization of their skills and abilities.

According to the Coleman Report[17] such nonintellectual measures as interests, self-concept and "sense" of environmental control have a higher relationship to the academic performance of Negro students than all other school factors together. Coleman suggests, however, that such attitudinal variables are probably more a consequence than a cause of scholastic achievement.

A very significant study has been reported by Farquhar which highlights research interests in the area of motivational factors related to academic achievement. In an effort to isolate motivational forces which initiate, direct, and sustain behavior toward scholarly goals, Farquhar developed the Michigan M-Scales on a predominantly white group of eleventh graders in the state of Michigan.[18] The four sub-tests of the M-Scales are designed to measure the following traits: (1) academic self concept (Word Rating List), (2) academic personality factors (Human Traits Inventory), (3) need for academic achievement (Generalized Situational Choice Inventory), and (4) occupational aspirations (Preferred Job Characteristics Scale). Based upon a sample of 254 males and 261 females the validity estimates of the total M-Scales are .56 and .40, respectively. The multiple correlation based on the total M-Scales and Differential Aptitude Test—VR estimates of grade point average are .69 and .73 for the male and .64 and .63 for the female validation and cross-validation samples. Furthermore, when the scores of either the sub-tests or total test were added to the D.A.T.—VR the precision of estimating the grade point criterion was significantly increased.

The data from a subsequent investigation by Green and Farquhar, however, show that the Michigan M-Scales more validly predicted the academic performance of eleventh grade Negro high school students than SCAT—verbal.[19] The Word Rating List proved to be the best predictor of academic achievement for both boys (.36) and girls (.64). Significant

---

[17] James S. Coleman, *Equality of Educational Opportunity* (Washington, D. C.: Government Printing Office, 1966), pp. 319–320.

[18] W. Farquhar, "A Comprehensive Study of Motivational Factors Underlying the Achievement of 11th Grade High School Subjects," Research Project No. 846 (8458). Supported by the U. S. Office of Education in Cooperation with MSU, 1959.

[19] R. L. Green, and W. Farquhar, "Negro Academic Motivation and Scholastic Achievement," *Journal of Educational Psychology*, LVI (1965), 241–243.

correlations were obtained for all sub-tests except the Human Trait Inventory for Males.

The research reviewed above became an impetus for a series of similar investigations which are being conducted by the writer. The following constitutes a preliminary report of the data collected thus far on the validity of the Michigan M-Scales in predicting the academic performance of Negro college students.

METHOD

Following the design of Green and Farquhar the writer administered two sub-tests from the Michigan M-Scales (Word Rating List and Human Trait Inventory) to 58 Negro females who were enrolled in his educational psychology courses. These M-Scales were administered to the students during the first semester of their sophomore year, with the explanation that the writer was standardizing the scales on college age students. Subsequently, the grade point average (G.P.A.) for each student was obtained from the following 27 semester hours of general education courses: English, Humanities, Biological Science, Physical Science, and Social Science. These courses were selected in determining G.P.A. because they are all academically based subjects, and within each department there exists a standard procedure for evaluating the performance of students enrolled in different sections of a course. Scores from the School and College Ability Test (SCAT) were obtained from records developed by the students upon their matriculation at the University. The correlations between G.P.A. and independent variables were computed.

RESULTS

The predictive validity of SCAT scores and two sub-tests of the M-Scales are shown in Table 1. It can be seen that each of the independent variables was valid for predicting the academic performance of students at the .05 level and above, with exception of the Human Trait Inventory (.10). However, the single best predictor of performance in academic subjects was SCAT—total which evidenced a correlation of .57 with G.P.A. SCAT—Q was a better predictor of G.P.A. ($r = .52$) than SCAT $-(r = .47)$.

When SCAT—total was combined in a multiple regression equation with the two M-Scales an R of .59 was achieved. Although R is significantly different from zero, it should be observed that the contribution of the two M-Scales to the validity coefficient is negligible. In fact, omitting the

TABLE 1

The Means, S.D. and T-Ratios on Predictive Validity of SCAT
and M-Scales for G.P.A.

Variable	Mean Score	Standard Deviation	df	t — ratio
SCAT — T	297	14.73	57	5.17***
SCAT — V	295	20.79	57	3.97***
SCAT — Q	298	16.43	57	4.56***
WRL	29.69	7.96	57	2.06**
HTI	18.43	3.60	57	1.40*

    * $p < .10$.
   ** $p < .05$.
 *** $p < .001$.

Human Trait Inventory from the regression equation does not alter the
R of .59, and retaining H.T.I. while omitting WRL merely reduces R to
.58. The correlation coefficients of H.T.I. and WRL with G.P.A. were
.18 and .27, respectively.

The academic self-concept and achievement motivation scores of these
Negro females are not significantly different from those presented for the
normative sample by Farquhar. As with the standardization group the
two measures of academic motivation correlated positively with each
other ($r = .55$), indicating some measurement overlap.

DISCUSSION

First, it is significant to note that the M-Scales do correlate positively
with the academic achievement of these students, even though they do
not contribute significantly to a multiple regression equation designed to
predict achievement.

The fact that these were primarily middle-class oriented female subjects with professional family backgrounds may partly explain the above
results. Within such a verbal group of students a test (such as SCAT)
which necessitates knowledge of and ability to manipulate concepts has
been found to be a good predictor of academic achievement. Green and
Farquhar reported SCAT to be a significant predictor of Negro female
scores in their study, although the validity of M-Scales was significantly
higher. In the present study, the lower correlation coefficients of the
M-Scales with G.P.A. may have resulted from the high homogeneity of
this middle-class group, and the resulting high level of academic competition which usually prevails among middle-class female students.

There is the possibility that the M-Scales may be more valid predictors of the academic performance of the less sophisticated high school students than for the college sophomores. The college sophomores should be more highly sensitive to the social desirability components inherent in many of the M-Scale items, and would probably (consciously or unconsciously) respond more so on the basis of their "ideal self" than "self concept."

However, additional validity studies are desirable which assess the usefulness of the total M-Scale battery on a more heterogeneous sample of college students. The extent to which the social desirability factor contaminates test results needs to be determined.

Bibliography for Part V

Ames, Louise B., and Ilg, Frances L. Search for children showing academic promise in a predominantly Negro school. *Journal of Genetic Psychology* (June, 1967), **110**, 217–231.

Bloom, Richard. Effects of racial and expressive cues on probability learning in children. *Psychological Reports*, 1969, **24**, 791–794.

Cipolla, Carlo M. *Literacy and Development in the West.* Baltimore: Penguin Books, 1969.

Clark, K. B. Educational stimulation of racially disadvantaged children. In A. H. Passow (Ed.), *Education in Depressed Areas.* New York: Teachers College Press, Columbia University, 1963. Pp. 142–162.

Coleman, James S., et al. *Equality of Educational Opportunity.* U. S. Department of Health, Education, and Welfare, Washington, D. C., 1966.

Conant, James B. *Slums and Suburbs: a Commentary on Schools in Metropolitan Areas.* New York: McGraw-Hill, 1961.

Criswell, Joan H. A sociometric study of race cleavage in the classroom. *Archeological Psychology*, N. Y., 1939, No. 235.

Crockett, Harry J. A study of some factors affecting the decision of Negro high school students to enroll in previously all-white high schools in St. Louis, 1955. *Social Forces* (May, 1957), **35**, 351–356.

Deutsch, M. Dimensions of the school's role in the problems of integration. In G. J. Klopf and I. A. Laster (Eds.), *Integrating the Urban School.* New York: Teachers College, Columbia University, Bureau of Publications, 1963. Pp. 29–44.

Deutsch, M., Katz, I., and Jensen, A. R. (Eds.). *Social Class, Race, and Psychological Development.* New York: Holt, Rinehart & Winston, 1968.

Equal Educational Opportunity. *Harvard Educational Review.* Cambridge: Harvard University Press, 1969.

Findley, W. G. *Learning and Teaching in Atlanta Public Schools.* Princeton, N. J.: Educational Testing Service, 1956.

Fuchs, Estelle. *Teachers Talk: Views from Inside City Schools.* New York: Doubleday, 1969.

Goodman, Yetta M. Metropolitan man and the social studies. *Social Education*, 1969, **33**(6), 700–702.

Gordon, Edmund W., and Wlkerson, Doxey, A. A critique of compensatory education. Compensatory Education for the Disadvantaged. New York: College Entrance Examination Board, 1966.

Gottlieb, D. Teaching and students: the views of Negro and white teachers. *Sociology of Education*, 1964, **37**, 345–353.

Jensen, A. R. Varieties of individual differences in learning. In R. M. Gagne (Ed.), *Learning and Individual Differences*. Columbus, Ohio: Merrill, 1967.

Katz, I., and Cohen, M. The effects of training Negroes upon cooperative problem solving in biracial teams. *Journal of Abnormal Social Psychology*, 1962, **64**, 319–325.

Kirkland, Hubert E. Teaching urban realities in primary classrooms. *Social Education*, 1969, **33**(6), 703–704.

Nichols, Robert. Schools and the disadvantaged. *Science* (December 9, 1966), **154**, 1312–1314.

Robins, Lee N., Jones, Robin S., and Murphy, George E. School milieu and school problems of Negro boys. *Social Problems* (Spring, 1966), **13**, 428–436.

Schwebel, M. *Who Can Be Educated?* New York: Grove, 1968.

Stodolsky, Susan, and Lesser, Gerald. Learning patterns in the disadvantaged. *Harvard Educational Review* (Fall, 1967), **37**, 546–593.

Thorndike, Robert L. Free choice open enrollment: junior high schools. Center for Urban Education. New York, August 31, 1966.

Warden, Sandra A. *The Leftouts: Disadvantaged Children in Heterogenous Schools*. New York: Holt, Rinehart & Winston, 1969.

Wiseman, S. Environmental and innate factors and educational attainment. In J. E. Meade and A. S. Parkes (Eds.), *Genetic and Environmental Factors in Human Ability*. New York: Plenum Press, 1966.

PART VI

Attitude, Personality, and Emotional Characteristics

It would seem reasonable to assume that the experience of growing up in a segregated, minority group setting would have some effect on such human attributes as attitude, personality, and emotional behavior. The papers in this section discuss the psychological implications of not being a member of the majority group in a given culture. The section opens with the very interesting work of Kenneth and Mamie Clark (1939) on consciousness of self and racial identification, and then both Roberts (1950) and Cameron (1967) discuss the emotional characteristics and needs of Black youth. Pierce-Jones and his associates (1959) report a survey of adolescent social attitudes and adjustment; Taylor (1962) and also Gore and Rotter (1963) examine personality structures of Black college students; and Bayton and his associates (1965) and Bayton and Muldrow (1968) examine the question of the perception of racial traits. Drs. Goins and Meenes (1960) contrast the ethnic and class preferences of Negro and white college students, Brazziel (1964) examines the appropriateness of psychological testing for Black college students, while Dr. Regina Goff (1962) looks at psychology and intercultural interaction. Finally, Dr. Wilson (1969) examines the whole process of counseling and suggests ways to render it more relevant for Black college students.

33 *The Development of Consciousness of Self and Emergence of Racial Identification in Negro Preschool Children*

KENNETH B. CLARK
Department of Psychology, Columbia University
&
MAMIE K. CLARK
Department of Psychology, Howard University

Perhaps the most significant and subtle question related to being a member of a particular racial group would concern the emergence of "racial identification" during the young child's development of self-awareness, and in this pioneer study Drs. Kenneth and Mamie Clark examine this question. Their research attempts to isolate the developmental period during which the majority of preschool children acquire racial identification, and is an interesting example of utilizing the projective technique in order to identify some of the basic attitude structures of children. The paper includes an excellent literature review, some interesting conclusions, and raises far more questions than it answers—the cardinal virtue of really productive research.

Speculations concerning the nature of the self and the development of consciousness of self have long been a significant part of psychology. Little experimental research has been done, however, in an attempt to raise this problem out of the maze of speculative conjectures. Piaget (9), elaborating upon Baldwin's (3) concept of a three-stage development of "personal consciousness" (transitions from a "projective" to a "subjective" to an "ejective" sense of personality—the final "ejective" stage being the social self wherein the child is aware of the fact that other people's bodies have similar experiences to his own), maintains that the child comes to

SOURCE. Reprinted from the *Journal of Social Psychology*, 1939, **10**, 591–599 by permission of the senior author and The Journal Press.

discover himself through a progressive comparison of his own body with other people's bodies. Concerning the psychical qualities of self, he states: "In the same way, with regard to psychical qualities, it is by imitating other peoples' behavior that the child will discover his own."

Lewin (7) emphasizes the formation of the concept of property as a feature of the development of self-consciousness.

". . . The 'I' or self is only gradually formed, perhaps in the second or third year. Not until then does the concept of property appear, of the belonging of a thing to his own person."

G. W. Allport (1), on the other hand, speaks of an earlier consciousness devoid of self-reference, while self-consciousness develops only after the age of four or five years.

"Until the child has a fairly definite conception of himself as an independent person, he cannot conceptualize his relationship to the surrounding world and hence lacks the subjective nucleus for the development of his own personality. . . . Even at the age of four or five the self is by no means firmly encapsulated. . . . The advent of self-consciousness is gradual, and its growth continuous, but a certain critical stage is reached around the age of two. . . . Its symptom is the period of negativism."

Some experimental work on the problem has been done. Bain (2) made daily observations and records of a child's speech in normal family situations from birth to one and one-half years. From an analysis of the "self" and "others" words of the child he concluded that self is social; it appears and develops rapidly and observably from five months on and begins to be verbalized after about the first year. Bain said of the child:

"It is out of his responses to others that his 'consciousness of self' arise, together with appropriate verbal symbols for naming it. . . . The 'I' is a social concept. It is quite different from the concept of self as object which arises much later."

Goodenough (4), assuming the use of the first personal pronoun to be evidence of having reached a primitive stage in the development of self-awareness, studied the use of certain specified pronouns by children in free play and control situations. Pronouns of the first person singular were used with far greater frequency during free play with other children than in the controlled situation. The same trend was shown for the possessions my and mine.

"Insofar as the use of these pronouns is indicative of something in the nature of an ego-consciousness, it is evident that this feeling is brought to the fore in the more competitive situations of group play far more frequently than is the case during the less socialized conditions of the controlled situation."

Moreno's (8) study is of interest in that it approaches the problem of the development of consciousness of self from the point of view of the dynamics of group development. He used a sociometric test wherein children chose from pictures of various racial groups the boy or girl whom they would like to have sit on either side of them. First and second choices were given. Moreno found that

"gradually from the first grade on the group develops a more differentiated organization. . . . From about the fifth grade . . . a greater number of Italian children begin to choose Italian neighbors . . . a larger number of white children reject colored children. . . . It indicates the beginnings of a racial cleavage."

Attacking the problem of consciousness of self from the point of view of determining the spatial localization of the self, E. L. Horowitz (5) found that he was unable to present a final statement describing where the self actually is. He concludes that

"the localization of the self . . . is not the basic phenomenon one might hope for to ease an analysis of the structure of the self and personality."

More recently, R. E. Horowitz (6) has been concerned with the problem of children's emergent awareness of themselves, with reference to a specific social grouping. Her study dealt with race-consciousness conceived as a function of ego-development. Her procedure is described in detail because of its similarity to the one used in the present study. Two picture techniques were used with 24 children from two to five years of age: (a) Choice tests—one pair of photographs for boys and girls respectively, showing a white child and a Negro child; one pair of line drawings showing a white boy and a Negro boy; one set of four-line drawings showing a white boy, a Negro boy, a chicken, and a clown. Boys were asked in each case to identify themselves. The form of the question was "Show me which one is you. Which one is ———" (using name of the subject). The girls, after having identified themselves in the first item, were asked to identify brothers or cousins in the three boys' items. (b) The Portrait Series—10 portrait pictures were exposed, one at a time. Children were asked, "Is this you? Is this ———?" (using name of child). This latter technique did not give as satisfactory results as the first. In the Choice Tests Horowitz found that 68.4 per cent children were "correct" and 31.6 per cent were "incorrect." In the second series of line drawings more errors on the whole were made, "but the balance of errors was weighted in the same direction." In the third series of this technique, four of five Negro boys made "correct" identifications and three out of seven white boys made "correct" identifications. The general limitations involved in the small number of cases are recognized by the author. She states: "Further work will, of course, have to be done to determine how common it is and within what framework of circumstances it operates."

THE PROBLEM

The present study is an attempt to investigate early levels in the development of consciousness of self in Negro preschool children with special reference to emergent race consciousness. The term consciousness of self may be considered as awareness of self as a distinct person; as distinct from other groups of things or individuals. The term race consciousness is here defined as consciousness of self as belonging to a specific group which is differentiated from other groups by obvious physical characteristics. It is hereby assumed that race consciousness and racial identification are indicative of particularized self-consciousness.

PROCEDURE

A modification of the Horowitz picture technique was used. There were three sets of line drawings as follows: Set A—one white boy, one colored boy, a lion and a dog; Set B—one white boy, two colored boys and a clown; Set C—two white boys, one colored boy and a hen. Combining all the line drawings there were four white boys and four colored boys. Each of the four pairs of white and colored boys was alike in every respect save skin color. The same white and colored boy never appeared in any one set of the pictures. Materials and instructions were presented in the same manner as in Horowitz's investigation. "*Show me which one is you. Which one is* ———?" (using name of subject); with girls "*Show me which one is* ———?" (using name of brother, boy cousin or boy playmate). Subjects were examined individually.

Subjects: 150 Negro children in segregated Washington, D. C., nursery schools (75 male and 75 female—50 three-year-old, 50 four-year-old, and 50 five-year-old children). These children were taken from five W.P.A. nursery schools, one private nursery school, and one public school kindergarten.

RESULTS

Table 1 presents the choices of subjects on the total picture series.

TABLE 1

Choices of Total Group on Picture Series

Line Drawings of	No. of Choices	% of Choices
Colored boy	225	50.9
White boy	195	44.1
Irrelevant*	22	4.9

* Lion, dog, hen, clown.

On the entire series of pictures the total group of 150 Negro children made more choices of the colored boy (50.9%) than of the white boy (44.1%) [CR 2.13]. This table, however, is meaningless from a genetic point of view, in that all age groups are combined. A mass presentation of the data completely disguises any factors which may be operative in the dynamics of self-consciousness and racial identification.

It is apparent that there is a consistent increase in the differences between choices of colored and white boys with age. The significance of these differences increases thus: —2.7 per cent at the three-year level (CR 0.4), to 10.9 per cent at the four-year level (CR 1.87), to 12.1 per cent at the five-year level (CR 2.08). These differences are in favor of the colored boy.

TABLE 2

Choices of Age Levels

	Three Years		Four Years		Five Years	
Line Drawings of	No. of Choices	%	No. of Choices	%	No. of Choices	%
Colored boy	61	41.2	81	55.4	83	56.0
White boy	65	43.9	65	44.5	65	43.9
Irrelevant	22	14.7	—		—	

The absolute number of choices of colored boy increase from the three-year level (41.2%) to the four-year level (55.4%) [CR 2.44] and slightly again at the five-year level (56.0%) [CR 1.03]. The number of choices of the white boy remain approximately the same at the three-, four-, and five-year levels.

Choices of the lion, dog, clown, and hen constitute 14.7 per cent of the total responses at the three-year level, but disappear at the four-year level and do not appear again at the five-year level. The increase in the percentage of choices of colored boy is at the expense of choices of the less relevant pictures of lion, dog, clown, and hen. Thus, beginning at the four-year level, these children cease to identify themselves in terms of the animals or the clown and consistently identify in terms of either the colored or white boys with a trend toward more choices of the colored boy.

The most significant aspect of the results presented in this table (Table 3) is the fact that the choices of the boys show significant trends whereas those of the girls seem to approximate chance. This fact can be best

TABLE 3

Choices of the Sexes at Each Age

Line Drawings of	Three Years				Four Years				Five Years			
	Male		Female		Male		Female		Male		Female	
	No.	%	No.	%	No.	%	No.	%	No.	%	No.	%
Colored boy	23	31.5	38	50.2	45	60.8	36	50.0	46	63.0	37	49.3
White boy	37	50.7	28	37.4	29	39.1	36	50.0	27	36.9	38	50.6
Irrelevant	13	17.6	9	12.2	—		—		—		—	

understood if it is remembered that the boys were making identifications of themselves while the girls were identifying brothers, cousins, and in a few instances a boy playmate. Because of this difference in response it would appear that either the technique used in this investigation has greater validity when used with boys than when used with girls, or that the dynamics involved when girls identify someone other than themselves is quite different from the self-identification of the boys.

In view of the fact that the reason for this difference is at present unknown it is necessary to compare the choices of the boys alone with the choices of the total group. For choices of the colored boy by the males alone at each age level, there is a consistent increase in these responses with age from 31.5 per cent at the three-year level, to 60.8 per cent at the four-year level, to 63.0 per cent at the five-year level. This is in agreement with the general trend of results found for the total group. For choices of the white boy by the males, there is a consistent decrease in these responses with age from 50.7 per cent at the three-year level, to 39.1 per cent at the four-year level, to 36.9 per cent at the five-year level. For the total group, however, there is no such consistent decrease in the choices of white boy. An examination of Table 2 will show that for the three-, four-, and five-year level the percentages of choices of the white boy are respectively 43.9, 44.5, and 43.9. This stability is obviously due to the non-differential responses of the females.

DISCUSSION

It is clear cut from the results that a definite delimitation of the self on the part of these children occurs between the three- and four-year age levels. The dropping out of irrelevant choices of the lion, dog, clown, and hen indicates the attainment of a developmental level where consciousness of self is in terms of a distinct person. This is undoubtedly a precursory level of development to the consciousness of belonging to one group as distinct from another. This latter contention appears to be justified by the increase in the number of choices of colored boy over white boy with age on the part of the total group, and is shown even more clearly in results for the males alone. The dynamic aspect in this development of self-consciousness is even more apparent if one conceives of this increase in the number of choices of colored boy over white boy with age to be an indication of the emergence of the still higher level of personal racial consciousness.

The fact that definite age trends in increased choices of colored boy were evident from the three-year to the four-year level but, while continuing the trend, were not as definite (statistically significant) from the four-year to the five-year level indicates the probability that this technique is inadequate when used with higher age levels.

An alternative explanation of this finding would assume that it is an indication of the facts as they are; that the greatest (most significant) amount of development in self-consciousness and racial identification occurs between the third and fourth years. After the fourth year there is relatively little development of the mechanisms operative. This explanation would assume that the ceiling had been approached if not actually reached. Obviously there must be a ceiling, but the data and incidental experiences of the investigators do not seem to warrant the assumption that the ceiling had been reached in this study by the technique used. In support of this belief is the fact that a few of the five-year-old children refused to identify themselves with any picture, saying *"I'm not on there,"* or *"That's not me,"* or *"I don't know them,"* etc. Some were hesitant, evidently because they thought the same. Some five-year-olds said before making identifications on the first set of line drawings: *"This is a white boy, this is a colored boy, this is a lion, and this is a dog."* These responses gave an inkling of the fact that these five-year-olds were developing ideas of themselves as intrinsic individuals. It appeared to be a conflict with this idea for them to identify themselves with either the white or the colored boy, just as most of the three-year-olds and all of the four-year-olds had not identified themselves with any of the irrelevant drawings.

A more refined technique, which would be as sensitive for the five-year-olds as this one is for the three- and four-year-olds, would undoubtedly yield more valid information concerning the operation of this mechanism in the older children. Identification of self from line drawings seems to be too great an abstraction of an emergent concrete entity for the five-year-old boys. The hesitancy in interpreting self in terms of the line drawings, but rather conceiving of it as an intrinsic, concrete entity, is suggestive of another stage in the development of self consciousness.

The fair degree of significance of the male responses and the seeming chance responses of the females indicate that the line drawings used in this study should have been used exclusively with males for greatest validity. Line drawings of girls should have been used with the girls. The dynamics involved in identification of a brother or cousin on the part of the girls is obviously different from those in identification of one's self. Further data on the problem will appear in a later paper.

Summary and Conclusions

In an effort to get some indication of the nature of development of consciousness of self in Negro preschool children, with special reference to emergent race consciousness, 150 Negro children in segregated schools were shown a series of line drawings of white and colored boys, a lion, a dog, a clown, and a hen and asked to identify themselves or others. The results were as follows:

The total group made more choices of the colored boy than of the white boy.

The ratio of choices of the colored boy to choices of the white boy increased with age in favor of the colored boy.

Choices of the lion, dog, clown, and hen were dropped off at the end of the three-year level, indicating a level of development in consciousness of self where identification of one's self is in terms of a distinct person rather than in terms of animals or other characters.

The seeming chance responses of the girl warrants further study of girls making identifications of themselves on similar line drawings of girls.

The fact that the sharpest increase in identifications with the colored boy occurred between the three- and four-year level and failed to increase significantly at the five-year level suggests that either this picture technique is not as sensitive when used with five-year-olds as when used with three- and four-year-olds, or that a plateau in the development of this function occurs between the ages of four and five, or that the five-year-olds have reached a stage in self-awareness which approaches a concept of self in terms of a concrete intrinsic self, less capable of abstractions or external representations.

References

1.   Allport, G. W. Personality: A Psychological Interpretation. New York: Holt, 1937. (Pp. 159–166.)

2.   Bain, R. The self-and-other words of a child. *Amer. J. Sociol.*, 1936, **41**, 767–775.

3.   Baldwin, J. M. Social and Ethical Interpretations in Mental Development. New York: Macmillan, 1897. (P. 7.)

4.   Coodenough, F. L. The use of pronouns by young children: A note on the development of self-awareness. *J. Genet. Psychol.*, 1938, **52**, 333–346.

5.   Horowitz, E. L. Spatial localization of the self. *J. Soc. Psychol.*, 1935, **6**, 379–387.

6.   Horowitz, R. E. Racial aspects of self-identification in nursery school children. *J. of Psychol.*, 1939, **7**, 91–99.

7.   Lewin, K. Dynamic Theory of Personality. New York: McGraw-Hill, 1935. (Pp. 106.)

8.   Moreno, J. L. Who Shall Survive? Wash., D. C.: Nervous and Mental Disease Publishing Co., 1934. (P. 61.)

9.   Piaget, J. The Moral Judgment of the Child. New York: Harcourt, Brace, 1932. (P. 393.)

34 *Some Mental and Emotional Health Needs of Negro Children and Youth*

S. OLIVER ROBERTS[1]
Associate Professor of Psychology and Education, Fisk University

It is sometimes the case that an author is able to develop a particularly broad perspective and contribute quite a bit to our understanding of his topic, and in this paper Dr. Roberts thoughtfully discusses the emotional and mental health needs of Negro children and young people. The paper is a highly readable literature review and critique of the many factors related to emotional stability and mental health. Particular attention should be paid to his analysis of the interaction between social or cultural factors and related psychological traits because it constitutes a significant feature of the article.

The title of this chapter is in large measure the theme of the forth-coming Midcentury White House Conference on Children and Youth. However, the specific purpose here is to summarize briefly selected literature and material related to the psychological aspects of personality and adjustment problems of the Negro American.[2] It is taken for granted

SOURCE. Reprinted from the *Journal of Negro Education,* 1950, 19, 351–362 with permission of the author and the publisher.

[1] The author wishes to express appreciation to Misses Anna P. Floyd and May Amritt for clerical assistance. Since it is not possible to specify them individually, general acknowledgment is given to those contributors whose research and writings have formed the substantial basis of this review.

[2] The term "Negro American(s)" is used throughout this paper to denote the almost exclusively American cultural background of this biologically heterogeneous minority in the United States and at the same time to give recognition to the sociological fact that this group is set apart from the larger society on the basis of possessing, among several other strains, varying and unspecified fractions of African ancestry. The order of the two words has been deliberately employed to emphasize the former rather than the later circumstance.

"White," unless qualified, is used in the general sense of the term as utilized in the United States to designate practically all other people who compose this Nation regardless of cultural background or biological ancestry.

that Negro American children and youth have, in general, similar if not identical problems and needs of their fellow Americans. Therefore, it is the intention of this paper to focus upon those needs and problems that are judged to arise primarily out of their minority status. The following topics will be discussed:

1. The psychological aspects of adjustment and personality problems.
2. The relation of psychiatric and social factors in adjustment.
3. The means of meeting the needs arising from the foregoing circumstances.

PSYCHOLOGICAL ASPECTS[3]

It is a truism that the actual reality of the child at birth consists of two fused and inseparable realities—the reality *with* which he is born (genetic and biological components), and the reality *into* which he is born (the social milieu). There is also a dynamic interdependent relationship between the child as a developing individual, his family, and the world in which they live; and so there is need for a description of the ways in which the child's life and total development are affected by that interrelated situation.

The literature in this field is voluminous concerning some questions and is very scanty for others. Much of the literature is also subject to controversy. Therefore, the generalizations set forth here are those which are drawn from selected studies or are those considered to be in line with the general weight of the evidence. No attempt has been made to make a definitive assessment of the total range of the available material in this field.

STATIC STUDIES

The term "static study" is used to refer to investigations which have been directed primarily towards the ascertainment of differences between

[3] Based largely upon "Negro American Youth, Mental Health and World Citizenship." Final Report for the International Conference on Mental Hygiene, London, Ag 1948, from the Local Preparatory Commission (S. O. Roberts, Chairman) Fisk University and Meharry Medical College.

The specific citations for this review are to be found in C. S. Johnson and H. M. Bond, "The Investigation of Racial Differences Prior to 1910." *Journal of Negro Education*, 3:328–339, 1934; Otto Klineberg, *Race Differences*. New York: Harper and Brothers, 1935; Robert L. Sutherland, *Color, Class, and Personality*. Washington: American Council on Education, 1942; S. O. Roberts, "The Measurement of Adjustment of Negro College Youth." Unpublished Doctoral Dissertation. Minneapolis: University of Minnesota, 1944; and studies by the author, his students, and others, since 1944.

samples of people without reference to causal or dynamic factors; the groups of particular concern in this paper are white and Negro Americans.

INTELLIGENCE. There have been, for example, hundreds of studies of mental ability. In general, the *average score* of Negro American groups has been somewhat lower than that of the compared white groups. This has been found to hold for children, adults, college groups, citizens in the armed forces, etc.

There has also been noted a wide range of average scores achieved by various groups within the Negro American minority. For instance, it has been observed that socio-economic status is positively related to intelligence. Also, Negro Americans living in the Northern part of the country do better on such tests than those who live in the South. Furthermore, Negro American soldiers in some Northern states have been found to surpass groups of white soldiers from certain Southern states. There is some evidence, but not without contradiction, that when more favorable environment is provided (such as moving from the South and living in the North) intelligence, as measured by test scores, tends to increase. In any case, there is unequivocal support for the view that these two groups in America have representatives at all levels of the intellectual distribution and that the range of *individual ability within* either group is of far greater magnitude and significance than the relatively small average differences that some samples may exhibit under specific circumstances.

PREJUDICE AND GENERAL PERSONALITY DIFFERENCES. Studies of prejudice against Negro Americans have yielded rather consistent results. It is generally agreed from numerous investigations that this group experiences more overt hostility and prejudice than any other minority within the United States. This unfavorable attitude is shared by several groups, including some other minorities. For example, it has been noted in one study that American Indians differ but little from whites in their unfavorable attitude towards Negro Americans. In another investigation it was discovered that Jews are remarkably free from prejudice towards Negro Americans, although their attitude became increasingly unfavorable if they (the Jews) had had frustrating anti-Jewish experiences. Even some Negro Americans have not been able to resist the subtle influence of the prevailing unfavorable attitude. Thus, students in one college were found to assign the same stereotypes to Negro Americans in general as white college students do. However, they were careful not to think of themselves in such terms.

Occasionally Negro American shave had the opportunity to express their preference for other groups. In one such instance it was found that Negro Americans placed themselves first and white Americans eighth—still very much higher than they are usually rated by whites, in such investigations. In other cases, white Americans have been placed even closer to themselves by Negro Americans. This finding suggests the absence of overt equivalent dislike or retaliatory feeling on the Negro American's part as determined in these studies.[4]

In order to justify these unfavorable attitudes towards this minority, whites have developed stereotypes that may be called "defensive beliefs" regarding the Negro American. Thus, the contentions that they are shiftless, happy-go-lucky, animal-like, or personally responsible for their economic and social position, etc., serve to soothe the conscience of those who do not wish or care to consider them as human beings differing in no essential respect from themselves. In keeping with this "defensive belief" concept, it was found in one survey that over the United States the opinion was more frequently expressed that the "Negro problem" is more likely to remain as it is than that there will be improvement. Northerners generally have a more favorable attitude than Southerners, but this difference may well be more superficial than genuine. There is substantial evidence that unfavorable attitudes towards minorities may develop as early as five to eight years, and are primarily generated in the *home from contact with the prevailing community or family sentiment* rather than through actual, personally unpleasant, experiences with these groups.

It has been shown that unfavorable and persistent attitudes can be induced, but can unfavorable attitudes be modified? The evidence is contradictory on this point. Thus, the amount of information possessed by individuals about the Negro American is generally associated with having a favorable attitude towards him. On the other hand, school children have been observed to show rather favorable attitudes in the fourth grade (the Negro American in seventh place), but in the fifth grade and from there on the Negro American is near the bottom in preference (eighteenth place or lower out of twenty-one rated groups). Efforts that have been made in college classes to change attitudes towards the Negro American have not been too successful.[5] However, a few investigators have found rather marked persistent changes in the direction of more favorable attitudes. No person should be discouraged on this score, since the adverse findings are based upon short-time, isolated experiments. Undoubtedly a broad program of inter-cultural education which touched every phase of the community's activities and one that

[4] Compare with Helen V. McLean, "The Emotional Health of Negroes," *Journal of Negro Education,* 18:283–290, Summer, 1949.

[5] *American Council on Race Relations.* Studies in Reduction of Prejudice. Chicago, Illinois, 1947.

reached into the home would do much to alleviate this anomalous condition in the country dedicated to the democratic ideal.

What are some of the direct effects of this prejudice and assigned inferior status upon the Negro American? Efforts to determine whether there are general personality differences or effects have resulted in a well-nigh hopelessly confused tangle of contradictory results. Part of this difficulty has emerged from the use of instruments (tests in particular) which were set up in one cultural situation and then used to evaluate individuals in quite a different cultural setting without reference to the cultural distinction. On the whole, it has been observed that in the general areas of adjustment, Negro Americans do not differ substantially or in any consistent fashion from their white colleagues. However, in the realm of attitudes as especially relating to questions of segregation and discrimination there are sharp differences compared with some groups of whites. This topic is more fully developed in Chapter XIII. There may be pointed out here specifically, however, that nearly all Negro American children have had some unpleasant experience regarding race relations,[6] usually at a very early age (eleven or twelve years). One study of the attitudes of Southern college students revealed an extremely unfavorable attitude towards the law. Since many of these students, either through direct knowledge or through experiences of others, have possibly had unpleasant contacts with the Southern legal system, the finding takes on added significance.

There are some who wish to rationalize their desire to segregate the members of this minority by claiming that they are happier with their own kind. When this statement was directed to the school system it was found, in one of the best investigations of the problem, that Negro American children were slightly better adjusted to all phases (except social activities) of their school life in mixed schools than in separate schools. Children in such mixed schools have been found to have as much racial pride as children have in separate schools.

Some investigations have revealed that more Negro American children than white engage in boxing and such "aggressive" sports. One worker observed a greater preference by Negro American children for more education, finer cars and other symbols of status than was true for a group of white children of comparable socio-economic status. These results have generally been interpreted as stemming from the circum-

---

[6] "Race" in this paper has no biological connotation, but it is a term frequently used to refer to either the white or Negro American group. "Race relations" generally denotes the adjustment problems arising out of the contacts of white and Negro Americans.

scribed nature of the Negro American child's participation in and therefore access to the rewards of the society in which he lives.

In reaction against this subordinate status, Negro Americans assume different attitudes. Some reject this minority and identify themselves psychologically with white Americans. Others do not feel wholly at ease with their own group, but are not willing to think of themselves as better. Still others dedicate themselves with fierce pride to their group and reject the friendship of whites. Obviously, these distinctions do not cover the whole gamut of attitudes, but serve simply to show some of the problems created by their minority status.

On the whole, the Negro American has taken over the values and attitudes of his white contemporaries. This inevitably sets the stage for personal conflict, since among these attitudes and values he occupies a very inferior position and one of relatively little value for most whites. The problem of skin color is one example which will be discussed more fully later.

ANALYTICAL STUDIES

In this type of research more attention is given to the dynamic and causal factors in the behavior under investigation.

One of the analytic concepts is that of "caste" as applied to Negro-white relations in the United States, and particularly in the South. Furthermore, the social anthropologists state that within the caste structure there is a "class" structure. Thus, a person has specific characteristics associated with his station in life—education, wealth or income, place of residence, family background, intimate friends, clubs, manners, speech, dress, and general behavior. These characteristics make easy the assignment of status or "class" by one's fellow citizens. There are three broad social classes— upper, middle, and lower. These, in turn, may be subdivided depending upon the complexity of the social differentiation and elaboration within a community. It should be noted, however, that these concepts have met considerable criticism on various points, and they are not fully accepted by all.

Geographic origin and skin color are other analytical concepts which have been utilized in some psychological research. There is good reason to believe that class, geographic region of residence, and skin color are indices of dynamic factors affecting the personality and adjustment of Negro Americans.

SOCIAL CLASS. Studies by Allison Davis and by others reveal that the training and attitudes of the Negro American child vary with the social class of his family. The lower-class family teaches the child to be subservient, since he must work for whites. However, if he is pushed too far by the demands of whites, he is taught to fight back physically. The middle-class child is taught, above all else, to be a "good child" and to keep out of trouble even at the expense of some personal humiliation. The upper-class family does all in its power to shield the child from the unpleasantness of inferior caste status. Thus, many of these families never patronize public carriers or amusement places operated by whites in the South. In a polite and socially acceptable manner, however, the child is taught to fight against race prejudice by means of education and propaganda. It has also been observed that middle-class white and Negro American mothers are more alike in child rearing practices than is either group like its own lower-class group.

In one interesting study of former slaves, it was found that household servants (often mulattoes) tended to identify themselves more with their owners than with their fellow-slaves who were field hands. Negro American slave owners and the substantial number of free Negro Americans during slavery are other historical factors which have helped to shape social class differentiation within this group.

These are differences in the merest outline; however, a glimpse may be caught of striking differences within this minority. This factor of differentiation is quite in contrast to the earlier bland assumption made by many of a socially undifferentiated mass of people.

GEOGRAPHIC FACTORS. It is not likely that the geographic concept is basic, but it is rather a shorthand way of saying that, by and large, persons who live in different sections of the country are subject to a variety of economic, political, social, and educational conditions which are quite different from the cultural influences in another section.

The full effects of such differences upon the personality and adjustment of Negro Americans have not been assayed, but there have been noted some differences. For example, Negro American children who have left the South and who have entered Northern public schools are said to present many adjustment problems, but the relative importance of the "racial" factor, over against the general problems of adjustment associated with social class and those occasioned by such migration, has not been fully evaluated.

One series of investigations has sought to relate the geographic and social class factors in groups of Negro American students from different regions of America attending a college in the South. These studies reveal, tentatively, that the differences on tests of ability and achievement associated with regional origin or residence are not overcome even when the groups are matched for social class. Differences regarding personality factors are not nearly so pronounced.

SKIN COLOR. Skin color is a biological factor which derives significance chiefly from the nature of the cultural evaluation placed upon it. In the wider American society, racial identification has become a status concept governing the nature of inter-racial relationships. In a somewhat similar manner, skin color has become a status concept regulating, to some extent, both the inter-racial and intra-racial relationships of Negro Americans.

Historically, Negro Americans of light complexion have occupied a more favorable position than the darker ones in the American social hierarchy. This can be largely attributed to the fact that the circumstances under which mixed bloods originated assured them superior social and economic opportunities. Being generally the offspring of white slave masters, the mixed bloods had more intimate contact with the dominant white culture, were more likely to be educated and emancipated, and were frequently bequeathed property or other economic goods. When their superior social and economic opportunities resulted in superior intelligence, achievement and leadership qualities, these superior qualities were attributed to their white blood rather than to the superior opportunities which white blood afforded them.

Another problem arises out of the fact that young Negro American children of very fair complexion tend to identify themselves with pictures of white children rather than with those of children with dark complexion. Accordingly, they must learn as they get older that their objective skin color is *not* the means by which they are identified socially.

Several studies conclude that by and large "brown skin" people are the best adjusted among Negro Americans with reference to color, since they deviate less markedly from the majority of people in this minority than do individuals at either of the color extremes. Various inventories designed to determine personal color preferences among Negro Americans generally reveal "light brown" or "brown" as the color most preferred. This attitude also extends to other persons in some instances. For example, in one college it was observed that the men expressed a general preference for mates with light brown complexion and "good hair;" while the women gave less evidence of being as much concerned with these physical traits.

Finally, it may be pointed out that some maintain that color becomes more painful in its consequences the closer a person approximates the behavior traits and standards of the larger society; and yet, because of "color" is not allowed to participate fully in the dominant culture. While color must be recognized as an important factor in the formation of personality, its importance must always be viewed in terms of the total situation; and as a factor in severe maladjustment it does not appear to be the determining or significant element.

On the basis of the preceding summary of some of the research and literature in this area, it can be seen that the general psychological situation is not a harmonious one. There are many pressures of external conditions and hostile attitudes with which this minority must contend. On the other hand, there are divisive factors (such as class, geographic residence, and physical characteristics) which have served in the past to create intra-group hostility. It is probable that external problems, extensive migration and economic mobility have tended to lessen the in-group tensions. There remain, however, problems attendant upon the conflict of minority and general cultural values and wide variation in the accommodative patterns adopted by Negro Americans in response to their imposed subordinate social status.

PSYCHIATRIC AND SOCIAL ASPECTS

The frustrating nature of socio-economic circumstances along with the associated disruptive effect upon family life and the lack of adequate opportunity for the development of "normal" (i.e., middle-class) values are reflected more sharply in social disorganization and severe personality disturbances than the previous survey would suggest. Figures are particularly difficult to secure for severe personality reactions, and even more difficult to interpret.[7] Regardless of the correct interpretation most authorities agree that the Negro American is disproportionately subject to unfavorable socio-economic influences and exhibits higher rates on many indices of social disorganization and for some classes of severe personality disorder than white Americans. The assessment of the balance sheet in this area is complicated by the availability of facilities, admission policies, mitigation, and so forth. While no disorder is peculiar to a particular group, there is the possibility that "racial" conflict or the circumstances associated with low economic and social status may be precipitating factors and may constitute a considerable core of the content of the behavioral disorder.

Other chapters of this Yearbook and the Report, referred to in the preceding section, both discuss in some detail the social circumstances and conditions which are related to, if not causative of, the adjustment problems experienced by Negro American children and youth. Furthermore, the importance of the social milieu is being increasingly stressed in both clinical work and experimental investigations related to personality development and adjustment. However, so little work has been sufficiently

---

[7] Ernest Y. Williams and Claude P. Carmichael, "The Incidence of Mental Disease in the Negro," *Journal of Negro Education*, 18:276–82, Summer, 1949.

analytical in keeping with this point of view that it is difficult to separate the factor of being "Negro American" from a complex of attendant social and economic forces. Nevertheless, few would deny that the problem of segregation serves to accentuate the gravity of the favorable socio-economic level of the bulk of the Negro American population.

Finally it should be pointed out that, in a sense, any problem of adjustment and personality associated with being "Negro American" has a certain social uniqueness. It may be true that other minorities have problems arising from varying degrees of non-acceptance by other groups and from conflicts between two different sets of cultural patterns and values. However, the Negro American minority, as pointed out earlier, is probably the most "American" in cultural background of any sub-group in the United States, by virtue of their length of residence and lack of continued contact and ties with any other original or foreign culture of any sort. Therefore, the "uniqueness" of their adjustment problems (compared with that of other minorities) stems from their attempt to exercise, despite strong opposition of custom or law, those very cultural habits, skills, and values which constitute their major cultural heritage. In short, the problem arises from the effort to deny, on artificial grounds, the privilege of being "American" to the very group of persons, who by virtue of their history are best entitled to it.

MEETING THE ENGENDERED NEEDS

Any sound and worthwhile effort to meet the mental and emotional health needs of people is necessarily predicated upon certain fundamental principles and must be directed towards the attainment of specific goals.

There may be advanced the reasoning that a sound society, and physically and mentally healthy personalities bear a circular relation to each other. Lack of attention to either creates the conditions of failure for both. Translated into more specific terms, this principle requires a society so constituted that the physical needs of all are met without discrimination. It postulates a society wherein differences can be settled by peaceful means and one which fosters a sense of security, and belonging, without artificial restrictions upon the full participation of the individual in local, national, and inter-national affairs .

Such a society sets the stage for individuals and a type of family life composed of persons sufficiently removed from economic and cultural marginality, so that they are capable of developing the warmth, affection, and sense of emotional security which are said to be so necessary to the development of normal personalities with sound emotional and mental health.

PROGRAMS AND PROCEDURES

Since this improved society will not emerge unaided, what are some of the specific steps that are being taken and which need to be further emphasized in the creation of this society better equipped to foster mental health?

EDUCATION. A stock but unavoidable part answer lies in education. The school has a real opportunity to provide its students with an atmosphere which is in accord with democratic and mental hygiene principles. Such schools are really indispensable for this minority, since it is only in the schools, the churches, and other such organized groups largely under the immediate and direct control of the minority that young people can learn the skills of democratic social participation and obtain the healthy ego-support which may be denied full play in the larger community. Some schools are moving in this direction, but in order to be fully effective education must also function in the wider community context. Parents can be educated and so can legislators concerning their responsibilities and obligations. Undoubtedly many parents are undemocratic and make mistakes in the rearing of their children due to insufficient understanding of the principles of child growth and development. Also, it may be assumed that better conditions of living and recreation might well be forthcoming if legislators and the general public could be made to understand the tragic cost of segregation in terms of physical and mental disease, social disorganization, uneducated people, and as a result—wasted human resources.

LEGISLATION AND ECONOMIC MEASURES. There are those who decry legislation since they say that attitudes and feelings can not be legislated. None would assert that laws wholly prevent homicides or robbery, but it is not likely that these false prophets would care to live in a society without the protection of such laws. It is also interesting to point out in this connection that it has been found that disapproval of legislation designed to improve the status of minorities is likely to be associated with a high amount of prejudice.

As President Johnson of Fisk University stated in a recent radio address, the single greatest barrier to improved "race relations" in America today is segregation. The removal of all forms of legal support for segregation would, therefore, seem to be called for; and there is increasing evidence that the legal sanctions are steadily crumbling. Public opinion polls can be very misleading in regard to this matter, since several studies have shown that the expressed view in the poll was not highly correlated with subsequent behavior *once a change had been effected* in a "racial" situation. As a further illustration, the record of the Negro American in all lines of endeavor where the barriers of segregation have been removed is ample demonstration, for all who are willing to see, of how human potentiality is released under even moderately favorable circumstances with beneficial rather than disastrous consequences for even the elements that may have originally objected.[8]

The aims of the FEPC, increased facilities of housing, recreational provisions, and child guidance centers, are other measures which may be obtained through legislation or through private support. In either case, these added facilities will contribute their share to healthier and happier people.

RESEARCH AND SUPPORT OF ORGANIZED GROUPS. Two final areas of activity involve research and support of organizations and groups working for the improvement of all of these areas. More research is needed to increase present knowledge, but of equal importance is work designed to show how to use more effectively the available information. Aside from local, state, and national bodies, there are such groups as UN UNESCO, WHO, and the International Congress on Mental Health (World Federation for Mental Health) which function at the international level, but which tend to influence conditions at the national and local levels.

EVALUATION OF PROGRAMS

The Midcentury White House Conference is providing the occasion for local groups and communities to assess their immediate situation from the point of view of the total contribution being made to the emotional and spiritual welfare and development of young people.

A specific program of evaluation has been provided by the Group for the Advancement of Psychiatry which outlines in detail the needed inventory of a community in order to determine whether it is meeting its mental hygiene needs.[9]

SUMMARY AND CONCLUSIONS

On the basis of the condensation and interpretation, set forth here, of a fairly wide range of research and literature in this field, it is believed that the following conclusions can be validly drawn.

1. The Negro American child and youth are subjected to a degree of

---

[8] The effort constantly expended by some in maintaining the conditions of segregation and discrimination influences the personality of those imposing as well as those subjected to such practices. However, that topic is beyond the scope of the present paper.

[9] "An Outline for Evaluation of a Community Program in Mental Hygiene," *Group for the Advancement of Psychiatry*. Topeka, Kansas. Report No. 8, Ap. 1949.

restricted cultural participation, by either law or custom, rarely experienced by other minorities in this country. This position is reflected in the generally unfavorable attitudes held by groups concerning Negro Americans.

2. The psychological effects of cultural marginality are difficult to determine scientifically because of the instrument used and the samples studied. Certain attitudes and a heightened social significance of some physical traits such as skin color and hair texture are probably the only psychological variables with a distinctive "racial" basis.

3. The more severe mental consequences and social disorganization can be analyzed in terms of the general social level of the Negro American population and of factors which bear more heavily upon this group. While the disentanglement of cultural and biological factors is particularly difficult in this area, there is evidence that "racial" conflicts may form part of mental disturbances, when such occur. Inadequate facilities, differing policies concerning arest or admission to institutions, etc., serve to complicate remedial and preventive measures.

4. The basic principle, in meeting the needs growing out of the foregoing facts, is the circular relation between a healthy society and an integrated, normal personality. The ameliorative measures and programs advanced in this connection include education in the broadest sense, legislation, and the provision of various psychological facilities and services. The removal of want and fear provides increased opportunity for the type of family life which fosters better mental health and meets more fully the emotional and mental health needs of the developing child. Support for research and of local, state, national, and international bodies devoted to peace and human welfare also serves to strengthen the efforts in this area.

5. The only sound social principle for mental health is the one of urging that *all* people should be permitted and encouraged to share in and contribute to the prevailing culture to the best of their abilities and interests while working for a better world. The continuation of a segregated pattern of life can not but serve to perpetuate the consequences set forth in this paper, and will thus continue to deny the full operation of the democratic principle and ideal upon which this nation is founded.

35 *A Review of Research and an Investigation of Emotional Dependency Among Negro Youth*

HOWARD K. CAMERON

Assistant Professor of Education, Howard University

Dr. Cameron discusses the concept of emotional dependency among Black youth, and attempts to examine the idea that there should be differences in regional as well as familial child-rearing patterns. Specifically he feels that the deep Southern states present an environment wherein overdependency would be fostered more than in either the Border or Northern states, and his data support his ideas rather clearly. The article is also valuable for its discussion of overdependency and child-rearing techniques.

INTRODUCTION

In this paper the writer proposes to consider an important topic in the area of personality theory—emotional overdependency. As used herein, the concept of emotional overdependency refers to the unusual reliance on others for approval and/or assistance, and conformity to the demands and opinions of others. Whereas such dependent behavior is somewhat common among children during the first years of life, its continuation into adolescence is perceived by developmental psychologists as indicative of the individual's failure to achieve one aspect of an important developmental task—independence.

It is a commonly held opinion that dependent behavior typifies most Negroes. However, the writer has been unable to locate any systematic and empirical research to validate this opinion. One might question whether those writers who have depicted Negroes as emotionally dependent individuals have duly considered the "Negro Revolt" which has been

SOURCE. Reprinted from the *Journal of Negro Education*, 1967, 36, 111–120 with permission of the author and the publisher.

in process during the past twenty years and the probable personality changes of Negro youth resulting therefrom.

Several important questions can be formulated relative to the above observation. Are Negro youths as emotionally dependent as it is frequently believed? If so, are there sex differences in the expression of emotional dependence? Do Negro youth express behavior which reveals significantly greater degrees of emotional overdependency than a comparable Caucasian group? Are there regional differences in the expression of emotional dependency? Do emotionally overdependent youth perceive the child-rearing practices of their parents as being significantly different from those youth characterized as emotionally independent?

There is general agreement among developmental psychologists that "early child-rearing practices" are the basic cause of emotional overdependence. Similarly, when such overdependent behavior continues to be exhibited by older Caucasian children and youths, these investigators generally postulate it to be the result of an overprotective mother or mother surrogate. However, in discussing causative factors in emotional overdependency among Negro youths, many of these investigators and sociologists single out socio-cultural conditions, and dwell on how such conditions directly or indirectly foster dependency. References are made to the effects of racial discrimination and segregation which Negroes encounter in various forms throughout the United States, and the influence such practices have on the ego structure of Negroes.

Before proceeding further with the topic, the point should be made that the writer intends for racial terms such as "Negro" or "Caucasian" to be interpreted in a restricted manner. The statements made above and hereafter are used in reference to only those members of an ethnic group to which the expressed idea applies. Such ethnic references should not be construed as a description of an entire group.

DEVELOPMENT OF EMOTIONAL OVERDEPENDENCY

Explanations on the cause of dependency behavior can be obtained from several sources. Psychoanalysts offer much clinical data on this topic. For instance, Abraham (1) believes that infancy is the critical stage for the development of dependency. Dependency is said to result from experiences of satisfaction and dissatisfaction the child has while interacting with his mother—the dependency object. Such erotic experiences first center around oral activities and later anal activities. Overdependency on the part of the adolescent is clinically linked to a fixation of oral activities and attitudes. In support of Abraham's hypothesis, the data of Levy (11) show a high incidence of oral fixation as a result of oral frustrations in infancy. Likewise, Sears and Wise (14) have found that children who experienced greater oral indulgence in the form of late weaning (which establishes a stronger oral drive) give more evidence of oral frustration and a higher incidence of oral fixations than those weaned early.

Explanations on the cause of emotional overdependency have also been given in the form of traditional reinforcement theory. Sears, et al. (13) state that as the mother interacts with the infant, the mother can acquire a secondary reward value. This is possible because the infant comes to associate his mother with the reduction of the hunger drive and the elimination of pain. Hence, the child eventually becomes dependent upon the mother for emotional succorance as well as the satisfier of his physical needs. The condition under discussion is one in which the child is continuously reinforced for exhibiting dependent behavior. This model for the development of overdependency would certainly seem to apply in cases where there exists an overprotective parent or authority figure who rewards dependent acts and punishes independent behavior.

The results from an investigation by Kagan and Moss (9) and Childs (3) suggest that dependent behavior which is learned during early childhood may continue to exist during adolescence, especially among females. These investigators suggest that such adolescent dependency may be the result of several factors. For instance, dependent behavior is less punished in females than males; hence, parental and peer group punishment of dependent behavior probably inhibits its occurrence among adolescent males. On the other hand, females are often encouraged to be passive and dependent. In summarizing their study, Kagan and Moss state:

"The results revealed that passive and dependent behaviors were quite stable for women, but minimally stable for men. Over sixty per cent of the correlations between childhood (ages 6–10) and adult ratings of dependency were statistically significant for females, while only nine per cent were significant for men. The correlations between the ratings for ages 3 to 6 and adulthood were considerably lower and not statistically significant."

The data of Merenda, et al. (12) also indicate a greater tendency for females to be more passively dependent than males. In their study of passive dependency among 181 adult males (ages 17 to 57 with a median of 22) and 90 adult females (age 17 to 62 with a median of 25), it was determined that 17 per cent of the males and 27 per cent of the females scored in the passive dependency category on the Kessler P D Scale.

In the discussion thus far, it has been emphasized that the development of emotional dependency during childhood is perceived as a general occurrence in American culture. Furthermore, it has been determined that overdependent behavior is often exhibited by adolescents, with its occurring significantly more often among girls than boys. On the other hand, the literature is replete with references to the American Negroes as being passive and overdependent individuals. In accounting for such passive and overdependent behavior, writers have theorized that the restrictive sociocultural conditions Negroes encounter are the basic causes.

Is there supportive data for this belief? Let us consider the common viewpoint which is often given on this topic. In Woodson's (15, pp. 87–88) discussion of the "slave codes" he depicts the predicament of slaves in servitude. Woodson states that the slaves were subjected to inhuman cruelties. In fact, according to American law during slavery, the Negro was not recognized as a human being, but was to be possessed, taxed, and disposed of as other chattel. Any slave who lifted his hand against a white man was frequently given the minimum punishment of thirty lashes on his bare back.

It is generally conceded that Negro males, more so than females, have been the specific targets of brutality and subjugations by those who had a vested interest in the so-called "Southern way of life." This way of life incorporates many customs, mores, and laws designed to demoralize the Negro male and disarm him of feelings of self respect, identity, and family cohesiveness. Such contemporary practices as addressing the Negro male by his first name or "boy," relegating Negroes to the menial and unskilled labors, differential wage patterns for Negroes and whites performing the same work—yet the last hired and the first fired, are intended to make the Negro male feel insecure, inferior, and inadequate. There is good reason to assume that such role demands have had deleterious effects upon the Negro male. According to Kardiner and Ovesey (10, p. 89), the effects of these experiences are overtly displayed in terms of ingroup aggression, suppressed hostility against white people, etc.

Dollard (5, p. 393) has hypothesized a direct relationship between the perceived dependency of Negroes and the luxuries accrued from their dependent relationship on the white authority figure. He poses a cultural conditioning process to account for the dependency of Negroes. The Negro, it is claimed, has been positively rewarded for exhibiting passive and dependent behavior, but punished for aggressive and nondeferent acts in his relationship with the white man. Whenever he was perturbed by economic problems, the "good Negro" in the South could always depend on his employer to extend credit until next pay-day—a contractual agreement which the lender knew frequently could not be fulfilled. Similarly, the Negro in the North could likewise depend upon a helping hand from the corner pawnbroker or loan shark, but in the end, the Northern Negro was more apt to wind up dispossessed of his property, or in jail for not fulfilling his end of the transaction. In both cases, however, the terms of such transactions were often extended with prohibitive interest rates and other binding and debilitating obligations.

Dollard (5, p. 174) concludes that conditions like those just described demanded that Negroes exhibit behavior which he depicts as "acts of deference" toward the white man. He gives the following motives to explain why the Negro reacted submissively and dependently in circumstances of this type. The first is based on the hypothesis that repressed antagonism is perceived as the safest answer to the initial demand for self-abnegation. The second possible motive is that the Negro identified with the socially powerful white person and took pride in serving him. In this regard, however, the writer suggests the importance of differentiating between dependent behavior which results from the realistic perception by Negroes of their "economic inadequacies," and emotional dependency which has a developmental basis.

PSYCHOLOGICAL STUDIES ON NEGRO DEPENDENCY

The data of Grossack (8) seem relevant to the discussion at this point. This investigator obtained personality measures on the Edwards Personal Performance Schedule from 108 females and 63 male Negro college students. His data revealed that the Negro males and females had significantly higher scores on the deference scale and lower scores on the autonomy scale than the white normative group. This finding can be interpreted to mean that the Negro subjcets showed a greater degree of emotional dependency. Grossack further states that five Jamaican males (which is such a small and highly selected sample) who also took the test scored significantly higher on the autonomy scale, but lower on the deference scale than his American Negro males. This statistical information is interpreted to be additional evidence to support the assumption that cultural restrictions have severely distorted the personality of American Negroes toward dependency.

There is additional evidence in psychological literature which applies to the problem under discussion. Clark and Clark's (4) data indicate that the Negro children in their study showed clear-cut rejection of "Negroid" looking dolls and a preference for white dolls. There was a tendency for Negro children to reject brown color, and to make irrelevant or escapist responses when asked to color a picture in a manner representative of themselves. The "escapist responses" were more marked among children living in the North, whereas the "rejection responses" were more characteristic of Southern children.

HYPOTHESES

On the basis of historical and socio-cultural data, it would seem proba-ble that the kind and pattern of racial segregation and discrimination en-countered by Northern Negroes would result in a different kind and degree of personality distortion than the racial segregation and discrimi-nation experienced by Negroes reared in border and deep Southern states. Such differential distortion should be perceptible on scales measuring traits which have a socio-cultural basis. It seems plausible that the more restrictive and stultifying environment would result in a higher incidence of over dependent behavior. The difficulty is realized, however, in delin-eating that degree and/or incidence of overdependent behavior which is caused by the immediate parent-child relationship from overdependency resulting from the larger socio-cultural environment. If one accepts the psychological studies on Negro dependency and historical data on the in-fluence of cultural conditions, the following research hypotheses seem plausible:

1. Emotional overdependency is more prevalent among Negroes reared and residing in deep Southern states than those reared and residing in border states.

2. Emotional overdependency is more prevalent among Negroes reared and residing in deep outhern states than those reared and residing in border states.

3. Emotional overdependency will be more prevalent among Negroes than within a comparable group of white youths within the same geo-graphical region.

4. A significantly greater number of Negro males will exhibit behavior characterized as emotional overdependency than Negro females.

5. Emotionally overdependent youth will differ significantly in their perception of child-rearing practices from emotionally independent youth.

PROCEDURE

The subjects in this pilot study consisted of 822 male and female Negro students between the ages of 18–22. The samples were selected from a group of prospective teachers at a southern state teachers college and a university located in a border state. The Southern sample was mostly com-prised of students from Louisiana, Mississippi and Texas; the Northern sample was equally represented by students from the Northeastern and Midwestern United States, and the border sample came primarily from the state of Maryland and Washington, D. C.

Each student was administered the Edwards Personal Preference

Schedule (P.P.S.) and the Perceived Parental Attitude Inventory (PPAI). The one hundred and fifty items on the PPAI (developed by Farquhar, 7) were used to measure the subjects' perception of child-rearing attitudes possessed by their parents. Responses to items on the PPAI were expressed in terms of a Likert type scale ranging from strongly agree to strongly disagree. Frequency data were obtained of agree and disagree responses in order to test for perceived differences in child-rearing between overdependent and independent subjects. The deference and autonomy scales of the P.P.S. were employed as a measure of emotional overdependency and independency. The reader can refer to the construct validation of EPPS by Bernadin and Jessor (2) as a measure of emotional overdependency. In order to test the hypothesis on racial differences in the expression of dependency behavior, data from this study will be compared with that of Merenda, et al. (12).

RESULTS

Regional Differences in Overdependency

The results from this study support the first hypothesis relative to regional difference in emotional overdependency among Negro youth. In Table 1 the reader will find percentage data on various degrees of emo-

TABLE 1

Emotional Overdependency Among Negro College Youth

Regional Groupings	A	B	C
Border Students N = 208			
Males n = 75	25	62	13
Females n = 133	25	52	23
Northern Students N = 157			
Males n = 64	22	51	27
Females n = 93	23	51	26
Southern Students N = 457			
Males n = 155	43	49	08
Females n = 302	40	50	10
Total Sample N = 822			
Males n = 294	34	53	13
Females n = 528	33	51	16

Key:
  A—Per cent of high dependency students.
  B—Per cent of average dependency students.
  C—Per cent of independency.

tional dependency. Chi square values for this frequency data are shown on Table 2. It is interesting to note the highly significant chi square values resulting from the test for independence between the Southern sample and the Northern and border samples for both males and females. Likewise,

TABLE 2

Frequency and Chi Square Values of Regional Differences in Dependency

Regional Groups	High Dependency	Average Dependency	Independence	Chi Square Values
Northern Males	14	33	17	
vs				
Border Males	19	46	10	3.86
Northern Males	14	33	17	
vs				
Southern Males	66	77	12	17.48**
Border Males	19	46	10	
vs				
Southern Males	66	77	12	7.01*
Northern Females	21	48	24	
vs				
Border Females	33	70	30	.357
Northern Females	21	48	24	
vs				
Southern Females	121	151	30	19.20**
Border Females	33	48	30	
vs				
Southern Females	121	151	30	16.86**
Total Males	99	156	39	
vs				
Total Females	175	269	84	1.06

* Chi square value is significant at .05 level of confidence.

** Chi square value is significant at .01 level of confidence.

the lack of significantly high chi values for Northern vs border comparisons is equally notable. In this category, the Northern male vs the border male test of independence yielded a chi square value approaching significance. The cross-regional hypotheses relative to the greater dependency of Southern Negroes in comparison with Negroes from other regions are supported. There were no within regional sex differences of a significant nature; therefore, the allegation that Negro males are more emotionally dependent than Negro females (within each geographical region) was not supported by data collected in this study. Likewise, when the total male and female samples are compared for differences in the incidence of emotional dependency no significant differences resulted. Regional differences in emotional dependency are quite apparent and the incidence increases in a north to south direction.

Racial Differences in Overdependency

What about racial differences in the expression of emotional overdependence? Although general and conclusive statements are not warranted on the basis of data presently available, some reflections seem to be in order. These reflections result from a comparison of data from this study with results of research performed on Caucasian subjects in California and Ohio, and the employment of different measures of dependency.

First, one should note that the occurrence of emotional overdependency is high among both Negro and Caucasian females. In the present study, 33 per cent of the Negro females were classified in this dependency category as compared to 27 per cent of the white females in the Merenda, *et al.* (12) study. In that study, only 17 per cent of the Caucasian male subjects were categorized as emotionally overdependent; whereas 34 per cent of the males in the present study were classified in this category. Similar results were obtained from comparing the data on Negro subjects with data based on the Caucasian sample in the Kagan and Moss study (9). It is realized that these comparisons are rough and statistically weak; at best they indicate a need for more valid data on this topic. The hypothesis on racial differences in the expression of emotional overdependency can neither be rejected nor accepted on the basis of data available.

Significant Differences in Child Rearing Techniques

Did highly dependent youth undergo rearing experiences which they perceived to be significantly different from the rearing experiences perceived by emotionally independent youth? In an effort to answer this question, highly overdependent and independent subjects were administered the Perceived Parental Attitude Inventory. Their responses to questions on this inventory were analyzed by computing chi square values for each item comprising the inventory. All of the differences discussed under the topic of "child rearing attitudes" were found to be significant at the .05 level of confidence.

Generally, the most outstanding differences in the perceived parental rearing attitude between overdependent and independent male subjects were in the area of discipline. Overdependent male subjects indicated that their parents tended to be more strict and demanded obedience to a greater extent than the parents of independent subjects. There were indications that parents of overdependent children were more concerned about the inability of other parents to control the behavior of their children. Parental strictness varied from "insisting that children take naps" to controlling study habits of children during afterschool hours. It is significant to note that parents of overdependent males were perceived to believe that "children were actually happier under strict training than under easier training." Overdependent males perceived their fathers as controlling child behavior through the use of physical punishment more so than independent males. Also, there was a stronger indication of parental rejection by overdependent males, although eighty-three per cent of all males rejected the idea of employing with their children the child rearing techniques which had been used by their parents. Males in the overdependent group indicated that their parents were more observant and rewarding than parents of independent male subjects. Although parents of overdependent male subjects are perceived to be more rewarding, these parents were also more exacting and demanded outstanding and greater accomplishment from their children than the parents of independent males.

In a similar manner to that of the male sample, the female subjects differed sharply in their perception of parental discipline. Again the parental strictness attributed by the overdependent males to their parents was quite perceptible, with a significantly greater number of these parents condoning spanking, prohibiting the expression of anger toward parents, and selecting the kinds of friends sons and daughters should have.

Within the overdependent female sample there appeared not only parental rejection, but somewhat of a rebellious conflict between the female students and their mothers. On the other hand, females in the emotionally independent group depicted their parents as less overprotective and more permissive than the parents of overdependent females. The parents of emotionally independent subjects were perceived to place significantly more emphasis on the principle that "happiness of the child is the most important thing in a family," and tended to express verbally more affection toward the emotionally independent daughter. In a similar manner, however, these parents also expect a greater amount of affection from their daughters than parents of overdependent children. In spite of the former difference, mothers of emotionally overdependent females tend to expect closer and more lengthy "emotional involvement" with their daughters. Considering this observation in respect to parental strictness and overprotection, one might deduce that the type of emotional relationship existing between the overdependent daughter and her mother is one which demands conformity behavior and obedience, even during the adolescent period. Support for this conclusion is also derived from the observation that parents of the overdependent females expect their children "to do as they say, *not* as their parents *do*."

CONCLUSIONS

An analysis of data from measures of emotional dependency and child-rearing attitudes of parents support the hypotheses regarding regional differences among Negro youths in the incidence of emotional overdependency. The highest incidence of overdependency among Southern Negroes might be a manifestation of the effects of an oppressive culture and/or a particular child-rearing pattern; the present data does not single out either factor as the decisive variable. This conclusion seems plausible when one considers the probability that parents in Southern, border, and Northern states might be culturally influenced to employ different techniques of child rearing. It appears, however, that when regional factors are controlled, there is no significant difference between males and females in the incidence of overdependent behavior. It is important to note that this finding not only contradicts popular opinion, but also the data collected by previous researchers on sex differences in overdependency among Caucasian youths. Further research seems desirable to ascertain if this and other findings are characteristic of non-teaching oriented Negro students.

Differences in the perceived child rearing attitudes of parents generally supported developmental theory regarding the continuation of overdependency past childhood. Techniques of parental discipline were perceived to be more physical and restrictive by overdependent males and females. The parents of overdependent youth exercised more rigid control over social and emotional behavior of their children and demanded greater accomplishments. There appeared to be some type of emotional attachment (of a holding-on nature) which mothers of dependent children exhibited.

References

1. Abraham, K. *Selected Papers*. London: Hogarth Publishing Co., 1942.
2. Bernadine, and Jessor, R. "Construct Validation of the E.P.P.S. as a Measure of Dependent Proneness," *Journal of Consulting Psychology*, 21:63–67, 1957.
3. Childs, I. *et al.*, "Children's Textbooks and Personality Development: An Exploration in the Social Psychology of Education," *Psychological Monographs*, LX, 1946.

4. Clark, K., and Clark M. "Emotional Factors in Racial Identification and Performance in Negro Children," *Journal of Negro Education*, 19:341–350, 1950.

5. Dollard, J. *Caste and Class in a Southern Town*. New York: Harper, 1937.

6. Edwards, A. *Manual for the Edwards Personal Preference Schedule*. Psychological Corporation, 1954.

7. Farquhar, William. *A Comprehensive Study of Motivational Factors Underlying the Achievement of Eleventh Grade High School Students*. Research Project No. 846 (8458) U. S. Office of Education, 1959.

8. Grossack, M. "Some Personality Characteristics of Southern Negro Students," *Journal of Social Psychology*, 46:125–131, 1957.

9. Kagan, J., and Moss, H. "Stability of Passive and Dependent Behavior from Childhood through Adulthood," *Child Development*, 31:577–591, 1960.

10. Kardiner, A., and Ovesey, L. *The Mark of Oppression: Exploration in the Personality of the American Negro*. New York: The World Publishing Co., 1962.

11. Levy, D. "Finger Sucking and Accessory Movements in Early Infancy— An Etiological Study," *American Journal of Psychiatry*, 7:881–918, 1928.

12. Merenda, P. "A.D.A. and Kessler P V Scale as Measures of Passive-Dependency," *Journal of Clinical Psychology*, 16:338–341, 1960.

13. Sears, R., *et al.* "Some Child Rearing Antecedents of Aggression and Dependency in Young Children," *Genetic Psychological Monograph*, 47:135–234, 1953.

14. Sears, R., and Wise, G. "Relation of Cup Feeding in Infancy to Thumb Sucking and Oral Drive," *American Journal of Orthopsychiatry*, 20:123–139, 1950.

15. Woodson, C. G. *The Negro in Our History*. Washington: Associated Publishers, 1931.

36 Adolescent Racial and Ethnic Group Differences in Social Attitudes and Adjustment

JOHN PIERCE-JONES, JACKSON B. REID, & F. J. KING
University of Texas

You might expect certain ethnic minorities in any culture to have some fairly trying experiences which would foster a negative orientation to the society, and such is the case in the data reported by Dr. Pierce-Jones and his associates. They examine adolescents' racial and ethnic differences in social attitudes and adjustment and find that a negative orientation to society is strongest in young Negroes, next most evident in young Mexican-Americans and, understandably, least pronounced in white youth. Certainly the events and unrest of the recent past have supported the many conclusions that could have been drawn from this particular study, and suggest the need for increased awareness of the more relevant findings of behavioral science research.

There is an evident hiatus in our knowledge of differences between racially identified groups with respect to personality and adjustment. Tyler (5) has pointed to the considerable sampling difficulties involved in research in this realm, and has said that "the few studies using questionnaire or projective methods . . . have shown no clear trends, [although] there may be interesting questions in this area." Most students of racial group differences have focused their investigations on dimensions of cognitive and psychomotor behavior as Anastasi's (1) recent summary shows.

The central purpose of this study was to test the hypothesis that Negro and white adolescent children, similar in their levels of intellectual ability, differ in several important social attitudes and in certain dimensions of personal and social "adjustment." In addition, differences between two

SOURCE. *Psychological Reports*, **5**, 549–552, 1959. Reprinted by permission of the senior author and publisher.

ethnic groups of white adolescents—Latin Americans and Anglo-Americans (neither Latins nor Negroes)—were examined, and each of these ethnic segments was compared with the Negro segment.

METHOD

Ss were 252 adolescents (84 Negroes, 84 Latin Americans, and 84 Anglo-Americans), drawn from the sample population of approximately 1600 seventh grade pupils now under longitudinal study in the Human Talent Research Project at The University of Texas.[1] These ethnic and racial group samples were selected so as to be equated on stanines for total reading grade placement as measured by the California Achievement Tests. This reading measure was found by factor analyses of the complex Human Talent Project test battery to be loaded (.91) only, and more heavily than any other test, on a clear-cut factor, "general intellectual ability." The equating of the samples on reading ability should have tended to control social status level also, since the Warner-type Index of Social Status (6) used was also loaded significantly (.44) on the same cognitive ability factor as was reading placement. Although the three samples are probably similar in their levels of complex verbal ability, they are also representative, in general, of populations which are somewhat below average levels of mental functioning.

The tests administered to all Ss in these samples for the purposes of the present study were, in the realm of "personal adjustment," the Children's Anxiety Scale (3) and the Texas Cooperative Youth Study (CYS) (4) Personal Adjustment Scale.[2] In the domain of "social adjustment," the Social Inadequacy scale of the CYS was employed. The social attitudes of interest here were measured by the following CYS scales: (a) Negative Orientation to Society, (b) Criticism of Education, and (c) Family Tensions. These scale names seem sufficiently self-explanatory, although further examination of them could wisely be undertaken by the interested reader.

The IBM Model 650 electronic computer was employed to obtain mean stanine scores for each of the samples on all of the social attitudes and the adjustment measures, and also to compute the t ratios used to compare

[1] This research was supported by funds from a grant, Project No. 025 (6431), by the United States Office of Education for the research program, *The Educational Utilization of Human Talent,* in which Professor Carson McGuire is the principal investigator.
   [2] This and all other CYS instruments utilized in the study were modified in such a way as to permit administration to seventh grade children.

and to evaluate Negro, Anglo, and Latin differences in these selected characteristics.

RESULTS

The mean stanine scores (adjustment and attitude scales) for Negroes, Latins, and Anglos are reported in Table 1 together with the *t* ratios obtained by comparing the means of these samples. The .05 level was accepted as the criterion of a statistically significant difference between paired means.

TABLE 1

Mean Stanine Scores for Anglo, Latin, and Negro Samples on Six Attitude and Adjustment Scales and *t* Ratios

	Means			*t* ratios		
Scales	Anglo	Latin	Negro	A-N	N-L	A-L
Children's Anxiety	5.03	5.54	5.10	.31	2.16*	2.39*
Personal Adjustment (CYS)	4.96	5.32	5.18	.93	.61	1.62
Social Inadequacy (CYS)	5.05	5.45	4.95	.42	2.35*	1.78
Family Tensions (CYS)	4.74	5.77	5.17	1.80	2.52*	4.31†
Negative Orientation to Society (CYS)	5.05	5.49	5.94	3.78†	2.14*	2.15*
Criticism of Education (CYS)	5.22	5.63	5.11	.50	2.61*	2.09*

* $F = 4.45$; $df = 1/464$; $p < .05$.
† Significant at .01 level.

Reference to Table 1 shows that in 10 of the 18 comparisons made, the differences between means were statistically reliable at the .05 level or beyond. The only measure not showing any differences was the CYS Personal Adjustment scale. Only one comparison, Negroes with Latins, yielded a significant difference on the CYS Social Inadequacy scale. Two dependable differences occurred in ethnic or racial comparisons involving the Children's Anxiety Scale, the CYS Family Tensions scale, and the CYS Criticism of Education scale. All three comparisons of ethnic racial samples showed statistically reliable differences between means for the CYS Negative Orientation to Society scale.

DISCUSSION AND CONCLUSIONS

In considering the results just presented, there are at least two kinds of sample comparisons which need to be interpreted: (a) those involving racial group membership (i.e., Anglo-Negro and Latin-Negro comparisons) and (b) those involving ethnicity (i.e., Anglo-Latin comparisons), but not racial group identification.

On only one of the measures employed in this research is there any basis for concluding that racial group membership as such is significantly related to adjustment or attitudes concerning society or social institutions. In this single instance, it appears that the Negro children are more "negatively oriented to society" than are either the Latin or the Anglo-American youngsters. But even this difference is not open to clean interpretation as one which is essentially linked to race *qua* race, for the Latin American sample is evidently more hostile toward society generally than is the Anglo-American group. At present, our thinking is that the tendency to be negatively oriented (or hostile) toward "society" hinges on the degree to which the individual's racial or ethnic membership assigns him visible distance from the modal characteristics of the dominant, or Anglo, American society.

If a negative orientation to society is interpretable in terms similar to those which we have just suggested, it is obviously important to examine the degree to which feelings of "social inadequacy" accompany racial group membership or ethnicity. The data in Table 1 indicate that the Latin American children, more than either the Anglo-Americans or the Negroes, report feelings of social ill-ease. Moreover, there is no reliable difference between the Anglos and the Negroes on this self-report measure of social inadequacy feelings. Thus, it is possible that this pattern of differences may mean that the Latin Americans, less visibly socially differentiated from both Anglos and Negroes than are the Anglos and Negroes from one another, function in a manifestly more ambiguous interpersonal environment. Otherwise stated, this means that the Negro and Anglo children are unambiguously classified, both by themselves and by society generally, into their clearly visible social groups, that their interpersonal activities occur essentially within their own identification groups, and that in their schools and communities they experience little need (or opportunity?) to mingle freely with others. The Latin American children, however, do have manifold opportunities to associate with the dominant (Anglo) society and to compete within it, but they also may be subject to social handicaps in these relationships because of deficiencies in dominant cultural socialization.

If the above intepretations are not too wide of the mark—and this we cannot discern from the present research alone—the essentially similar pattern of ethnic-racial group differences obtained with the manifest anxiety measure, the criticism of education scale, and the measure of family tensions might fall into place quite rationally. Regarding the pattern of means and differences on the family tensions measure, it may be noted in passing that modern treatments of adolescent behavior, as exemplified by Ausubel (2), summarize much evidence indicating that "family tensions" are generally characteristic at this age-grade level, but there is little information bearing on this area of adolescent adjustment for racially or ethnically identified groups. A need for test of the hypotheses generated as a result of these findings is definitely indicated.

Apparently, personal adjustment, as we have measured this construct, is not the same psychological attribute as that sampled by the Children's Anxiety Scale, for reliable racial and ethnic differences are entirely absent from our findings on personal adjustment, but present for anxiety. However, the pattern of means and difference is the same for both variables. At this juncture, having in mind the notions about intergroup relationships essayed above, an hypothesis worth testing might be that the "anxiety" measured by Castaneda's scale is influenced to some unknown degree by real factors over and above the interpersonal anxiety it is intended to measure.

SUMMARY

The main purpose of this investigation was to test the prediction that white (i.e., Anglo and Latin American) and Negro adolescents of similar mental ability levels differ in selected orientations toward society and its institutions and in personal-social adjustment. Ss were 252 Texas seventh grade pupils—84 Negroes, 84 Anglos, and 84 Latin Americans. The Anglos were those Ss not identified as either Latin Americans or Negroes and were, further, treated as the dominant cultural segment. The self-report instruments used in this study were the Children's Anxiety Scale and several Cooperative Youth Study scales designed to measure (a) negativism toward society, (b) criticism of education, (c) family tensions, (d) feelings of social inadequacy, and (e) personal adjustment status. The only measure which distinguished reliably between white (both Anglo and Latin Americans) and Negroes was the CYS scale, "Negative Orientation to Society," on which Negroes scored highest (or most negativistic) and Anglos lowest. This difference was interpreted in terms of intergroup relations and socialization theory rather than by means of any bio-racial concepts. Other significant differences obtained in this research appeared to be interpretable within a framework emphasizing the relations of the Latin Americans to more clearly socially visible, accessible, and psychologically unified cultural groups, i.e., the culture-dominant Anglo-Americans, and the clearly visible, but perhaps socially devalued, Negro caste.

References

1. Anastasi, A. *Differential psychology*. New York: Macmillan, 1958.
2. Ausubel, D. *Theory and problems of adolescent development*. New York: Grune & Stratton, 1954.
3. Castenada, A., McCandless, B. R., and Palermo, D. S. The children's form of the Manifest Anxiety Scale. *Child Developm.*, 1956, **27**, 317–326.
4. Moore, B. M., and Holtzman, W. H. What Texas knows about youth. *Nat. Parent-Teacher*, 1958, **53**, 22–24.
5. Tyler, L. E. *The psychology of human differences*. New York: Appleton-Century-Crofts, 1956.
6. Warner, W. L., Meeker, M., and Eells, K. *Social class in America*. Chicago: Science Research Assoc., 1949.

37 The Relationship Between Authoritarianism and Ethnocentrism in Negro College Students[1]

DALMAS A. TAYLOR
Research Fellow, Department of Psychology, University of Delaware

World War II made the world painfully aware of the brutality and sense of dictatorial purpose of totalitarianism, so that it was only natural for the social scientists of the time to attempt to better comprehend such an obviously destructive and threatening form of government. The pioneer works in this field, *The Authoritarian Personality* (Adorno, Frenkl-Brunswik, Levison, and Sanford, 1950); *Escape from Freedom* (Fromm, 1941); and *Totalitarianism* (Ahrendt, 1951) had all shown that certain kinds of personalities could proliferate under such governments and had discussed the psychological and social implications of such majorities. The research related to these viewpoints showed that very authoritarian persons tended to be quite ethnocentric or group oriented since they would much prefer to relate to a very restricted group of people. In this paper, Dr. Taylor examines the relationship between authoritarianism and ethnocentrism in Negro college students. His work is valuable in that it attempts to clarify the ways in which Negroes would display such personality attributes as fascism, ethnocentrism, and anti-Semitism; and also demonstrates that Black college students exhibit an understandable sympathy toward other minority groups.

INTRODUCTION

One landmark of a great study is the amount of interest and controversy that it inspires. *The Kinsey Report* (5) and *The American Dilemma* (6)

SOURCE. Reprinted from the *Journal of Negro Education*, 1962, 31, 455–459 with permission of the author and the publisher.

[1] This paper is adapted from a Master's thesis written at Howard University under the Guidance of Dr. James A. Bayton, to whom the author is deeply grateful.

are two cases in point. Similar to these two studies, in prestige and influence, is *The Authoritarian Personality* (1). A major tribute to its vitality is that it has inspired such a tremendous volume of research (7). Initially, the study was conducted as an investigation of anti-Semitic attitudes, but was later expanded to include the relationship between personality, socio-economic attitudes and political ideology. These traits were explored by correlating scale scores with data obtained in psychoanalytic interviews. The four scales utilized to this end are:

1. The F (fascism or authoritarianism) Scale
2. The E (ethnocentrism) Scale
3. The A-S (anti-Semitism) Scale
4. The PEC (politico-economic conservatism) Scale

Since the publication of *The Authoritarian Personality* in 1950, much research has been conducted using one or more of the four scales. The most widely used of these has been the F scale. In spite of subsequent revisions, modifications and criticisms, it is still considered to be a very valid indicator of anti-democratic or fascistic (authoritarian) thinking.

The focus of the present paper is to investigate the relationship between ethnocentrism and authoritarianism among Negroes. A further undertaking is to compare this finding with those in *The Authoritarian Personality*.

Since the original purpose of *The Authoritarian Personality* was to measure anti-Semitism and later prejudice in general, the standardization of its several scales excluded Negroes and Jews. This was necessary because the wording of the scales was such that it would have been obvious to Jews and Negroes that the statements were directed against them. Therefore, it would have been impossible to get an indirect measure of prejudice among these subjects. Thus, the generalizations of its findings were considered to hold fairly well for non-Jewish, white, native born, middle-class Americans only.

The authoritarian personality (anti-democratic or pro-fascist) is distinguished by anti-Semitism, ethnocentrism, and political conservatism. Since the present endeavor is concerned with ethnocentrism and authoritarianism, a brief discussion of the two scales that measure these traits is in order.

ETHNOCENTRISM

Ethnocentrism refers to strong identification with an "ingroup" and a sympathetic attitude for hostility directed toward an "outgroup" which is seen as a menace to ingroup solidarity. Or more generally, ethnocentrism refs to acceptance of the culturally "alike" and rejection of the "unlike." In general, ingroups are seen as superior in all respects to outgroups, and if outgroups attempt to improve their status, this is viewed as threatening to the ingroup. Further, what is seen as power-seeking and clanishness in outgroups is rationalized into virtues for ingroups.

An inspection of E scale items suggests that it may not be the most valid measure of ethnocentrism among Negroes. The scale is divided into three areas—attitudes toward Jews, toward Negroes and toward other minorities. Since ethnocentrism deals with ingroup-outgroup distinctions, that portion of the E scale referring to Negroes would tend to minimize the overall results when administered to Negro subjects. Therefore, in order to get a good measure of ethnocentrism, it is necessary to use a scale giving ingroup-outgroup distinctions, but omitting attitudes against Negroes. For this purpose, it was decided to use the A-S (anti-Semitism) scale. Anti-Semitism among Negroes can be considered a "specialized" ethnocentrism. The substitution is further enhanced by the fact that the authors of the original text reported a correlation of .68 between the A-S and E scales. Therefore, in investigating the relationship between ethnocentrism and authoritarianism among Negroes, scores on the A-S scale will be used as a measure of ethnocentrism.

AUTHORITARIANISM

The construction of the F scale, developed from the ideology of the PEC, A-S, and E scales, was an attempt to measure prejudice without appearing to do so. Therefore, its items were chosen from the clinical material collected in association with the previously mentioned scales (PEC, A-S, and E). Thus, it intended to measure anti-Semitism and ethnocentrism without mentioning minority groups. During its construction, another purpose, which became its major purpose, began to emerge. That is, the desire to quantify anti-democratic trends at the level of personality. This was so because it became apparent that anti-Semitism and ethnocentrism were expressions of more than mere surface opinion. Therefore, as mentioned above, the F scale is considered a valid indicator of fascism or anti-democratic trends coupled with an indirect assessment of anti-Semitism and ethnocentrism.

Considering the fact that Negroes are an "outgroup" with respect to American culture, and an "ingroup" with regards to themselves, it would be of interest to know where they stand on an attitude scale measuring ethnocentrism and how this measure would correlate with F scale scores. Adorno et al. (1), using an all white population, reported a high correlation between these two scales. The aim of the present study is to determine whether or not a high positive correlation between these two scales exists in a Negro population.

It would be quite difficult to challenge some of the negative effects a segregated society leaves on its outgroup. Karon (4) provides a valuable scientific insight into this problem. His thesis is that Negro Americans differ from white Americans as a result of living and working in a segregated culture. These differences are manifested in low self-esteem, self-abnegation, cautious and apologetic behavior, apathy, hedonism (living for the moment) or turning to a life of crime. On the other hand, the low self-esteem is often compensated for by a quest for status. Frazier (3) maintains that Negroes tend to handle their frustrations through mass consumption of material things and rigid adherence to white middle-class values.

Since the authors of the original study found a high correlation between the E and F scales in the white middle-class, it is possible that Negroes who identify with this class will show a similar correlation between authoritarianism and an analogous measure of ethnocentrism. But since Negroes exist in the framework of outgroup pressures, there are at least two possibilities as to how this would affect the correlation between these two measures.

1. If the defense mechanism of reaction formation is employed as a result of the pressures and frustrations encountered through membership in a minority group, the level of ethnocentrism will increase, thereby giving a high correlation.

2. If Negroes are especially sensitized to and sympathetic with the problems represented by questions on the E scale, you would expect a lower correlation.

This author feels that on the basis of the information in the literature, it would be difficult to predict which one of these two phenomena would be evidenced in a middle-class Negro population. Therefore, it was decided to proceed as though Negroes did not differ from whites, in this respect. If a difference is found, it will be explained on the basis of one of the above two possibilities.

PROCEDURE

SUBJECTS. One hundred and sixty-two Negro undergraduate freshmen (male and female) in the introductory psychology courses at Howard University served as subjects.

SCALES. The following scales were used:

1. F (Fascism) Scale

2. E (Ethnocentrism) Scale
3. A-S (Anti-Semitism) Scale

In order to disguise the intent of the scales, each was introduced as a Public Opinion Questionnaire. The directions for the A-S scale stated further that the statements were about Jewish people. A critical evaluation of these scales and the method of scoring can be found in Jahoda and Christie's *Studies in the Scope and Method of "The Authoritarian Personality"* (2). However, an inspection of the scale items can be found in *The Authoritarian Personality* by Adorno *et al.*

RESULTS

Since the subjects from the original study were middle-class whites, only middle-class Negroes could be used for this study. Therefore, of the 162 subjects tested, 19 were disqualified because their socio-economic and/or ethnic group memberships were not suited to the conditions necessary here. The correlations between the F scale and the A-S and the E scales are given in Table 1 along with correlations of these same measure-

TABLE 1

Correlations Between the F Scale with the A-S and E Scales from the Two Studies

	F-Scale
A-S Scale (Present Study)	.55
E Scale (Present Study)	.58
E Scale (Original Study)	.77

ments obtained by the original authors. As was mentioned earlier, anti-Semitism is being used as a measure of ethnocentrism. At the same time, the actual ethnocentrism scale is being used as a check on the logic and validity of this substitution.

Further analysis revealed that each of the correlations in the present study was significantly lower than the correlation between the F scale and the E scale reported in the original research.

Table 2 gives the correlations between the A-S and E scales and the F and A-S scales from both studies. First of all, it should be noted that the correlation between the A-S and E scales in the present study is sufficiently high enough to suggest that the two scales may be measuring approximately the same thing. Next, the difference between the correlation obtained here and the one reported by Adorno *et al.* is not significant. Therefore, it might be concluded that there is some consistency and stability in the findings of these two studies. The correlations between the F and A-S scales were also approximately the same in both studies. These data suggest that perhaps the scale items were as valid for a middle-class Negro population today as they were for a white, non-Jewish middle-class population ten years ago.

TABLE 2

Correlation Between the A-S, E and F Scales from the Two Studies

	r	t
A-S Scale and E Scale	.71	.60
A-S Scale and E Scale	.68	p > .05
F Scale and A-S Scale	.55	.30
F Scale and A-S Scale	.53	p > .05

The correlation of .55 between the F and A-S scales (Table 1) is indicative of a low relationship between authoritarianism and ethnocentrism among Negro subjects. Therefore, it can be concluded, that the second alternative is the proper explanation of the relationship between authoritarianism and ethnocentrism among Negroes. That is: if Negroes are especially sensitized to and sympathetic with problems represented by questions on a scale measuring ethnocentrism (outgroup rejection), you would expect a lower correlation with "F scale attitudes" than that obtained in a white population.

DISCUSSION

Using anti-Semitism as a critical measure of ethnocentrism among Negroes, the present author found a lower correlation with the F scale than the original authors reported, even though the correlations between the A-S and E scales in the two studies were similar. This seems to indicate that rather than employing the Freudian defense mechanism of reaction formation, resulting in greater ethnocentrism, Negroes are sympathetic to problems experienced by another minority group.

The problems involved in giving a confirmation for the alternative offered can be remedied by using more indirect techniques for measuring the variables involved, and employing an interview situation as a follow-up for the findings. Projective techniques and clinical interviews would be suitable to the kind of information desired here and such is suggested for any further research in this area.

SUMMARY

The present study was concerned with the relationship between ethnocentrism and authoritarianism among Negroes. Further, there was an interest in how Negroes would compare with whites in this respect. To this end, attitude scales of the Likert (2) type were administered to 162 undergraduate students in introductory psychology courses at Howard University.

The scales used were: (1) F (Fascism) Scale; (2) E (Ethnocentrism) Scale; and (3) A-S (Anti-Semitism) Scale.

On the basis of the literature, the author was unable to predict how Negroes would compare with whites. However, the data obtained suggest that Negroes tend to be sympathetic with problems experienced by other minority groups, rather than being more ethnocentric.

Bibliography

1. T. W. Adorno, Else Frenkel-Brunswick, Daniel J. Levison, and R. Nevitt Sanford. *The Authoritarian Personality*. New York: Harper & Brothers, 1950.
2. R. Christie, and M. Johoda, *Studies in the Scope and Method of "The Authoritarian Personality."* Illinois: Free Press, 1954.
3. E. Franklin Frazier. *Black Bourgeoisie*. Illinois: Free Press and Falcon's Wing Press, 1957.
4. Bertram P. Karon. *The Negro Personality*. New York: Springer Publishing Co., Inc., 1958.
5. Alfred C. Kinsey, *et al. Sexual Behavior in the Human Male*. Philadelphia: W. B. Sanders Co., 1948.
6. Gunnar Myrdal. *An American Dilemma*. New York: Harper and Bros., 1944.
7. H. Edwin Titus, and R. P. Hollander. "The California F Scale in Psychological Research: 1950–55," *Psychol. Bulletin*, 54:47–64, 1957.

38 A Personality Correlate of Social Action[1]

PEARL MAYO GORE[2] & JULIAN B. ROTTER
Ohio State University

Who will act? Who will revolt, develop new ways, begin a new school of thought, or significantly change his existing way of life? Such questions have fascinated psychologists for quite some time, because they involve the prediction of how different types of people will behave in various situations. In this paper the authors have attempted to isolate certain personality characteristics of Negroes who were very active in the Civil Rights Movement. Drs. Gore and Rotter show that persons who see themselves as controlling their own behavior from within are more likely to be strongly committed to social action than are persons who see their behavior generally under the control of external forces or other persons.

Social scientists have long been interested in the conditions under which the initiation of social change will take place. It has fallen to the social psychologist in particular to attempt predictions of individual differences in behavior directed toward a changing of the social structure. Usually, the problem has been approached through the measurement of the intensity or strength of attitudes. However, it is now widely recognized that the apparent desirability of some social outcome is a poor predictor of the degree to which an individual will commit himself toward action to obtain the desired goal. This is particularly true when the social action runs counter to majority opinion and entails risk of rejection, failure, or other punishment.

SOURCE. Reprinted from *The Journal of Personality*, 1963, 31, 58–64 with permission of the senior author and Duke University Press.

[1] This research was supported in part by the United States Air Force under Contract No. AF 49 (638)-741 monitored by the Air Force Office of Scientific Research, Office of Aerospace Research. This paper was read at the Midwestern Psychological Association Meeting, 1962.

[2] Now at the University of Illinois.

The concept of internal vs. external control of reinforcement may be of value in predicting social action behavior. This dimension distributes individuals according to the degree to which they attribute what happens to themselves to their own behaviors or characteristics vs. the degree to which they attribute what happens to themselves to forces outside their own control. Such forces would be represented by ideas of fate, chance, powerful others, or a general inability to understand the world. In social learning theory (Rotter, 1954), this variable is viewed as a generalized expectancy relating behavior to reinforcement in a large number of learning situations, cutting across specific need areas. In other words, it involves a higher-level learning skill affecting behavior in a wide variety of problem-solving situations.

Previous research by Phares (1957, 1962), James and Rotter (1958), James (1957), Rotter, Liverant, and Crowne (1961) and others has shown unequivocally that the growth and extinction of expectancies for reward vary considerably in different laboratory tasks if the tasks are perceived by S as chance, luck, or controlled by E vs. those which are seen as skill tasks with reinforcement dependent upon the individual's ability.

In addition to the findings from studies of expectancy changes, it has been hypothesized that individuals differ in a stable personality characteristic of whether they expect reward in a large variety of situations to be the function of external forces or their own behavior or attributes. The first attempt to measure such a generalized characteristic was made by Phares (1957). His test was revised by James (1957) into a longer Likert type scale, and Liverant, Rotter, Crowne, and Seeman have developed successive forms of a forced choice scale starting from the James-Phares test (Rotter, Seeman, & Liverant, 1962). The test now being used at Ohio State for research with adults consists of twenty-three items with six filler items (I-E Scale). Illustrative items are as follows.

I more strongly believe that:
   6. a. Without the right breaks one cannot be an effective leader.
      b. Capable people who fail to become leaders have not taken advantage of their opportunities.
   9. a. I have often found that what is going to happen will happen.
      b. Trusting to fate has never turned out as well for me as making a decision to take a definite course of action.
   17. a. As far as world affairs are concerned, most of us are the victims of forces we can neither understand, nor control.
       b. By taking an active part in political and social affairs the people can control world events.

23. a. Sometimes I can't understand how teachers arrive at the grades they give.
   b. There is a direct connection between how hard I study and the grades I get.

Approaches to the assessment of individual differences along these lines with children have been developed by Bialer (1961), Crandall and Katkovsky (in press), and Battle (1962). Previous studies with adult and child scales have shown predictiveness in some learning situations (Phares, 1957; James, 1957; Bialer, 1961), an achievement situation (Crandall & Katkovsky, in press), a conformity situation (Crowne & Liverant, in press), risk taking tasks (Liverant & Scodel, 1960), logical relationships to other tests (Holden, 1958; Simmons, 1959), and mean differences among known groups (Battle, 1962; Cromwell, Rosenthal, Shakow, & Zahn, 1961).

The most closely related research to the present study, however, was conducted by Seeman and Evans (in press) who related the concept and measure of internal vs. external control to the sociological concept of alienation, in the sense of powerlessness. Using one revision of the current test, Seeman and Evans studied patients in a tuberculosis hospital. They found statistical support for their general hypothesis that those patients who scored toward the internal control end of the dimension would know more about their own condition, would be better informed about the disease of tuberculosis in general, and would be regarded by the ward personnel as being better patients and better informed about their own condition. These predictions held in spite of the fact that none of the items in the questionnaire dealt with tuberculosis specifically or any disease or attitude toward disease. If patients' efforts to find out about their own serious physical condition can be affected by such a generalized attitude, it seems likely that where people are highly involved in desire for certain social change, as Negroes are in desegregation, social action-taking behavior could be likewise predicted from a generalized attitude of internal vs. external control of the locus of reinforcement. This is the major hypothesis of the present study. It should be emphasized that no test items in the I-E Scale deal directly with political liberalness,[3] prejudice, attitudes toward Negro rights, or the Ss' own present or past social action behavior.

In addition, it was hypothesized that predictiveness of this behavior would be improved by a knowledge of the social desirability motives of

[3] Data recently collected by Rotter show no significant difference in the I-E Scale scores of Ohio State University students who identify themselves as Republicans from those who identify themselves as Democrats.

the Ss. Hence, a secondary hypothesis was that Ss high in measured social desirability motive (high SD) would be less likely to participate in actions toward social change than Ss low in this trait.

Since it appeared likely that the assumed high reinforcement value of the social change might be differentially affected by the individual's social class membership, a measure of social class was included in the investigation. The direction of the relationship between social class membership and social action taking behavior was not hypothesized.

METHOD

Ss of the present study were students of a Southern Negro college that has featured prominently in recent social protest movements. Three psychology classes, including 62 males and 54 females, were given the Internal-External Control of Reinforcements Scale (I-E), and the Marlowe-Crowne Social Desirability Scale (S-D) (Crowne & Marlowe, 1960). Socioeconomic status and religious preference data were also obtained.

Four weeks (including two weeks of vacation) after the questionnaires were given, a student confederate went into all three classes on the same day, five minutes prior to dismissal and made the following statements,

TABLE 1

Questionnaire to Determine Degree of Social Action-taking Behavior

---

Students for Freedom Rally

Please check any or all aspects of our program in which you would be willing to participate.

I would be interested in: Check here:

(A) Attending a rally for civil rights.   _____

(B) Signing a petition to go to local government and/or news
    media calling for full and immediate integration of all
    facilities throughout Florida.   _____

(C) Joining a silent march to the capitol to demonstrate our
    plea for full and immediate integration of all facilities
    throughout Florida.   _____

(D) Joining a Freedom Riders Group for a trip during the
    semester break.   _____

(E) I would not be interested in participating in any of the
    foregoing.   _____

                    Signature: _____
                    Address: _____
                    Tel. No.:   _____

"Thank you, Dr. ———, for allowing me this time. I would like to ask the cooperation of each of you in a Students for Freedom Movement. To that end, I will pass out slips for you to fill out and hand back to me as you leave." The questions on the slip are shown in Table 1. Class attendance was used to identify Ss who turned in slips without signing them.

Ss were divided into groups according to their category of social action-taking behavior. If a S checked more than one item, he was placed in the category of highest commitment, in the order A, B, C, D. The mean I-E, S-D, and Social Class (Warner) of each group was then determined. F and t tests were computed.

RESULTS

The means and sigmas for each category of social action-taking are given in Table 2. Using the "mean square ratio" for unequal N's (Lindquist, 1953), a significant F relationship between scores on the I-E scale and social action-taking behavior was found. ($F = 2.89$, $df = 4$ and 111, $p = < .05$.)

TABLE 2

Mean Scores by Categories of Commitment

Category	I-E		S-D		Social Class		N
	Mean	Sigma	Mean	Sigma	Mean	Sigma	
A	10.3	3.1	18.10	6.4	4.76	1.6	20
B	9.2	3.4	17.05	5.5	5.00	1.5	20
C	7.4	2.9	16.95	6.4	5.95	1.3	24
D	8.1	3.8	16.82	4.4	5.29	1.5	20
E*	10.0	3.9	18.74	4.9	5.50	1.4	32

* E category includes those who did not sign a slip but were present.

The following t tests were significant (all two-tailed): categories of high commitment B, C, and D vs. little commitment A ($p = <.05$); category of no commitment E vs. high commitment B, C, and D ($p = .05$); category A vs. category C alone ($p = <.01$), and category C vs. category E ($p = < .01$). In general, it can be seen that the means on the I-E test follow closely the order of degree of social action-taking involved in the various alternatives shown in Table 1.[4] The order is C

---

[4] Shortly before the time of testing, a large number of Negroes were arrested and placed in jail for a similar march on the state house of a nearby state.

and D most; B in the middle; and A and E least. Those individuals who were more inclined to see themselves as the determiners of their own fate tended to commit themselves to more personal and decisive social action. There was a trend, not reaching statistical significance, for persons high in measured social desirability motive to commit themselves to less social action.

An analysis of these data by sex indicates that the same trend was present for males and females. The males provided slightly more differentiation of groups than females.

Little class difference in this essentially homogeneous population was present. Class V was the modal class position (Warner scale). A nonsignificant curvilinear trend was noted. Ss at both extremes of the social action-taking continuum obtained the lowest social class ratings.

SUMMARY

Students in a Southern Negro college very much involved in the current social protest movement against segregation were used as Ss of a study of prediction of social action-taking behavior. A forced choice test of a generalized attitude toward internal or external control of reinforcements, not specifically dealing with the issue studied, predicted the type and degree of commitment behavior manifested to effect social change. The social desirability motive and social class showed a weak trend in the predicted direction in the case of the former and a logically consistent one on an ad hoc basis in the case of the latter. These findings may serve as an impetus for much needed research in the important area of ongoing social action and social change.

References

Battle, Esther. The relationship of social class and ethnic group to the attitude of internal vs. external control of reinforcement in children. Unpublished master's thesis, Ohio State Univer., 1962.

Bialer, I. Conceptualization of success and failure in mentally retarded and normal children. *J. Pers.*, 1961, **29**, 303–320.

Crandall, V. J., and Katkovsky, W. A conceptual formulation for some research on children's achievement development. *Child Develpm.*, in press.

Cromwell, R. L., Rosenthal, D., Shakow, D., and Zahn, T. P. Reaction time, locus of control, choice behavior, and descriptions of parental behavior in schizophrenic and normal subjects. *J. Pers.*, 1961, **29**, 363–380.

Crowne, D. P., and Liverant, S. Conformity under varying conditions of personal commitment. *J. of abnorm. soc. Psychol.*, in press.

Crowne, D. P., and Marlowe, D. A new scale of social desirability independent of psychopathology. *J. consult. Psychol.*, 1960, **24**, 349–354.

Holden, K. Attitude toward external vs. internal control of reinforcement and learning of reinforcement sequences. Unpublished master's thesis, Ohio State Univer., 1958.

James, W. H. Internal vs. external control of reinforcement as a basic variable in learning theory. Unpublished doctoral dissertation, Ohio State Univer., 1957.

James, W. H., and Rotter, J. B. Partial and 100% reinforcement under chance and skill conditions. *J. exp. Psychol.*, 1958, **55**, 397–403.

Lindquist, E. F. *Design and analysis of experiments in psychology and education.* Boston: Houghton Mifflin, 1953.

Liverant, S., and Scodel, A. Internal and external control as determinants of decision making under conditions of risk. *Psychol. Reports*, 1960, **7**, 59–67.

Phares, E. J. Expectancy changes in skill and chance situations. *J. abnorm. soc. Psychol.*, 1957, **54**, 339–342.

Phares, E. J. Perceptual threshold decrements as a function of skill and chance expectancies. *J. Psychol.*, 1962, **53**, 399–407.

Rotter, J. B. *Social learning and clinical psychology.* New York: Prentice Hall, 1954.

Rotter, J. B., Liverant, S., and Crowne, D. P. The growth and extinction of expectancies in chance controlled and skilled tasks. *J. Psychol.*, 1961, **52**, 161–177.

Rotter, J. B., Seeman, M., and Liverant, S. Internal versus external control of reinforcement: A major variable in behavior theory. In N. F. Washburne (Ed.), *Decisions, values and groups*, Vol. 2. London: Pergamon Press, 1962.

Seeman, M., and Evans, J. W. Alienation and learning in a hospital setting. *Amer. sociological Review*, in press.

Simmons, W. L. Personality correlates of the James-Phares Scale. Unpublished master's thesis, Ohio State Univer., 1959.

39 *Negro Perception of Negro and White Personality Traits*

JAMES A. BAYTON, LETTIE J. AUSTIN, & KAY R. BURKE
Howard University

Although seeing is often believing, it sometimes happens that we tend to see what we want to, or, given a certain person or object we may attribute characteristics (e.g., bad, mean, pleasant, dangerous, nice, etc.) to them simply on the basis of physical appearance. Dr. Bayton and his associates have developed a model of the perception of racial personality traits that suggests that there are three separate factors involved, the trait of being stereotyped, the sex of the group being evaluated, and the sex of the person doing the judging.

Male and female Negro Ss answered the Guilford-Zimmerman Temperament Survey in terms of how they thought "the average Negro male," "the average Negro female," would reply to the items. The results show that 3 dimensions are involved in the perceptions of racial personality— the trait being "stereotyped," sex of the group being assessed, and the sex of S. For 6 of the 10 traits, the means for whites, in contrast to those for Negroes, were in the direction indicative of better personality adjustment.

There have been several studies of the attitudes and stereotypes which minority group members hold with respect to their own races. These studies consistently show that members of minority groups tend to have attitudes and stereotypes concerning their respective groups which are similar to those held by the white majority. Using the adjective list procedure developed by Katz and Braly (1933), Bayton (1941), and

SOURCE. Bayton, J. A., Austin, Lettie, J. and Burke, Kay, "Negro Perception of Negro and White Personality Traits," *Journal of Personality and Social Psychology,* I, 1965, 3, 250–253. Copyright 1965 by the American Psychological Association, and reproduced with permission.

Meenes (1943) found that Negroes stereotype "the Negro" as being lazy, superstitious, musical, loud, and very religious. These items also appear in the stereotype which white Americans have of the Negro. Sarnoff (1951) found Jewish college students with the same anti-Semitic attitudes observed in majority-group bigots. Engel O'Shea, Fischl, and Cummings (1958) reported that an "outwardly loyal" group of Jewish subjects showed the same pattern of negative attitudes toward their own group as that found among white Protestants. In these latter studies, the Jewish Anti-Semitism Scale developed by Sarnoff was used.

From these investigations arises the question of what dynamics would lead minority group members to possess negative attitudes toward their own race, attitudes which are quite similar to those held by the majority group. Sarnoff (1951) regards anti-Semitic attitudes in Jews as being a symptom of identification with the aggressor. These anti-Semitic attitudes are viewed as being expressions of hostility toward one's own social group and appropriation of the attitudes of those in the white majority who aggress against them. At the level of personality characteristics, this symptom was related to negative attitudes toward the self and one's parents and passivity in the face of interpersonal hostility. This same concept—identification with the aggressor—might provide an explanation of the negative stereotype of the Negro found among Negro subjects.

The identification-with-the-aggressor theory, as stated by Sarnoff, includes only one direction of influence—incorporation on the part of the minority group members of the negative attitudes that the majority group holds toward their race. Since the fundamental process is supposed to be identification, another direction of influence could be operating, namely, a tendency to idealize the aggressor. The two influences could be operating simultaneously. In the latter case, the attitudes and stereotypes which the minority group holds toward the majority should be characterized by highly positive components. Evidence for this point of view is found in the stereotypes which Negroes have of "white Americans"—intelligent, industrious, ambitious, progressive, etc. (Bayton, 1941; Meenes, 1943).

Utilizing several approaches that differ from those in other studies, the present research attacks the problem of how a minority group perceives itself and the majority group. Whereas earlier investigators have used either adjective lists to determine stereotypes or scales to assess attitudes, in this research the instrument was a standardized personality test (Guilford-Zimmerman Temperament Survey—GZTS) on which Negro subjects answered the items as they thought both Negroes and whites would. This basic design permits investigation of the data to see whether there are indications of the two directions of influence in the identification-with-the-aggressor concept.

Bayton, McAllister, and Hamer (1956) have shown that stereotypes are a function of dimensions other than race. In their research, stereotypes were obtained in terms of race-class differentiation of the groups being stereotyped—upper-class Negroes and whites; lower-class Negroes and whites. The results indicated that stereotypes as held by white and Negro subjects were more class linked than race linked. In the current research, perceptions of racial characteristics were investigated in the dimension of sex, as well as race. The subjects (all Negroes) answered the personality inventory in terms of "the average Negro male," "the average white male," "the average Negro female," and "the average white female." Moreover, since male and female subjects were used, the interaction of the sex of subject and the perception of the personalities of race-sex groups was investigated.

METHOD

SUBJECTS. The subjects were 240 Negro students at Howard University (120 male, 120 female).

DESIGN. The subjects were randomly assigned to one of four groups. Each group of 60 subjects was given the GZTS. The instructions given to the respective groups were: "How do you think the Average Negro Male [Average Negro Female, Average White Male, Average White Female] would answer these items?" (It should be noted that a given subject responded to only one of the above instructions.)

RESULTS

A three-way classification analysis of variance was used to evaluate the data of each of the 10 traits in the GZTS. (The within-groups variance was used as the error term.) The results for five of the traits (G, R, A, S, E) are given in Table 1.

The Negro subjects gave whites a significantly higher score on general activity than they did Negroes (white $M = 15.63$, Negro $M = 13.01$). They "saw" whites as being more restrained than Negroes (white $M = 14.22$, Negro $M = 11.87$). However, the Sex Stereotype × Race Stereotype interaction for restraint was significant—the Negro subjects saw white males as being more restrained ($M = 15.27$) than Negro males ($M = 10.55$). There was no difference in the stereotypes for this trait for the two groups of females (white females $M = 13.18$, Negro females $M = 13.18$). The original racial difference for restraint is created by the difference in the stereotype for Negro and white males on this trait (restraint).

TABLE 1

Analysis of Variance: Race-Sex Personality Trait Stereotyping
for Factors G, R, A, S, E

	F				
Source	General Activity	Restraint	Ascendance	Sociability	Emotional Stability
Sex of subject (A)	0.29	0.12	0.56	0.25	0.22
Sex stereotype (B)	3.58	0.15	0.83	10.71**	4.55**
Race stereotype (C)	14.44**	10.30**	27.17**	1.10	4.84**
A × B	0.41	0.71	3.02	2.90	1.76
A × C	0.47	0.19	1.95	2.03	1.36
B × C	2.29	10.30**	0.11	0.86	0.03
A × B × C	0.35	0.01	0.31	1.57	3.06

Note.—Respective within-group variances used as error terms. $N = 240$ (120 male, 120 female).

** $p < .01$.

Whites were seen as having more ascendance than Negroes (white $M = 17.46$, Negro $M = 13.55$). For the trait of sociability, the stereotype is a function of sex rather than of race; females ($M = 19.31$) were seen as being more sociable than males ($M = 16.63$).

For emotional stability, significant differences were found for the sex stereotypes and the race stereotypes. Males ($M = 13.65$) were perceived as being more emotionally stable than females ($M = 12.07$); whites ($M = 13.68$) were stereotyped as being more emotionally stable than Negroes ($M = 12.00$).

The results for the remaining five traits O, F, T, P, M) are shown in Table 2. Whites were scored as having a greater degree of objectivity than Negroes ($M = 12.08$ and 10.51, respectively).

For friendliness, two of the interactions showed significance—Sex of Subject × Sex Stereotype and the triple interaction. Male subjects saw greater friendliness in males ($M = 9.12$) than in females ($M = 7.42$). For female subjects the reverse was true; they perceived greater friendliness in females ($M = 9.92$) than in males ($M = 8.07$).

Inspection of the data involved in the triple interaction for friendliness indicates that the male Negro subjects made their besic differentiation on this trait in terms of racial stereotyping. For them the group with the highest degree of this trait was white males ($M = 10.90$), second was white females ($M = 8.17$), third was Negro males ($M = 7.33$), and last was Negro females ($M = 6.67$), the first two groups being white, the last two being Negro. In contrast, the female Negro subjects made their basic

TABLE 2

Analysis of Variance: Race-Sex Personality Trait Stereotyping
for Factors O, F, T, P, M

	F				
Source	Objectivity	Friend-liness	Thought-fulness	Personal Relations	Masculinity
Sex of subject (A)	2.68	1.03	0.23	1.69	0.28
Sex stereotype (B)	0.79	0.01	0.01	0.02	92.53**
Race stereotype (C)	4.57*	0.91	1.86	5.61*	1.68
A × B	0.35	6.02*	0.59	0.48	1.08
A × C	3.40	1.37	0.63	3.40	4.48*
B × C	1.69	1.41	1.74	0.12	0.02
A × B × C	0.01	5.23*	0.70	0.32	3.81

Note.—Respective within-group variances used as error terms. $N = 240$ (120 male, 120 female).

  * $p < .05$.

  ** $p < .01$.

differentiation on the basis of sex stereotyping. Their highest friendliness score went to Negro females ($M = 10.87$), next to white females ($M = 8.97$), third to Negro males ($M = 8.27$), and last to white males ($M = 7.87$). For the female subjects, the two highest means were assigned to females; the two lowest means were for males.

No significant results were obtained for the analysis of the data for the trait of thoughtfulness. For personal relations, these Negro subjects assigned a greater degree of "tolerance and understanding of people" to whites ($M = 10.58$) than to Negroes ($M = 9.07$).

The validity of our general procedure is seen in the data on masculinity. If the subjects were responding differentially in accordance with the differences in instructions, the sex stereotype for masculinity should be significant. The results satisfied this demand. The subjects gave males a mean of 15.96 on masculinity and females a mean of 8.73 on this trait.

For masculinity, the Sex of Subject × Race Stereotype was significant. The male Negro subjects attributed greater masculinity to whites ($M = 13.18$) than to Negroes ($M = 10.75$). The female Negro subjects, however, saw Negroes ($M = 12.63$) as having more masculinity than whites ($M = 12.05$). Although the triple interaction missed being significant at $p = .05$, the data are strongly suggestive of such an effect. Negro male subjects gave white males a mean masculinity score of 17.63; they gave Negro males a mean of 13.90. In contrast, Negro female subjects gave Negro males a mean masculinity score of 16.43; they gave white males a mean masculinity score of 15.87. Finally, both groups of subjects, male and female, gave slightly higher femininity, scores to Negro females than to white females.

DISCUSSION

These results demonstrate that members of a minority group do differentiate in the perception of the personality characteristics of their own group and of the majority group, as measured by a standardized personality test. However, at least three dimensions are involved in this process—the trait being "stereotyped," the sex of the members of the group being assessed, and the sex of the individuals doing the "stereotyping." Race was the sole differentiating factor for only 4 of the 10 traits—general activity, ascendance, objectivity, and personal relations. Sociability was differentiated solely on the basis of sex. Interaction of race and sex was found for restraint, emotional stability, friendliness, and masculinity. Thoughtfulness showed no differentiation on the dimensions used in this research.

In terms of basic impressions, some of these data seem to be in the same direction as those obtained in earlier studies (Bayton, 1941; Meenes, 1943). With an adjective list, Negro subjects characterized Negroes as being "lazy" and whites as being "industrious." In the present research the Negro subjects gave whites a higher score on general activity (having more energy, vitality, and productivity). (True, they did not say specifically that Negroes are "lazy.") In another instance, the present Negro subjects saw Negroes as having less restraint (less serious-minded; more happy-go-lucky). "Happy-go-lucky" is a trait that is nearly always assigned to Negroes, when an adjective check list is used. The present data, however, indicate that, for Negro subjects, this particular stereotype is more associated with Negro males (as against white males) than with Negro females (as against white females).

Although we have no explicit data on this point, there seems to be some evidence of the operation of the two directions of influence in the identification-with-the-aggressor theory. In every instance where differentiation of racial groups, per se, occurred (general activity, restraint, ascendance, emotional stability, objectivity, and personal relations), the means for whites were in the direction representing better personality adjustment. This might result from the combined tendencies to idealize the aggressor and to incorporate his negative views toward the minority group.

References

Bayton, J. A. Racial stereotypes of Negro college students. *Journal of Abnormal and Social Psychology,* 1941, **36**, 97–102.

Bayton, J. A., McAllister, Lois B., and Hamer, J. Race-class stereotypes. *Journal of Negro Education,* 1956, **25**, 75–78.

Engel, G., O'Shea, H. E., Fischl, M. A., and Cummings, G. M. An investigation of anti-Semitic feelings in two groups of college students: Jewish and non-Jewish. *Journal of Social Psychology,* 1958, **48**, 75–82.

Katz, D., and Braly, K. Racial stereotypes of 100 college students. *Journal of Abnormal and Social Psychology,* 1933, **28**, 280–290.

Meenes, M. A comparison of racial stereotypes of 1930 and 1942. *Journal of Social Psychology,* 1943, **17**, 327–336.

Sarnoff, I. Identification with the aggressor: Some personality correlates of anti-Semitism among Jews. *Journal of Personality,* 1951, **20**, 199–218.

40 Interacting Variables in the Perception of Racial Personality Traits

JAMES A. BAYTON & TRESSIE W. MULDROW
Howard University

This paper examines the interaction between self-perception and the perception of others in order to clarify the role that skin color may play in the way in which we see each other. Four hundred and eighty Black college students took a personality test, answering the questions as they thought others would (e.g., those who were very light-skinned, very dark-skinned, etc.) and then rated themselves in terms of the degree of blackness of their own skin. Dr. Bayton and Mrs. Muldrow found that the light-skinned male is more sensitive to the skin color of the role-playing situation than either medium- or dark-skinned Blacks. They discuss the role that skin color may play in the development of self-perception.

Four hundred and eighty Negro college students took the Guilford-Zimmerman Temperament Survey in terms of how they thought "very light-skinned Negro males," "very dark-skinned Negro males," "very light-skinned Negro females," and "very dark-skinned Negro females" would reply to the items. The sex and self-judgments of the subjects' own skin color were used in the analysis. Attributes of the subjects interacted with cues concerning "the observed" in determining the personality assessments. Differentiation of observer-attributes seemed especially related to determination of the traits of "the observed." Light-skinned Negro males seem to have some difficulties in their self-concept vis-à-vis dark-skinned Negroes.

Vernon (1964) cites six sets of cues which form the basis for an individual's judgment as to the personality characteristics of another person:

SOURCE. *Journal of Experimental Research in Personality*, 3, 39–44, 1968. Reprinted by permission of the senior author and Academic Press, Inc.

(1) static or physical factors, (2) dynamic or expressive factors, (3) content factors, (4) situational factors, (5) communications from other people, and (6) communications from the person himself. This classification refers to only one of the two general categories of influence operating as one individual evaluates another's personality, namely, cues or attributes linked to the person being judged. The second general category of influence could be particular aspects or attributes of the observer's own personality. It would seem reasonable to assume that aspects of the observer's own characteristics play a role in how he selects and uses cues emanating from the person he is evaluating, in terms of personality.

Given that a set of attributes of the observer and a set of cues linked to the person being observed operate in the naive assessment of personality, one should be alert to the possibility that the final judgment is a function of interactions occurring within and between the two general sets of attributes or cues. The present research was designed to explore these interacting relationships. The specific cues used were race (Negro) of observer and observed, sex of the two, and skin color of the two. The personality characteristics evaluated were those represented in the Guilford-Zimmerman Temperament Survey—General Activity, Restraint, Ascendance, Sociability, Emotional Stability, Objectivity, Friendliness, Thoughtfulness, Personal Relations, and Masculinity.

It has been demonstrated that changing the set of cues linked to the persons being judged can evoke differential judgements as to those persons' personality traits (Bayton, McAllister, and Hamer, 1956; Bayton, Austin, and Burke, 1965). For example, Negroes and whites perceive different personality characteristics in lower-class as against upper-class Negroes, and in lower-class versus upper-class whites.

The particular attributes or cues operating in the observer-observed relationship most likely do not operate as static factors. Certain of these attributes or cues can bring into play dynamic forces within the observer. A racial cue might instigate identification-with-the-aggressor responses within an observer (Sarnoff, 1951), for example. Several studies have shown that the skin color of a Negro can operate as a functional cue, tapping positive or negative reactions within the observer (Clark and Clark, 1940; Marks, 1943; Seeman, 1946; Secord, Bevan, and Katz, 1956). There have been few, if any, systematic studies of how the skin color of Negro observers influences their perception of the personality characteristics of other Negroes, defined in terms of the latter's skin color. Added to this set of attributes (race and skin color), in the observers and "the observed," was sex of observer and of "the observed." The objective of this research was to determine how these factors (three defined as attributes of "the observer" and three defined as attributes of "the observed") interact in the perception of racial personality characteristics.

METHOD

SUBJECTS. The subjects were 480 Negro students at Howard University. A "background" questionnaire permitted elimination of white students and foreign-born Negroes.

DESIGN. The Guilford-Zimmerman Temperament Survey was used to obtain the personality evaluations. The subjects were randomly assigned instructions as to the type of person they were characterizing. The specific instructions were:

"This is a test which is designed to reveal an individual's personality traits. Usually you would be asked to answer these questions in terms of how YOU would react to the test items. However, this time you are being asked to do something different. Instead of answering the questions as you would answer them yourself, answer them as you think a Very Dark-Skinned (or Light-Skinned) Negro male (or Negro Female) would answer them."

Each subject was asked to respond to only one of the four groups— e.g., *Very Light-Skinned Negro Female, Very Dark-Skinned Negro Female,* etc.

After completing the Guilford-Zimmerman, the subjects were given the "background" questionnaire. This asked for the subjects' sex, home town, age, and race. The last item in this questionnaire was an unstructured scale consisting of ten squares arranged vertically on the page. Above the top square was *"Very Light"*; below the bottom square was *"Very Dark."* The subjects were instructed to check the square they thought best described their own skin color.

RESULTS

One particular result points to the effectiveness of the instructions. The difference in perception of masculinity-femininity was directly related to the instructions given in terms of whether the group being described was male or female. The mean on masculinity was 13.10 when the group was defined as being male; it was 10.07 when the group was defined as being female. This difference is significant at $p = .01$.

Table 1 is a summary of the results of the subjects' judgments of their own skin color. There was a sex difference; somewhat fewer Negro females perceived themselves as being "dark" than did Negro males (7% versus 17%).

The subjects were divided into "light" and "dark" groups, using a scale value of 5 as the criterion. The data for each of the ten Guilford-Zimmer-

TABLE 1

Self-Description of Skin Color

Own Skin Color	Negro Male Subjects (%)	Negro Female Subjects (%)
"Light" (Scale 1–3)	23	25
"Medium" (Scale 4–7)	60	68
"Dark" (Scale 8–10)	17	7
	100	100
N	240	240
Chi-square	11.335 ($p < .01$)	

man traits were then subjected to a $2 \times 2 \times 2 \times 2$ analysis of variance (Sex of Subject × Color of Subject × Sex "Observed" × Color "Observed"). Because the authors believe that the procedure is a way of determining stereotypes, the data on the persons observed are referred to as either sex or color stereotypes (concerning Negroes). Since the key issue is the interaction of the attributes or cues as they relate to perception of racial personality characteristics, the analysis of the results concentrates upon the highest order significant interactions obtained.

SEX OF SUBJECT × COLOR OF SKIN × COLOR STEREOTYPE. The two attributes of the observer (sex and perceived skin color) interacted with the color of the observed (stereotype) for Objectivity ($F = 6.00$; $p < .05$), Friendliness ($F = 4.65$; $p < .05$), and Personal Relations ($F = 6.74$; $p < .01$). Light-skin males saw dark Negroes as being less hypersensitive and more "thick-skinned" than light Negroes. Dark males, and both light and dark females, did not make this distinction.

Light males also perceived dark Negroes as having better Personal Relations (tolerance of people in contrast to suspiciousness of others) than light Negroes. Again, none of the other groups showed this difference in perception. Light-skin and dark-skin male subjects, as well as dark-skin female subjects, saw dark Negroes as having a greater degree of Friendliness than light Negroes. Light-skin female subjects did not perceive such a difference. In fact, the light-skin female subjects did not perceive any differences between light and dark Negroes on these three particular traits (Table 2).

COLOR OF SKIN OF SUBJECT × SEX STEREOTYPE × COLOR STEREOTYPE. The perception of G (activity, energy, enthusiasm) in Negroes was related to the skin color of the observers, and the sex and skin color of the groups being stereotyped ($F = 5.54$; $p < .05$). Light-skin Negro subjects perceived light Negro females as having a greater degree of General Activity than dark Negro females. These particular subjects did not see this differ-

TABLE 2

Sex of Subject × Color of Skin of Subject × Color Stereotype (Means)

Characteristic	Male Subjects		Female Subjects	
	Light-skin Subjects	Dark-skin Subjects	Light-skin Subjects	Dark-skin Subjects
Objectivity (O)*				
Light Negroes	12.85$_a$	13.91$_a$	14.33$_a$	14.63$_a$
Dark Negroes	15.98$_b$	12.38$_a$	12.08$_a$	12.48$_a$
Friendliness (F)**				
Light Negroes	10.23$_a$	10.91$_a$	10.00$_a$	9.33$_a$
Dark Negroes	15.50$_b$	13.05$_b$	10.56$_a$	11.66$_b$
Personal Relations (P)***				
Light Negroes	11.28$_a$	12.08$_a$	12.12$_a$	10.43$_a$
Dark Negroes	13.86$_b$	11.55$_a$	11.25$_a$	11.65$_a$

Note—Paired means, within columns, having the same subscript are not significantly different at $p = .05$.

  * $F = 6.00$; $df = 1/464$; $p < .05$.
 ** $F = 4.65$; $df = 1/464$; $p < .05$.
*** $F = 6.74$; $df = 1/464$; $p < .01$.

ence in light and dark Negro males. The dark-skin subjects, however, saw
the difference as applying to Negro males; the light Negro males were
seen as having more General Activity than dark Negro males (Table 3).

SEX OF SUBJECT × SEX STEREOTYPE × COLOR STEREOTYPE. Among male
subjects, light Negro females were seen as being more Objective than
dark Negro females. Male subjects did not see any difference between
light and dark Negro males in this respect. Similarly, female subjects did

TABLE 3

Color of Skin of Subject × Sex Stereotype × Color Stereotype (Means)

Characteristic	Light-skin Subjects		Dark-skin Subjects	
	Negro Males	Negro Females	Negro Males	Negro Females
General Activity (G)*				
Light Negroes	16.53$_a$	17.11$_a$	17.68$_a$	16.30$_a$
Dark Negroes	15.63$_a$	15.06$_b$	14.75$_b$	15.90$_a$

Note—Paired means, within columns, having the same subscript are not significantly different at $p = .05$.

 * $F = 5.536$; $df = 1/464$; $p < .05$.

not perceive any difference in Objectivity between light and dark Negro males. They also saw no difference on this trait between light and dark Negro females ($F = 6.17$; $p < .05$). Female subjects perceived a difference between light and dark Negro males on Friendliness; light Negro males were seen as being more friendly than dark Negro males. The female subjects did not show a difference on this trait for light and dark females. The male subjects showed no difference in perception of Friendliness for light versus dark males or females ($F = 5.04$; $p < .05$) (Table 4).

TABLE 4

Sex of Subject × Sex Stereotype × Color Stereotype (Means)

	Male Subjects		Female Subjects	
Characteristic	Negro Males	Negro Females	Negro Males	Negro Females
Objectivity (O)*				
Light Negroes	14.35$_a$	14.23$_a$	12.41$_a$	14.73$_a$
Dark Negroes	13.21$_a$	12.51$_b$	15.56$_a$	12.05$_a$
Friendliness (F)**				
Light Negroes	12.40$_a$	9.36$_a$	14.75$_a$	10.00$_a$
Dark Negroes	13.76$_a$	10.93$_a$	8.78$_b$	11.25$_a$

Note—Paired means, within columns, having the same subscript are not significantly different at $p = .05$.
* $F = 6.17$; $df = 1/464$; $p < .05$.
** $F = 5.04$; $df = 1/464$; $p < .05$.

COLOR OF SKIN OF SUBJECT × COLOR STEREOTYPE. Dark-skin subjects perceived dark Negroes as having more Restraint (deliberative; self-control) than light Negroes. Light subjects made no such distinction on this trait ($F = 10.43$; $p < .01$). Light Negro subjects saw dark Negroes as having a greater degree on Masculinity than light Negroes. Dark Negroes did not differentiate between the two skin color groups on this trait ($F = 4.35$; $p < .05$) (Table 5).

SEX STEREOTYPE × COLOR STEREOTYPE. The subjects (male and female; light and dark) saw dark Negro females as having more thoughtfulness (reflectiveness; mental poise) than light Negro females. No such difference was seen between light and dark Negro males ($F = 4.45$; $p < .05$) (Table 6).

COLOR STEREOTYPES; SEX STEREOTYPES. Ascendance, Sociability, and Emotional Stability were related only to single effects and not to any interac-

TABLE 5

Color of Skin of Subject × Color Stereotype (Means)

Characteristic	Light-skin Subjects	Dark-skin Subjects
Restraint (R)*		
Light Negroes	14.39_a	13.22_a
Dark Negroes	14.73_a	16.10_b
Masculinity (M)**		
Light Negroes	12.40_a	13.00_a
Dark Negroes	14.87_b	13.55_a

Note—Paired means, within columns, having the same subscript are not significantly different at $p = .05$.
* $F = 10.43$; $df = 1/464$; $p < .01$.
** $F = 4.35$; $df = 1/464$; $p < .05$.

TABLE 6

Sex Stereotype × Color Stereotype (Means)

Characteristic	Negro Males	Negro Females
Thoughtfulness (T)*		
Light Negroes	16.77_a	15.50_a
Dark Negroes	15.60_a	17.50_b

Note—Paired means, within columns, having same subscript are not significantly different at $p = .05$.
* $F = 4.45$; $df = 1/464$; $p < .05$.

TABLE 7

Color Stereotype (Means)

Characteristic	All Subjects
Ascendance (A)*	
Light Negroes	17.95
Dark Negroes	14.04
Sociability (S)**	
Light Negroes	21.23
Dark Negroes	15.77
Emotional Stability (E)***	
Light Negroes	15.78
Dark Negroes	13.46

* $F = 48.66$; $df = 1/464$; $p < .01$.
** $F = 86.97$; $df = 1/464$; $p < .01$.
*** $F = 15.94$; $df = 1/464$; $p < .01$.

tions. All subjects tended to perceive light Negroes as having more Ascendancy, more Sociability, and more Emotional Stability than dark Negroes (Table 7).

All subjects tended to see Negro females as having more Sociability than Negro males; they also tended to perceive Negro males as having a greater degree of Emotional Stability than Negro females (Table 8).

TABLE 8

Sex Stereotypes (Means)

Characteristic	All Subjects
Sociability (S)*	
Negro males	18.37
Negro females	19.00
Emotional Stability (E)**	
Negro males	15.74
Negro females	14.29

* $F = 9.36$; $df = 1/464$; $p < .01$.
** $F = 6.85$; $df = 1/464$; $p < .01$.

DISCUSSION

The results of this research demonstrate that the perception of personality characteristics, or the naive assessment of personality, can be an interaction of specific sets of attributes of the observer and a specific set of attributes of the person being observed. In this particular instance, the attributes involved were race (Negro), sex, and self-perception of skin color of "the observer," and the race (Negro), sex, and designated skin color of "the observed."

When we look at the results in terms of the skin color and sex of the Negro subjects, we find an indication that Negro males who perceive themselves to be relatively light-skinned seem to be the most sensitive group. In the first place, these subjects show differentiation in their perception of the Negro personality on three of the ten traits—Objectivity, Friendliness, and Personal Relations. Second, for each of these traits, the light-skin Negro males perceived dark Negroes as having the more desirable characteristic. Dark-skin Negro males and dark-skin Negro females, in contrast, were "sensitive" to only one of these traits—Friendliness. In this trait, each of the latter groups saw dark Negroes possessing it to a greater degree than light Negroes. Light-skin Negro females did not differentiate between light and dark Negroes on any of these three traits.

These data strongly suggest that light-skin Negro males occupy some psychologically marginal status which makes them especially responsive to skin color cues emanating from other Negroes. Furthermore, they see dark Negroes as having certain more desirable personality characteristics than light Negroes possess. The data further suggest that light-skin Negro males are somewhat "uncomfortable" in their position vis-à-vis dark Negroes. The authors are not in a position to speculate upon the source of these reactions among light-skin Negro males and as to why they are found least of all, apparently, among light-skin Negro females.

Seven of the ten traits showed interaction effects operating in the perception or assessment of "another's" personality. In six of these seven instances, the interactions involved attributes of "the observer" and attributes of "the observed"—General Activity, Restraint, Objectivity, Friendliness, Personal Relations, and Masculinity. There were no traits, in the set of ten, for which no differentiation in assessment of personality occurred in terms of the skin color of "the observed." This indicates that research based upon global definitions of the groups being assessed can be misleading, since the observer might demonstrate differentiation if a relevant pattern of cues were presented to him. Research on impressions of personality must take into consideration the attributes of the people on both sides of the observation system—"the observer" and "the observed."

References

Bayton, J. A., McAllister, and Hamer, T. Race-class stereotypes. *Journal of Negro Education,* 1956, **25**, 75–78.

Bayton, J. A., Austin, L. J., and Burke, K. R. Negro perception of Negro and white personality traits. *Journal of Personality and Social Psychology,* 1965, **1**, 250–253.

Clark, K. B., and Clark, M. P. The development of consciousness of self and emergence of racial identification in Negro pre-school children. *Journal of Social Psychology,* 1939, **10**, 591–599.

Marks, E. Skin color judgments of Negro college students. *Journal of Abnormal and Social Psychology,* 1943, **38**, 370–376.

Sarnoff, I. Identification with the aggressor: some personality correlates of anti-Semitism among Jews. *Journal of Personality,* 1951, **20**, 199–218.

Secord, R. F., Bevan, W., and Katz, B. The Negro stereotype and perceptual accentuation. *Journal of Abnormal and Social Psychology,* 1956, **53**, 78–83.

Seeman, M. A situational approach to intra-group Negro attitudes. *Sociometry,* 1946, **9**, 199–206.

Vernon, P. E. *Personality assessment.* New York: John Wiley, 1964.

41 Ethnic and Class Preferences Among College Negroes[1]

ALVIN E. GOINS
Naval Research Laboratory, Washington, D. C.

MAX MEENES
Professor of Psychology, Howard University

Drs. Goins and Meenes report an interesting study in which they contrast
ethnic and class preferences of Negro college students to those of comparable whites. After assessing the preferences of Black students, they found
considerable disparity between Black and white preferential rankings
and suggest that Blacks tended to rank ethnic groups from most to
least desirable in terms of the amount of racial prejudice and distance
typically experienced from a particular group. Thus, Black students
ranked each other as most preferred, white Northerners next, and white
Southerners well down in the preference hierarchy. The study is particularly valuable for its insight into the inadequacy of the notion of a fixed
preference within a culture based on the majority viewpoint.

PROBLEM

Beginning with the classical study of social distance by Bogardus in
1925[2] it has been repeatedly shown that American students readily arrange
a list of group denominations such as English, American, Chinese, Negro,
Jew, into a rank order of preference which does not vary in its essentials
among different groups of subjects studied at different times and places.
In general the order of preference obtained for white college students is:

SOURCE. Reprinted from the *Journal of Negro Education*, 1960, 29, 128–133 with
permission of the author and the publisher.
[1] The data on which this article is based were collected and analyzed by Alvin E.
Goins and is contained in his unpublished M.S. dissertation, Howard University,
May 1955.
[2] E. S. Bogardus, "Measuring Social Distance," *Journal of Applied Sociology,*
9: 299–308, 1925.

American, English, Northern and Western Europeans, Southern and Eastern Europeans, Asiatics, Negroes. The regularity with which these results have been reported has led Hartley to suggest that these preferences are an integral part of American culture.[3]

The present study was designed to determine: (a) if Negroes would adopt the order of preference, and if not, how different would their preferences be? (b) do American Negroes differentiate between Northern white Americans and Southern white Americans? (c) does class of the group to be ranked have any influence upon the preferences? and (d) how reliable are these patterns of preference?

A review of Rose, Frazier, and others[4] would lead to the inference that most Negroes have high group identification, and should have high preference for their own group. Simpson and Yinger, and Horowitz pointed out that American Negroes accepted the prevailing American attitude with some variation, and Myrdal[5] stated that this may be even toward himself in some instances. Bayton and Byoune[6] also concluded from a study of Negro stereotypes held by Negroes that these stereotypes were not indicative of a high degree of intragroup morale.

Rose[7] further suggested that Negroes differentiated between whites depending upon their attitude toward the Negro, and Star, Williams and Stouffer[8] found that Negro soldiers preferred to serve under Northern white lieutenants to Southern white lieutenants. Regarding the Negro's preferences for other groups, Rose stated that (a) Negroes had a secondary identification with Africans, (b) literate Negroes express a high degree of sympathy for the underdog and other darker races in different parts of the world, and (c) although the Negro press is favorable toward Jews, Negroes on the whole cannot be said to be very favorable to the Jewish group, though some public opinion polls show that they are less anti-Semitic than white Christians.

In three actual studies reported on Negro preferences for ethnic groups, Bogardus in 1928, Meltzer in 1937, and Gray and Thompson[9] in 1953,

---

[3] E. L. Hartley, *Problems in Prejudice,* Kings Crown Press, 1946.

[4] A. Rose, *The Negro's Morale: Group Identification and Protest,* 1953; E. F. Frazier, *The Negro in the United States*—New York: Macmillan, 1940; S. A. Star, R. M. Williams, Jr., and S. A. Stouffer, *The Negro Soldier,* Princeton: Princeton University Press, 1949. Vol. I.

[5] G. Myrdal, *An American Dilemma,* New York: Harper and Bros., 1944.

[6] J. A. Bayton, and E. Byoune, "Racio-National Stereotypes Held by Negroes," *Journal of Negro Education,* 16: 49–56, 1947.

[7] *Op. cit.*

[8] *Op. cit.*

[9] J. Gray and A. Thompson, "The Ethnic Prejudice of White and Negro College Students," *Journal of Abnormal Social Psychology,* 48: 311–313, 1953.

found that the Negro preferences were similar to those of the white pattern, except that Negroes (American) were preferred first rather than near the end.

Ethnic preference is the manifestation of a certain type of attitude toward the group in question, and is related to ethnic stereotype, social distance, and ethnic prejudice. However, what this relationship is has never been adequately pointed out. Klineberg[10] stated that there was little direct relationship between the definiteness of the stereotype and the amount of prejudice against any group. Katz and Braly[11] suggested that the preferential order, reported by Bogardus and Thurstone, may reflect attitudes toward race names and may not arise from animosity toward the specific qualities inherent in the real human beings bearing a given racial label; however, in a later article Katz and Braly[12] concluded that the whole attitude of race prejudice toward the Negro is more than a simple conditioned response to the race name. At any rate, ethnic preference does not seem to be the exact reciprocal of ethnic prejudice.

These reported preferences may be influenced by both the class of the respondent and the class of the groups to be ranked, but few studies have been reported concerning this relationship. However, several investigators have reported substantial psychological differences among social classes, and Centers[13] has stated that the differences among the various occupational strata often exist in such a degree and pattern as to indicate a tendency toward two distinct poles of attitude and behavior. Perhaps class may be even more important than ethnic background in preferential patterns.

METHOD

A sample of 161 students at Howard University in 1955 were given a list of 18 ethnic groups and asked to rank order them by preference. These groups represented Negro groups, American minority groups, "darker races," dominant American sub-groups, white groups, and groups with outspoken anti-Negro attitudes. The subjects were also asked to rank order 15 ethnic classes, representing the upper-, middle- and lower-classes of

[10] O. Klineberg, *Characteristics of the American Negro*. New York: Harper and Bros., 1944.

[11] D. Katz, and K. Braly, "Racial Stereotypes of 100 college students," *Journal of Abnormal & Social Psychology* 28: 280–290, 1933.

[12] D. Katz, and K. Braly, "Verbal Stereotypes and Racial Prejudice," in Newcomb, Hartley, *et al.*, (eds.) *Readings in Social Psychology*. Henry Holt and Co. 1947.

[13] E. Centers, *The Psychology of Social Classes*. Princeton: Princeton Univ. Press, 1949.

five of these ethnic groups. No effort was made to define class. The mean and standard deviation scores were determined for each of these scales and Kendall's coefficient of concordance W was obtained.

RESULTS

One group of 24 subjects was used to test the reliability of the rankings shown in Table 1 and Table 2. They were asked to rank the same groups two months after their first rankings. The rank order correlation between the two sets of rankings for "ethnic" preferences was .94, and for class pref-

TABLE 1

Preference for Ethnic Groups as Indicated by 161 Negro College Students

Ethnic Group	Mean	S.D.
American Negro	1.81	2.31
American white, Northern	5.02	3.99
West Indian Negro	6.09	4.10
French	6.43	3.44
African Negro	7.15	4.43
South American	7.64	3.55
English	8.08	4.25
Italian	8.45	3.72
Mexican	8.84	4.12
Jew	9.08	4.30
German	11.16	4.19
Hindu	11.36	3.75
Chinese	11.41	3.76
Japanese	11.60	3.88
West Indian white	12.87	3.20
American white, Southern	14.04	4.77
Russian	14.67	3.50
South African white	15.33	2.87

erences was .92. The results obtained by this adaptation of the Bogardus scale may therefore be accepted with confidence in their reliability; these rank ordered preferences are not determined by chance nor do they fluctuate haphazardly.

The rank order preference for the 18 ethnic groups was determined by the sum of their ranks and is shown in Table 1. An analysis of variance by ranks indicated that the order of preference was significant at $P = <.01$, and the coefficient of concordance (Kendall's W) showed that there was a significant agreement among the subjects for this order of preference ($P = <.01$).

The rank order of preferences of these subjects places "American Negro" in the first rank, with "American white, Northern" in the second position. The order of preference reflects the combined identification of these subjects with the American culture and Negro group membership. Thus among the first five ranks are all three Negro groups, white American Northern, and French. The last three groups consist of those conceived as most antagonistic to the United States (Russia) and to Negroes (American white, Southern and South African white).

Gray and Thompson,[14] studying the preferences of Negro college students in Georgia also obtained first rank for American Negro. Their subjects ranked the American white in position ten out of a possible twenty-four. The subjects of the present study were not provided with the opportunity of ranking American white. Instead, they were asked to rank American white (Northern) and American white (Southern). The results are striking; American white Northern is ranked in number two position and American white Southern is placed near the very bottom of the preferential rating.

Table 2 shows the rank order of preferences for five groups, American Negro, American white (Northern), African Negro, American white (Southern), and South African white when these are arranged in terms of upper-, lower- or middle-class.

For the data of Table 2, an analysis of variance by ranks indicates that the order of preference is significant (P = <.01) and the coefficient of concordance showed highly significant agreement among subjects for this order of preference (P = <.01).

The mean rank order of preference for upper-, middle- and lower-class American Negroes is 3.3. The composite rank for American white (Northern) is 5.3, the African Negro, 8.7, American white (Southern), 11.7 and South African white, 12.7. Thus the relative rank order of the ethnic groups as composed of three separate classes is the same as when the ethnic groups are ranked without regard to class (Table 1).

With respect to class alone, upper-class is generally ranked first with a mean rank of 6, middle-class second with a mean rank of 7 and lower-class with a decidedly wider difference as shown by the mean rank of 11. The difference between upper- and middle-class is small and not significant but the difference between either of these and the lower-class is significant. For the two most favored ethnic groups the results of this study show a preference for middle-class above upper-class; for the least favored ethnic groups especially those felt to show high antiNegro prejudice, the upper-class is preferred above the middle class.

[14] Op. cit.

TABLE 2

Rank Order Preference by Ethnic Group and Social Class

Ethnic and Social Class	Mean	S.D.	Rank
Middle-Class American Negro	2.19	1.70	1
Upper-Class American Negro	2.68	1.87	2
Middle-Class American white (Northern)	4.04	2.29	3
Upper-Class American white (Northern)	4.55	3.24	4
Upper-Class African Negro	5.63	2.40	5
Middle-Class African Negro	6.31	2.47	6
Lower-Class American Negro	7.61	3.79	7
Upper-Class American white (Southern)	9.12	3.66	8
Lower-Class American white (Northern)	9.40	2.85	9
Lower-Class African Negro	10.09	2.64	10
Upper-Class South African white	10.37	2.66	11
Middle-Class American white (Southern)	10.43	2.91	12
Middle-Class South African white	10.57	2.50	13
Lower-Class South African white	12.57	2.17	14
Lower-Class American white (Southern)	13.87	1.87	15

DISCUSSION

Many of the questions concerning Negro preferences were answered by the results of this study. Since practically all of these subjects thought of themselves as belonging to the middle-class, high group identification (race pride) was evidence by the highest preference for their own group. Perhaps lower-class Negroes will have low group identification and a significantly different order of preference for ethnic groups and social classes. This offers an interesting area for research. Star, Williams and Stouffer[15] found that the Negro soldier representing a cross section of American Negroes and therefore having a high percentage of lower-class Negroes in large majority preferred to serve under Negro lieutenants than under white lieutenants. However, the better educated Negroes were somewhat more likely than the lesser educated to express a preference for serving under Negro lieutenants.

When the American white was divided into Northern and Southern subgroups, the results are indeed interesting. The Northern group seems to correspond to the high ranking of the American white group in the previous studies. Perhaps the American white Northerner is symbolic of America for the American Negro while the American white Southerner may symbolically represent the antiNegro attitudes in America. At any

[15] Op. cit.

rate, this differentiation gave the subjects a chance to reject, and still remain attached to the dominant group.

The results of this study demonstrate that it is possible to use the Bogardus social distance technique for a more refined analysis of attitude than is usually attempted. Attitudes toward white Americans can be shown, as here, to be a composite of attitudes toward Northern and Southern white Americans. Attitudes toward American Negroes can be broken down into attitudes toward upper-, middle- and lower-class American Negroes. In the same way it is possible to analyze attitudes toward any ethnic group. It is quite possible to show some day that the attitude of American Negro college students toward African Negroes is a composite of attitudes toward the several distinct nations of Africa. The fact that an attitude may be expressed toward an ethnic group as a whole does not indicate that the subjects are unable to differentiate between component parts toward which different attitudes may be demonstrated.

Ethnic attitudes are complex and depend upon a variety of factors. The rank orders obtained in using the Bogardus social distance scale depend in the first place upon the groups chosen for study; that is, the preferences shown depend upon the groups selected for study. Another influence on ethnic rankings is the current national attitude. Before Pearl Harbor Howard students were shown, by Meenes,[16] to favor the Japanese over the Chinese but the attitudes toward these groups were reversed after the Japanese attack on the United States. Still another influence is group identification and a rejection of group enemies. The subjects of this study identify with middle class American Negroes and indicate a preference for non-American groups also. The lowest rankings were given to those groups that are considered as antagonistic to the United States or to Negroes in the United States or elsewhere in the world. It should be possible to devise further studies to demonstrate the relative influence of each of these factors upon ethnic attitudes.

SUMMARY

Although numerous studies have been made to determine social distance, preferences, and prejudice toward various ethnic groups, the majority of the studies used American whites as subjects and found a rather consistent pattern of preferences. However, few studies have been conducted using the American Negro as subjects.

It was the purpose of this investigation to seek clarification of and an-

[16] M. Meenes, "A comparison of racial stereotypes of 1935 and 1942," *Journal of Social Psychology,* 17: 327–336, 1943.

swers to some questions concerning Negro ethnic and class preferences, to check the reliability of these preferences, and to compare the results with previous studies.

Two rank order preference scales were used, one to determine ethnic group preference and one to determine ethnic class preference. Also a small sample was used to determine the reliability of the preferences. The subjects were 161 Negro college students at Howard University in 1955.

The results showed that ethnic preferences are influenced by identification of these subjects with Americans and with American Negroes. White American (Northern) was ranked in second place, next to American Negro, while white American (Southern) was ranked near the bottom of the list of ethnic groups. The rankings show that those groups regarded as unprejudiced toward Negroes are given preferential rankings and those felt to be prejudiced toward Negroes were given low ranks.

Attitudes are complex and ethnic preferences are composites of a variety of influences. The fact that subjects rank ethnic groups as totalities does not mean that they conceive of them as unitary. In this study it has been demonstrated that ethnic attitudes can be analyzed by the use of the social distance technique.

42 Correlates of Southern Negro Personality

WILLIAM F. BRAZZIEL

Dr. Brazziel's thoughtful paper seriously questions the relevance of much of the content of the Edwards Personal Preference Scale for Negro youth, and in so doing clarifies one of the problems of psychological testing by asking for whom are they appropriate? Dr. Brazziel observes that such criterion tasks as writing a great novel, being a recognized authority, etc. have little actual meaning in the life of someone who visualizes graduation from college and adapting to a hostile social environmental as nearly insurmountable tasks. The data in this paper also suggest that there are "kinds" of Southern Negroes, and proposes further research that would clarify the effect of caste-system membership on both the development and change of personality structure.

How and at what price has the American Negro accommodated to his caste status in American society? How can we estimate the impact of this social system on Negro personality development and change? Clearly this problem is relevant to the more general concern of sociologists, psychologists and educators with the issue of how social structure and personality development interact. Yet, while a good deal of cross-cultural research has been generated very little work has been done comparing the personality structure of different Negro sub-cultures and their relevance to the social system.

A review of the literature reveals a small number of excellently conceived studies which made use of psychoanalytic and projective techniques to investigate the dynamics of emotional disturbances caused by caste sanctions. Most of these, however, used relatively small size samples (25–50 cases) to which such techniques are necessarily limited. Few studies have attempted to identify types of character formation resulting from the problems faced by Negro youth and the substructure of emo-

SOURCE. Reprinted from the *Journal of Social Issues*, 1964, XX, 2, 45–52 with permission of the author and the Society for the Psychological Study of Social Issues.

tional upheaval resulting therefrom, and still fewer have investigated these dynamics in the increasingly large Negro urban, middle class group.

Some early studies which utilized objective paper and pencil instruments, while quite adequate sample-wise, were seriously hampered by the validity of the instruments used. Klineberg (1944) noted in his review of research in the area: "satisfactory research in this field will have to wait until psychologists have devised more adequate measures for the study of personality" (p. 138). Dreger and Miller (1960) compiled a review of studies of Negro personality done since 1944. In the area of temperament and personality, they noted that most instruments with the exception of the Murray TAT had been seriously questioned with regard to the cultural aspects of their validity. They concluded that the self-concept seems to suffer in the Negro subculture but that this research needed further cross-cultural support.

Several researches have reported similar findings with respect to the direct effects of discrimination on the personalities of Negroes: namely, the lowering of self-esteem, various forms of hostility impulses. There is some consensus among investigators that the most serious emotional problem of the American Negro is the control over felt needs for aggression (Dollard, 1937, Guba et al., 1959, and Havighurst, 1951). Other types of secondary effects that have been posited are apathy, hedonism, shortened time perspective, and delinquent behavior. More specifically, with regard to the middle class Negro, other effects posited are self hate, success and cleanliness phobias and an overconformity to white ideals in sex.

PURPOSE

This study sought to explore some of the differences in need structure between samples of Negro and white college students. In addition, comparisons were made between differing groups of Negroes in order to assess the influence of such demographic factors as geographic residence, social class and occupational choice. The instrument chosen for this purpose was the Edwards Personal Preference Schedule (EPPS, Edwards, 1953). By employing a forced-choice technique in which persons are asked to choose between items matched for social desirability values, the EPPS provides some internal control over test-taking attitudes; particularly, the tendency to project a favorable self-image. Unfortunately, however, the measurement of item social desirability value was based upon white student samples.

PROCEDURE

A total of 262 Negro students completed the Edwards Personal Preference Schedule. The group consisted of 87 students from the college of education and 53 from the college of liberal arts of a Negro institution in the lower-south and 52 students from the division of education and 70 students from liberal arts and business administration divisions from a Negro institution in the upper-south. The entire lower-south sample of 140 students were residents of the state in which the institution was located and consisted of both rural and urban students. The upper-south sample (122 students) was composed entirely of residents of the large metropolitan area (687,000 persons) in which the institution was located. Both were state institutions and admitted all graduates from state-approved high schools. The instrument was administered in groups of 20–25 students and the t test was used to identify significant differences. Data for the white normative college sample was derived from liberal arts colleges drawn from all parts of the country (Edwards, 1959).

FINDINGS

The need structure of the total group from both institutions (262 students) differed significantly (.01 levels of confidence) from the white norm group in 8 of 15 variables yielded by the instruments. This data is presented in Table 1. The majority of the variables were of a type involving direct ascendance-submission in human relationships, i.e., deference, dominance, etc. Grossack conducted (1957) a similar study with the EPPS using a smaller group of lower-south Negro college students.

SEX DIFFERENCES

When sex comparisons are made for the lower-south group, females exhibit significantly higher needs for achievement, endurance and intraception, but are lower in deference, autonomy and heterosexuality. This finding parallels that of Grossack (1957). On the other hand, there are only two significant differences between the sexes in the upper-south sample; the females score lower on needs for dominance and heterosexuality.

Most significant concerning sex difference, perhaps, is the relative absence of such differences in this group when compared to the norm group. Sex differences are present in twelve of fifteen variables in the general college norms but are revealed in only two instances in the upper-south and six instances in the lower-south. It must be further noted that the pattern of sex differences does not coincide with the norm group.

Achievement differences, for instance, are reversed in this sample with women revealing the higher need. Deference is also reversed with men exhibiting a higher need. Endurance which was not significantly different according to sex in the norm group is revealed as significant in the lower-south sample in favor of women. This pattern of ascendance on the part of

TABLE 1

A Comparison of Mean Scores of Negro College Students and Norm Groups on the Edwards Personal Preference Schedule

Need Variables	White-Norm		Negro Upper-South		Negro Lower-South	
	M	F	M	F	M	F
Achievement	15.7*	13.1	14.0	12.0	12.8	16.2*
Deference	11.2	12.4*	13.6	12.8	18.0*	12.0
Order	10.2	10.2	11.0	11.3	13.0	13.0
Exhibition	14.4	14.3	14.4	14.0	13.5	13.3
Autonomy	14.3*	12.3	10.0	10.0	12.2*	9.9
Affiliation	15.0	17.4*	14.8	17.0	15.6	16.3
Intraception	16.1	17.3*	16.0	16.0	17.0	19.9*
Succorance	10.7	12.5*	11.0	13.0	10.7	12.3
Dominance	17.4*	14.2	13.0*	10.3	12.0	11.0
Abasement	12.2	15.1*	12.6	12.5	12.7	12.6
Nurturance	14.0	16.4*	14.3	15.0	16.4	18.8
Change	15.5	17.2*	15.0	16.4	16.0	16.0
Endurance	12.7	12.6	13.6	13.1	16.2	18.8*
Heterosexuality	17.7*	14.3	15.5*	11.0	12.0*	8.0
Aggression	12.8*	10.6	12.0	11.0	12.0	11.0
Consistency Score	11.5	11.7	11.3	11.0	11.5	11.5
N	760	749	60	62	60	80

* This mean is significantly larger (at the one percent level) than the corresponding mean for the opposite item.

women might give some credence to the widely asserted belief than one result of the attrition of the caste system is the suppression of the dominant, driving tendencies on the part of the Negro male and the subsequent emergence of the matriarchal family pattern. It tends to support the notion that the deference shown by the Negro college student is the result of a great fear of showing a real need for aggression.

SOCIAL CLASS DIFFERENCES

To achieve a useful dichotomous measure of social class, the EPPS need scores were grouped according to the occupation of the parent or guardian. Professional, managerial, farm owners and skilled laborers constituted a middle-income group; and semi-skilled, farm tenant and day laborers constituting a lower-middle income group. Table 2 contains the data for this analysis.

TABLE 2

Social Class Differences on the EPPS

	Upper-South				Lower-South			
	Middle Income		Lower-Middle Income		Middle Income		Lower-Middle Income	
Variables	Male	Female	Male	Female	Male	Female	Male	Female
Achievement	15.0*	14.0*	12.0	12.0	13.3	16.0	13.5	16.3
Order	12.0*	12.0*	10.0	10.6	15.0*	15.2*	12.0	12.3
Autonomy	10.0	11.0	8.5	8.9	9.8	9.9	11.0*	12.1*
Nurturance	12.0	13.0	15.3	15.5*	14.0	15.6	16.4*	18.8*
Dominance	13.0*	10.5*	10.0	10.3	12.0	11.0	12.0	12.0
Endurance	64.3	14.1	12.6	12.9	17.0*	19.8*	15.0	17.0

* This mean is significantly larger (at the 1 percent level) than the corresponding mean.

The upper-south, middle-income group revealed significantly higher needs for achievement, order and dominance and lower needs for nurturance. The lower-south middle-income group revealed higher needs for order and endurance and lower needs for autonomy and nurturance.

When the data were grouped according to rural-urban, only the lower-south group revealed differences. They were higher in nurturance and lower in exhibition than their urban counterparts.

Sex differences by social class were not pronounced. Lower-middle income females in the lower-south group revealed higher needs for nurturance and endurance than their male counterparts. Both social classes in this region revealed higher female needs for achievement. Middle-income males in the upper-south group scored higher on dominance.

DISCUSSION

Perhaps the most revealing lesson of these data is that there is more than one south and more than one Negro college student. The findings of the study suggest that Negro students from the upper-south urban areas where caste sanctions are less severe when compared to lower-south students, seem to be motivated by need structures which are more similar to their white liberal arts counterparts. The first hypothesis of this study, that the Negro student as a group would differ significantly, must, with the exception of the heterosexual variable, be rejected or at least severely qualified. The results for the lower-south sample of this study differ only slightly from the findings of Guba, Bidwell and Jackson (1959) who studied 110 Negro college students along with three other college types but the pattern

406 The Psychological Consequences of Being a Black American

of differences is quite similar. Using the EPPS these researchers also found significant differences in thirteen of the fifteen variables as compared to the eight found in the present total group of this study and to the one difference revealed for the urban, upper-south liberal arts group. It is also important to note here that the broader criterion of the .05 level of confidence was used in the tests of the Guba et al., study as compared to the more restrictive .01 level for the present study. The second hypothesis of the study: that the need structure would vary significantly with the demography of the samples studied can thus be regarded as tenable.

Portraits of the lower-south Negro college student as a deferent, orderly, submissive, intraceptive, persistent person with low needs for heterosexuality and exhibition focus perhaps the workings that the forces on environment have wrought. While the attributes listed above might, with the exception of submissiveness, seem worthy goals for personal development, their adequacy of fit must be questioned when it is noted that the needs for aggression for this group was comparable to white students while the need to defer was high and to dominate and have autonomy low. This unique syndrome of conflicting needs is consistent with the findings of Dollard (1937), Kardiner and Ovesey (1951) and Karon (1958). It could be as these authors have suggested that regardless of social class, one of the more difficult lessons that the Negro adolescent must learn is to suppress his aggressions and to erect a facade of contentment with the status quo of the caste system.

Sex differences which portray the lower-south Negro female as more ambitious, persistent and intraceptive than her male counterpart present a familiar theme to most students of matriarchal Negro life and its exigencies. However, the deference, dominance and sex patterns which in this study show male ascendancy offers an interesting commentary on the fact that these attributes are often associated with the Negro female in the studies of low income groups usually with a conjectural note that the middle classes might present a different picture.

To one who has worked with or observed closely the rural deep south Negro adolescent, the total of two differences revealed in this study might seem surprisingly small although one would expect the greater degrees of reticence and nurturance which they revealed in relation to their urban counterparts. It seems, then, that beneath their gentle and almost over-polite manner, rural student's needs to assert themselves are present in at least the same degree of intensity as urban students.

The writer's observations of the dynamics of sit-down demonstrations greatly substantiated this thesis. Passive resistance seemed to have caught the energies of deep south rural students in no small measure because of less suitable outlets in a hostile land for pent-up aggressions against the caste system. Here was a way to fight back. This opportunity to resist persecution and oppression is also held by Karon to be a contributing factor in the significant differences in the types of psychiatric disorders found in northern and southern Negro patients.

Since the revelations of the researches of Davis, Havighurst and others, attunement to social class differences in motivation and achievement have become rather widespread. The portraits presented in this study of the lower-middle income student as a rather disorderly and highly nurturant person in relation to his middle income counterpart can best be understood by those familiar with the unscheduled, highly communal and offtime chaotic life in the lower-income Negro groups. The need to have meals organized, to keep letters and files according to some system and even to have written work neat and organized all suggested as criterions of order by the instrument would perhaps seem foreign to the participants of the "latch-key," "large family—little money" groups from whence the lower-middle income family sample was drawn. To help friends when they are in trouble, to treat others with kindness and sympathy and to show a great deal of affection toward one another all as suggested as criteria for nurturance by the instrument, assume high priority and is perhaps one of the few beautiful things in the life of a poverty-yoked and often troubled people.

The significantly low needs for achievement in the upper-south low middle-income group and for endurance in the lower-south group can perhaps be interpreted in the same light as above. The criterion tasks of writing a great novel, solving problems and puzzles, being a recognized authority, etc., as suggested by the instrument might seem unrealistic to an adolescent to which the prospect of simply graduating from college presents a formidable, financial and academic challenge to say nothing of finding employment in the overcrowded Negro teaching corps or in the often hostile educational, governmental, and industrial structure of a wider society.

CONCLUSION

Caste sanctions, as investigated in this study, undoubtedly make a difference in the need patterns of Negro college students.

The areas most affected are those personal attributes which serve as equipment for relating in an ascendance or submission pattern to others. Generally, middle-income students from urban areas in the upper-south who were preparing for careers in business and industry seemed less affected than were lower-south students in most categories.

John Dollard observed in his *Caste and Class in a Southern Town* (1937) that the southern Negro's approach to the caste system correlated most closely with the method he had worked out for relating to his elders as a child. Staunch, self-directive adult types were usually products of democratic-permissive homes, churches and schools. Submissive, deferent, accommodative types were products of rigid and harshly authoritarian social institutions. While this is perhaps an over-simplification of an extremely complex development, the thesis merits study by those who work to develop the talents and aspirations of Negro youth.

Interesting problems for study in this area might include the effects of caste sanction on need structures of white youth and the unresolved questions of the impact of institutions upon need structure. Further investigation in the years to come, might also attempt to ascertain the degree of change in ascendancy-submission patterns as Negro youth gain more fully their rights as human beings in a democracy.

References

Davis, A. *Social Class Influence on Learning*. Cambridge: Harvard University Press, 1948.

Dollard, J. *Caste and Class in a Southern Town*. New Haven: Yale University Press, 1937.

Dreger, R., and Miller, S. "Comparative Studies of Negroes and Whites in the United States," *Psychological Bulletin*. 1960, pp. 57, 361–403.

Edwards, A. L. Edwards Personal Preference Schedule. New York: Psychological Corporation, 1953.

Grossack, M. "Some Personality Characteristics of Negro College Students." *Journal of Social Psychology*, 1957, Vol. 46, pp. 125–131.

Guba, E., Jackson, P., and Bidwell, C. "Occupational Opportunities and the Teaching Career." *Educational Research Bulletin*, 1959, XXXVIII, #1, pp. 1–13.

Havighurst, R. *Developmental Tasks and Education*. New York: Longmans-Green Company, 1951.

Kardiner, A., and Ovesey, L. *The Mark of Oppression*. New York: Norton Company, 1951.

Karon, B. *The Negro Personality*. New York: Springer Company, 1958.

Klett, C. J. "A Study of the Edwards Personal Preference Schedule in relation to Socio-Economic Status." Unpublished Doctor's Dissertation. University of Washington, 1956.

Taylor, B. H. "The Use of the Edwards Personal Preference Schedule in Establishing Personality Profiles for Three College Majors." Unpublished Master's Thesis, University of Washington, 1957.

43 *Psychology and Intercultural Interaction*[1]

REGINA M. GOFF

Department of Education, Morgan State College

Often, an enlarged viewpoint toward a particular group or attitude or belief results in an accompanying increase in understanding. Dr. Regina Goff has emphasized the cross-cultural approach in order to examine the operation of certain cultural beliefs and psychological principles. By interviewing nearly 300 Iranian male teachers she has provided us with a more general look at "intercultural interaction" because the same phrase might well be applied to groups from two distinctly different neighborhoods in the same town. She finds, among other things, that the Iranian culture focuses little attention and value on "liberty" and "independence" and relates this to the generally authoritarian nature of leadership in underdeveloped countries (see Taylor, 1962, this collection). The paper is particularly significant because it shows how different are the perceptions and values of a group of Iranian men from the typical "American way." The implications for American Blacks are relatively clear-cut, and should be considered by the reader.

A. INTRODUCTION

The purpose of this study is to indicate the use which may be made of psychological data in intercultural interaction. By way of illustration a specific question is posed and an answer sought in responses made to self-reference questions by Nationals of a Middle East culture.

The question: In what manner may values held by a people be utilized in positive intercultural interaction? It is hypothesized that successful interaction is a function of psychological management; that such management is dependent upon skillful use of knowledge of defensive attitudes of a people, the nature of values held, and protective patterns of action

SOURCE. Reprinted from the *Journal of Social Psychology*, 1962, **58**, 235–240 with permission of the author and The Journal Press.

[1] Received in the Editorial Office on June 19, 1962 and given prior publication in accordance with our policy on cross-cultural research.

sanctioned by them. Further, that reconditioning in terms of incorporation of any desired new features, attitudes or action patterns must be achieved without threat of removal of internalized security defenses or displacement of values and sanctioned behavior; a people must be positively motivated to want to relearn.

B.   METHOD OF GETTING ANSWER

A group of teachers in Iran were asked to respond to a series of questions designed to obtain in indirect manner the nature of values held. Responses were then considered in terms of cues to values revealed and in terms of the relevance of content to positive interaction.

C.   THE INSTRUMENT AND THE SUBJECTS

Two hundred and seventy-five male, elementary school teachers considered to be between the ages of 18 and 35 were administered 14 questions of which, due to space limitations, but three are mentioned here. The teachers were in attendance in the 1956 summer sessions held in the sharestans of Shahrekard, Nain, Golpaygan, Yazd, and the city of Isfahan. These areas represented a cross between traditional thought and tempered inroads of Western stimulation.

Questions, which were simply and indirectly stated, may suggest superficiality. However, this simplicity was necessary in order to achieve clarity with a population totally unfamiliar with exploratory investigation and its techniques and to eliminate misunderstandings involved in attempts to conceptualize words for which the culture provided no content comparable to our own.

D.   LIMITATIONS INHERENT IN THE STUDY

A limiting factor is the absence of knowledge of personal attributes or emotional status of individuals responding. Too, the accuracy of responses may be affected by unconscious or conscious omissions. Nevertheless, a great effort was made to create in each setting an atmosphere which fostered freedom of expression. Interviewees were satisfied that no ulterior motives were involved in questioning and that the identity of papers would remain anonymous. Introductory remarks, circulation and collection of papers were handled entirely by instructed and capable Iranian personnel. It is probable that responses are as accurate as those usually obtained in this manner.

E. FINDINGS AND DISCUSSION

Table 1 represents findings in answer to the question: "Think of a person whom you like very much. Why do you like that person? I like him because—(list traits)."

Most Admired Traits

Trait	Frequency	Percentage
National pride	51	19
Spirituality	47	18
Personal usefulness	47	18
Respect, courtesy	46	17
Trustworthiness	26	10
"Good mind"	20	7
Good temper	14	5
Humor	8	3
Dependability	1	.75
Economic wisdom	1	.75
Persistence	1	.75
Efficiency	1	.75
Total	263	100.00

Heading the list as the most admired trait, in a wide range of categories and thin spread of responses, is that which has been termed a spirit of national pride. Typical answers were, "I like a person who is interested in the country; respects our King." "I like a person who is interested in the progress of Iran." The social inference or nationalist sentiment is motivated by protective attitudes embedded in individual security systems. The severities of living, confusion and conflict causing near crisis within, and fear of "colonialism" or "imperialism" from without provoke feelings of vulnerability and weakness. A collective security is envisioned in an autonomous nation implied in the statements of admiration for those who revere the country.

Group behavior in the instance of insecurity is characterized by gullibility, a swaying back and forth toward the profitable; in essence, the spirit of the opportunist. The reversal of agreed upon decisions and the employment of face-saving techniques are an expectancy where prestige is at stake. Successful interaction requires anticipation of substitute action patterns in place of original plans and, therefore, subsequent readiness with pre-planned alternatives.

The nationalist strain is a component of a cluster which includes spirituality and, within the context of this study, is allied to personal usefulness, respect and trustworthiness found in the second through the fourth categories. Islamic philosophical thought is a common heritage which has shaped cultural practices, tenaciously guarded tradition, and given the nation its single thread of unity amid the diversity of classes and ethnic groups. Spirituality as expressed by the respondents, within the inscription of Islam, is not only a unifying force but psychologically serves the function of provoking democratic tenets within the Moslem framework; mainly, brotherhood and respect for human dignity. "I like a person who gives me what I need." ". . . a person who helps me with my debts." ". . . a person I can trust and who gundes me."[2] All these are statements indigenous to Moslem Obligation. Our foreign aid program to under-developed areas, with cultural features similar to Iran, is consistent with social inclinations and rewarding in terms of group approval. Giving with too many strings, however, suggests among other things a paternalistic attitude which conflicts with the prestige motive.

Appearing at the bottom of the list of admired traits are the characteristics of dependability, efficiency, economic wisdom, and persistence in work effort. Judged by hierarchal arrangement, these are values of low intensity discharging little pressure toward stabilizing fundamentals as conceived by the West. While it is a cultural privilege to choose a response to phenomena, realistically, the demands of present day competitive national powers dissuades laissez-faire attitudes. In order to achieve the potential of the values named without the punitive effects of disapproval of existing views, the function of competence must be understood and its rewards objectively experienced.

Examination of the range of responses of Nationals to the question directs attention to the concept of overdeterminism in group behavior; the simultaneous expression of different complexes or the relationship existing among psychic tensions expressed as values and which become controlling factors in the selection and regulation of intensity of response patterns.

A second question posed was, "Think of someone whom you do not admire. List the traits which you do not like." It was assumed in this instance that traits contrary to accepted codes or values elicit unfavorable reactions.

The largest number of responses, accounting for almost one-fourth of the total, is found in the category labeled "bad character" inclusive of "vile," "base," "non-spiritual," "treacherous," "hypocritical," and "defamers of character." The selection of the terms themselves suggests the depth of emotion which accompanies reactions to this unadmired behavior. Sensitivity to ill treatment was indicated by twenty per cent who admired least

---

[2] These and other quotes are direct responses made by Nationals.

persons of "bad temper," "ill humor," "egotistical," "arrogant," "unjust," "impolite" and "demagogic" behavior. Such behavior from any source, interpreted as belittlement, violates ego strivings and blocks compatible relations.

A third disliked trait was that of "selfish money-seeking" which though set forth as a separate entity is allied to unjust and non-spiritual behavior indicated in the above-mentioned categories, and is probably reacted to by a larger number than specifically identified it as such. Considered in its wider cultural context, this unadmired trait has significance. Recent uprisings within Iran, participated in by members of the rising middle class against political and social conditions judged unfair and corrupt, may be attributed to the presence of hidden discharges or accumulated tensions resulting from deficits to need satisfaction. They also reflect absence of intergroup communication except at the level of mutual resistance. When groups overcome isolation, values are communicated even if not accepted. The same procedure follows in intercultural relations in which instance, however, understandings are sought without the negative effect of violence.

Table 2 shows responses to the question, "If you could have anything you wanted, what would you wish for?" It was assumed that preferences, inclinations, and partialities are indirect reflectors of values held.

TABLE 2
Wishes

Wish	Frequency	Percentage
Prestige, status, power	64	31
Leadership	49	24
Knowledge	40	20
Peace of mind; spiritual progress	24	12
Health	15	7
Land ownership	5	2
Good character	3	1.5
Mental ability	2	1
Good personality	2	1
Liberty and independence	1	.5
Total	205	100.00

The desire for prestige and power ranked first though leadership and land ownership might well have been included in a larger "power" category which would then have included fifty-seven per cent of the total responses.

The expressed wishes have vital and deeply rooted connections understood through the dimension of time extending from the historical past to the concrete present. Reverence continues today for Cyrus the Great, Darius, Nadir Shah, Shah Abbas and like leaders. In ancient cultures, the glory and power of the past has not dimmed with the years. Unfortunately, as in the case of Iran, coincident with the urge for personal power are existing conditions in which few positive valences are present for need fulfillment. "There is loneliness, poverty, and obvious gradual dying." Unleashed tensions expressed as deep-seated wishes infer unrest. Impulse energy is available for press toward salient social change or impulse drainage may occur by means of displaced aggression and social disequilibrium.

It is noted that twelve per cent of the responses were concerned with desire for "peace of mind and spiritual progress."

The scant mention of liberty and independence causes pause for thought. Democracy has not been dominant, historically, in the political and social theories of under-developed nations. Authoritarian leadership has more often been the practice. Unless the skills and techniques of democratic leadership can rapidly be converted into felt material growth for a people, their attention and allegiance may be drawn to a more circumscribed and regulated political control but one which promises more immediate relief. This point of view is not new having been reiterated on many occasions. Responses of individuals included in this study document the point of view. It is incumbent in positive intercultural relations to give priority to concepts of reward as conceived by a particular people rather than to assume an immediate internalization of values which represent cultural contrasts.

F. SUMMARY STATEMENT

All cultures have traditional values which have been institutionalized and which, as indicated in the data, are subject to discovery. Psychic tensions, expressed as values, serve as discriminatory forces and lead to the abstracting of tension reducing stimuli from a wide field of stimulating elements.

The nature of responses of a people in intercultural interaction may be anticipated in terms of personal values and protective attitudes which are at stake and which seek expression as motivators of group behavior. Though the term "cultural values" has been used, in actuality this is but collective reference to individual psychic systems in which values are embedded. Violations of values or of defensive attitudes disturb psychic tensions and cause disequilibrium, frustration, and resistance.

A deficit-tension hypothesis would suggest the coincidence of social need and the immediacy of environmental provisions for need satisfaction.

In the absence of positive factors, substitute responses are made in keeping with available tension outlets.

Responsiveness in intergroup relations, inclusive of the learning of new attitudes, depends upon giving power to personal and group defenses through sanctioning of deserving cultural features and approval, with reasoned judgment, of prevailing internalized values.

44 The Significance of Communication in Counseling the Culturally Disadvantaged

MILTON E. WILSON
Kent State University

Historically, a number of problems have emerged that show either psychotherapy or counseling to be less effective with lower social classes than high and with minority groups than standard Americans. Such were the conclusions of Hollingshead and Redlich's *Social Class and Mental Illness* (1958), and in this paper Dr. Wilson poses many of the same problems in America's attempts to counsel the culturally disadvantaged. He carefully reviews language differences, the role of language and values in communication, and then proposes the need for real "communication" in counseling the disadvantaged. The suggestions regarding ways to more efficiently counsel such unique groups are sound, and indicate the nature of the changes in counseling that are required to render it meaningful for culturally disadvantaged persons.

Since we are concerned with communication, let us begin with a translation exercise:

John: "Man, you should dig my float."
Paul: "Yea, baby, the bread came just in time."
John: "I see you got a short with your loot."
Paul: "Easy, baby, if we don't watch out, we'll get a rock on our checks."
John: "Say, you sure are cool."
Paul: "I dig your threads. Do you dig my front?"
John: "Hey, I see the man. Let's cool it. Split, baby."
Paul: "See you later—you old dozens' player."

Perhaps it occurred to you that "float" and "short" referred to cars; that "bread" and "loot" refer to money; that "front" and "threads" refer to suits;

SOURCE. Presented at the annual meeting of the American Personnel and Guidance Association, Las Vegas, 31 March 1969. Reprinted with permission of the author.

416

that "dig" refers to understanding and appreciation; that "rock on our checks" means garnishment; that "cool" means smart and A-OK; that "cool it" and "split" mean to depart in a controlled fashion; and that "dozens" refers to a game in which the players devaluate each other's mother in an unconscious effort to develop the kind of frustration tolerance that will enable them to cope with the problems that confront and will confront them.

Perhaps it also occurred to you that many counselors experience difficulty in communicating with clients who are culturally different. In fact, some counselors devaluate clients who communicate with nonstandard English.

Moreover, the values of counselors and their clients might differ, and these differences, rather than being understood and accepted by counselors, may be misunderstood, unappreciated, and rejected.

Because language and values are central to communication, I am going to focus on these factors. Before doing so, however, I want to discuss briefly what I consider to be the current orientation in counseling the "disadvantaged." In my concluding remarks, I will suggest some guidelines for effecting more facilitative communication with persons handicapped by cultural differences.

GOALS IN COUNSELING THE CULTURALLY DISADVANTAGED

In counseling, we seek to help clients to become aware of and to actualize their potentials for functioning more effectively in the area or areas that concern them.

Our models of effectiveness consist of standards or criteria for judging deviancy from and movement toward the standards of effectiveness.

Existing models, as you might guess, are generally cast in terms of middle-class values.

Counseling, therefore, is value-oriented. This is true of vocational, educational, and personal-social counseling. The basic goal is to help the client to modify his thinking, feeling, and behaving in the direction of middle-class effectiveness.

The main tool employed in counseling is verbal communication. While nonverbal communication is important, it is generally a lesser tool. Through both verbal and nonverbal exchange of concepts and feelings, including values, the client is helped to conceptualize his problems, examine alternative solutions, and to take the steps needed for realizing a more effective adjustment.

In the counseling process, certain assumptions are made about the client. It is assumed that the client knows he has a problem, wants to solve the problem, has the resources to learn how to solve the problem, and needs a warm, friendly relationship to accelerate the gaining and working through of insight. Furthermore, it is assumed that the client can solve his problems through talking, relating, and responding to a trained counselor. And it is generally assumed that the counselor and the client have similar communication and value orientations.

In counseling persons who are disadvantaged by cultural differences, these assumptions may not hold. The language and value orientations of the counselor and the client may differ. These differences may hinder the movement of the client toward human effectiveness as defined by middle-class standards or by the standards of the client's cultural group. The relationship and the expectations sought by both the counselor and the client, therefore, may not be achieved. In brief, the facilitative or therapeutic communication associated with the counseling process may not occur.

THE SIGNIFICANCE OF LANGUAGE DIFFERENCES IN COMMUNICATING WITH CULTURALLY DIFFERENT PERSONS

According to Reusch (1961), "Language is composed of a plurality of signs or symbols, the significance of which must be known to a number of interpreters" (p. 457).

In other words, language is composed of shared meanings which can be exchanged through verbal and nonverbal acts. Language consists of meaningful referents to thoughts, feelings, and things.

To a large extent, persons disadvantaged by cultural differences are conceptualized as persons with language differences which handicap them. Baratz (1968), for example, lists three orientations to the language problems of disadvantaged persons in her review of relevant literature. These are: verbal destitution; underdeveloped language; and full but nonstandard language development.

In terms of the verbal destitution frame of reference, studies comparing culturally disadvantaged persons with middle-class persons find the former to be less verbal; to have greater vocabulary deficits, descriptive and qualifying word deficits, and deficits in the comprehension of figurative language. Studies also find the culturally disadvantaged to have greater deficits in grammar, pronunciation, articulation, and syntactical form than their middle-class counterparts. In other words, from the verbal destitution frame of reference, culturally disadvantaged persons are viewed as having less language than middle-class persons, and the insufficiency of language is viewed as hindering them from functioning effectively in the larger society.

In terms of the underdeveloped language frame of reference, persons who are culturally disadvantaged are viewed as having underdeveloped language systems that thwart the development and utilization of higher cognitive processes in adjusting to the demands of daily living. The research used to support this frame of reference suggests that the language used by culturally disadvantaged persons is not conducive to the expression of abstractions; logical, spatial, and temporal relationships; generalizations; and individual differences and feelings. Research findings also suggest that persons with cultural disadvantages have difficulty in using syntactic devices to express complex ideas and in using language to inform, interpret, explain, analyze, and evaluate.

If the verbal destitution and underdeveloped language frames of reference are correct, we would have to conclude that persons with cultural disadvantages are not very intelligent when compared to middle-class standards. We would have to say that they have difficulty in planning, thinking rationally, reasoning by analogy, and in acting purposefully in dealing with human and environmental problems.

Moreover, we would have to conclude that persons with cultural disadvantages are who they are and where they are because language has not been learned and/or language has been learned faultily.

Fortunately, an examination of the methodologies used in the research to support the verbal destitution and underdeveloped language frames of reference indicate that the findings are explained better by experimental procedures than by the constructs of "destitution" and/or "underdevelopment." In these studies, as Baratz (1968) indicates, the materials, settings, and orientations constitute a built-in middle-class bias.

Moreover, the investigators utilized a restricted view of language. For example, the prevalence of significant differences in language between middle-class and culturally disadvantaged persons suggests the presence of different language systems. If large numbers of persons, for example, use the same form, this suggests that the form used must be part of the syntax of a culture. It does not mean that the syntax employed by disadvantaged persons is incorrect. Indeed, it may be very correct in that it represents shared meaning and significance and facilitates the reciprocal exchange of signals for a group of people.

That brings us to the third approach which regards the language of persons with cultural disadvantages as developed but nonstandard language when compared to middle-class persons. From this frame of reference, the omission of sounds, like the /d/ in "hand" is interpreted as being similar to our omission of the /ps/ in "psychology." That is, the sound does not blend with the dialect being used. Because of general acceptance among the persons in the community, the omission is not an articulation error or mispronunciation. Moreover, the nonstandard language of persons with cultural disadvantages, particularly the Southern Negro, is similar in structure to other languages and follows well-ordered but different grammatical rules than standard English (Stewart, 1964). Here is an example given by a linguist:

"Speakers of nonstandard American Negro dialects make a grammatical distinction by means of *be,* illustrated by such constructions as *he busy;* 'He is busy' (momentarily); or, *he workin';* 'He is working' (right now) as opposed to *he be busy;* 'He is (habitually) busy' or *he be workin';* 'He is working' (steadily), a contrast which the grammar of standard English is unable to make." (Stewart, 1967).

In the case of Negro nonstandard speech, rules governing the formation of the possessive, the plural, the negative, and the past and future tense appear to be different from standard English (Stewart, 1967).

In looking at the significance of language in facilitating interpretation, analysis, synthesis, and evaluation, Baratz (1968) reports that while many of the transformational forms of culturally disadvantaged persons are similar to standard English transformational forms, the majority of transformations are not. Nevertheless, developmental research suggests that culturally disadvantaged children can function at transformational levels.

Certainly, the culturally different, as a group, are not intellectually dull. Wherever I go, I find some very, very bright children, adolescents, and adults who manifest their brightness in many problem-solving situations but have been labelled as being disadvantaged because they have difficulty communicating their brightness in standard English. Many also have difficulty communicating their feelings and experiences to middle-class social workers, physicians, lawyers, and counselors.

Although they may not communicate effectively with professional workers, they do communicate effectively among themselves. Middle-class persons who are not highly sensitive to language differences do not receive the culturally disadvantaged effectively because they do not understand the language they speak. Language differences, therefore, are important, for they may affect any realization of desired behavioral changes through counseling. Left unresolved, language differences can generate mutual rejection.

THE SIGNIFICANCE OF VALUE DIFFERENCES IN COMMUNICATING WITH CULTURALLY DIFFERENT CLIENTS

Values play a significant role in communication. This is particularly true in counseling persons who have cultural disadvantages.

A linguist once told me that when we communicate, we always communicate two things. We send a message; and we send an image of who we are and what we believe. In brief, our message is always accompanied by some expression of personality and values.

The communication of personality and values, especially in face-to-face encounters, occurs through our appearance, gestures, looking, listening, and other mannerisms. More than ten years ago, Routh (1958) pointed out the importance of nonverbal factors in an article for vocational counselors. He wrote:

"The look in the eyes, the set of the mouth, the flare of the nostrils, the sneer, the frown, the upturned lip, the way the hands are used, the gait, stance, or walk—these factors help to communicate feelings, attitudes, and emotional reactions between people." (p. 135).

Certainly values are important determinants of behavior. Values are central to the survival of a culture or subculture and are transmitted to and reinforced consciously and unconsciously in those persons encapsulated in a culture.

Value orientations are cognitive-affective directive elements, which according to Kluckhohn (1964), "give order and direction to the ever-flowing stream of human acts and thoughts as these relate to the solution of common human problems."

Put another way, value orientations are generalized and organized sets of principles which orient man toward nature, toward his place in nature, toward his relationship with other human beings, and toward the desirable and undesirable as they relate to his environment.

These orientations govern man's expectations and relationships to such phenomena as health and illness, professional services, including counseling, activity and work, education, and family relationships. They govern his behaviors toward time, change, frustration, and dependency. They predispose him to act in certain ways as he experiences trouble, toughness, smartness, excitement, and as he considers fate.

To illustrate the point, let us draw on an article concerned with differences between dominant American middle-class value orientations and dominant value orientations of Spanish surnamed persons who are disadvantaged by cultural differences. The following excerpt from an article written by Sanchez (1964), a psychiatrist, is illustrative:

"In the U.S.A., we find a middle class culture characterized by the following value orientations: (1) for the 'Relational' (interpersonal) orientation, we find individualism (i.e., emphasis of the individual ahead of any group considerations); (2) for the 'Time' orientation, we find future time orientation (i.e., anything new is clearly better than anything old and hopes are usually cast for the time to come); (3) for the relation of 'Man to Nature' orientation, we find an over nature orientation (i.e., nature can be tamed to man's will and control of his fate resides within his own skill and resources); (4) for the 'Activity' orientation we find a doing orientation (i.e., strivings for competence and achievement, as measured by outside standards, are the important factors on the road to success); (5) for the 'Human Nature' orientation, we find a human but perfectible nature orientation (i.e., roughly the puritan notion).

"Let us examine now the dominant lower class Latin American value orientations. There we find a culture characterized by the following: (1) in the 'Relational' sphere we find a strong lineality orientation (i.e., the vertically structured group hierarchy is stressed) and collaterality orientation (i.e., the horizontally structured group, 'one for all and all for one' aspect of group loyalty, and the existence of the extended family). I mention both because they alternate as first order and second order orientations depending on the groups within the lower classes being considered. In any case both stress group rather than individual goals. (2) For the 'Time' orientation, we find a present time orientation (i.e., stress on the present with little or no regard for the future or past, and therefore, with scarce planning ahead of time). (3) For the relation of 'Man to Nature' we find a subjugated to nature orientation (i.e., the stress is on the helplessness and weakness of man, factors that he has to recognize in order to gain any control at all over his fate). (4) In the 'Activity' sphere we find a being orientation (i.e., the is-ness of behavior, the spontaneous inclination to act in accordance with one's mood, feelings, desires and impulses). (5) For the 'Human Nature' orientation, we find a *mixed good and evil* conception of human nature (i.e., roughly the characteristic Judeo-Christian notion).

"I have here portrayed only the first order and not the second or third order value orientations held by both groups and it becomes apparent that they are almost mirror images. In any case, they are opposed." (pp. 1–2.)

Although I have contrasted dominant American middle-class value orientations with dominant value orientations of culturally disadvantaged Spanish surnamed persons, I could have made similar contrasts of American middle-class value orientations with the dominant value orientations of American Blacks, Indians, and Appalachian Whites.

But what does this have to do with the communication of counselors with persons who have cultural differences.

Rokeach (1960) gives us a clue. He advanced the hypothesis, which subsequent research has reinforced (Rokeach, Smith, and Evans, 1960;

Stein, Hardyck and Smith, 1965), that prejudice may be in large part the result of perceived dissimilarity of belief systems. Put another way, "the prejudiced person does not reject a person of another race, religion, or nationality *per se*, but rather because he perceives that the other differs from him in important beliefs and values" (Stein, Hardyck, and Smith, 1965).

In other words, people—and this includes counselors—are highly committed to those persons, processes, and things that are in agreement with their values.

Since counselors come from and have been conditioned to the values of American middle-class culture and operate in programs generated by middle-class interests designed to foster middle-class outcomes, they will confront and communicate to the client, both consciously and unconsciously, middle-class expectations.

As Sanchez (1964) has put it:

"They will encourage in and expect from the patient autonomy and independence in the making of choices and decisions and a clear feeling that the future will be different from and better than the past and present. They will expect that each patient will take individual responsibility in seeing that this is so. They will further expect the patient to have a clear notion about the therapist as a professional involved in helping him technically without having any other ax to grind. The patient will be expected and encouraged to consider activities, work and labor as something good and desirable in itself that must be measured by what is accomplished. Hopefully the patient will develop confidence in the use of words rather than physical action in expressing himself. All this, which is only part of the expectation of the therapist, will fit wonderfully well a middle-class American patient who, by holding roughly the same values, will be oriented to the *future* (hopes), to *doing*, to conquering nature (*over nature*), and being an independent autonomous individual (*individualism*)." (p. 3).

These values will be communicated by the counselor to the client. They will not necessarily be accepted by the client.

The client's values will be communicated to the counselor. They will not necessarily be accepted by the counselor.

The outcome may well be that the counselor and the client will reject each other and retreat defensively.

SOME IMPLICATIONS

What I have tried to do is to take two dimensions of communication—language and value orientations—and indicate their significance in counseling persons who are disadvantaged by cultural differences. Although there are other dimensions to the communication process, these two dimensions, in my opinion, are the most important dimensions in face-to-face counseling with persons who are culturally disadvantaged. Moreover, time does not permit further analysis.

What are the implications of this analysis? The major implication is that counselors should relate to clients with cultural differences in ways that will enhance the cultural identities of their clients. Counselors should relate to clients in ways which will permit the cultural identities of their clients to become positive sources of pride and major motivators of behavior (Sanchez, 1964; Gross, 1968). To do less is to denigrate a client's identity. To do less is to ask a client to give up his values in order to participate in the dominant culture. To do less is to contribute to the destruction of life; and our mission is not to destroy life but to enhance life.

Here are some specific implications stemming from the major conclusion:

1. Counselors need to understand how and why clients think, feel, and behave the way they do. Counselors need to understand the ways clients learn, that is, the socialization process. Counselors need more than a superficial understanding. They need to see, smell, hear, and taste the culture of their clients until they can grasp some of the deeper meanings of the language and the deeper meanings of values guiding the clients. When counselors can honestly accept culturally different clients as individuals of dignity and worth, when counselors are accepted by the clients as effective human beings who will not dehumanize them, then counselors can practice their profession effectively in helping clients to become aware of and realize their potentials. Although counselors need to learn all they can by reading about cultural differences, they especially need to interact with and to gain an understanding of and appreciation for people who are culturally different. On the job, they need to study their interactions with culturally different persons and to analyze and synthesize their successes and failures.

2. Counselors need to understand the conditions under which clients with cultural differences relate to human service personnel and the expectations they bring to such relationships.

3. In the language area, counselors should permit culturally different clients to use nonstandard English. Counselors should not criticize the primary language of their clients. They must not try to obliterate the language being used but help the clients to see that knowledge of and skills in using standard English as a second language can make a sig-

nificant difference in some types of employment and in some situations related to the satisfaction of the needs of the clients. Clients should be allowed to maintain their nonstandard language because it is necessary to them in the majority of their experiences outside the middle-class culture. To devalue a client's language or to argue that standard English is better is to devalue the client and his culture and to reveal a shocking ignorance concerning language. The work of the counselor, then, is to help the client to see the value of a second language system without denying the legitimacy of his own system. The use of effective models and examples from the client's cultural group may facilitate these outcomes.

4. In the value orientation area, some suggestions may be helpful. Many clients, for example, expect to be told what to do. I believe that the counselor, in many instances, should tell the clients what they should do and why. Many clients, because of their life style, expect authority figures to advise them. If the counselor feels uncomfortable about this role, he may not have an understanding of the cultural background and expectations of his client. The counselor should learn to feel comfortable in pointing out alternatives to the client and in being active in helping the client to weigh the alternatives. The use of authority, however, should not conflict with the authority of significant others (e.g., the church and parents for Spanish surnamed persons; the authorities to whom Blacks are committed, such as a particular peer group, church, or mother).

5. Counselors should engage in short, frequent counseling sessions and focus on short-range planning with fairly quick payoffs. Since the time orientation of disadvantaged clients is likely to be in terms of a *now* frame of reference, the counselor should focus on the *now*. The counselor should be particularly sensitive to the immediate gratification expectations of the client. The counselor should be strongly committed to quick action or to a series of quick actions that will enable the client to move toward the goals being sought.

6. If a client's peer group is important to him, consideration should be given to work that will help the client to be perceived by his peer group with enhanced status.

7. In line with the attitudes of culturally different clients toward authorities, counselors who behave paternalistically or brotherly and guide clients along kindly may be the most effective counselors in working with disadvantaged persons with cultural differences. Clients should feel about counselors as they feel about friends. Clients should be able to say, "His door was always open; he was never too busy; he understands." Above all, the counselor should be honest. He should be a person who can be trusted. And he should be a person who has courage to work as an advocate for his clients in the securing of equal opportunity.

8. For upward mobile clients—that is, individuals moving toward full acceptance of the values and language of the dominant culture, the counselor should assume a followship rather than a leadership role. The counselor should follow closely his clients, providing reinforcement and support when needed. Understanding, acknowledgement, and acceptance of minimal gains is the rule, not the exception.

Now, I realize that some of my suggestions are not consistent with current counselor education values and practices. But what I have said is consistent with the value orientations of culturally different persons with whom I have worked. And what I have said is being said by others with greater frequency today than ever before.

In counseling culturally different persons, we really have only three choices. We must either seek to change the values of clients through our traditional counseling approaches, or we must change our counseling approaches to adapt to the self-defined needs and values of persons with cultural differences, or we must achieve some middle course.

While I advocate some middle course for the culturally different clients who are strongly oriented toward embracing the dominant culture, for all others I strongly believe that we must change our counseling approaches to adapt to their self-defined goals. This is not only the path of least resistance but it is also the most effective course. The resistance of values to change, the potential, maladjustive effects associated with forced change, the strong commitment of the culturally different to responsible self-determination, and our commitment to the dignity of each person should enable us to see clearly who has the most changing to do.

Communication in counseling the culturally disadvantaged is tremendously important. Let us, therefore, embrace the kind of facilitative communication with our clients that will keep the light of hope and dignity burning.

References

Baratz, J. "Language in the Economically Disadvantaged Child: A Perspective." *ASHA*, 1968, April, 143–145.

Gross, E. "Counseling Special Populations." *Employment Service Review*, 1968 Jan.–Feb., 14–19, 29.

Kluckhohn, C. *Culture and Behavior*. New York: Macmillan, 1964.

Rokeach, M. (Ed.) *The Open and Closed Mind*. New York: Basic Books, 1960.

Rokeach, M., Smith, P. W., and Evans, R. I. "Two kinds of prejudice or one?" In M. Rokeach (ed.), *The Open and Closed Mind*. New York: Basic Books, 1960, pp. 132–168.

Routh, T. "The Importance of Body Language in Counseling." *Vocational Guidance Quarterly*, 1958, *6*, 134–137.

Ruesch, J. *Therapeutic Communication*. New York: W. W. Norton, 1961.

Sanchez, V. "Relevance of Cultural Values for Occupational Therapy Programs." *American Journal for Occupational Therapy*, 1964, *28*, (1), 1–5.

Stein, D. D., Hardyck, J. A., and Smith, M. B. "Race and Belief: An Open and Shut Case." *Journal of Personality and Social Psychology*, 1965, *1*, 281–289.

Stewart, W. (Ed.). *Nonstandard Speech and the Teaching of English*. Washington, D. C.: Center for Applied Linguistics, 1964.

————. "Sociolinguistic Factors in the History of American Negro Dialects." *Florida Foreign Language Reporter*, 1967, 5. Cited by J. Baratz, "Language in the Economically Disadvantaged Child: A Perspective." *ASHA*, 1968, April, 144.

Bibliography for Part VI

Barron, F. An ego-strength scale which predicts response to psychotherapy *Journal of Consulting Psychology,* 1953, **17**, 327–333.

Byrne, D., Barry, J., and Nelson, D. Relation of the revised repression-sensitization scale to measures of self-description. *Psychological Reports,* 1963, **13**, 323–334.

Caffrey, Bernard, Anderson II, Sims, and Garrison, Janet. Change in racial attitudes of white Southerners after exposure to the atmosphere of a Southern university. *Psychological Reports,* 1969, **25**, 555–558.

Caffrey, Bernard, and Capel, Wm. C. Negro and war attitudes of the same persons assessed at three points over a thirty-three year period. *Psychological Reports,* 1969, **25**, 543–551.

Caffrey, B., Jones, C., and Holcombe, J. C. Racial attitudes of seniors in two Southern high schools. *Journal of Social Psychology,* in press.

Carr, L., and Roberts, S. O. Correlates of civil rights participation. *Journal of Social Psychology,* 1965, **67**(2), 259–267.

Crowne, D. P., and Marlowe, D. A new scale of social desirability independent of psychopathology. *Journal of Consulting Psychology,* 1960, **24**, 349–354.

Crowne, D. P., and Marlowe, D. *The Approval Motive: Studies in Evaluative Dependence.* New York: John Wiley & Sons, 1964.

Deutsch, M. Minority group and class status as related to social and personality factors in scholastic achievement. *Social Applied Anthropology Monograph,* 1960, No. 2.

Eysenck, H. J. *The Biological Basis of Personality.* Springfield, Ill.: Charles C Thomas, 1967.

Freeman, Howard E., Armor, David, Ross, J. Michael, and Pettigrew, T. F. Color gradation and attitudes among middle income Negroes. *American Sociological Review* (June, 1966), **31**, 365–374.

Goodman, M. E. *Race Awareness in Young Children.* New York: Collier, 1964.

Gross, Theodore L. The idealism of Negro literature in America. *Phylon, Atlanta University Review of Race and Culture,* 1969, **30**(1), 5–10.

Hackney, Sheldon. Southern violence. *American Historical Review,* 1969, **74**(3), 906–925.

Jenkins, W. An experimental study of the relationship of legitimate and illegitimate birth status to school and personal and social adjustment of Negro children. *American Journal of Sociology,* 1958, **64**, 169–173.

Karon, B. P. *The Negro Personality: a Rigorous Investigation of the Effects of Culture.* New York: Springer, 1958.

Kinnick, B. C., and Plattor, S. D. Attitudinal change toward Negroes and school desegregation among participants in a Summer training institute. *Journal of Social Psychology,* 1967, **73**, 271, 283.

Krech, D., Crutchfield, R. S., and Ballachey, E. L. *Individual in Society*. New York: McGraw-Hill, 1962.

Nuttall, R. L. Some correlates of high need for achievement among urban northern Negroes. *Journal of Abnormal and Social Psychology*, 1964, **68**, 593–600.

Pettigrew, Thomas F. Negro American personality: Why isn't more known? *Journal of Social Issues* (April, 1964), **20**, 4–23.

Plant, W. T. Changes in intolerance and authoritarianism for sorority and non-sorority women enrolled in college for a year. *Journal of Social Psychology*, 1966, **68**, 79–83.

Radke, Marian, Sutherland, Jean, and Rosenberg, Pearl. Racial attitudes of children. *Sociometry*, 1950, **13**, 154–171.

Stevenson, H. W., and Stewart, E. G. A developmental study of racial awareness in young children. *Child Development*, 1958, **29**, 399–409.

Stott, D. H. *Studies of Troublesome Children*. New York: Humanities Press, 1966.

Strickland, Bonnie R. The prediction of social action from a dimension of internal-external control. *Journal of Social Psychology*, 1965, **66**, 353, 358.

Yarrow, Marian R. (Issue Ed.) Interpersonal dynamics in a desegregation process. *Journal of Social Issues*, 1958, *14*(1, entire issue).

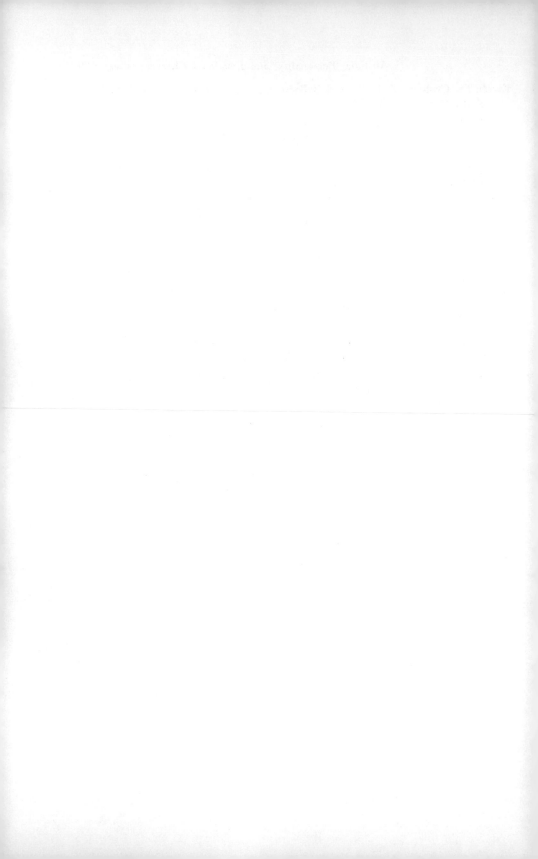

PART VII

Psychology as a Study
and as a Profession

This section specifically examines psychology as an academic and occupational possibility, and begins with the extremely thoughtful review
by Dr. Herman G. Canady (1938) of the status of psychology in Negro
institutions during the mid-1930's. Dr. Condell's (1954) provocative survey enumerates the numbers of Black patients and professional workers
in Southern mental hospitals; and then Wispe and his associates (1969)
review the status of Black psychologists and students within American
psychology. Their collective remarks are understandably critical, and
need careful consideration. It might be noted that Bernard Harleston had
delivered a speech to the American Psychological Association in which
he had called for (1) a clearer understanding of how students become
undergraduate psychology majors, (2) the development of more effective
recruiting programs for Black students, and (3) the need to train many
more Black psychologists. Many of the same points are covered in the
Wispe et al. paper. This section closes with Dr. Martin Luther King Jr.'s
(1968) challenging statement of the role of behavioral scientists in the
Civil Rights Movement which he delivered as an address to the American
Psychological Association.

45 *Psychology in Negro Institutions*[1]

HERMAN G. CANADY

> The development and history of the Negro university is one of the truly significant and interesting events in the growth of American education. In a sense they represent the beginning of the search for equality, so it is fitting that we look back to see what the all-Black colleges and universities were doing in the areas of psychology and the social sciences prior to World War II. Dr. Canady had surveyed 47 all-Black colleges which resulted in an excellent review of the status of psychology in the mid-1930's. Among Dr. Canady's conclusions were the following observations: (1) there was a lack of laboratory courses and equipment, (2) there was a lack of research by the faculty, (3) only 30% of the schools surveyed had departments of psychology, (4) psychology was seen as largely applying to education, and (5) only one college offered a course entitled "The Psychology of the Negro." The paper furnished the basis upon which many colleges and universities were to develop and update their own psychology programs.

PROBLEM

For our own information and as a service to the institutions themselves, the Department of Psychology at West Virginia State College proposed to make a study of the status of Psychology in the curricula of some forty or more of the better Negro institutions in the United States. The specific information sought in connection with this problem concerned, (a) the status of psychology in the curriculum; (b) nature of the introductory course; (c) undergraduate courses in psychology; (d) provisions for laboratory work; (e) library equipment; (f) teaching personnel; and (g) research in psychology.

SOURCE. Reprinted from the *Journal of Negro Education,* 1938, **7**, 165–171 with permission of the author and the publisher.

[1] The writer desires to express his thanks for the assistance of Harry W. Greene and David A. Lane, Jr., and the coöperation of the institutions which made this study possible.

PROCEDURE

The data of this study were secured by means of a carefully prepared questionnaire covering the items in the preceding paragraph forwarded to fifty of the better Negro colleges during the fall of 1936. A letter was sent out over the signature of David A. Lane, Jr., then Dean of West Virginia State College, to the deans or other responsible officials, or directly to the heads of the departments of psychology or divisions which included psychology, suggesting the nature of the study and requesting the coöperation of the various institutions. A summary of the returns was promised the participating institutions. Enclosures were a copy of the questionnaire and a self-addressed, stamped envelope.

Replies were received from forty-seven of the institutions. This study is based, then, on 94 per cent return from a total of fifty colleges. The response is considerably larger than is ordinarily found in studies of this type and shows an encouraging interest in the question under consideration.

RESULTS

For each of the topics the information from some institutions was incomplete, and the number of replies is accordingly less than the number of institutions participating in the study. On several of the principal questions the replies are tabulated for different institutions on the basis of size.

The Status of Psychology in the Curriculum

Our data reveal that only 14, or 30 per cent, of the 47 institutions included in this study have departments of psychology, with an enrollment of 1,292 students. These departments are found in the larger Negro institutions. The 33 institutions which do not have departmental facilities combine psychology with the following departments: education, 31; philosophy, 7; and sociology, 5.

Four of the institutions reporting (including two that combine psychology with philosophy) offer the major in psychology. The remaining 43 do not offer the major either because of insufficient number of courses or inadequate preparation of instructors or both. The quantitative requirements for majors in psychology, in the four institutions which offer them are, as follows: 24 semester hours, 1; 20 semester hours, 1; 18 semester hours, 1; and 12 semester hours, 1.[2]

---

[2] In some cases the institution reported quarter hours. In all cases, here and hereafter, quarter hours were reduced to semester hours.

The requirements in psychology for graduation in 47 Negro institutions are given in Table 1.

TABLE 1

Requirements in Psychology

Size of Institution	No. Reporting	No. Requiring Psychology	Per Cent	Teachers Colleges	Range of Hours Required	Median Requirement
Over–599	9	5	55	1	3–6	4.33
400–599	15	11	73	2	2.5–9	5.00
300–399	6	5	83	1	3–5	4.00
200–299	12	8	66	0	2.5–6	3.31
100–199	3	3	100	1	3–6	4.00
Under–100	2	2	100	0	5–6	5.00
All Institutions	47	34	72	5	2.5–9	4.36

It will be noted from the table that 13, or 28 per cent, of the institutions which offer degrees do not require psychology. All the teachers colleges, however, require psychology. Of the 13 institutions which do not require psychology for graduation, we find that they tend to place it in a group from which requirements are made, or it is required by certain departments, or it may be offered as an elective.

The distribution of the subjects grouped with psychology in the 6 institutions (the largest from the point of view of enrollment) which place psychology in a group of subjects from which requirements are made, and the number of times that each appears are: philosophy, 4; education, 3; history, 2; sociology, botany, chemistry, pre-medicine, social anthropology, home economics, mathematics, physics, English, foreign language, each 1. The size of the groups range from 3 subjects to 6, and the number of semester hours required range from 2 to 12.

The five institutions in which psychology is required by certain departments unavoidably overlap with those in which psychology is placed in a group from which requirements are made. The number of times that psychology is a requirement in other departments is, as follows: education, 4; sociology, 2; economics, 1.

Nature of the Introductory Course

LENGTH OF INTRODUCTORY COURSE. Psychology has, over the years, swiftly changed from a series of interesting and wise chats to a body of scientific knowledge of great scope and considerable depth. In current scientific psychology, the same general methods of investigation are used as in other sciences, and a large number of variations of the scientific method are employed that are of particular significance in gathering the material pertinent to an understanding of human activity.

Not only, then, does psychology have an intensive subject-matter, it also has a wide repertoire of methods. Some teachers of the science have concluded, therefore, that at least six semester hours are required to cover adequately a general survey of the field. Their position is supported by the American Psychological Association. Current practice in the Negro institutions studied, however, still favors a one semester beginning course. In 46 institutions the introductory course ranges from 2 to 7 semester hours: 32 institutions, or 70 per cent, require 3 semester hours; 5, or 10 per cent, require 2; 2, or .04 per cent, require 5; and 7, or 15 per cent, require 7.

EXPERIMENTAL WORK IN INTRODUCTORY COURSE. The opinion is pretty well established, we believe, that traditionally, at least, the first course in psychology has contained too much dialectic, too many fine verbal distinctions, and too many technical definitions; and that it has made too little appeal to concrete, objective, experimental work. Psychology should integrate the experimental approach with the first course taken by the student through stressing experimental methods, thereby giving the student some idea how psychological facts have been discovered.

Our replies show an appreciation of the importance of experimental work for elementary students. Twenty-seven of our respondents said that they would give laboratory work with the first course if facilities permitted, but only one institution reports a definite laboratory course as part of the beginning work. Out of 46 institutions reporting, 19, or 41 per cent, include laboratory work of some kind often in the form of demonstrations or selected experiments.

Courses Offered in Psychology in Negro Institutions

A total of 28 courses were named in the reports. Table 2 gives the names of the courses and number of times each is offered. It is of interest to note the large number of courses of an applied nature and the relatively few in pure or theoretical psychology; also, that only two institutions offer a course in Race Psychology, and that no institution offers a course with the distinct title of "The Psychology of the Negro."

There is obviously some overlapping in titles. Those that normally cover the same content might have been combined; but because of the small number of courses reported and the possibility that in some instances the courses might constitute a particular organization of material, we decided to list the titles as given.

TABLE 2

Courses Offered in Psychology in Negro Institutions

Name of Course	Times Offered
Educational Psychology	41
General Psychology	40
Child Psychology	30
Social Psychology	22
Adolescent Psychology	22
Abnormal Psychology	14
Experimental Psychology	7
Statistical Methods	5
Applied Psychology	4
Psychology of Religion	4
Psychological Test	3
Differential Psychology	3
Race Psychology	2
Genetic Psychology	2
Business Psychology	2
Psychology of Learning	2
Recent Schools of Psychology	2
Clinical Psychology	2
Elementary Psychology for Nurses	1
Medical Psychology	1
Legal Psychology	1
Psychological and Psychiatric Social Work	1
Psychology of Personal Adjustment	1
Psychology of Selling and Adjusting	1
Mental Psychology	1
Human Behavior	1
Nations Psychology	1
Comparative Psychology	1

Laboratory Equipment for Psychology

Psychology is not only a science, but a laboratory science. Adequate laboratory facilities, therefore, are essential for effective work in Psychology. It is necessary that the student not only be taught what is known in psychological science (factual content as in the typical beginning course), but also how what is known is discovered (experimental methods and laboratory).

Table 3 gives the equipment in laboratory apparatus and supplies.

In the 47 institutions there were varying numbers of rooms set aside for laboratory work. The following table (Table 4) will show the number

TABLE 3

Value of Psychological Laboratory Apparatus and Supplies

Size of Institution	No. of Institutions	Median Value of Apparatus	Range in Value of Apparatus
Over–599	2	$4,000	$3,000–$5,000
400–599	4	94	50– 200
300–399	4	378	60– 700
200–299	2	225	200– 250
100–199	1	250	
Under–100	1	56	
All Institutions	14	$ 834	$ 50–$5,000

of rooms set aside and, also, the number of institutions in which these rooms are found.

Thirteen institutions, or 28 per cent, report that a dark room is available in connection with their laboratory work.

TABLE 4

Rooms Set Aside for Laboratory Work

No. of Rooms	No. of Institutions
0	29
1	14
2	2
3	1
4	0
5	1
Total	47

Teaching Personnel in Psychology

The study of the teaching personnel is a very difficult topic. We asked in detail the preparation both in terms of degrees and the particular major for each degree and, also, the people with whom the major work was done. The answers were definite in a sufficient number of instances to permit the following tabulations (Table 5).

This table shows that only 27, or 32.6 per cent, of the instructors who teach the first year's course in psychology, educational psychology and other branches of psychology in Negro institutions, have had the training represented by major work in psychology. Two, or .07 per cent, of these hold the bachelor's degree, eighteen, or 66 per cent, the master's, and seven (three of which are white), or 30 per cent the doctor's.

TABLE 5

Major Fields of Graduate and Undergraduate Training and the Highest Degree Held by Negro Instructors in Psychology

Major Field of Training	No. of Instructors	Ph.D. Ed.D.	M.A. M.S.	B.A. B.S. Ph.B.	B.D.
Psychology	20	5*	13	2	
Ed. Psychology	7	2	5		
Education	38	5	28	5	
Philosophy	5	2	2		1
Sociology 7 Theology 1 Relig. Ed. 1 Spanish 1	10	2	8		
Dept. Omitted	2		2		
Degree Omitted	6				
Totals	88	16	58	7	1
Trained in approved fields	27	7	18	2	
Per cent approved	(27/88) 32.6				

* Three of these are white.

Our data do not reveal the number of years of graduate training. It is quite possible that many of these instructors have had the training equivalent of a doctor's degree.

Research in Psychology

Research in Psychology should be carried on by scientists regardless of race and relative to any psychological problem; but whereas such problems in the field of Negro collegiate education are many and a fertile, almost unexplored, field is offered the researcher, few investigations are being carried on by Negro psychologists. Then, again, there is the field of Racial Psychology which bristles with problems.

Only 8 instructors (three of which are white) out of the 88 report significant published research in psychology during the past five years. This means that the burden of research is carried by a small per cent of the Negroes trained to carry on systematic studies.

SUMMARY AND CONCLUSIONS

The following statements summarize and conclude the most significant findings of the study:

1. Only 14, or 30 per cent, of the 47 institutions report departments of psychology. The 33 institutions which do not have department facilities combine psychology with the following departments: education, 31; philosophy, 7; and sociology, 5.

Four of the institutions reporting offer the major in psychology. The remaining 43 do not offer the major either because of an inadequate number of courses, or inadequate preparation of instructors, or lack of an appreciation of the importance of psychology in the program of study. This means, of course, that *there are only 4 Negro institutions in the country where one can get an undergraduate major in psychology.*

2. Current practice in the Negro institutions studied still favors a one semester beginning course, although the American Psychological Association recommends six semester hours or a full year course before electives are permitted in advance fields. Our replies show an appreciation on the part of the institutions of the importance of integrating the experimental approach with the first course taken by the student; but, owing to inadequate equipment in many institutions, effective work is almost impossible. Twenty-seven of our respondents said that they would give laboratory work with the first course if facilities permitted, but only one institution reported a definite laboratory course as part of the beginning work.

3. From a study of the courses offered, it appears that most of them are selected on the basis of their usefulness to students of education. Altogether 28 courses were named in the reports. Among those mentioned fourteen times or over and the number of times each was mentioned, were educational psychology, 41; general psychology, 40; child psychology, 30; social psychology, 22; adolescent psychology, 22; and abnormal psychology, 14.

The conclusion that psychology is usually thought of in terms of its application to education seems to be brought out again when it is recalled that education was the most popular department with which to combine psychology.

Too many of the courses offered seem to be of an applied nature, and not a sufficient number are in pure or theoretical psychology. From a study of courses in an undergraduate curriculum thus arranged, one scarcely can expect the major student to leave the institution with a cogent idea of fundamental principles of human activity.

Only two institutions offer a course in Race Psychology, and not one offers a course having the distinct title of "The Psychology of the Negro."

4. Negro institutions lack adequate laboratory facilities, and most of them do not have even the very simple and inexpensive instruments.

5. The library facilities (also the laboratory) are related to the work the institution is offering; an institution with a small range of courses

might be better equipped with a few books and periodicals than another which attempted to teach a wide range of courses with the same material. In this connection, therefore, we shall merely summarize our results and offer some suggestions for checking library equipment.

The median annual appropriation for books and periodicals in 13 institutions was $138 with a range in appropriation of $25 to $500.

The median number of volumes in psychology in 32 institutions was 269. The number of volumes ranged from 32 to 1,500. In selecting books for their libraries, the institutions might consider the list of books on psychology suggested by the American Library Association and, also, the Carnegie Corporation Advisory Group list.[3] A total of twenty-six periodicals on psychology are in the libraries of Negro institutions. Twelve, or 26 per cent, of the institutions report that they keep the files of the journals in bound form.

6. Only 27, or 32.6 per cent, of the 88 instructors who teach the first year's course in psychology, educational psychology and other branches of psychology, have had the training represented by major work in psychology. Two, or .07 per cent, of these hold the bachelor's degree; eighteen, or 66 per cent, the master's; and seven (three of which are white), or 30 per cent, the doctor's.

The attention of Negro administrative officers is called to the fact that there are different types of preparation for instructors in psychology, even among people who hold the same academic degrees. The high standard of training required of teachers in education, chemistry, history, et cetera, should not be ignored in selecting teachers of psychology.

7. Only 8 instructors (three of which are white) reported significant published research in psychology during the past five years. This means that the burden of research is carried on by only 5 Negroes trained to carry on systematic studies. We feel that Negroes should be as active as others in advancing the science of psychology; and when one recalls that the vast majority of studies in Race Differences and Racial Psychology (just to mention two fields) have been made by members of the other race, one wonders what Negro psychologists have been and are doing besides teaching.

[3] For detailed information see *Books and Pamphlets on Library Work* (1937), esp. pp. 4 and 5, American Library Association, 520 N. Michigan Avenue, Chicago, Illinois.

45a   Psychology as a Study and as a Profession

HERMAN G. CANADY, PH.D.
Professor Emeritus of Psychology
West Virginia State College

Although definitions of psychology have varied considerably over the years as a result of the theoretical orientations of particular "schools," most contemporary psychologists would agree on a definition that characterizes psychology as a science of the behavior of organisms. It had its beginnings in primitive reflection, it grew under the fostering solicitude of philosophy, and made its debut as a science in connection with developments in physics, physiology, and medicine. Today psychology, like many other sciences no longer relegated to classroom and laboratory, plays an important part in many phases of society. Examples of its practical value are evident in its application to vocational guidance, personnel administration, medicine, business, industry and education.

I believe that most of the important problems of war and peace, exploitation and brotherhood, hatred and love, sickness and health, understanding and misunderstanding, and the happiness and unhappiness of mankind will yield only to a better understanding of human behavior. For example, let us reflect on what psychologists have done in the past to improve race relations and inter-cultural education.

When I entered the field of psychology forty-five years ago, the theory of the inborn inferiority of the American Negro was dominant, and the prevailing opinion was that no amount of training or social opportunity would enable Black people to do noble deeds and obtain a place of usefulness and honor among men. Moreover, the ruling class acted on these beliefs and denied Negroes many of those opportunities, privileges, and responsibilities accorded other citizens. About this time, however, the heavily prejudiced position of science on the race problem was being undermined by the change toward environmentalism in the behavioral sciences of anthropology, sociology and psychology. Increasingly, we began to gain insights into the social dependency of behavior; to establish

SOURCE. Postscript to "Psychology in Negro Institutions" reprinted with permission of the author.

evidence that social influences enter every action of the individual, even actions which seem to have nothing to do with society; and, finally, to demonstrate the fundamental, direct, and widespread role of social and cultural effects on personality.

I am happy to have contributed to this recent trend in scientific thought. Although my research was concerned with social action directed toward the problem of being Black, it does not differ essentially from research of other American psychologists, as we were all interested in behavior and its determinants, regardless of race, color, or creed. I hope that in the future persons can and will work in this field as psychologists without having such descriptions as Black placed before their titles. My present thought is that I am a *Psychologist* who by accident of birth happens to be Black. There are about 25,000 psychologists in the American Psychological Association, and the number is rapidly increasing. Nearly half of these teach and do research in colleges and universities. Others are employed in various areas of practical application of their science while a few devote all of their time to research. But all psychologists should be, and many are concerned with the development of the understanding of behavior so that the Civil Rights Movement will succeed because mankind is more aware and therefore more humane.

46 The Negro Patient and Professional Worker in the State-Supported Southern Mental Hospitals

JAMES F. CONDELL
Department of Psychology, Florida A. & M. University

This is an extremely interesting paper in that it takes a most thoughtful look at both Negro professionals and patients in Southern mental hospitals prior to 1950. The paper needs careful study since it is essentially a series of tables, and among its possible conclusions simply shows the extent to which the South had failed to come to grips with the mental health needs of Blacks. In this regard, see especially the footnotes to Table 1 because they are somewhat unbelievable. The significance of the paper's being included here lies in the fact that both Harleston (1968, this volume) and Wispe and his associates (1969, this volume) report very little improvement in the recruitment and development of Black persons for American psychology.

There is currently an increasing awareness of the role of psychology in the Southern states. A great part of this concern is and should be of the role of the Negro patient and professional in the area of psychology due to the number of Negroes living in the South. It is to be expected that the Southern Negroes represent an equal portion of the mentally ill as in other streams of life in the South.

This study is designed to investigate the proportionate status of Negroes as both patients and professional workers in the state supported mental hospitals in the seventeen Southern states which practice legal segregation. With the present increased emphasis on all phases of mental health, much effort is being placed on increasing facilities and adding personnel in the various mental health programs. It is the pattern in Southern prac-

SOURCE. Reprinted from the *Journal of Negro Education*, 1954, **23**, 193–196 with permission of the author and the publisher.

tices to provide "separate but equal facilities." With this approach then, it is of interest to know what equality of opportunity exists in the employment of the Negro professional workers in proportion to the number of patients in the state tax supported hospitals for the mentally ill.

The data of this study were obtained by sending a letter and questionnaire to the superintendent of the mental hospitals in the Southern states. A follow-up questionnaire was sent to the hospitals which failed to answer the first request. Complete returns were received from thirteen states. Only one hospital of the three in the state of Tennessee returned the completed questionnaire. West Virginia, Georgia and Delaware did not return their questionnaires. For those states which failed to return the questionnaire, the statistics for the total population of the mental hospitals were obtained from a Public Health Service Report.[1] The questionnaire asked for data on the total number of patients in state-supported mental institutions, and the total number of Negroes in state-supported mental institutions, and the total number of Negro physicians including psychiatrists, psychiatric nurses, psychiatric social workers and clinical psychologists. Table 2 is included to show the percentage of nonwhites, who in the South are predominantly Negroes, in the total population.

In Table 1 can be seen the total number of patients in the South in mental hospitals, the white population, the Negro population, and the percentage of Negroes in the hospitals. Florida, Kentucky, Maryland, Mississippi and Virginia have a greater number of Negroes in their mental hospitals than they are in proportion to the general population. The remaining states reporting have a smaller number of Negroes in the mental hospitals than they have in proportion to the general population. Two states, Oklahoma and Missouri, have both small percentages of Negroes in the mental hospitals and the general population. The information in Table 1 may or may not be indicative of the true picture of the ratio of Negroes to whites in the mentally ill segment of our Southern population. "It has been said that it was the practice of Southern institutions to admit only the more severe Negro mental cases."[2] It is also believed that as yet, "The Negro community is not as aware as the white community of psychiatry and of the fact that emotional illness and behavior disorders can be alleviated . . . . If and when there is sufficient number of both Negro and white psychiatrists to cope with emotional illness in all its various manifestations, it will be necessary to educate the Negro concerning

[1] Federal Security Agency, *Patients in Mental Institutions,* 1949. Washington: Public Health Service Publication, No. 233, U. S. Government Printing Office, 1952.
[2] Ernest Y. Williams, and Claud P. Carmichael, "The Incidence of Mental Disease in the Negro," *Journal of Negro Education,* 18: 276–282, No. 3, Summer, 1949.

TABLE 1

A Comparison of Negro and White Mental Patients in Southern
State-Supported Mental Hospitals

States	Total	White	Negro	Per Cent Negroes
Alabama	9,098	6,665	2,443	27
Arkansas (1)	5,681	4,635	1,046	18
Delaware	1,263 (2)			
Florida (4)	9,401	7,093	2,308	25
Georgia	9,586			
Kentucky	9,040	7,873	1,167 (3)	13
Louisiana	9,930	7,338	2,592	26
Maryland	11,923	9,715	2,208	19
Mississippi (5)	4,760	2,210 (2)	2,550	53
Missouri	13,704	12,218	992	8
North Carolina	13,704	10,788	2,916	21
Oklahoma (6)	8,745	7,878	867	9
South Carolina	7,914	5,336	2,578	33
Tennessee (7)	6,451 (2)		(147)	
Texas (8)	25,964	23,770	2,194	8
Virginia	16,718	12,364	4,349	26
West Virginia (9)	4,503 (2)			
Total	167,882	117,878	28,210	24

(1) Arkansas has 17 Negro Psychiatric aids.
(2) Data are taken from—Patients in Mental Institutions, 1949, Fed. Sec. Agency,
      U. S. Public Health Service.
(3) Figures as of October 31, 1951.
(4) The State of Florida has 425 Negro workers in its mental institutions at non-
      professional levels.
(5) The State of Mississippi has never received an application from Negro psychi-
      atrists, physicians, or social workers. They have approximately 265 Negroes
      in the nursing service.
(6) Oklahoma has a Negro hospital.
(7) Tennessee has three state hospitals. Eastern State Hospital returned the only
      questionnaire.
(8) Texas has one Negro social worker—non-psychiatric.
(9) West Virginia has a Negro hospital. No response came from this state.

psychiatry. For the Negro, it seems frightening and smacks of trickery
on the part of the white doctor. It may seem like another device of the
white majority to deceive and keep the Negro in his place."[3]

[3] Helen V. McClean, "The Emotional Health of Negroes," *Journal of Negro
Education,* 18: 283–290, No. 3, Summer, 1949.

TABLE 2

The Number of Negroes in the General Population in
the Seventeen Southern States*

State	Total	Non-White	Per Cent Non-White
Alabama	3,061,743	982,243	32
Arkansas	1,909,511	428,003	22
Delaware	318,085	44,207	14
Florida	2,771,305	605,258	22
Georgia	3,444,578	1,064,005	31
Kentucky	2,944,806	202,876	7
Louisiana	2,683,516	886,968	33
Maryland	2,343,001	388,014	17
Mississippi	2,178,914	990,485	46
Missouri	3,954,653	299,066	8
North Carolina	4,061,929	1,078,814	27
Oklahoma	2,233,351	200,796	9
South Carolina	2,117,027	823,624	39
Tennessee	3,291,718	531,468	16
Texas	7,711,194	984,963	13
Virginia	3,318,680	737,038	22
West Virginia	2,005,552	115,268	6

* From the U. S. Census—1950.

In Table 3 is shown the number of Negro professional workers in the Southern mental hospitals. Three of the states have no Negroes in the professional category. Three of the states employ Negro physicians with a high of four in one of the three states. Seven of the states employ Negro psychiatric nurses with a range from one to eleven. Negro psychiatric social workers are found in three of the states. Only two states employ Negro clinical psychologists. In the fourteen states which responded to the questionnaire there is a total of fifty-four Negro physicians, nurses, social workers and psychologists working in the mental hospitals. Twenty-three of these are employed in one state.

One of the Southern states reports a non-discriminatory hiring policy. In the mental hospitals of this state, the Negro professional represents twenty-six per cent of the total professional group, yet, Negroes are just seventeen per cent of the total state population.

That there is a small number of Negro professionals in the field of mental health is generally known. It is significant, however, that some Southern states employ no Negro workers classified as professionals. One state institution reported that they have received no applications from Negro

TABLE 3

The Number of Negro and White Professionals Employed in
the Southern State-Supported Mental Hospitals

	Physicians		Graduate Nurses		Social Workers		Psychologists	
State	Total	Negro	Total	Negro	Total	Negro	Total	Negro
Alabama	12	0	9	0	1	0	0	0
Arkansas	23	0	19	1	4	0	1	0
Delaware	8	—	31	—	4	—	5	—
Florida	14	0	26	0	0	0	2	0
Georgia	22	—	40	—	0	—	0	—
Kentucky	28	1	12	0	6	0	0	0
Louisiana	15	0	17	0	6	0	1	0
Maryland	43	4	9	2	20	11	9	6
Mississippi	18	0	12	1	4	0	—	1
Missouri	22	0	31	0	7	0	5	0
North Carolina	36	0	48	2	6	0	4	0
Oklahoma	21	3	14	0	3	1	2	0
South Carolina	12	0	17	8	1	1	0	0
Tennessee	15	—	4	—	4	—	4	—
Texas	44	0	24	1	20	0	7	0
Virginia	21	0	40	11	5	0	4	0
West Virginia	18	0	2	0	5	0	2	0
Total	372	8	355	26	96	13	46	7

psychiatrists, physicians, or social workers. In another report it was stated that, "Many administrators seem to fear that the employment of Negro personnel will cause 'trouble,' in that some of their other personnel might leave."[4]

This study reveals that Negroes represent an equal proportion of the mental patients in the state-supported mental hospitals as they are represented in the population of the Southern states. Negroes are not employed in the mental hospitals of four Southern states and in some several categories in other Southern states. Only one state in the South employs Negroes in all four professional areas and in this state they are hired on a non-segregated basis. There is a definite need to alter the employment pattern in the state-supported mental hospitals to include Negro professional workers in all areas, especially in view of the segregated patterns that exist in the South.

[4] Rutherford B. Stevens, "Interracial Practices in Mental Hospitals," *Mental Hygiene*, 36: 56–65, No. 1, 1952.

47 The Negro Psychologist in America[1]

LAUREN WISPÉ
University of Oklahoma

JOSEPH AWKARD
Florida Agricultural and Mechanical University

MARVIN HOFFMAN
Field Foundation, New York City

PHILIP ASH
University of Illinois, Chicago Circle

LESLIE H. HICKS[2]
American Psychological Association

JANICE PORTER
Temple University Hospital

This paper reports a survey that was undertaken by the Committee on Equality of Opportunity in Psychology in order to clarify the role and significance of the Negro psychologist in America. The survey is so lengthy that no attempt will be made to review it here. However, some of the major conclusions are well worth restating, and are: (1) Negro psychologists are excluded from the mainstream of American psychology. (2) To be Black in America is a terrible handicap and to be a Black psychologist is only slightly better. (3) The American Psychological Association is ultimately responsible for the leadership that will eradicate this inequality.

SOURCE. Wispé, L., Ash, P., Awkard, J., Hicks, L., Hoffman, M., and Porter, Janice, "The Negro Psychologist in America," *American Psychologist*, 24, 1969, 2, 142–150. Copyright 1969 by the American Psychological Association and reproduced by permission.

[1] The authors acknowledge the contributions of Martin Deutsch and Thomas Pettigrew, who were members of the Committee when the survey was begun, and to Harley Preston, at that time APA Administrative Officer for Public Affairs. The Committee also wishes to thank Doris Chandler for work beyond the call and Angus Campbell for a critical reading of the preliminary report.

Reprints available from Wispé, Department of Psychology, University of Oklahoma, Norman, Oklahoma.

[2] Formerly at Howard University.

Little is known about the origins, education, and training of Negro psychologists. Even less is known about the discrimination they have faced in the course of their professional careers. To obtain this kind of information, which would be valuable in itself and could also serve as a basis for recommendation to the Board of Directors of the APA, the Committee on Equality of Opportunity in Psychology undertook to survey psychologists in America who are Negro.[3] The findings reported below are the results of this survey. Because of the difficulty in obtaining information about race and discrimination, these findings must be taken as the best possible tentative answers under the present conditions to very complex problems.

PROCEDURE

To obtain the names and addresses of Negro psychologists and graduate students currently working and studying in the United States, requests for this information were sent to 94 Negro colleges and universities, to the chairmen of 216 psychology departments with graduate training programs listed in the *American Psychologist* (Ross & Harmon, 1966), to the deans and chairmen of the 78 largest Colleges of Education listed in the *Educational Directory* (Office of Education, United States Department of Health, Education and Welfare, 1965), to the 50 State Psychological Associations, and to about 15 of the larger government departments and centers where psychologists were employed. A 6-page questionnaire containing items about family background, undergraduate and graduate education, occupational history, and present earnings was mailed to the 492 Negro psychologists whose names were obtained in this way. The questionnaire also contained items about ethnic factors which were professionally advantageous or disadvantageous to Negroes, and about ways the APA could help to counter professional discrimination.

The questionnaires, with a covering letter, were mailed July 1966. An unusually energetic telephone campaign, three follow-up letters, and

[3] The Committee on Equality of Opportunity in Psychology was established by the Board of Directors in 1963. The Board had received a proposal from Division 9 relative to the training and employment of Negroes in psychology. The Committee was charged with exploring the possible problems encountered in training and employment in psychology as consequence of race. (Proceedings of the Seventy-First Annual Business Meeting, August 30 and September 3, 1963. Reported in the *American Psychologist*, 1963, 18, 769.) The Committee is presently a standing committee under the Education and Training Board. The conclusions drawn in the paper are the sole responsibility of the authors, as are the analysis and interpretation of the data.

additional airmail-special questionnaires raised the response rate from 61% in January 1967 to 81% by July 1967.

A one-third sample of the 398 usable returns showed that 27% were members of APA. This appeared to compare unfavorably with the percentage of non-Negro psychologists who belong to the APA. Of the 94 nonrespondents, only 15% were listed in the 1967 *APA Directory*, so that nonrespondent bias was almost impossible to check. Their refusal to respond to the questionnaire, however, despite repeated personal and telephone contacts, suggested that they may have differed in critical ways from respondents.

RESULTS

Origins and Background

POPULATION COMPARISONS. As Table 1 clearly indicates, the distribution of Negro psychologists closely parallels the distribution of Negroes in the United States. Over half (52.8%) the American Negroes live in the Southeast and over half of the respondent Negro psychologists (51%) live in the Southeast. The distribution of APA members, however, differs significantly from the distribution of the total United States population; psychologists are overrepresented in the Northeast (36.1% to 24.5%) and underrepresented in the Southeast (15.4% to 23.7%). Even if allowance is made for the difference in dates of the various distributions, Table 1 shows clearly that Negro psychologists are distributed in a significantly different way from APA members.

AGE. The median age for male respondents was 38.8 years, and for female respondents, 38.1 years. Regional differences in age were slight.

PLACE OF BIRTH AND RESIDENCE. Almost 60% of the Negro psychologists were born in the Southeast, and two thirds of that group still live there. Table 2 shows, however, that there has been a significant net migration out of the Southeast. Of all respondents born in the Southeast, one third moved out; while of all those now living there, slightly under one fourth are in-migrants. The major movement, similar to the national trend, has been to the Western States, with an in-migration that resulted in a net increase of 71%.

OCCUPATIONAL STATUS OF PARENTS. Table 3 indicates that both the fathers and mothers of Negro respondent psychologists were, on the average, of higher occupational status than the general 1965 Negro population. Only 34.2% of the fathers and 9.4% of the mothers of respondents were manual laborers, compared with population estimates of 74.5% and 34.7%, respectively. More of the fathers of respondents were in the

TABLE 1

Percentage of Negro–White Population and Responding Negro and APA Psychologists Compared by United States Regions

Region	Total United States Population[a]	Total Negro United States Population[b]	Total APA Psychologists[c]	Responding Negro Psychologists[d]
West	22.3	12.9	24.0	13.3
Midwest	28.3	18.3	24.4	17.0
Southeast	23.7	52.8	15.4	51.0
Northeast	24.5	16.0	36.1	14.8
Outside USA	1.3	—	0.1	1.7
National Register	—	—	—	2.0

[a] $N = 185,890$. United States Bureau of the Census. *Statistical abstract of the United States, 1967.* (88th edition) Washington, D. C., 1967. Table No. 10, p. 12. (In thousands.)

[b] $N = 18,872$. United States Bureau of the Census. *Statistical abstract of the United States, 1967.* (88th edition) Washington, D. C., 1967. Table No. 27, p. 29. (In thousands.)

[c] $N = 24,604$. In 1966 Count, United States members only (includes Puerto Rico).

[d] $N = 398$.

TABLE 2

Migration Patterns of Responding Negro Psychologists in Percentages

	Residence						
Birthplace	West ($N = 53$)	Midwest ($N = 68$)	Southeast ($N = 203$)	Northeast ($N = 59$)	Outside United States ($N = 7$)	National Register ($N = 8$)	Total %
West	4.0	1.0	1.5	1.0	—	.3	7.8
Midwest	3.0	7.0	5.5	2.0	.3	.3	18.1
Southeast	4.8	8.0	39.2	4.8	—	1.5	58.3
Northeast	1.5	1.0	4.0	6.3	—	—	12.8
Outside USA	—	—	.5	.8	1.5	—	2.8
National Register	—	—	.3	—	—	—	.3
Total %	13.3	17.0	51.0	14.9	1.8	2.1	
Net change	+22	−4	−29	+ 8	− 4	—	
% change[a]	+71.0	−5.6	−12.4	+15.7	−36.4	—	

[a] Birthplace/migrant = % change.

TABLE 3

Distribution of Parents' Occupations Compared with 1965 Distribution
of United States Negro Population in Percentages

Occupation	Respondent's Father	Negro Men	Respondent's Mother	Negro Women
Housewife	—	—	57.6	39.7
Manual labor	34.2	74.5	9.4	34.7
Skilled labor	25.6	10.7	4.9	0.3
Clerical and technical	6.5	6.7	6.6	6.0
Managerial and professional[a]	33.0	8.2	21.4	5.0
Other[b]	—	—	—	14.3
Total %	99.3	100.1	99.9	100.0

[a] Includes self-employed.

[b] In school, etc.

managerial and professional category, and more of the mothers kept house
than Negroes in the general population.

Education

REGIONAL DIFFERENCES. Table 4 shows the percentage of bachelor's,
master's, and doctor's degrees in psychology earned by Negro psychologists from schools in different regions of the United States. In the last
column of Table 4 is the distribution of doctoral degrees in psychology
for all graduates during the years 1960–1966 (National Science Foundation, 1967b). Most Negro psychologists received their bachelor's degree
in the region of their birth. This explains the large proportion (62%) of

TABLE 4

Geographic Distribution by Educational Degrees of Respondent Negro
Psychologists and All 1960–65 Doctorates in Psychology

Region of Degree Granting School	BA ($N = 59$)	MA ($N = 173$)	PhD ($N = 166$)	All 1960–66 PhDs ($N = 6,443$)
Southeast	62%	32%	11%	13%
Northeast	12%	28%	33%	31%
Midwest	19%	31%	42%	30%
West	7%	9%	14%	26%
Total N	59	173	166	—
Total %	14.8%	43.5%	41.7%	100%

Note.—National Science Foundation (1967b).

bachelor's degrees in the Southeast. Master's degrees were more equally distributed among geographic regions, reflecting the geographic differences in availability of the bachelor's and master's degrees. The geographic distribution of doctoral degrees for Negroes showed the closest similarity to that of the total group of psychologists who received PhD degrees between 1960–1966. Nevertheless, proportionately more of the Negro psychologists received doctorates in the Midwest and proportionately fewer in the West. Although the percentage of Negro doctorates from the Southeast is not different from the percentages of all 1960–1966 doctorates in psychology (11% versus 13%), because of the large percentage (62%) of Negro bachelor's degrees from the Southeast, one would have expected a much larger proportion of Negro PhDs from this region. This low figure for the Southeast is again a product of a history of segregated colleges and the absence of a single Negro university which offered the PhD in psychology.

REGION, RACE, AND NEGRO COLLEGES. Since most of the Negro colleges are located in the South, the question arises whether the reason so few Negroes pursue the PhD in psychology is regional or educational. To try to answer this question a group of 28 non-Negro colleges were matched as well as possible with 28 Negro colleges on public-private control, geographic region, number of faculty and students, operating income, and value of buildings. According to available data from the 28 Negro colleges (National Science Foundation, 1967b), 76 graduates received their doctorates in psychology during the period 1920–1966. The NSF data show that during the same period the matched non-Negro colleges produced 167 bachelors who later obtained the PhD degree in psychology. Thus when one controls such important factors as geographic region, student-faculty ratio, etc., it may be seen that students from white institutions pursue the PhD in psychology more frequently than do students from Negro colleges. Although the issue is a complex one, this analysis suggested that factors inherent in Negro colleges militated against the Negro students' pursuit of the PhD in psychology.

Table 5 presents the number and percentage of responding Negro psychologists who received their bachelor's degrees from Negro and non-Negro colleges and universities. This table shows that a majority (57.1%) of the respondents received their undergraduate training at Negro colleges and universities, and among respondents over 40 years old this proportion was much higher. If, for whatever reason, graduates of Negro colleges have not pursued the doctorate in psychology, the fact that Negroes are now increasingly attending non-Negro schools could be viewed as favorable for psychology.

DOCTORAL INSTITUTIONS. Table 6 presents the 25 institutions granting

TABLE 5

Respondents' Ages and Bachelor's Degrees Classified by Type of Institution

Age	% Negro Colleges/Universities	% Non-Negro Colleges/Universities	Total %
60 and older	71.4	28.6	100.0
50–59	66.7	33.3	100.0
40–49	71.1	28.9	100.0
30–39	49.6	50.4	100.0
20–29	47.4	52.6	100.0
National Register	14.3	85.7	100.0
Total	57.1	42.9	100.0

the largest number of doctorates in psychology, 1920–1966 (National Science Foundation, 1967b), and the number of Negro doctorates granted by these schools to the respondents in the present study. It can be seen that several Midwestern schools ranking quite low in the total number of doctorates granted have produced disproportionately more Negro doctorates. Moreover, as Table 7 shows, if the rated quality of psychology departments (Cartter, 1966) is related to total doctorates produced and to Negro doctorate production, it is clear that few Negro PhDs in psychology have come from the 10 presently best-rated psychology departments. The top 10 departments produced 24% of the total doctorates in psychology between 1920 and 1966, but only .5% of the total Negro doctorates in psychology. Closer inspection of Table 7 shows, moreover, that seven of the eight Negro doctorates from these 10 leading departments were produced by three Midwestern schools. Those Ivy League schools among the 10 leading departments produced none of the Negro doctorates in the present study. It is doubtful that these trends would be much affected even if all Negro psychologists in the United States were included.

Salary

Median annual salaries provided one of the few measures comparing Negro and non-Negro psychologists on the same dimension. The median annual salaries of the responding Negro psychologists, Negro psychologists who were included in the National Register, and all National Register respondents were used for this purpose. The National Register data were obtained in March 1966 by the APA, in cooperation with NSF's continuing study of the nation's scientific manpower. The results were based on 19,027 individuals who responded to the National Register form and were classified as psychologists. Of the National Register respondents, 64% were APA members, as contrasted with an estimated 27% of the present sample; 66% had the doctorate, as contrasted with 41% in the present study; 78% were male, as compared with 72%; and the median age was 41 years, as compared with 38 years for the present group. The criteria for inclusion in the National Register study, as established by the APA, would probably not include respondents with bachelor's degrees comparable to the respondents in the present study. The studies, there-

TABLE 6

Negro and Non-Negro Psychology Doctorates Granted by the 25 Universities Producing the Largest Number of Doctorates in Psychology, 1920–1966

Universities	Total No. Psychology PhDs 1920–1966	No. Negro PhDs among Respondents
New York	804	13
Columbia	770	10
Chicago	680	9
Michigan	651	3
Ohio State	647	4
Minnesota	615	3
Iowa	583	0
Purdue	533	1
Berkeley	405	1
Harvard	383	0
UCLA	307	0
Illinois	302	0
Yale	293	0
Stanford	292	0
Texas	285	3
Cornell	261	0
Penn State	257	4
Northwestern	246	6
Southern California	245	2
Michigan State	240	6
Pittsburgh	234	1
Western Reserve	229	4
Indiana	223	14
Boston	217	4
Pennsylvania	212	5
Total	9,914	93

Note.—National Science Foundation (1967a).

TABLE 7

Negro Doctorates in Psychology from Leading Psychology Departments

Rank[a]	Universities	Total Psychology PhDs 1920–1966[b]	No. Negro PhDs among Respondents
1	Harvard	383	0
2	Stanford	292	0
3	Michigan	651	3
4	Berkeley	405	1
5	Yale	293	0
6	Illinois	302	0
7	Minnesota	615	3
8	Wisconsin	206	1
9	Brown	87	0
10	Iowa	533	0
Total		3,767	8

[a] Carter (1966).

[b] National Science Foundation (1967a).

fore, are comparable for the PhDs but not the BAs, although information for both degrees is presented in Table 8. Moreover, not all of the respondents in either study provided salary information, and it is impossible to know the effects of these selective omissions. In order to answer questions arising out of possible differences in samples and procedures, therefore, a subsample of Negro respondents to the National Register was drawn.[4] This subsample included 87 psychologists who responded to both studies, and 6 psychologists who responded to the National Register but not to the present study. The National Register data provide about as representative a basis for salary comparison as is available, but interpretations must be made with caution because, in one case, the comparisons are being made between two different studies and, in the other case, the subsample size is very small. Nevertheless, certain differences emerged with sufficient consistency to warrant serious consideration.

Table 8 gives the characteristics on which the three samples were compared. For the Equal Opportunities questionnaire, 92% of the respondents provided salary information. The median salary for these Negro psychologists was $7,775.00. This is considerably less than the median salary for all psychologists responding to the National Register, but this difference must not be taken literally because of the larger number of

[4] The authors wish to thank Alan Boneau (1968) for his cooperation in obtaining and analyzing these data.

younger respondents with only bachelor degrees in the present study. The median salary for Negro psychologists in the National Register sample was $11,500.00, which is the same as the median salary for all respondents to the National Register. In general, for Negro as well as for non-Negro psychologists, men earn more than women, older psychologists earn more than younger psychologists, psychologists with the PhD earn

TABLE 8

Median Annual Salary of Responding Negro Psychologists and Negro and Non-Negro Psychologists in the 1966 National Register (NR)

Characteristics	Negro Psychologists[a]	Negro Psychologists in NR[b]	All Psychologists in NR[c]	% Differences Negro and NR Psychologists
Total	7,775 (365)	11,500 (89)	11,500 (19,027)	−32
Sex				
Male	8,425 (264)		12,000	−19
Female	6,200 (101)		10,000	−26
Age				
60–64	13,125 (15)	11,800 (7)	12,700	+3
55–59	12,475 (25)	13,300 (10)	12,600	−1
50–54	11,250 (30)	12,500 (17)	13,000	−14
45–49	12,150 (52)	11,200 (16)	13,000	−7
40–44	10,475 (65)	10,200 (17)	12,400	−16
35–39	10,500 (68)	10,400 (15)	11,400	−8
30–34	8,495 (69)	10,000 (8)	9,900	−14
25–29	6,075 (49)		8,300	−27
Highest degree				
PhD	12,625 (166)	12,100 (60)	12,100	+4
MA	8,275 (173)	9,700 (93)	9,800	−16
Type of employer				
College or university (calendar year)	10,325 (233)	12,000 (39)	12,000	−14
Federal Government	12,850 (52)	12,700 (12)	13,400	−4
State and local government	8,600 (29)	11,800 (11)	10,400	−17
Industry and business	8,750 (10)	—	15,100	−42
Academic rank				
Professor	12,225 (56)	13,400 (20)	15,600	−22
Associate professor	10,000 (18)	11,100 (2)	12,500	−20
Assistant professor	9,750 (31)	10,200 (10)	10,600	−8
Instructor	8,225 (21)	10,900 (4)	8,900	−8

Note.—Number in parentheses are Ns for that median.

[a] $N = 398$.

[b] $N = 93$.

[c] $N = 19,027$.

more than those with less than the doctorate, and psychologists employed with the Federal Government earn more than those employed by universities.

A closer perusal of Table 8 reveals a tendency for the disparity in median annual salaries between Negro and non-Negro psychologists to decrease with age, and this is true regardless of the type of employer. Although the younger age cohorts are not comparable between studies, for the ages over 40 there is a steady, if slight, improvement in Negro salaries so that by age 55 equity has nearly been achieved. Table 8 shows that Negro doctorates in psychology earned as much as non-Negro doctorates, although Negro MA psychologists in the present study earned less than the National Register MA respondents, and this was true regardless of type of employer.

The comparison of the salaries of psychologists in the present study and National Register psychologists working in universities presented an interesting apparent contradiction to the idea that the disparity between Negro and non-Negro salaries decreased with age. Table 8 shows that professors and associate professors earned about 20% less annually, while assistant professors and instructors earned about 8% less. Academic rank is, of course, related to age. Further analysis revealed, however, that a large proportion (71%) of these professors and associate professors were teaching in Negro colleges in the Southeast, 77% were over 40 years old, and 18% had only the master's degree. By contrast, most (58%) of the assistant professors and instructors were younger, already had their PhDs, and were teaching in colleges and universities in the West, Midwest, and Northeast. It should be remembered from the analysis of educational background that more of these younger respondents received their baccalaureate degrees from non-Negro colleges. These statistics serve not only to explicate this apparent contradiction, but also to illuminate the greatly disadvantaged teaching positions of many of the older Negro psychologists, and the sharp disparity between the median annual salaries of Negroes and non-Negroes at the higher academic ranks. On the other hand, it is worth noting that this situation may be changing for the assistant professors and instructors.

Discrimination

Nearly half of the respondents (48.2%) stated race had limited their professional opportunities. When regional differences were examined this pattern was the same whether the question was asked of those presently living in a region, or of those who had been born and presumably grew up within the area. Table 9 shows that more respondents in the West

TABLE 9

Opinions about Limitations of Professional Opportunities and Respondents' Present Residence

Present Residence	"Do you feel your professional opportunities have in any way been circumscribed... because of your race?"			
	% Yes (N = 192)	% No (N = 177)	% No Response (N = 29)	Total %
West (N = 53)	58.5	37.7	3.8	100
Midwest (N = 68)	44.1	47.1	8.8	100
Southeast (N = 203)	53.2	39.9	6.9	100
Northeast (N = 59)	33.9	54.2	11.9	100
Outside USA (N = 7)	.0	100.0	.0	100
Region unknown (N = 8)	37.5	63.5	.0	100
% total (N = 398)	48.2	44.5	7.3	—

(58.5%) than in any other region, including the Southeast (53.2%), reported that race had limited their opportunities.

One hypothesis to account for these regional differences in reported racial discrimination is that this discrepancy reflected not an actual difference in experience as much as a difference in expectation, and a greater candor about the disadvantages of being black. Unimpeded by those employment barriers which traditionally exist in the South, western Negroes felt free to compete in a wider job market where race supposedly would less often bar them from obtaining a job. Given these expectations, Negroes living in the West paradoxically encountered more discrimination

TABLE 10

Kinds of Professional Restrictions Reported and Respondents' Region of Birth

Region of Birth	Kinds of Professional Restrictions					
	% Employment	% Training	% Negative Self-Image	% Professional Discrimination	% Other	Total
West (N = 18)	27.8	27.8	27.8	16.7	0	100.1
Midwest (N = 30)	60.0	10.0	10.0	3.3	16.7	100.0
Southeast (N = 111)	53.2	12.6	14.4	13.5	6.3	100.0
Northeast (N = 16)	50.0	0	6.3	12.5	31.3	100.1
% total (N = 175)	51.1	12.5	14.2	11.9	10.2	

than they were prepared for, and proved more sensitive to the handicap of being Negro than those respondents residing in the South.

Table 11 shows that fewer young Negroes reported racial barriers than did older ones. Whether this finding is to be interpreted as a relaxing of racial barriers or as a function of the youthfulness of the group, many of whom have not yet been exposed to those employment and professional situations where they might find race a handicap, is a moot question. That so large a percentage within this age group gave no response to this item (three times as many as in the preceding age groups did not answer this item) may reflect the group's awareness of its lack of experience.

One interesting sex difference ought to be noted. Although the number of respondents in each age cohort was not large, Table 11 shows that fewer younger women respondents reported restrictions on their professional opportunities than did men in their own age group, older men, or older women. For example, 22 of the 31 women aged 21–30 (71%) said their opportunities had not been circumscribed by race, while only 28 of the 64 men (43.8%) in the same age cohort would agree. Moreover, there was an interesting parallel between age and percentage of women respondents reporting circumscribed job opportunities; the younger women consistently reported fewer professional restrictions. This was not true for the male respondents. These findings may suggest the greater acceptability of Negro females to the culture. If this interpretation is valid, then it would appear that it is the younger Negro woman psychologist more than the Negro male psychologist who has benefited from the lowering of racial barriers.

Further analysis of these data showed that more older psychologists, with PhDs and higher incomes, reported that race had been a limiting factor in their careers. This finding suggested that reports of circumscribed professional opportunities were not the rationalizations of the less successful among the respondents. These data are harder to interpret without comparable reports from non-Negro psychologists. It may be that there is less "room at the top" for anybody, Negro or white; or it may mean that the higher one moves in the professional hierarchy, the more race becomes a limiting factor. Whatever the interpretation, these data were doubly interesting because the comparison of median annual salaries suggested that these were the psychologists who, despite their perception of racial barriers, were doing as well financially as their non-Negro peers.

DISCUSSION

The Committee was not unaware that of all possible approaches the questionnaire was among the most likely to underestimate the depth of

TABLE 11

Opinions about Limitations of Professional Opportunities and Respondents' Age and Sex

"Do you feel your professional opportunities have in any way been circumscribed . . . because of your race?"

Respon-dent Age	N (N = 398)			% Yes (N = 192)			% No (N = 177)			% No Answer (N = 29)			Total %		
	M	F	T	M	F	T	M	F	T	M	F	T	M	F	T
51-74	45	18	63	64.4	61.1	63.5	28.9	33.3	30.2	6.7	5.6	6.3	100	100	100
41-50	76	26	102	48.7	61.5	52.0	44.7	38.5	43.1	6.6	—	4.9	100	100	100
31-40	101	37	138	47.5	56.8	50.0	48.5	40.5	46.4	4.0	2.7	3.6	100	100	100
21-30	64	31	95	37.5	19.4	31.6	43.8	71.0	52.6	18.8	9.7	15.8	100.1[a]	100.1[a]	100

Note.—Abbreviations: M = male; F = female; T = total.
[a] Net equal to M% and F% because of rounding.

feelings of many, if not most, of the respondents. The unusual effort the Committee expended to raise the response rate to an acceptable 81% indirectly reflected the amount of resistance many of the respondents felt, and some expressed. Many of the nonrespondents, for example, wrote long letters, but refused to return a completed questionnaire! Many felt it was unutterably naive to ask if race had limited their opportunities. Of course it had. Others, after long-distance calls, agreed reluctantly to complete the questionnaire, but expressed doubts about its efficaciousness. The intensity of the frustrations and resentments of both the respondents and the nonrespondents cannot be quantified, but these facts must be kept in mind as we turn now to what we believe are the main implications of this study.

Negro Psychologists Are Excluded from the Mainstream of American Psychology

For the most part, the Negro has received his early training in Negro schools. He moved outside the Negro institution to get an MA and PhD, since no Negro schools granted the higher degree in psychology. Having obtained a PhD, he then usually returned to the Negro college to work, if pursuing an academic career. Of all respondents employed by colleges or universities, for example, 154 worked in Negro institutions, 46 in white.

A sense of inadequacy and fear has worked hand in glove with actual discrimination to insure the isolation of most black psychologists. As one respondent put it, "Recognizing the limitations of a segregated society, I protected my ego by enrolling in predominantly Negro institutions and by seeking employment only in Negro institutions." We are not here taking a stand on the Negro college or its future. Our point is that Negro schools are by and large divorced from the mainstream of psychology. As many respondents stated, facilities, research monies, and professional contacts are almost nonexistent in the Negro institution.

The isolation of Negro psychologists is further revealed by the finding that although 85% of the sample had obtained either the doctorate or master's degree only an estimated 27% of them were members of APA. A clue to the reason for this low percentage is provided by the respondent who wrote, "I have never been active in the APA, since I have always felt it was part of the white academic club. Besides, the ghetto colleges don't know what it [APA] means, and usually don't even know what psychology means." It is not so much to actual instances of discrimination that we point, depressing as these are to read, but rather to the fact that most black psychologists feel themselves, and until recently were, alienated from American psychology because of the totality of what it means to be black.

To Be Black in America Is a Terrible Handicap, and To Be a Black Psychologist Is Not Much Better

It was at least discomforting to learn that nearly half the respondents felt race had limited their professional opportunities in psychology. It was even more devastating to recognize that this percentage is probably an underestimation of the true figure. Even respondents who said their own experiences had been good, often added, as in the quotation above, that they had deliberately restricted their lives to avoid the possibility of rejection. Social as well as professional factors were expressed. Many respondents feared segregated housing were they to teach in a predominantly white college; many wondered whether their families would find friends, and how hard they would have to work to prove themselves equal. The inescapable conclusion to be drawn from this study, therefore, is that being a Negro psychologist may reduce the handicap of being black, but it does not remove it.

The Responsibility of APA for Affirmative Action

Many respondents suggested that the APA first put its own house in order. Respondents noted the absence of Negroes holding APA office and presenting papers at conventions. One respondent said, "Negroes play a relatively minor role in its [APA] organization and functions to the point that only a few . . . apply for offices. . . ."

The question, "How can the APA correct professional discrimination?" was not answered by 58% of the respondents. Moreover, there were no significant age or sex relationships to this failure to respond. In light of the many comments like the one above, this high percentage of no answers could be interpreted as a lack of faith in the APA's willingness or ability to take corrective action. Of those respondents who indicated ways in which the APA might help, over half suggested that the APA enforce nondiscrimination in employment and training, refuse to list such openings in APA employment literature, refuse to grant advertising space to those who would not comply with a nondiscriminatory policy, etc. Such policies could also be adopted for internship programs in clinical psychology.

This report cannot conclude without addressing itself most strongly to the issue of making more flexible the opportunities for Negro graduates to enter psychology. As one respondent wrote, "The real problem is, as I see it, making opportunities for quality education available. We are still guilty of a serious failure to develop and nurture the talents of a sizable group of promising but disadvantaged youngsters who are Negro." This could be the most exciting and rewarding undertaking of all.

References

Boneau, A. Psychology's manpower: Report on the 1966 National Register of scientific and technical personnel. *American Psychologist,* 1968, **23**, 325–334.

Cartter, A. M. *An assessment of quality in graduate education.* Washington, D. C.: American Council on Education, 1966.

National Science Foundation. *American science manpower 1966.* Report No. 68–7. Washington, D. C.: Author, 1967. (a)

National Science Foundation. *Doctorate recipients from United States universities 1958–1966.* Publication No. 1489. Washington, D. C.: Author, 1967. (b)

Office of Education, United States Department of Health, Education and Welfare. *Educational Directory, 1964–1965, Higher education.* Washington, D. C.: United States Government Printing Office, Document No. FS 5.25: 964–65/Part III, 1965.

Ross, S., and Harmon, J. J. Educational facilities and financial assistance for graduate students in psychology: 1966–67. *American Psychologist,* 1966, **21**, 52–77.

48 *The Role of the Behavioral Scientist in the Civil Rights Movement*[1]

MARTIN LUTHER KING, JR.
Southern Christian Leadership Conference

I have chosen to conclude this collection with the speech by Dr. Martin Luther King, Jr. in order to end with the ringing and positive challenge to the Behavioral Sciences to assume their leadership position in furthering the Civil Rights Movement. Dr. King's comments are scholarly and direct, and they clearly outline the form that the contribution of the Behavioral Sciences should take in order to augment the growth of civil rights for Blacks. It is also hoped that the article will inspire many young Black Americans to devote their lives to a career as social or behavioral scientists capable of making significant contributions toward the goal of a meaningful and functional social equality. Blacks, as Black behavioral scientists, must assist American psychology toward a more realistic and mature understanding of the meaning and consequences of being Black so that together we can provide the intellectual and scholarly leadership so necessary to the ultimate success of the Civil Rights Movement.

It is always a very rich and rewarding experience when I can take a brief break from the day-to-day demands of our struggle for freedom and human dignity and discuss the issues involved in that struggle with concerned friends of good will all over this nation. It is particularly a great privilege to discuss these issues with members of the academic community, who are constantly writing about and dealing with the problems that we face and who have the tremendous responsibility of moulding the minds of young men and women all over our country.

SOURCE. King, Martin Luther, Jr., "The Role of the Behavioral Scientist in the Civil Rights Movement," *American Psychologist*, **23**, 1968, 180–186. Copyright 1968 by the American Psychological Association and reproduced by permission.

[1] Invited Distinguished Address presented to the meeting of the Society for the Psychological Study of Social Issues, American Psychological Association, Washington, D. C., September 1967. Martin Luther King, Jr., is President of the Southern Christian Leadership Conference, Atlanta, Georgia.

In the preface to their book, *Applied Sociology,* S. M. Miller and Alvin Gouldner (1965) state: "It is the historic mission of the social sciences to enable mankind to take possession of society." It follows that for Negroes who substantially are excluded from society this science is needed even more desperately than for any other group in the population.

For social scientists, the opportunity to serve in a life-giving purpose is a humanist challenge of rare distinction. Negroes too are eager for a rendezvous with truth and discovery. We are aware that social scientists, unlike some of their colleagues in the physical sciences, have been spared the grim feelings of guilt that attended the invention of nuclear weapons of destruction. Social scientists, in the main, are fortunate to be able to extirpate evil, not to invent it.

If the Negro needs social science for direction and for self-understanding, the white society is in even more urgent need. White America needs to understand that it is poisoned to its soul by racism and the understanding needs to be carefully documented and consequently more difficult to reject. The present crisis arises because, although it is historically imperative that our society take the next step to equality, we find ourselves psychologically and socially imprisoned. All too many white Americans are horrified not with conditions of Negro life but with the product of these conditions—the Negro himself.

White America is seeking to keep the walls of segregation substantially intact while the evolution of society and the Negro's desperation is causing them to crumble. The white majority, unprepared and unwilling to accept radical structural change, is resisting and producing chaos while complaining that if there were no chaos orderly change would come.

Negroes want the social scientist to address the white community and "tell it like it is." White America has an appalling lack of knowledge concerning the reality of Negro life. One reason some advances were made in the South during the past decade was the discovery by northern whites of the brutal facts of southern segregated life. It was the Negro who educated the nation by dramatizing the evils through nonviolent protest. The social scientist played little or no role in disclosing truth. The Negro action movement with raw courage did it virtually alone. When the majority of the country could not live with the extremes of brutality they witnessed, political remedies were enacted and customs were altered.

These partial advances were, however, limited principally to the South and progress did not automatically spread throughout the nation. There was also little depth to the changes. White America stopped murder, but that is not the same thing as ordaining brotherhood; nor is the ending of lynch rule the same thing as inaugurating justice.

After some years of Negro-white unity and partial successes, white

America shifted gears and went into reverse. Negroes, alive with hope and enthusiasm, ran into sharply stiffened white resistance at all levels and bitter tensions broke out in sporadic episodes of violence. New lines of hostility were drawn and the era of good feeling disappeared.

The decade of 1955 to 1965, with its constructive elements, misled us. Everyone, activists and social scientists, underestimated the amount of violence and rage Negroes were suppressing and the amount of bigotry the white majority was disguising.

Science should have been employed more fully to warn us that the Negro, after 350 years of handicaps, mired in an intricate network of contemporary barriers, could not be ushered into equality by tentative and superficial changes.

Mass nonviolent protests, a social invention of Negroes, were effective in Montgomery, Birmingham, and Selma in forcing national legislation which served to change Negro life sufficiently to curb explosions. But when changes were confined to the South alone, the North, in the absence of change, began to seethe.

The freedom movement did not adapt its tactics to the different and unique northern urban conditions. It failed to see that nonviolent marches in the South were forms of rebellion. When Negroes took over the streets and shops, southern society shook to its roots. Negroes could contain their rage when they found the means to force relatively radical changes in their environment.

In the North, on the other hand, street demonstrations were not even a mild expression of militancy. The turmoil of cities absorbs demonstrations as merely transitory drama which is ordinary in city life. Without a more effective tactic for upsetting the status quo, the power structure could maintain its intransigence and hostility. Into the vacuum of inaction, violence and riots flowed and a new period opened.

Urban riots must now be recognized as durable social phenomena. They may be deplored, but they are there and should be understood. Urban riots are a special form of violence. They are not insurrections. The rioters are not seeking to seize territory or to attain control of institutions. They are mainly intended to shock the white community. They are a distorted form of social protest. The looting which is their principal feature serves many functions. It enables the most enraged and deprived Negro to take hold of consumer goods with the ease the white man does by using his purse. Often the Negro does not even want what he takes; he wants the experience of taking. But most of all, alienated from society and knowing that this society cherishes property above people, he is shocking it by abusing property rights. There are thus elements of emotional catharsis in the violent act. This may explain why most cities in which riots have occurred have not had a repetition, even though the causative conditions remain. It is also noteworthy that the amount of physical harm done to white people other than police is infinitesimal and in Detroit whites and Negroes looted in unity.

A profound judgment of today's riots was expressed by Victor Hugo a century ago. He said, "If a soul is left in darkness, sins will be committed. The guilty one is not he who commits the sin, but he who causes the darkness."

The policy makers of the white society have caused the darkness; they created discrimination; they structured slums; and they perpetuate unemployment, ignorance, and poverty. It is incontestable and deplorable that Negroes have committed crimes; but they are derivative crimes. They are born of the greater crimes of the white society. When we ask Negroes to abide by the law, let us also demand that the white man abide by law in the ghettos. Day-in and day-out he violates welfare laws to deprive the poor of their meager allotments; he flagrantly violates building codes and regulations; his police make a mockery of law; and he violates laws on equal employment and education and the provisions for civic services. The slums are the handiwork of a vicious system of the white society; Negroes live in them but do not make them any more than a prisoner makes a prison. Let us say boldly that if the total violations of law by the white man in the slums over the years were calculated and compared with the law breaking of a few days of riots, the hardened criminal would be the white man. These are often difficult things to say but I have come to see more and more that it is necessary to utter the truth in order to deal with the great problems that we face in our society.

There is another cause of riots that is too important to mention casually —the war in Vietnam. Here again, we are dealing with a controversial issue. But I am convinced that the war in Vietnam has played havoc with our domestic destinies. The bombs that fall in Vietnam explode at home. It does not take much to see what great damage this war has done to the image of our nation. It has left our country politically and morally isolated in the world, where our only friends happen to be puppet nations like Taiwan, Thailand, and South Korea. The major allies in the world that have been with us in war and peace are not with us in this war. As a result we find ourselves socially and politically isolated.

The war in Vietnam has torn up the Geneva Accord. It has seriously impaired the United Nations. It has exacerbated the hatreds between continents, and worse still, between races. It has frustrated our development at home by telling our underprivileged citizens that we place insatiable military demands above their most critical needs. It has greatly contributed to the forces of reaction in America, and strengthened the military-industrial complex, against which even President Eisenhower solemnly warned us. It has practically destroyed Vietnam, and left thousands of American and Vietnamese youth maimed and mutilated. And it has exposed the whole world to the risk of nuclear warfare.

As I looked at what this war was doing to our nation, and to the domestic situation and to the Civil Rights movement, I found it necessary to speak vigorously out against it. My speaking out against the war has not gone without criticisms. There are those who tell me that I should stick with Civil Rights, and stay in my place. I can only respond that I have fought too hard and long to end segregated public accommodations to segregate my own moral concerns. It is my deep conviction that justice is indivisible, that injustice anywhere is a threat to justice everywhere. For those who tell me I am hurting the Civil Rights movement, and ask, "Don't you think that in order to be respected, and in order to regain support, you must stop talking against the war?" I can only say that I am not a consensus leader. I do not seek to determine what is right and wrong by taking a Gallup Poll to determine majority opinion. And it is again my deep conviction that ultimately a genuine leader is not a searcher for consensus, but a molder of consensus. On some positions cowardice asks the question, "Is it safe?"! Expediency asks the question "Is it politic?" Vanity asks the question, "Is it popular?" But conscience must ask the question, "Is it right?" And there comes a time when one must take a stand that is neither safe, nor politic, nor popular. But one must take it because it is right. And that is where I find myself today.

Moreover, I am convinced, even if war continues, that a genuine massive act of concern will do more to quell riots than the most massive deployment of troops.

The unemployment of Negro youth ranges up to 40% in some slums. The riots are almost entirely youth events—the age range of participants is from 13 to 25. What hypocrisy it is to talk of saving the new generation —to make it the generation of hope—while consigning it to unemployment and provoking it to violent alternatives.

When our nation was bankrupt in the '30s we created an agency to provide jobs to all at their existing level of skill. In our overwhelming affluence today what excuse is there for not setting up a national agency for full employment immediately?

The other program which would give reality to hope and opportunity would be the demolition of the slums to be replaced by decent housing built by residents of the ghettos.

These programs are not only eminently sound and vitally needed, but they have the support of an overwhelming majority of the nation—white and Negro. The Harris Poll on August 21, 1967, disclosed that an astounding 69% of the country support a works program to provide employment to all and an equally astonishing 65% approve a program to tear down the slums.

There is a program and there is heavy majority support for it. Yet, the administration and Congress tinker with trivial proposals to limit costs in an extravagant gamble with disaster.

The President has lamented that he cannot persuade Congress. He can, if the will is there, go to the people, mobilize the people's support, and thereby substantially increase his power to persuade Congress. Our most urgent task is to find the tactics that will move the Government no matter how determined it is to resist.

I believe we will have to find the militant middle between riots on the one hand and weak and timid supplication for justice on the other hand. That middle ground, I believe, is civil disobedience. It can be aggressive but nonviolent; it can dislocate but not destroy. The specific planning will take some study and analysis to avoid mistakes of the past when it was employed on too small a scale and sustained too briefly.

Civil disobedience can restore Negro-white unity. There have been some very important sane white voices even during the most desperate moments of the riots. One reason is that the urban crisis intersects the Negro crisis in the city. Many white decision makers may care little about saving Negroes, but they must care about saving their cities. The vast majority of production is created in cities; most white Americans live in them. The suburbs to which they flee cannot exist detached from cities. Hence powerful white elements have goals that merge with ours.

Now there are many roles for social scientists in meeting these problems. Kenneth Clark has said that Negroes are moved by a suicide instinct in riots and Negroes know there is a tragic truth in this observation. Social scientists should also disclose the suicide instinct that governs the administration and Congress in their total failure to respond constructively.

What other areas are there for social scientists to assist the Civil Rights movement? There are many, but I would like to suggest three because they have an urgent quality.

Social science may be able to search out some answers to the problem of Negro leadership. E. Franklin Frazier (1957), in his profound work, *Black Bourgeoisie,* laid painfully bare the tendency of the upwardly mobile Negro to separate from his community, divorce himself from responsibility to it, while failing to gain acceptance into the white community. There has been significant improvement from the days Frazier researched, but anyone knowledgeable about Negro life knows its middle class is not yet bearing its weight. Every riot has carried strong overtone of hostility of lower class Negroes toward the affluent Negro and vice versa. No contemporary study of scientific depth has totally studied this problem. Social science should be able to suggest mechanisms to create a wholesome black unity and a sense of peoplehood while the process of integration proceeds.

As one example of this gap in research, there are no studies, to my knowledge, to explain adequately the absence of Negro trade union leadership. Eighty-five percent of Negroes are working people. Some 2,000,000 are in trade unions, but in 50 years we have produced only one national leader—A. Philip Randolph.

Discrimination explains a great deal, but not everything. The picture is so dark even a few rays of light may signal a useful direction.

The second area for scientific examination is political action. In the past 2 decades, Negroes have expended more effort in quest of the franchise than they have in all other campaigns combined. Demonstrations, sit-ins, and marches, though more spectacular, are dwarfed by the enormous number of man-hours expended to register millions, particularly in the South. Negro organizations from extreme militant to conservative persuasion, Negro leaders who would not even talk to each other, all have been agreed on the key importance of voting. Stokely Carmichael said black power means the vote and Roy Wilkins, while saying black power means black death, also energetically sought the power of the ballot.

A recent major work by social scientists Matthews and Prothro (1966) concludes that "The concrete benefits to be derived from the franchise— under conditions that prevail in the South—have often been exaggerated," . . . that voting is not the key that will unlock the door to racial equality because "the concrete measurable payoffs from Negro voting in the South will not be revolutionary."

James A. Wilson (1965) supports this view, arguing, "Because of the structure of American politics as well as the nature of the Negro community, Negro politics will accomplish only limited objectives."

If their conclusion can be supported, then the major effort Negroes have invested in the past 20 years has been in the wrong direction and the major pillar of their hope is a pillar of sand. My own instinct is that these views are essentially erroneous, but they must be seriously examined.

The need for a penetrating massive scientific study of this subject cannot be overstated. Lipsit (1959) in 1957 asserted that a limitation in focus in political sociology has resulted in a failure of much contemporary research to consider a number of significant theoretical questions. The time is short for social science to illuminate this critically important area. If the main thrust of Negro effort has been, and remains, substantially irrelevant, we may be facing an agonizing crisis of tactical theory.

The third area for study concerns psychological and ideological changes in Negroes. It is fashionable now to be pessimistic. Undeniably, the freedom movement has encountered setbacks. Yet I still believe there are significant aspects of progress.

Negroes today are experiencing an inner transformation that is liberating them from ideological dependence on the white majority. What has penetrated substantially all strata of Negro life is the revolutionary idea that the philosophy and morals of the dominant white society are not holy or sacred but in all too many respects are degenerate and profane.

Negroes have been oppressed for centuries not merely by bonds of economic and political servitude. The worst aspect of their oppression was their inability to question and defy the fundamental percepts of the larger society. Negroes have been loath in the past to hurl any fundamental challenges because they were coerced and conditioned into thinking within the context of the dominant white ideology. This is changing and new radical trends are appearing in Negro thought. I use radical in its broad sense to refer to reading into roots.

Ten years of struggle have sensitized and opened the Negro's eyes to reaching. For the first time in their history, Negroes have become aware of the deeper causes for the crudity and cruelty that governed white society's responses to their needs. They discovered that their plight was not a consequence of superficial prejudice but was systemic.

The slashing blows of backlash and frontlash have hurt the Negro, but they have also awakened him and revealed the nature of the oppressor. To lose illusions is to gain truth. Negroes have grown wiser and more mature and they are hearing more clearly those who are raising fundamental questions about our society whether the critics be Negro or white. When this process of awareness and independence crystallizes, every rebuke, every evasion, become hammer blows on the wedge that splits the Negro from the larger society.

Social science is needed to explain where this development is going to take us. Are we moving away, not from integration, but from the society which made it a problem in the first place? How deep and at what rate of speed is this process occurring? These are some vital questions to be answered if we are to have a clear sense of our direction.

We know we have not found the answers to all forms of social change. We know, however, that we did find some answers. We have achieved and we are confident. We also know we are confronted now with far greater complexities and we have not yet discovered all the theory we need.

And may I say together, we must solve the problems right here in America. As I have said time and time again, Negroes still have faith in

America. Black people still have faith in a dream that we will all live together as brothers in this country of plenty one day.

But I was distressed when I read in the *New York Times* of August 31, 1967, that a sociologist from Michigan State University, the outgoing President of the American Sociological Society, stated in San Francisco that Negroes should be given a chance to find an all Negro community in South America: "that the valleys of the Andes Mountains would be an ideal place for American Negroes to build a second Israel." He further declared that "The United States Government should negotiate for a remote but fertile land in Equador, Peru, or Bolivia for this relocation." I feel that it is rather absurd and appalling that a leading social scientist today would suggest to black people, that after all these years of suffering and exploitation as well as investment in the American dream, that we should turn around and run at this point in history. I say that we will not run! Loomis even compared the relocation task of the Negro to the relocation task of the Jews in Israel. The Jews were made exiles. They did not choose to abandon Europe, they were driven out. Furthermore, Israel has a deep tradition, and Biblical roots for Jews. The Wailing Wall is a good example of these roots. They also had significant financial aid from the United States for the relocation and rebuilding effort. What tradition do the Andes, especially the valley of the Andes mountains have for Negroes?

And I assert at this time that once again we must reaffirm our belief in building a democratic society, in which blacks and whites can live together as brothers, where we will all come to see that integration is not a problem, but an opportunity to participate in the beauty of diversity.

The problem is deep. It is gigantic in extent, and chaotic in detail. And I do not believe that it will be solved until there is a kind of cosmic discontent enlarging in the bosoms of people of good will all over this nation.

There are certain technical words in every academic discipline which soon become stereotypes and even clichés. Every academic discipline has its technical nomenclature. You who are in the field of psychology have given us a great word. It is the word maladjusted. This word is probably used more than any other word in psychology. It is a good word; certainly it is good that in dealing with what the word implies you are declaring that destructive maladjustment should be destroyed. You are saying that all must seek the well-adjusted life in order to avoid neurotic and schizophrenic personalities.

But on the other hand, I am sure that we all recognize that there are some things in our society, some things in our world, to which we should never be adjusted. There are some things concerning which we must always be maladjusted if we are to be people of good will. We must never adjust ourselves to racial discrimination and racial segregation. We must never adjust ourselves to religious bigotry. We must never adjust ourselves to economic conditions that take necessities from the many to give luxuries to the few. We must never adjust ourselves to the madness of militarism, and the self-defeating effects of physical violence.

In a day when Sputniks, Explorers, and Geminies are dashing through outer space, when guided ballistic missiles are carving highways of death through the stratosphere, no nation can finally win a war. It is no longer a choice between violence and nonviolence, it is either nonviolence or nonexistence. As President Kennedy declared, "Mankind must put an end to war, or war will put an end to mankind." And so the alternative to disarmament, the alternative to a suspension in the development and use of nuclear weapons, the alternative to strengthening the United Nations and eventually disarming the whole world, may well be a civilization plunged into the abyss of annihilation. Our earthly habitat will be transformed into an inferno that even Dante could not envision.

Thus, it may well be that our world is in dire need of a new organization, the International Association for the Advancement of Creative Maladjustment. Men and woman should be as maladjusted as the prophet Amos, who in the midst of the injustices of his day, could cry out in words that echo across the centuries, "Let justice roll down like waters and righteousness like a mighty stream"; or as maladjusted as Abraham Lincoln, who in the midst of his vacillations finally came to see that this nation could not survive half slave and half free; or as maladjusted as Thomas Jefferson, who in the midst of an age amazingly adjusted to slavery, could scratch across the pages of history, words lifted to cosmic proportions, "We hold these truths to be self evident, that all men are created equal. That they are endowed by their creator with certain inalienable rights. And that among these are life, liberty, and the pursuit of happiness." And through such creative maladjustment, we may be able to emerge from the bleak and desolate midnight of man's inhumanity to man, into the bright and glittering daybreak of freedom and justice.

I have not lost hope. I must confess that these have been very difficult days for me personally. And these have been difficult days for every Civil Rights leader, for every lover of justice and peace. They have been days of frustration—days when we could not quite see where we were going, and when we often felt that our works were in vain, days when we were tempted to end up in the valley of despair. But in spite of this, I still have faith in the future, and my politics will continue to be a politic of hope. Our goal is freedom. And I somehow still believe that in spite of the so-called white backlash, we are going to get there, because however untrue it is to its destiny, the goal of America is freedom.

Abused and scorned though we may be, our destiny as a people is tied up with the destiny of America. Before the Pilgrim fathers landed at Plymouth, we were here. Before Jefferson scratched across the pages of history the great words that I just quoted, we were here. Before the beautiful words of the "Star Spangled Banner" were written, we were here. For more than 2 centuries, our forebears labored here without wages. They made Cotton King. They built the home of their masters in the midst of the most humiliating and oppressive conditions.

And yet out of a bottomless vitality, they continued to grow and develop. If the inexpressible cruelties of slavery could not stop us, the opposition that we now face will surely fail. We shall win our freedom because both the sacred heritage of our nation, and the eternal will of the almighty God, are embodied in our echoing demands.

And so I can still sing, although many have stopped singing it, "We shall overcome." We shall overcome because the arch of the moral universe is long, but it bends toward justice. We shall overcome because Carlysle is right, "No lie can live forever." We shall overcome because William Cullen Bryant is right, "Truth crushed to earth will rise again." We shall overcome because James Russell Lowell is right, "Truth forever on the scaffold, wrong forever on the throne, yet that scaffold sways a future." And so with this faith, we will be able to hew out of the mountain of despair a stone of hope. We will be able to transform the jangling discords of our nation into a beautiful symphony of brotherhood. This will be a great day. This will not be the day of the white man, it will not be the day of the black man, it will be the day of man as man.

References

Frazier, E. F. *Black bourgeoisie*. Glencoe, Ill.: Free Press, 1956.

Lipsit, M. Political sociology. In, *Sociology today*. New York: Basic Books, 1959.

Matthews, and Prothro. *Negroes and the new southern politics*. New York: Harcourt & Brace, 1966.

Miller, S. M., and Gouldner, A. *Applied sociology*. New York: Free Press, 1965.

Wilson, J. A. The Negro in politics. *Daedalus*, 1965, Fall.

49 Reprise: In the Light of Increased Awareness

Since this anthology features only experimental analyses of certain facets of Black psychology it would seem worthwhile to survey and contrast some of the major issues considered in the light of the alternative viewpoints concerned with the understanding and furthering of Black people. Without question the major issue concerning us all is the fostering of true equality among the different groups that comprise America. The articles presented here have discussed certain observed differences between racial or ethnic groups; an approach that is in distinct contrast to the viewpoint of the membership of the Association of Black Psychologists who have begun to lobby for a moratorium on research designed to either clarify or enumerate differences between the races. The Association has also proposed a general boycott of standardized psychological testing programs that assess intelligence and achievement. Like nearly everything else, psychological tests can be vastly improved and in the process rendered more suitable for the various ethnic groups. My personal feeling is that a major effort to culturally update the available testing programs will, in the long run, be a more constructive approach than simply boycotting the testing programs themselves.

As the section on Higher Education made quite clear, there is a tremendous need for increased numbers of Black students in psychology at all levels up to the Ph.D., and both the Association of Black Psychologists and the newly chartered Black Student Psychological Association are demanding increased recruiting among Black students to encourage interest in psychology as a profession. As Green points out in Reading 27, there are a number of difficult and as yet unresolved problems in this area, but progress is being made and increasing numbers of Black students are enrolled in psychology programs.

By now it is obvious to even the casual reader that Arthur Jensen's article, reviewed by Brazziel in Reading 17, has revived the old and universally destructive arguments regarding "racial intelligence" and the future of this particular controversy is stormy and uncertain. However, some of the emerging models of human intelligence, particularly J. P. Guilford's *The Nature of Human Intelligence* (1967) are complex enough to allow for considerable human intellectual diversity without featuring the conclusion of "superior-inferior" which is such a needlessly harmful aspect of Jensen's viewpoint. There is actually no argument with the proposition that people can differ enormously from each other, but for the time being our failure in psychology has been an inability to describe and measure human differences in ways that are instructive without being demeaning and of potential value to the more determined of the segregationists. This is assuredly the most critical and significant charge to the profession of psychological measurement, and one that is capable of a meaningful resolution.

A number of emerging viewpoints regarding Black people are of interest, and among them are: Black psychiatry as seen in the work of Franz Fanon, Alvin Poussaint, William Grier and Price Cobbs; Black sociology as exemplified by the writing of C. Eric Lincoln and E. Franklin Frazier; Black history via the distinguished work of John Hope Franklin; together with the enlightened militancy of the Association of Black Psychologists and the Black Students Psychological Association.

Since the issue of the research moratorium as well as the closely related movement to boycott psychological testing are of such significance to psychology, I would like to briefly consider the implications of such approaches to socially disturbing issues. The fundamental success of the psychological testing movement has its origins in Sir Francis Galton's (1883) concern with the nature of individual differences, Alfred Binet (1909) and later Lewis Terman's (1916) work with the Binet and Stanford-Binet Tests of Intelligence, together with the work of Hermann Rorschach (1921) and Starke R. Hathaway and J. Charnley McKinley (1943) in the analysis of personality. These represent monumental efforts in that they supported the hope for an objective, descriptive approach to human nature in contrast to largely subjective and unreliable characterizations based on such humn attributes as body type, facial features, and handwriting samples. The urgent problem of today is that the results of many psychological assessment programs have been detrimental to the welfare of Black Americans because they are among the criteria used for admission to colleges, graduate, professional, and training schools. Since Blacks have not tended to score as well as whites on such tests, the scores have functioned to exclude Black students from many beneficial educational experiences. This unfortunate circumstance highlights the distinction that must be made between the results of psychological tests and the utilization of those same results because the two differ considerably. It would seem advisable to reassess the utilization of the results of psychological tests and propose quite stringent regulations for their dissemination and use. To simply boycott testing programs as the Association of Black Psychologists has proposed is to retard progress in the area of being able to more effectively assist students and others through counseling based on refined standardized testing programs.

A workable compromise might take the form of the continuation of psychological testing programs wherein the results are leavened by the more extensive weighting of such nonintellective traits as one's motivation to learn, dedication to succeed in a particular career, and meaningful interest in the subject-matter field. Obviously these are difficult traits to measure effectively but with diligent effort considerable success could be realized. For examples of such approaches, the work of Mednick (1962), Verplanck and his associates (1967, 1968), Wilcox (1969, 1970), and Whitlock (1965) suggest viable methods whereby available measurement techniques could be adapted to assist in the meaningful assessment of some of the nonintellectual characteristics of man. The tradition and importance of psychological measurement are among the most significant achievements in the history of psychology, and as such can be of considerable utility in this time of dire social need. We simply must begin to ask what can be done by psychology that will be of service to the Civil Rights Movement rather than what not to do because some are at a disadvantage by virtue of the sometimes destructive utilization of the results of psychology's endeavors. To deny the development of the potential for enlightened change within American psychology at such a time seems inadvisable in view of the urgent necessity to solve our manifold problems in training, education and human development.

Professor Canady says it best when he argues:

"I believe that most of the important problems of war and peace, exploitation and brotherhood, hatred and love, sickness and health, understanding and misunderstanding, and the happiness and unhappiness of mankind will yield only to a better understanding of human behavior."

And then:

"I hope that in the future persons can and will work in this field as psychologists without having such descriptions as Black placed before their titles . . . . But all psychologists should be, and many are, concerned with the development of the understanding of behavior so that the Civil Rights Movement will succeed because mankind is more aware and therefore more humane."

List of References

Binet, Alfred. *The Experimental Psychology of Alfred Binet,* selected papers, Robert Pollack and Margaret W. Bunner (Eds.) New York: Springer Publishing Co., 1969.

Fanon, Frantz. *Black Skin, White Masks,* Charles Markmann (Transl.) New York: Grove Press, 1967.

Fanon, Frantz. *Studies in a Dying Colonialism,* Haakon Chevalier (Transl.) New York: Monthly Review Press, 1965.

Frazier, Edward Franklin. *Black Bourgeoisie,* Glencoe, Illinois: Free Press, 1957.

Frazier, Edward Franklin. *The Negro Family in the U. S.* (4th ed.), Nathan Glazer, Chicago: University of Chicago Press, 1967. (a)

Frazier, Edward Franklin. *Negro Youth at the Crossways, Their Personality Development in the Middle States,* prepared for the American Youth Commission, American Council on Education, New York: Schocken Books, 1967. (b)

Frazier, Edward Franklin. *The Free Negro Family,* New York: Arno Press, 1968.

Galton, F. *Inquiries into Human Faculty and Its Development,* London: Macmillan, 1883.

Grier, William H., and Price M. Cobbs. *Black Rage,* New York: Basic Books, 1968.

Guilford, Joy Paul. *The Nature of Human Intelligence,* New York: McGraw-Hill, 1967.

Hathaway, Starke Rosencrans. *An Atlas of Juvenile MMPI Profiles,* Minnesota: University of Minnesota Press, 1961.

Lincoln, Charles Eric. *The Black Muslim in America,* Boston: Beacon Press, 1961.

Lincoln, Charles Eric. *My Face Is Black,* Boston: Beacon Press, 1964.

Lincoln, Charles Eric. *Is Anyone Listening to Black America,* New York: Seabury Press, 1968.

Lincoln, Charles Eric. *Martin Luther King Jr., A Profile,* New York: Hill and Wang, 1970.

Mednick, S. A. "The Associative basis of the creative process," *Psychological Review,* 1962, 69:220–232.

Poussaint, Alvin. "A Negro psychiatrist explains the Negro Psyche," *New York Times Magazine,* August 20, 1967.

Rorschach, Hermann. *Psychodiagnostics: A Diagnostic Test Based on Perception,* New York: Grune and Stratton, 1921.

Terman, L. M. *The Measurement of Intelligence,* Boston: Houghton Mifflin, 1916.

480

Verplanck, W. S. *Associations and Connected Discourse,* paper presented to Psychonomic Society Meetings, 1967, Niagara Falls, New York.

Verplanck, W. S. *Associations and Connected Discourse: Further Results,* paper presented to Psychonomic Society Meetings, 1968, St. Louis, Missouri.

Whitlock, Gerald. *The Critical Incident Technique as a Model for Teacher Assessment,* unpublished manuscript, 1965, The University of Tennessee, Knoxville.

Wilcox, R. C. "From word associations to more interesting English composistions," *College Composition and Communication,* 1969, XX, 5:329–332.

Wilcox, R. C. "Racial differences in associative style," *Language and Speech* (England), 1971.

Bibliography for Part VII

Brown, Morgan C. The status of jobs and occupations as evaluated by an urban Negro sample. *American Sociological Review* (October, 1955), **20**, 561–566.

Institutional Affiliation of Black Psychologists

Philip Ash
University of Illinois
Chicago Circle, Illinois

Dr. Calvin O. Atchison
Professor and Director
Educational Research
Tennessee A & I State University
Nashville, Tennessee

Lettie J. Austin
Howard University
Washington, D. C.

Dr. Joseph C. Awkward
Professor and Head
Department of Psychology
Florida A & M University
Tallahassee, Florida

Dr. James A. Bayton
Professor of Psychology and
Vice President of
Universal Marketing Research
Howard University
Washington, D. C.

William F. Brazziel
Coordinator of General Studies
Norfolk Division of the
Virginia State Colleges
Norfolk, Virginia

Kay R. Burke
Howard University
Washington, D. C.

Howard K. Cameron
Associate Professor
Educational Psychology
Howard University
Washington, D. C.

Dr. Herman G. Canady
Professor Emeritus
Department of Psychology
West Virginia State College
Institute, West Virginia

Kenneth B. Clark
Department of Psychology
University of Rochester
New York, New York

Mamie K. Clark
Department of Psychology
Howard University
Washington, D. C.

Spurgeon Cole
East Carolina University
Greenville, North Carolina

James F. Condell
Professor and Chairman
Moorhead State College

Moorhead, Minnesota (or)
Department of Psychology
Florida A & M University
Tallahassee, Florida

Perry E. Crump
Professor and Chairman
Department of Pediatrics
Meharry Medical College
Nashville, Tennessee

Pearl Mayo Gore Dansby
Tennessee Agriculture and
Industrial State University
Nashville, Tennessee

William A. Dansby
Tennessee Agriculture and
Industrial State University
Nashville, Tennessee

James De Shields
Institute for Youth Studies
Howard University
Washington, D. C.

Ann E. Dickerson
Psychologist
Department of Pediatrics
Meharry Medical College
Nashville, Tennessee

Edgar G. Epps
Tuskegee Institute
Alabama

William W. Farquhar
Professor
College of Education
Michigan State University
East Lansing, Michigan

Otis D. Froe, Director
Research and Evaluation
Morgan State College
Baltimore, Maryland

Dr. Regina M. Goff
Professor
Department of Education
Morgan State College
Baltimore, Maryland

Dr. Alvin E. Goins

NIMH, Director Extramural
Res. Program
5454 Wiss Avenue
Chevy Chase, Maryland
Room 10 A 02

Robert Lee Green
Professor of Educational
Psychology and
Associate Director, Center
for Urban Affairs
Michigan State University
East Lansing, Michigan

Dr. Bernard W. Harleston
Provost Lincoln University
Lincoln University
Pennsylvania

Leslie H. Hicks
Associate Professor
Howard University
Washington, D. C.

Marvin Hoffman
Field Foundation
New York, New York

Louis J. Hofmann
Yeshiva University
New York, New York

Carrell Horton
Statistical Analyst
Department of Pediatrics
Meharry Medical College
Nashville, Tennessee

Martin D. Jenkins
Director, Urban Affairs Program
American Council on Education
Washington, D.C.

Dr. Reginald L. Jones
Professor of Education
University of California
Riverside, California

Dr. Roy J. Jones
Assistant Research Director
Central Community Studies
Assistant Professor
Department of Psychiatry

Howard University
Washington, D. C.

Irwin N. Katz
Professor and Director
Research Center of Human Relations
New York University
New York, New York

F. J. King
University of Texas
Austin, Texas

Martin Luther King Jr. (Deceased)
Southern Christian
Leadership Conference
Atlanta, Georgia

Florence (Shelton) C. Ladd
Research Associate
Department of Education
Harvard University
Cambridge, Massachusetts

Harold O. Lewis
Professor of History
Howard University
Washington, D. C.

Max Meenes
Head, Department of Psychology
Howard University
Washington, D. C.

Robert F. Morgan
Hawaii State Hospital (or)
St. Bonaventure University
New York

Tressie W. Muldrow
Howard University
Washington, D. C.

James S. Peters II, Ph.D.
Director, Division of
Vocational Rehabilitation
Connecticut State Department of
Education
Hartford, Connecticut

Dr. John Pierce-Jones
Psychology Department
University of Texas
Austin, Texas

Janice Porter
Department of Psychiatry
Temple University Hospital
Philadelphia, Pennsylvania

Constance M. Randall
Department of Education
Howard University
Washington, D. C.

Jackson B. Reid
Professor, Associate Dean
Graduate Studies College
Education
University of Texas
Austin, Texas

S. Oliver Roberts
Professor and Chairman
Department of Psychology
Fisk University
Nashville, Tennessee

James Robinson

Julian B. Rotter
Professor of Psychology
University of Connecticut
Storrs, Connecticut

Dr. Dalmas A. Taylor
Research Fellow
Department of Psychology
University of Delaware
Newark, Delaware

David L. Terrell
Research Associate
Howard University Center for
Youth Community Studies
Washington, D. C.

Mary Terrell
First Grade Teacher
E. A. Harrold School
Millington, Tennessee

Patricia Waly

Robert L. Williams
National Chairman
Association of Black Psychologists
Washington, D. C.

Also Chairman
Department of Black Studies
Washington University
St. Louis, Missouri
Milton E. Wilson
Dean, Human Relations

Kent State University
Kent, Ohio
Lauren G. Wispé
Chairman, Department of Psychology
University of Oklahoma
Norman, Oklahoma

Name Index

Ahrendt, H., 363
Alsop, J., 158
Ash, P., 449
Atchison, C. O., 16, 227
Austin, L. J., 377
Awkard, J., 449

Bayton, J. A., 186, 377, 384
Bogardus, E. S., 393–394
Brazziel, W. F., 25, 154, 401, 477
Bunche, R., 63, 178
Burke, K. R., 377

Cameron, H. K., 302, 310, 345
Canady, H. G., v, 89, 169, 433, 442, 479
Carver, G. W., 63
Cattell, R. B., 312
Chisum, G. T., viii
Clark, K. B., 323
Clark, M. B., 323
Cobbs, P. M., 478, 480
Cole, S., 221
Coleman, J. S., 314
Condell, J. F., 444
Crump, E. P., 126, 138

Dansby, P. M., 288
Dansby, W. A., 288
Davis, A., 29
DeShields, J. I., 20
Dickerson, A. E., 1, 138

Epps, E. G., 107

Fanon, F., 478, 480
Farquahar, W. W., 216, 351, 356
Franklin, J. H., 478, 480
Frazier, E. F., 478, 480
Froe, O. D., 233

Goff, R. M., 30, 292, 409
Goins, A. E., 393

Gore, P. M., 370
Green, R. L., 3, 57, 74, 216, 261
Grier, W. H., 478, 480
Guilford, J. P., 477, 480

Harleston, B. W., viii, 175, 431
Herskovits, M. J., 94–96, 99
Hicks, L. H., viii, 449
Hoffman, M., 449
Hofmann, L. J., 3
Horowitz, R. E., 325–326, 331
Horton, C. P., 126, 138, 146

Jenkins, M. D., 45, 102, 198
Jensen, A. R., 154, 311, 319, 477
Jones, R. J., 20
Jones, R. L., viii, 277

Katz, I., 84, 107, 112
King, F. J., 357
King, M. L., Jr., viii, 466

Ladd, F. S., 248
Lewis, H. O., 186
Lincoln, C. E., 478, 480

Mednick, S. A., 479, 480
Meenes, M., 393
Morgan, R. F., 3, 74
Moynihan, D. P., 153
Muldrow, T. W., 384

Peters, J. S., II, 114
Pierce-Jones, J., 357
Porter, J., 449
Poussaint, A., 478, 480

Randall, C., 198
Reid, J. B., 357
Roberts, S. O., 138, 146, 332
Robinson, J. M., 107
Rotter, J. B., 370, 376

487

Subject Index

Abstractions, historical and social, 190–191
Academic integration, 68–73
    emotional conflict over, 71–72
Achievement, critical age period, 12
    of Jewish children, 8
    negative teacher characteristics, 11
    perceptual deprivation experiments and, 12
    personal characteristics and, 9
    predictors of, 218, 219–220, 263–270
    school deprivation and, 59, 74–83
    social context factors, 9–10
    standardized testing programs for Negro
        children, 171
Advancement associations, American Council
        on Human Rights, 55
    National Association for the Advancement
        of Colored Peoples, 55, 63
    National Urban League, 55
American Psychological Association, 443
Aspiration levels, effects of rejection upon,
        30–38
    social class and, 31
    sports, role of in, 36

Berkeley Daily Gazette, 158
Black colleges and universities, 50
    and degrees granted, 177
    and integration, 184
    land grant institutions, 50–51, 173, 175–178
    need for change in, 184
    organization and function, 191–195
    psychology in, 433–441
        courses offered in, 437
    remedial training programs, 189
    teaching faculties of, 196–197, 438–439
Black psychologists, 449–465
    Association of, 477–478
    with degrees from leading universities, 457
    limitations on professional growth, 460–462,
        463–464
    salary levels of, 458

Black Student Psychological Association,
        477–478
Board of Education, New York City, 310
Broken home, 141
    and mental ability, 144, 149–150

Children, 16
    decline in mental ability, 144
    developing school-readiness, 25–29
    family situation and mental ability, 144,
        149–150
    mentally defective, 16–19, 59
    effects of mentally retarded mother upon,
        121
    negative orientation to society, 360
    pre-school, 20–24
    race and honesty about handicaps of, 37–38
    racial integration of, 65–66
    self-concept, development of, 329–330, 349
    teachers' views of, 59–61
Coleman Report, 158, 314
College students, Negro, 167–273
    academic motivation and achievement, 216–
        220
    admissions criteria, new, 269
    attitudes of, Southern, 221–226
    counseling of disadvantaged, 416–427
    "disadvantaged freshmen," 233–247
    family characteristics of, 201–202, 239–240
    at Harvard University, 248–260
    parents of, occupational and educational status,
        203–207
    personality differences, 403–405
    "philosophies" of education, 237–238
    predicting performance of, 310–317
    secondary school experience of, 207–210
    superior versus unselected, 211
    whites, motivation to learn, 217–219
Committee on Equality of Opportunity in Psy-
        chology, 449–450
Conference on the Courts and Racial Integra-
        tion in Education, 45–56

489